German Philosophers

Roger Scruton is Visiting Professor at Birkbeck College, University of London. His books include *Spinoza, Sexual Desire,* and *Modern Philosophy,* along with several works of fiction.

Peter Singer is DeCamp Professor of Bioethics at Princeton University. He is best known for his book *Animal Liberation,* sometimes called 'the Bible of the modern animal movement'. His other books include *Practical Ethics, Marx, How are we to live?, Ethics into Action* and *A Darwinian Left?* He is also the author of the major article on ethics in the current edition of the Encyclopaedia Britannica.

Christopher Janaway is Senior Lecturer in Philosophy at Birkbeck College, University of London, and author of *Self and World in Schopenhauer's Philosophy* (1989) and *Images of Excellence: Plato's Critique of the Arts* (1995).

Michael Tanner is a Fellow of Christ College and a University Lecturer in Philosophy. He is author of *Wagner* (Modern Masters, London, 1995).

D1075963

German Philosophers

Kant
Roger Scruton

Hegel
Peter Singer

Schopenhauer
Christopher Janaway

Nietzsche
Michael Tanner

OXFORD
UNIVERSITY PRESS

OXFORD
UNIVERSITY PRESS

Great Clarendon Street, Oxford OX2 6DP

Oxford University Press is a department of the University of Oxford.
It furthers the University's objective of excellence in research, scholarship,
and education by publishing worldwide in

Oxford New York

Auckland   Cape Town   Dar es Salaam   Hong Kong   Karachi
Kuala Lumpur   Madrid   Melbourne   Mexico City   Nairobi
New Delhi   Shanghai   Taipei   Toronto
With offices in
Argentina   Austria   Brazil   Chile   Czech Republic   France   Greece
Guatemala   Hungary   Italy   Japan   South Korea   Poland   Portugal
Singapore   Switzerland   Thailand   Turkey   Ukraine   Vietnam

Oxford is a registered trade mark of Oxford University Press
in the UK and in certain other countries

Published in the United States
by Oxford University Press Inc., New York

ISBN 978-0-19-285424-7

Foreword

THE German universities of the eighteenth century were the first to produce academic philosophers of a recognizably modern kind. There had been universities since the Middle Ages, but relatively few contributions to speculative thought had been made by their members. Aquinas, Bacon, Descartes, Hobbes, Spinoza, and Leibniz were not academics. Only when the universities took on the task of advancing knowledge rather than merely conserving it did they begin to monopolize philosophical activity; and it was in Germany that this new conception of the university first established itself.

The four philosophers whose ideas are discussed in this book were products of this academic revolution. They were all born in Germany, wrote in German, and were, or intended to be, university professors. Immanuel Kant (1724–1804) spent an uneventful life teaching at the university in his native Königsberg. G. W. F. Hegel (1770–1831) studied in Tübingen and eventually became a professor at the University of Berlin. Arthur Schopenhauer (1788–1860) studied at Göttingen, Berlin, and Jena, and would have become an academic at Berlin, had he not been disillusioned by failing to attract an audience because his lectures were given at the same time as those by Hegel. Friedrich Nietzsche (1844–1900) was a professor of classics at Basle until he resigned his chair because of ill health.

Of the four, Kant has been much the most influential, at least among philosophers. With Plato and Aristotle, he is one of the three giants who did most to define what philosophy is about. His work was the culmination of the Enlightenment, a synthesis which reunited the two opposed streams of Baconian empiricism and Cartesian rationalism, and which formed the starting-point for a great deal of subsequent philosophical inquiry. He is an overwhelmingly difficult writer, but Roger Scruton provides an admirably lucid guide to the nature of the

Kantian enterprise, embodied in the three great *Critiques*: of *Pure Reason*; of *Practical Reason*; and of *Judgement*. In the first, Kant attempted to establish the scope and limits of all objective knowledge. In the second, he outlined the principles of the 'categorical imperative', a universal moral law which was based on reason and was a precondition of human freedom. In the third, he established the modern discipline of aesthetics.

Very soon after his death, Kant's philosophy was being taught in every German university. Hegel inevitably formed his own ideas in reaction to those of the master. His *Phenomenology of Mind*, for example, was an attempt to argue that ultimate reality was the creation of the mind, and therefore not forever beyond knowledge, as Kant had argued. Like Kant, Hegel is formidably difficult to understand, but Peter Singer's account is so crystal-clear that it may even deceive the student into thinking that Hegel is easier than he really is. He explains the nature of Hegel's absolute idealism and the meaning of the dialectic. He also clarifies his preoccupation with the achievement of human freedom and of a community in which the individual's interests are in harmony with those of the whole. Hegel's belief that history is moving inexorably in one direction and that all parts of a culture are organically related to each other have been perhaps his most powerful legacies to later social and historical thought.

Schopenhauer greatly disliked Hegel, whom he compared to 'a cuttle-fish creating a cloud of obscurity around itself so that no one sees what it is'. But he recognized his debt to Kant, whose project he saw himself as correcting and completing. In *The World as Will and Representation* he constructed a metaphysical system which, in the words of Christopher Janaway, 'collapses under the gentlest analytical probing'. Yet his insights foreshadow some key preoccupations of modern thought. Writing before Darwin, he believed that our thought-processes are the product of our biological nature and thus subject to the limitations of human egotism and sexuality. Long before Freud, he was aware of the influence of the unconscious upon the intellect. Rationality, he believed, was an illusion: the only means by which the human animal could hope to overcome his limitations were disinterested aesthetic experience and the renunciation of individual desire. His was a pessimism so profound that he believed that it would have been better for every individual not to have been born. Yet no philosopher has written better about music.

It was the work of Schopenhauer which drew Nietzsche to philosophy, though eventually he reacted against him. In place of the ascetic renunciation which Schopenhauer had recommended, he urged self-affirmation: 'become who you are!' Individuals, he thought, should deliberately give 'style' to their character. Though a prolific writer, he was not a systematic one and much of his thought is expressed in aphorisms and epigrams. He was a merciless critic of such accepted verities of the nineteenth century as Christianity, nationalism, and social respectability; this no doubt accounts for his neglect in his own lifetime and his popularity today. Michael Tanner convincingly argues that Nietzsche's fundamental concern was to plot the relationship between suffering and culture. Hence his interest in tragedy, his preoccupation with the heroic, and his attack on all religions that teach the existence of an afterlife. Of the many striking remarks in *The Genealogy of Morals*, perhaps the most arresting is the assertion that Christianity as a dogma has been destroyed by its own morality.

The four self-contained essays in this volume were originally written for the Past Masters series, which sets out to expound the ideas of notable thinkers of the past in a lucid, accessible, and authoritative manner. Because they are necessarily short, they do not attempt to discuss every aspect of their subjects' lives and works. But readers will find that they offer iluminating guides to the complex and demanding thought of four exceptional individuals.

Corpus Christi College   KEITH THOMAS
Oxford   *General Editor*
       Past Masters

Contents

Kant

Roger Scruton

Preface

I have tried to present Kant's thought in a modern idiom, while presupposing the least possible knowledge of philosophy. Since Kant is one of the most difficult of modern philosophers, I cannot hope that I have made every aspect of this thought intelligible to the general reader. It is not clear that every aspect of his thought has been intelligible to *anyone*, even to Kant. The depth and complexity of Kant's philosophy are such that it is only after complete immersion that the importance of its questions, and the imaginative power of its answers, can be understood. Kant hoped to draw the limits of the human understanding; he found himself compelled to transcend them. The reader should therefore not be surprised if he has to read this introduction more than once in order to appreciate Kant's vision. To share that vision is to see the world transformed; to acquire it cannot be the labour of a single day.

The first draft of this book was written in Prague. I am grateful to Dr Ladislav Hejdánek, not only for the invitation to speak to his seminar on the topic of The Categorical Imperative, but also for the example he has set in obeying it. I have benefited from Ruby Meager, Mark Platts and Dorothy Edgington, who commented on a later draft, and from the students of London University who have, over the last decade, made the teaching of Kant's philosophy so rewarding. I have also benefited, in more ways than I can express, from the kindness of Lenka Dvořáková, to whom this book is dedicated.

London
May 1981

Contents

Abbreviations

Quotations are mostly from the English translations referred to below. However, where these translations have seemed to me to be misleading or inelegant, I have used my own.

A   *Critique of Pure Reason*, First Edition, tr. N. Kemp-Smith

B   *Critique of Pure Reason*, Second Edition, tr. N. Kemp-Smith

P   *Critique of Practical Reason*, tr. T. K. Abbott

J   *Critique of Aesthetic Judgement*, tr. J. C. Meredith

T   *Critique of Teleological Judgement*, tr. J. C. Meredith

F   *Foundations of the Metaphysic of Morals*, tr. T. K. Abbott

For the editions of the above works referred to, see notes on further reading.

I   'Inaugural Dissertation', contained in G. B. Kerferd, D. K. E. Walford, and P. G. Lucas (eds): *Kant: Selected Pre-Critical Writings* (Manchester, 1968)

K   *The Kant-Eberhard Controversy*, by H. E. Allison (Baltimore and London, 1973)

L   *Lectures on Ethics*, tr. L. Infield, new edition (New York, 1963)

M   *Prolegomena to any Future Metaphysics*, tr. P. G. Lucas (Manchester, 1953)

C   *Kant's Philosophical Correspondence: 1759–99* ed. and tr. Arnulf Zweig (Chicago, 1967)

All italics that appear in quotations from Kant are his own.

1 Life, works and character

The greatest modern philosopher was moved by nothing more than by duty. His life, in consequence, was unremarkable. For Kant, the virtuous man is so much the master of his passions as scarcely to be prompted by them, and so far indifferent to power and reputation as to regard their significance as nothing beside that of duty itself. Having confined his life so that he could act without strain according to this ideal, Kant devoted himself to scholarship, entirely governed by congenial routines. The little professor of Königsberg has thus become the type of the modern philosopher: bounded in a nutshell, and counting himself king of infinite space.

Immanuel Kant was born in Königsberg in 1724, the fourth of the nine children of a poor harness-maker. Kant's parents were simple people and devout pietists. At that time, pietism, a reformist movement within the Lutheran Church, held powerful sway among the lower and middle classes in Germany, consoling hardship with the idea of the sacredness of work, duty and prayer; its vision of the sovereignty of conscience was to exert a lasting influence on Kant's moral thinking. Although in some respects anti-intellectual, it was also one of the major forces behind the spread of education in late seventeenth-century Germany, and a pietist school had been stablished in Königsberg. To this school Kant, whose talents had been recognised by a wise and benevolent pastor, was sent at the age of eight. It is fortunate for posterity that such an education should have been offered to one of Kant's lowly origins; it was perhaps less fortunate for the young Kant himself, whose gratitude towards his tutors was so mingled with distaste for their oppressive zeal that in later years he forbore all mention of his

early schooling. Some impression of its nature can be gathered
from a remark in the little treatise on education, edited from
Kant's lecture notes late in his life:

Many people imagine that the years of their youth are the
pleasantest and best of their lives; but it is not really so. They are
the most troublesome; for we are then under strict discipline,
can seldom choose our friends, and still more seldom have our
freedom.

In a letter sent to Kant by a former schoolfriend, at a time when
both had become famous, the philologist David Ruhnken remarked: 'thirty years have passed since the two of us groaned
beneath the pedantically gloomy, but not entirely worthless,
discipline of those fanatics'. And it is undeniable that Kant
emerged from his schooling with a considerable weight of
gloom, together with a remarkable self-discipline. His early
manhood was partly devoted to using the second to overcome
the first. In this he was almost completely successful. Despite
straitened circumstances, a deformed and diminutive body, and
the loss both of a father whom he respected and of a mother
whom he deeply loved, Kant soon became one of the most
popular citizens of Königsberg, welcomed everywhere for his
grace, wit and ready conversation.

Kant entered the university of his native city at the age of
sixteen and graduated from it six years later. Being unable to
secure an academic position, he took work as a private tutor in
various households. It was not until the age of thirty-one that
he obtained a post at the university, as private docent, an
unsalaried employment which conferred the privilege of giving
public lectures, and the chance of securing a meagre reward
through private tuition. By then Kant had already published
works on dynamics and mathematics. He had also acquired,
through the connections which his position as private tutor
made available, the social ease which was to earn him the title
of *der schöne Magister*.

Königsberg was then a city of some dignity, with 50,000
inhabitants and an important garrison. As a seaport serving the

trading interests of Eastern Prussia it contained a bustling and variegated population, including Dutch, English, Poles and Russians. The university, founded in 1544 as the Collegium Albertinum, was a cultural centre of some importance, although so much sunk in provincial obscurity by the mid-eighteenth century that Frederick the Great, visiting the city as crown prince in 1739, described it as 'better suited to the training of bears than to becoming a theatre of the sciences'. Frederick ascended the throne the following year, and did his best to spread into this corner of his kingdom the high culture and intellectual toleration which characterised his reign. Kant, who had already determined to value truth and duty above all things, was therefore fortunate to find that his university offered no major impediments to the pursuit of either. It was perhaps this, as much as his passionate attachment to his birthplace, that prompted him to wait so long for his first appointment, and to continue waiting thereafter, for another fifteen years, before being granted the professorship which he desired. During this period Kant several times refused offers from other German universities, and continued conscientiously to deliver, in the house where he lodged, the lectures which established his reputation. His intellectual labours were devoted mainly to mathematics and physics, and at the age of thirty-one he published a treatise on the origin of the universe which contained the first formulation of the nebular hypothesis. His duties required him, however, to lecture on a wide variety of subjects, including physical geography, about which he became, perhaps because of his reluctance to travel, an acknowledged authority and, in the opinion of one Count Purgstall (who admired the philosopher greatly), a conversational bore.

It is to some extent by chance that Kant's professorship was in metaphysics and logic, rather than in mathematics or natural science. From this point in his career, however, Kant devoted his energies entirely to philosophy, rehearsing in his lectures the thoughts which he was to publish, ten years later, in works which earned him a reputation as the greatest luminary in Germany. The philosopher J. G. Hamann records that it was necessary to arrive in Kant's lecture room at six in the morning, one hour before the professor was due to appear, in order to obtain a place, and Kant's pupil Jachmann has this to say of the performance:

Kant had a peculiarly skilful method of asserting and defining metaphysical concepts, which consisted, to all appearances, in carrying out his inquiries in front of his audience; as though he himself had just begun to consider the question, gradually adding fresh determining concepts, improving bit by bit on previously established explanations, and finally arriving at a definitive conclusion of his treatment of the subject, which he had thoroughly examined from every angle, having given the completely attentive listener not only a knowledge of the subject, but also an object lesson in methodical thought . . .

And in a letter to a friend, the same writer speaks of Kant's lectures on ethics:

In these he ceased to be merely a speculative philosopher and became, at the same time, a spirited orator, sweeping the heart and emotions along with him, as well as satisfying the intelligence. Indeed, it was a heavenly delight to hear his sublimely pure ethical doctrine delivered with such powerful philosophic eloquence from the lips of its very creator. How often he moved us to tears, how often he stirred our hearts to their depths, how often he lifted up our minds and emotions from the shackles of self-seeking egoism to the exalted self-awareness of pure free-will, to absolute obedience to the laws of reason and to the exalted sense of our duty to others!

Jachmann is more fulsome than false, and Kant's fame as a speaker, both in private and in public, earned him wide recognition, long before the publication of his greatest works.

Kant's private life is often parodied as one of clockwork routine, fastidious, donnish and self-centred. It is said (because Heine said it) that the housewives of Königsberg would set their clocks by his time of passing; it is said (because Kant once said it) that his constant concern for his bodily condition displayed a morbid hypochondria; it is also said that the bareness of his house and furnishings displayed and indifference to beauty, and that the punctuality of his routine disguised a cold and even frozen heart.

It is true that Kant's life was, if not mechanical, at least highly disciplined. His manservant had instructions to wake him each morning at five and to tolerate no malingering. He would work until seven at his desk, dressed in nightcap and robe, changing back into these garments at once when he had returned from his morning lectures. He remained in his study until one, when he took his single meal of the day, following it, irrespective of the weather, by a walk. He took this exercise alone, from the eccentric conviction that conversation, since it causes a man to breathe through the mouth, should not take place in the open air. He was averse to noise, twice changing lodging in order to avoid the sound of other people, and once writing indignantly to the director of police, commanding him to prevent the inmates of a nearby prison from consoling themselves with the singing of hymns. His aversion to music other than military marches was indeed notorious, as was his total indifference to the visual arts—he possessed only one engraving, a portrait of Rousseau, given to him by a friend.

Kant was aware of the accusations which the intellect draws to itself. And it was to the subject of this engraving that he turned in self-justification, saying that he should have regarded himself as much more worthless than the common labourer, had not Rousseau convinced him that the intellect could play its part in restoring the rights of man. Like all people given to the life of the mind, Kant was in need of the discipline which he imposed on himself. Far from crippling his moral nature, his routine enabled him to flower in the ways best suited to his genius. His love of solitude was balanced by an equal love of company. He would invariably have guests at his midday meal, inviting them on the same morning lest they should be embarrassed by the need to refuse some other invitation, and providing for each a pint of claret, and, if possible, some favourite dish. He conversed, to the delight and instruction of his companions, until three, endeavouring to end the meal in laughter (as much, however, from a conviction that laughter promotes digestion, as from any natural inclination towards it). Kant's writings contain many flashes of satire, and satire, indeed, was his favourite reading. His indifference to music and painting must be set against his love of poetry; even his concern for his health was little more than a consequence of the Kantian philosophy of duty. He neither admired nor enjoyed the sedentary life, but regarded it, nevertheless, as indispensable to the exercise of his intellect. Herder, one of the greatest and most passionate writers of the romantic movement, attended Kant's lectures and afterwards vigorously opposed their influence. He nevertheless thought highly of Kant himself, and summarised his character in these words:

I had the good fortune to make the acquaintance of a philosopher, who was my teacher. Though in the prime of life, he still had the joyful high spirits of a young man, which he kept, I believe, into extreme old age. His open brow, built for thought, was the seat of indestructible serenity and gladness. A wealth of ideas issued from his lips, jest and wit and good humour were at his bidding, and his instructional lecture was also the most fascinating entertainment.

With the same spirit with which he examined Leibniz, Wolff, Baumgarten, Crusius and Hume, and analysed the laws of nature expounded by the physicists Kepler and Newton, he appraised the currently appearing writings of Rousseau, his *Émile* and his *Héloise*, as he did every fresh discovery in natural science which came to his notice, estimated their value and returned, as always, to an unbiased knowledge of nature and of the moral worth of man.

The history of mankind, of nations and of nature, natural science, mathematics and his own experience were the well-springs which animated his lectures and his everyday life. He was never indifferent to anything worth knowing. No intrigue, no sectional interests, no advantage, no desire for fame ever possessed the slightest power to counteract his extension and illumination of truth. He encouraged and gently compelled people to think for themselves: despotism was alien to his nature. This man, whom I name with the deepest gratitude and reverence, is Immanuel Kant; I recall his image with pleasure.

Kant's duties as a university teacher required him to lecture on all aspects of philosophy, and for many years he devoted the major part of his intellectual efforts to teaching, publishing short and undeveloped books and papers. His greatest achievement—the *Critique of Pure Reason*—was also his first major publication, appearing in 1781, when Kant was fifty-seven. Of this work he wrote to Moses Mendelssohn: 'although the book is the product of twelve years of reflection, I completed it hastily, in perhaps four or five months, with the greatest attentiveness to its content but less care about its style and ease of comprehension' (C 105–6). In an attempt to alleviate the difficulties presented by the *Critique* he published a short *Prolegomena to any Future Metaphysic which shall lay Claim to being a Science* (1783), in which brilliant polemic is combined with an obscure condensation of the *Critique*'s most offending passages. For the second edition of the *Critique*, in 1787, Kant rewrote the most forbidding sections; since the result is equally difficult, commentators have come to agree that the opacity of Kant's work stems not so much from the style as from the thought itself. Despite its difficulty, however, the work rapidly became so famous that the 'critical philosophy' was being advocated, taught, opposed, and sometimes even censored and persecuted, throughout the German-speaking world. Kant's self-confidence increased, and he was able to write in 1787 to K. L. Reinhold (who did much to popularise Kant's ideas): 'I can assure you that the longer I continue in my path the less worried I become that any contradiction . . . will ever significantly damage my system' (C 127). The influence of Kant's first *Critique* is justly summarised by Mme de Staël, when, thirty years after the first edition, she wrote that 'when at length the treasures of thought which it contains were discovered, it produced such a sensation in Germany, that almost all which has been accomplished since, in literature as well as in philosophy, has flowed from the impulse given by this performance'.

During the twelve years of reflection to which Kant refers in his letter to Mendelssohn he published almost nothing, and his earlier ('pre-critical') writings are of peripheral interest to the student of his mature philosophy. However, once the critical philosophy had achieved expression, Kant continued, with increasing confidence, to explore its ramifications. The *Critique of Pure Reason* dealt in a systematic way with metaphysics and the theory of knowledge; it was followed by the *Critique of Practical Reason* (1788), concerned with ethics, and the *Critique of Judgement* (1790), concerned largely with aesthetics. Many other works were added to those, and Kant's collected writings in the so-called *Berliner Ausgabe* now fill twenty-seven volumes. Of these other works, two will particularly concern us: the *Prolegomena*, already mentioned, and the *Foundations of the Metaphysic of Morals*, which appeared in 1785, before the second *Critique*, and contains a compelling expression of Kant's moral theory.

During the reign of Frederick the Great Königsberg breathed the air of enlightenment, and Kant enjoyed the esteem of Frederick's ministers, in particular of von Zedlitz, the minister of education, to whom the *Critique of Pure Reason* is dedicated. A marked change occurred when Frederick William II ascended the throne. His minister, Woellner, exerted great influence, and, becoming responsible for religion in 1788, attempted to bring religious toleration to an end. Kant's *Religion Within the Limits of Reason Alone* was published in 1793, under the imprint of the Königsberg philosophy faculty, thus escaping censorship on a point of law. Woellner, mightily displeased, wrote in the King's name to Kant, charging him to give an account of himself. Kant replied with a solemn promise to his sovereign not to engage in public discussion of religion, either through lectures or through writings. Kant regarded himself as absolved from this promise by the monarch's death. Nevertheless this conflict with authority caused him much pain and bitterness. Kant prided himself on being a loyal subject, despite republican sympathies which he once expressed in the presence of an Englishman with such vivacity as to call forth a challenge to a duel, and with such eloquence as to overcome both the challenge and the opinions of the man who had offered it. (The man in question, Joseph Green, was a

merchant in Königsberg, and subsequently became Kant's closest friend.)

Kant enjoyed the company of women (provided that they did
not pretend to understand the *Critique of Pure Reason*) and
twice contemplated marriage. On each occasion, however, he
hesitated long enough to ensure that he remained unwed. One
day, his disreputable and drunken manservant appeared at table
in a yellow coat. Kant indignantly ordered him to take it off and
sell it, promising to make good the financial loss. He then
learned with amazement that the servant had been married,
was a widower, and was now to marry again, the yellow coat
having been purchased for the occasion. Kant was appalled at
these revelations, and never again looked on his servant with
favour. It seems that he was unable to persuade himself of the
normality of marriage, which he once described as an agreement between two people for the 'reciprocal use of each other's
sexual organs' (C 235). However, in his early *Observations on
the Sentiment of the Beautiful and the Sublime* (1764), Kant
had written eloquently on the distinction between the sexes.
He was radically opposed to the view that men and women
partake of a common nature which alone suffices to determine
the character of their relations; instead, he assigned to women
a charm, beauty, and capacity to melt the heart which are
foreign to the more 'sublime', 'principled' and 'practical' sex to
which he belonged. This description of women accords with
Kant's description of natural beauty. It was nature, above all,
that stirred his emotions, and it was to scenes of natural beauty
that his mother had taken him as a child, so as to awaken his
feelings towards the things she loved. It is possible to discern in
his evocations, both of feminine charm, and of natural beauty,
the residue of erotic feelings which, had they been more actively expressed, might well have broken the routine to which
our intellectual history is so heavily indebted.

Kant gave his last official lecture in 1796. By that time his
faculties had begun to decline and a sombre melancholy had
replaced his former gaiety. Fichte describes him as seeming to
lecture in his sleep, waking with a start to his half-forgotten

subject-matter. Soon he lost his clarity of mind, his ability to recognise old friends, even his ability to complete simple sentences. He faded into insensibility, and passed from his blameless life on 12 February 1804, unaccompanied by his former intellectual powers. He was attended to his grave by people from all over Germany, and by the whole of Königsberg, being acknowledged even in his senility as the greatest glory of that town. His grave crumbled away and was restored in 1881. His remains were moved in 1924, to a solemn neo-classical portico attached to the cathedral. In 1950 unknown vandals broke open the sarcophagus, and left it empty. By that time Königsberg had ceased to be a centre of learning, had been absorbed into the Soviet Union, and had been renamed in honour of one of the few of Stalin's henchmen to die of natural causes. A bronze tablet remains fixed to the wall of the Castle, overlooking the dead and wasted city, bearing these words from the concluding section of the *Critique of Practical Reason*:

Two things fill the heart with ever renewed and increasing awe and reverence, the more often and the more steadily we meditate upon them: *the starry firmament above and the moral law within.*

It is fortunate for the inhabitants of Kaliningrad that they are daily reminded of two things that they may still admire.

2 The background of Kant's thought

The *Critique of Pure Reason* is the most important work of philosophy to have been written in modern times; it is also one of the most difficult. It poses questions so novel and comprehensive that Kant judged it necessary to invent technical terms with which to discuss them. These terms have a strange beauty and compellingness, and it is impossible to acquire a full appreciation of Kant's work without experiencing the order and connectedness that his vocabulary imposes upon the traditional problems of philosophy. Nevertheless, the gist of Kant's thought can be expressed in a lowlier idiom, and in what follows I shall try to eliminate as many of his technicalities as I can. The task is not easy, since there is no accepted interpretation of their meaning. While a 'picture' of the Kantian system is common to all who have commented on it, there is no agreement whatsoever as to the strength, or even as to the content, of his arguments. A commentator who presents clear premises and clear conclusions will invariably be accused of missing Kant's argument, and the only way to escape academic censure is to fall into the verbal mannerisms of the original. It has become, in recent years, slightly easier to risk this censure. Contemporary Kantian studies—in particular in Britain and America—have tended to the view that the obscurity of Kantian scholarship is often a product of its confusion. In order not to attribute the confusion to Kant, scholars have laboured hard to elicit from, or at least to impose upon, the first *Critique*, an interpretation that renders it intelligible. I shall try to do the same, and shall be more influenced by these contemporary studies than I am able to acknowledge.

The first problem posed by the interpretation of the *Critique of Pure Reason* is this: what are the questions which it hopes to answer? Kant wrote, in the preface to the first edition:

In this enquiry I have made completeness my aim, and I venture to assert that there is not a single metaphysical problem which has not been solved, or for the solution of which the key at least has not been supplied. (A xiii)

While this represents the ambition, if not the achievement, of the first *Critique*, Kant was in fact motivated by more specific interests. If we turn to the historical antecedents of Kant's argument, we can extract from the philosophical controversies which influenced him certain major subjects of dispute. The most important we find to be the problem of objective knowledge, as this had been posed by Descartes. I can know much about myself, and this knowledge often has a character of certainty. In particular it is senseless, according to Descartes, to doubt that I exist. Here, doubt only confirms what is doubted. *Cogito ergo sum*. In this case, at least, I have objective knowledge. The fact that I exist is an objective fact; it is a fact about the world and not just about someone's perception. Whatever the world contains, it contains the thinking being who I am. Kant's contemporary Lichtenberg pointed out that Descartes ought not to have drawn this conclusion. The 'cogito' shows that there is a thought, but not that there is an 'I' who thinks it. Kant, similarly dissatisfied with Descartes's argument, and with the doctrine of the soul that flowed from it, felt that the certainty of self-knowledge had been wrongly described. It is true that, however sceptical I may be about the world, I cannot extend my scepticism into the subjective sphere (the sphere of consciousness): so I can be immediately certain of my present mental states. But I cannot be immediately certain of what I am, or of whether, indeed, there is an 'I' to whom these states belong. These further propositions must be established by argument, and that argument had yet to be found.

What is the character of this immediate and certain knowledge? The distinguishing feature of my present mental states is that they are as they seem to me and seem as they are. In the subjective sphere being and seeming collapse into each other. In the objective sphere they diverge. The world is objective because it can be other than it seems to me. So the true question of objective knowledge is: how can I know the world as it is? I can have knowledge of the world as it *seems*, since that is merely knowledge of my present perceptions, memories, thoughts and feelings. But can I have knowledge of the world that is *not* just knowledge of how it seems? To put the question in slightly more general form: can I have knowledge of the world which is not just knowledge of my own point of view? Science, common sense, theology and personal life all suppose the possibility of objective knowledge. If this supposition is unwarranted then so are almost all the beliefs that we commonly entertain.

Among Kant's immediate predecessors two in particular had provided answers to the question of objectivity which were sufficiently decisive to command the attention of the intellectual world. These were G. W. Leibniz (1646–1716) and David Hume (1711–76); the first claimed that we could have objective knowledge of the world uncontaminated by the point of view of any observer, the second claimed (or at least seemed to his contemporaries to claim) that we could have objective knowledge of nothing.

Leibniz was the founding father of Prussian academic philosophy. His thought, left to the world in succinct and unpublished fragments, had been built into a system by Christian von Wolff (1679–1754), and applied and extended by Wolff's pupil, the former pietist, A. G. Baumgarten (1714–62). The Leibnizian system had met with official censure during Kant's youth, since it made such claims for reason as to threaten those of faith; for a time Wolff was forbidden to teach. But the system was restored to favour under Frederick the Great, and became the orthodox metaphysics of the German Enlightenment. Kant respected this orthodoxy, and to the end of his days would use Baumgarten's works as texts for his lectures. But Hume's scepticism made a deep impression on him, and introduced new problems which he felt could be answered only by overthrowing the Leibnizian system. These problems, concerning causality and a priori knowledge (i.e. knowledge not based in experience), were combined with the question of objectivity to form the peculiar subject-matter of the first *Critique*.

Leibniz belonged to the school of thought now generally labelled 'rationalist', and Hume to the school of 'empiricism' which is commonly contrasted with it. Kant, believing that both philosophies were wrong in their conclusions, attempted to give an account of philosophical method which incorporated the truths, and avoided the errors, of both. Rationalism derives all knowledge from the exercise of reason, and purports to give an absolute description of the world, uncontaminated by the experience of any observer. Empiricism argues that knowledge comes through experience alone; there is therefore no possibility of separating knowledge from the subjective condition of the knower. Kant wished to give an answer to the question of objective knowledge which was neither as absolute as Leibniz's nor as subjective as Hume's. The best way to make his unique position intelligible is to begin by summarising the two views which he strove to reject.

Leibniz believed that the understanding contains within itself certain innate principles, which it knows intuitively to be true, and which form the axioms from which a complete description of the world can be derived. These principles are necessarily true, and do not depend upon experience for their confirmation. Hence they lead to a description of the world as it is, not as it appears in experience or to a circumscribed 'point of view'. At the same time the 'points of view' which are characteristic of individuals can be fitted into the rational picture of the world. Leibniz recognised a division in thought between subject and predicate; (in the sentence 'John thinks' the subject-term is 'John', and the predicate-term is 'thinks'). He believed that this division corresponds to a distinction in reality between substance and property. The fundamental objects in the world are substances. These, he thought, must be self-dependent, unlike the properties which inhere in them: for example, a substance can exist without thinking, but no thinking can exist without a substance. Being self-dependent substances are also indestructible, except by a miracle. He called them 'monads', and his model for the monad was the individual soul, the thinking substance, as this had been described by Descartes. From this idea, he derived his 'perspectiveless' picture of the world, relying on two fundamental laws of reason: the Principle of Contradiction (a proposition and its negation cannot both be true), and the Principle of Sufficient Reason (nothing is true which has no sufficient explanation). By means of ingenious and subtle arguments and making the fewest possible assumptions, he arrived at the following conclusions.

The world consists of infinitely many individual monads which exist neither in space nor in time, but eternally. Each monad is different in some respect from every other (the famous 'identity of indiscernibles'). Without that assumption objects cannot be individuated in terms of their intrinsic properties; a point of view then becomes necessary from which to tell things apart, and it is Leibniz's contention that the real nature of the world can be given from no point of view. The point of view of each monad is simply a way of representing its internal constitution; it does not represent the world as it is in itself. Each monad mirrors the universe from its own point of view, but no monad can enter into real relation, causal or otherwise, with any other. Even space and time are intellectual constructs, through which we make our experience intelligible, but which do not belong to the world as such. However, by the principle of 'preestablished harmony', the successive properties of every monad correspond to the successive properties of every other. So we can describe our successive states of mind as 'perceptions', and the world will 'appear' to each monad in a way which corresponds to its appearance to every other. There is a system among appearances, and within this system it makes sense to speak of spatial, temporal and causal relations; of destructible individuals and dynamic principles; of perception, activity and influence. These ideas, and the physical laws which we derive from them, depend for their validity on the underlying harmony among points of view which they describe.

They do not yield knowledge of the real world of monads except indirectly, on account of our assurance that the way things appear bears the metaphysical imprint of the way things are. When two watches keep exact time together I might be tempted to think that the one causes the other to move. This is an example of a merely apparent relation. In some such way Leibniz argued that the whole world of common-sense belief and perception is no more than an appearance or 'phenomenon'. But it is, Leibniz said, a 'well-founded' phenomenon. It is no illusion, but a necessary and systematic offshoot of the operation of those rational principles which determine how things really are. The real substances, because they are described and identified from no point of view, are without phenomenal characteristics. Reality itself is accessible to reason alone, since only reason can rise above the individual point of view and participate in the vision of ultimate necessities, which is also God's. Hence reason must operate through 'innate' ideas. These are ideas which have been acquired through no experience and which belong to all thinking beings. They owe their content not to experience but to the intuitive capacities of reason. Among these ideas is that of substance, from which all Leibniz's principles ultimately flow.

Hume's vision is in some measure the opposite of Leibniz's. He denies the possibility of knowledge through reason, since reason cannot operate without ideas, and ideas are acquired only through the senses. The content of every thought must be given, in the last analysis, in terms of the experiences which warrant it, and no belief can be established as true except by reference to the sensory 'impressions' which provide its guarantee. (This is the general assumption of empiricism.) But the only experience that can confirm anything for *me* is *my* experience. The testimony of others, or of records, the formulation of laws or hypotheses, the appeal to memory and induction—all these depend for their authority on the experiences which guarantee them. My experiences are as they seem, and seem as they are, for here 'seeming' is all that there is. Hence there is no problem as to how I can know them. But in basing all knowledge on experience Hume reduces my knowledge of the world to knowledge of my point of view. All claims to objectivity become spurious and illusory. When I claim to have knowledge of objects existing externally to my perceptions, all I can really mean is that those perceptions exhibit a kind of constancy and coherence which generates the (illusory) idea of independence. When I refer to causal necessities all I am entitled to mean is the regular succession among experiences, together with the subjective sense of anticipation which arises from that. As for reason, this can tell us of the 'relations of ideas': for example, it can tell us that the idea of space is included in that of shape, or that the idea of a bachelor is identical with that of an unmarried man. But it can neither generate ideas of its own, nor decide whether an idea has application. It is the source only of trivial knowledge derived from the meanings of words; it can never lead to knowledge of matters of fact. Hume took his scepticism so far as to cast doubt upon the existence of the self (that entity which has provided the model for Leibniz's monad), saying that neither is there a perceivable object that goes by this name, nor is there any experience that would give rise to the idea of it.

Such scepticism, reaching back into that very point of view from which scepticism begins, is intolerable, and it is not surprising that Kant was, as he put it, aroused by Hume from 'dogmatic slumbers' (M 9). The parts of Hume's philosophy which most disturbed him concerned the concept of causality. Hume had argued that there is no foundation for the belief in necessities in nature: necessity belongs to thought alone, and merely reflects the 'relations of ideas'. It was this that led Kant to perceive that natural science rests on the belief that there are real necessities, so that Hume's scepticism, far from being an academic exercise, threatened to undermine the foundations of scientific thought. Kant did indeed have a lasting quarrel with Leibniz, and with the Leibnizian system. But it was the sense that the problems of objectivity and of causal necessity are ultimately connected that led him towards the outlook of the *Critique of Pure Reason*. It was only then that he perceived what was really wrong with Leibniz, through his attempt to show what was really wrong with Hume. He came to think as follows.

Neither experience nor reason are alone able to provide knowledge. The first provides content without form, the second form without content. Only in their synthesis is knowledge possible; hence there is no knowledge that does not bear the marks of reason and of experience together. Such knowledge is, however, genuine and objective. It transcends the point of view of the man who possesses it, and makes legitimate claims about an independent world. Nevertheless, it is impossible to know the world 'as it is in itself', independent of all perspective. Such an absolute conception of the object of knowledge is senseless, Kant argues, since it can be given only by employing concepts from which every element of meaning has been refined away. While I can know the world independently of my point of view on it, what I know (the world of 'appearance') bears the indelible marks of that point of view. Objects do not depend for their existence upon my perceiving them; but their nature is determined by the fact that they *can* be perceived. Objects are not Leibnizian monads, knowable only to the perspectiveless stance of 'pure reason'; nor are they Humean 'impressions', features of my own experience. They are objective, but their character is given by the point of view through which they can be known. This is the point of view of 'possible experience'. Kant tries to show that, properly understood, the idea of 'experience' already carries the objective reference which Hume denied. Experience contains *within* itself the features of space, time and causality. Hence in describing my experience I am referring to an ordered perspective on an independent world.

In order to introduce this novel conception of objectivity (to which he gave the name 'transcendental idealism') Kant began from an exploration of a priori knowledge. Among true propositions, some are true independently of experience, and remain true however experience varies: these are the a priori truths. Others owe their truth to experience, and might have been false had experience been different: these are the a posteriori truths.

(The terminology here was not invented by Kant, although it owes its popularity to Kant's frequent use of it.) Kant argued that a priori truths are of two kinds, which he called 'analytic' and 'synthetic' (A 6–10). An analytic truth is one like 'All bachelors are unmarried' whose truth is guaranteed by the meaning, and discovered through the analysis, of the terms used to express it. A synthetic truth is one whose truth is not so derived but which, as Kant puts it, affirms something in the predicate which is not already contained in the subject. It is a truth like 'All bachelors are unfulfilled' which (supposing it to be true) says something substantial about bachelors and does not merely reiterate the definition of the term used to refer to them. The distinction between the analytic and the synthetic involved novel terminology, although similar distinctions can be found in earlier philosophers. Aquinas, inspired by Boethius, defines a 'self-evident' proposition as one in which the 'predicate is contained in the notion of the subject', and a similar idea is to be found in Leibniz. What is original, however, is Kant's insistence that the two distinctions (between the a priori and the a posteriori, and between the analytic and the synthetic), are of a wholly different nature. It is mere dogmatism on the part of empiricists to think that they must coincide. And yet for the empiricist view to be true, there cannot be synthetic a priori knowledge: synthetic truths can be known only through experience.

The empiricist position has been taken in our time by the logical positivists of the 'Vienna circle', who argued that all a priori truths are analytic, and drew the conclusion that any metaphysical proposition must be meaningless, since it could be neither synthetic nor a posteriori. It was already apparent to Kant that empiricism denies the possibility of metaphysics. And yet metaphysics is necessary if foundations are to be provided for objective knowledge: without it, there is no conceivable barrier against the scepticism of Hume. So the first question of all philosophy becomes 'How is synthetic a priori knowledge possible?' Or, to put it another way, 'How can I come to know the world through pure reflection, without recourse to experience?' Kant felt that there could be no explanation of a priori knowledge which divorces the object known from the perspective of the knower. Hence he was sceptical of all attempts to claim that we can have a priori knowledge of some timeless, spaceless world of the 'thing-in-itself' (any object defined without reference to the 'possible experience' of an observer). I can have a priori knowledge only of the world that I experience. A priori knowledge provides support for, but it also derives its content from, empirical discovery. Kant's *Critique* is directed against the assumption that 'pure reason' can give content to knowledge without making reference to experience.

All a priori truths are both necessary and absolutely universal: these are the two signs whereby we can discern, among our claims to knowledge, those items which, if they are true at all, are true a priori. For it is obvious that experience could never confer necessity or absolute universality on anything; any experience *might* have been otherwise, and experience is necessarily finite and particular, so that a universal law (which has indefinitely many instances) could never be truly confirmed by it. No one should really doubt that there is synthetic a priori knowledge: Kant gave as the most conspicuous example mathematics, which we know by pure reasoning, but not by analysing the meanings of mathematical terms. There ought to be a philosophical explanation of the a priori nature of mathematics, and Kant attempted to provide it in the opening sections of the *Critique*. But he also drew attention to other examples, of a more puzzling kind. For instance, the following propositions seem to be true a priori: 'Every event has a cause'; 'The world consists of enduring objects which exist independently of me'; 'All discoverable objects are in space and time.' These propositions cannot be established through experience, since their truth is presupposed in the interpretation of experience. Moreover, each claims to be true, not just on this or that occasion, but universally and necessarily. Finally, it is just such truths as these that are required for the proof of objectivity. Hence the problem of objectivity and the problem of synthetic a priori knowledge are ultimately connected. Moreover, the vital role played by the truths given above in all scientific explanation persuaded Kant that a theory of objectivity would also provide an explanation of natural necessity. Such a theory would then give a complete answer to the scepticism of Hume.

What, then, are Kant's aims in the first *Critique*? First, in opposition to Hume, to show that synthetic a priori knowledge is possible, and to offer examples of it. Secondly, in opposition to Leibniz, to demonstrate that 'pure reason' alone, operating outside the constraints placed on it by experience, leads only to illusion, so that there is no a priori knowledge of 'things-in-themselves'. It is normal to divide the *Critique* into two parts, in accordance with this division of the subject, and to describe the first part as the 'Analytic', the second as the 'Dialectic'. While this division does not correspond exactly to Kant's division of chapters (which is exceedingly complex and bristles with technicalities), it is sufficiently close not to be misleading. The terms 'analytic' and 'dialectic' are Kant's: and so is the bifurcation of the argument. In the first part Kant's defence of objectivity is expounded, and it is with the argument of the 'Analytic' that I shall begin, for until it is grasped, it will be impossible to understand the nature either of Kant's metaphysics, or of the moral and aesthetic doctrines which he later brought within its purview.

3 *The transcendental deduction*

Kant's answer to the fundamental question of metaphysics—
'How is synthetic a priori knowledge possible?'—contains two
parts. I shall call these, following Kant's own terminology (A
xvi), the 'subjective' and the 'objective' deductions. The first
had been partly adumbrated in Kant's inaugural dissertation of
1770 (I 54 ff.), and consists in a theory of cognition. It tries to
show what is involved in making a judgement: in holding
something to be true or false. It concentrates on the nature of
the mind, in particular on the nature of belief, sensation and
experience. Its conclusions are presented as part of a general
theory of the 'understanding' (the faculty of judgement). Kant
repeatedly emphasises that the theory is not to be construed as
empirical psychology. It is not, nor does it purport to be, a
theory of the workings of the *human*, as opposed to some other,
intelligence. It is a theory of the understanding as such, telling
us what it is, and how it must function if there are to be
judgements at all. In all philosophical discussion of these matters, Kant argues, we are talking 'not about the origin of experience, but about what lies in it' (M 63). And he compares
such purely philosophical questions to that 'analysis of concepts' which has since become so fashionable. Kant wishes to
draw the limits of the understanding. If there are things which
cannot be grasped by the understanding, then all assertions
about them are meaningless.

The objective deduction consists in a positive attempt to
establish the content of a priori knowledge. The argument here
proceeds, not by an analysis of the faculties of knowledge, but
by an exploration of its grounds. What are the presuppositions
of experience? What has to be true if we are to have even that

bare point of view which the sceptics ascribe to us? If we can identify these presuppositions, then they will be established as true a priori. For their truth follows, not from the fact that we have this or that experience, but from the fact that we have experience *at all*. Hence they depend upon no particular experience for their verification, and can be established by reasoning alone. They will be true in every world where the sceptical question can be asked (in every comprehensible world). And this is tantamount to their being necessary. I cannot conceive of their falsehood, since I cannot conceive *myself* as part of a world which refutes them.

Kant calls this argument the 'transcendental deduction', and the resulting theory 'transcendental idealism'. The word 'transcendental' needs some explanation. An argument is transcendental if it 'transcends' the limits of empirical enquiry, so as to establish the a priori conditions of experience. We must distinguish transcendental from, empirical argument (B 81); the former, unlike the latter, leads to 'knowledge which is occupied not so much with objects as with the mode of our knowledge of objects *in so far as this mode of knowledge is possible a priori*' (B 25). The word 'transcendental' is also used by Kant in another sense, to refer to 'transcendental objects'. These are objects which transcend experience, i.e. which are not disclosed to empirical investigation, being neither observable themselves, nor causally related to what is observable. These 'transcendental objects' present a problem of interpretation to which I shall return in Chapter 4.

I shall also return to the interpretation of 'transcendental idealism'. Briefly, this theory implies that the laws of the understanding, laid down in the subjective deduction, are the same as the a priori truths established in the objective deduction. It implies, in other words, a very special kind of harmony between the capacities of the knower and the nature of the known. It is because of this harmony that a priori knowledge is possible.

It follows from this theory that the 'forms of thought' which govern the understanding, and the a priori nature of reality, are in exact correspondence. The world is as we think it, and we think it as it is. Almost all the major difficulties in the interpretation of Kant depend upon which of those two propositions is emphasised. Is it our thought which determines the a priori nature of the world? Or is it the world which determines how we must think of it? The answer, I believe, is 'neither, and both'. But only at the very end of this essay will that answer be clear.

Self-consciousness

I have referred, adopting Kant's usage, to 'our' understanding and experience. Who are 'we'? Kant's use of the first person plural is a device of a very special character. He is not, as I said, engaging in a psychological study of 'creatures like us'. Nor is he speaking with some abstract authorial voice for which no true subject can be found. He means the term 'we' to denote indifferently any being who can use the term 'I': anyone who can identify *himself* as the subject of experience. The starting-point of all Kant's philosophy is the single premise of self-consciousness, and his three *Critiques* concern themselves respectively with the questions: 'What must a self-conscious being think?', 'What must he do?' and 'What must he find agreeable?' Self-consciousness is a deep phenomenon, with many layers and aspects: different features of it are invoked as we tackle each of those questions. In the case of the first *Critique* the feature is that which Kant regarded as providing common ground between himself and the empiricists whom he sought to refute: self-conscious experience. It is not every being that can know his own experience (for whom the 'I think' can accompany all his perceptions), as Kant expresses his crucial emendation of Descartes (B 131–2). But it is only such a being who can pose the sceptical question: 'Are things as they seem to me (as my experience represents them)?' The argument explores, therefore, the presuppositions of this self-consciousness. Kant's conclusion can be summarised thus: the conditions which make scepticism possible also show that it is false.

The transcendental synthesis

I shall deal first with the subjective deduction—the theory of the 'subjective conditions' of judgement. There are two sources from which our knowledge is drawn: sensibility and understanding. The first is a faculty of intuitions (*Anschauungen*): it includes all the sensory states and modifications which empiricists think to be the sole basis of knowledge. The second is a faculty of concepts. Since concepts have to be *applied* in judgements, this faculty, unlike sensibility, is active. It is a mistake of empiricism, Kant argued, not to have understood this crucial point, and to have construed all concepts of the understanding on the model of sensations. (Thus for Hume a concept is simply a faded relict of the 'impression' from which it derives.) The corresponding mistake of rationalism is to think of sensation as a kind of confused aspiration towards conceptual thought. Thus Kant summarised the famous dispute between Leibniz and Locke in the following way: 'Leibniz *intellectualised* appearances, just as Locke ... *sensualised* the concept of the understanding'. In fact, however, there are two faculties here, irreducible the one to the other; they 'can supply objectively valid judgements of things only in *conjunction* with each other' (A 271, B 327).

Judgement requires, then, the joint operation of sensibility and understanding. A mind without concepts would have no capacity to think; equally, a mind armed with concepts, but with no sensory data to which they could be applied, would have nothing to think *about*. 'Without sensibility no object would be given to us, without understanding no object would be thought. Thoughts without content are empty; intuitions without concepts are blind' (A 51, B 75). Judgement requires what Kant calls a 'synthesis' of concept and intuition, and only in this synthesis is true experience (as opposed to mere 'intuition') generated. This synthesis is somewhat confusingly described by Kant: sometimes it seems to be a 'process' whereby experience is generated, at other times a kind of 'structure' which experience contains. In any event, it seems to have two stages: the 'pure' synthesis, whereby intuitions are grouped together into a totality, and then the act of judgement, in which the totality is given form through a concept (A 79, B 104). This synthesis is not meant to be a psychological fact; it is a 'transcendental' as opposed to an 'empirical' synthesis. In other words, it is *presupposed* in (self-conscious) experience, and not derived from it. I do not lay hold of my experience and then subject it to synthesis. For the very act of 'laying hold' presupposes that this synthesis has occurred. Suppose I attempt to describe how things seem to me, as I sit writing at this desk. I am at once engaged in the activity of subsuming my sensory awareness under concepts (such concepts as those of desk and writing). I can represent my experience to myself only by describing 'how things seem': and that is to use the concepts of the understanding. Conversely, none of my concepts would be intelligible without the experiences which exhibit their application.

A priori concepts

It is an assumption of empiricism that all concepts are derived from, or in some manner reducible to, the sensory intuitions which warrant their application. There can be no concept without the corresponding sensory stimulus, and it is in terms of such stimulus that the meaning of a concept must be given. Kant argued that this assumption is absurd. The empiricists confuse experience with sensation. Experience can provide the grounds for the application of a concept, because it already contains a concept, in accordance with the 'synthesis' just described. Sensation, or intuition, contains no concept, and provides grounds for no judgement. Until transformed by mental activity, all sensation is without intellectual structure, and therefore provides grounds for no belief. If we understand experiences, then it is because they already contain within themselves the concepts which we supposedly derive from them. Whence came these concepts? Not from the senses. There must therefore be some repertoire of concepts contained within the understanding itself, and which defines the forms of its activity.

It follows that the Leibnizian theory of 'innate ideas' is substantially correct. There are concepts which cannot be given *through* experience because they are presupposed *in* experience. They are involved in every apprehension of the world that I can represent as mine; not to possess them is to have, not experience, but mere intuition, from which no knowledge can be derived. These 'a priori concepts' of the understanding prescribe the basic 'forms' of judgement. All other concepts can be seen as 'determinations' of them—that is, as special cases, more or less adulterated by the reference to observation and experiment.

Kant called these fundamental concepts 'categories', borrowing a term that had been put to similar (but less systematic) use by Aristotle. The categories are our forms of thought. One such category is the concept which lies at the origin of the Leibnizian system: the category of substance. A substance is that which is able to exist independently, and which supports the properties which depend upon it. The concept 'chair' is a special, empirical determination of the general concept of substance. It can be acquired only by someone who already grasps that general concept, for only such a person would be able to interpret his experience in the requisite way. Another category is the one that had been subjected to such sceptical attack by Hume: the category of cause. It is not surprising that much of the argument of the Analytic concerns the ideas of substance and causality, as Kant wished us to understand them. However, he gave a list of twelve categories in all, and found to his satisfaction that they corresponded to all the disputes of traditional metaphysics.

The subjective deduction

It seems to follow from the above account that if we are to have knowledge at all, our intuitions must permit application of the categories. To speak more directly: it must seem to us that we are confronted by substances, causes and the rest. So we can know a priori that every comprehensible world (every world which could contain self-consciousness) must also have the appearance dictated by the categories. It can have that appearance only if it appears to obey certain 'principles'. A principle specifies the conditions under which a category gains application. The sum of all principles defines the extent of our claims to a priori knowledge.

What does this 'subjective deduction' of the categories establish? The answer seems to be this: we must think in terms of the categories, and must therefore accept as true the principles which govern their application. So the world must ordinarily appear to us in such a way that we *can* accept these principles. Self-consciousness requires that the world must appear to 'conform to the categories'. This assertion contains the essence of what Kant called his 'Copernican Revolution' in philosophy. Previous philosophers had taken nature as primary, and asked how our cognitive capacities could lay hold of it. Kant takes those capacities as primary, and then deduces the a priori limits of nature. This is the first important step in his answer to Hume. It is well for Hume to assert that our knowledge has its foundation in experience. But experience is not the simple concept that Hume supposed it to be. Experience contains intellectual structure. It is already organised in accordance with the ideas of space, time, substance and causality. Hence there is no knowledge of experience that does not point towards a world of nature. Our point of view is intrinsically a point of view *on* an objective world.

But does that answer the sceptic? Surely, he will say, even if Kant were right, and the world must appear to us in this way, does it also have to *be* as it *appears*? Even if we are compelled to think that the categories apply, it does not follow that they really *do* apply. We have yet to pass from the description of our point of view to a description of the world. The problem therefore remains, how 'subjective conditions of thought can have objective validity' (A 89, B 122). As Kant argues (B 141), there can be no judgement without objectivity. Clearly then, an 'objective deduction' of the categories is required: an argument that will show that the world, and not just our experience of the world, is in conformity with the a priori principles of the understanding.

Forms of thought and forms of intuition

Before proceeding to that objective deduction we must return to the earlier sections of the *Critique of Pure Reason*, in which Kant writes in general terms about the nature of sensibility. Kant believed that he had arrived at his list of categories by a process of abstraction. Suppose I describe what I now see: a pen writing. The concept 'pen' is a special 'determination' of the wider concept 'artifact', itself a determination of 'material object', and so on. The limit of this train of abstraction is the a priori concept which each stage exemplifies: the concept of substance. Beyond that point we cannot abstract further, without ceasing to think. Likewise 'writing' is a determination of 'action', which is a determination of 'force', and so on: the category here being that of cause or explanation, beyond which the understanding cannot proceed. By these, and similar, thought-experiments, Kant supposed that he had isolated, through his list of the twelve categories, all the forms of judgement, and so given an exposition of the concept of objective truth. Hence the proof of the objectivity of our claims to knowledge involves the demonstration of the 'objective validity' of the categories, and of the principles presupposed in their application.

There are two ideas, however, which, despite their importance to science and to the objective view of the world, are not included in Kant's list of categories. These are the ideas of space and time, which he described, not as concepts, but as forms of intuition. Space and time are discussed in the opening section of the first *Critique*, the 'Transcendental Aesthetic'. The word 'aesthetic' here derives from the Greek for sensation, and indicates that the subject-matter of this section is the faculty of sensibility, considered independently of the understanding.

Kant argued that space and time, far from being concepts applicable to intuitions, are basic *forms* of intuition, meaning that every sensation must bear the imprint of temporal, and sometimes of spatial, organisation.

Time is the form of 'inner sense', that is, of all states of mind, whether or not they are referred to an objective reality. There could not be a mental state that is not in time, and time is made real to us through this organisation in our experience. Space is the form of 'outer sense'—that is, of those 'intuitions' which we refer to an independent world and which we therefore regard as 'appearances' of objective things. Nothing can appear to me as independent of myself without also being experienced as 'outside', and therefore as spatially related to myself. Space, like time, forms part of the organisation of my sensibility. My very sense-impressions bear the form of space, as is evidenced in the phenomenon of the 'visual field'.

But why deny that space and time are a priori concepts? They are a priori, but they cannot be concepts, since concepts are general, admitting of a plurality of instances. Kant argued that there is of necessity only one space, and only one time. All spaces form parts of a single space, and all times parts of a single time. Kant sometimes expresses this point by saying that space and time are not concepts but 'a priori intuitions'.

There is, in Kant's philosophy, a rage for order that leads him to attempt to solve as many philosophical questions as possible through each distinct part of his system. One motive for treating space and time separately from the categories of the understanding is in order to suggest an explanation for the fact that there are two kinds of synthetic a priori truth: mathematics and metaphysics. It seems that there ought to be a different explanation for each, since mathematics is self-evident, and obvious to all thinking beings, whereas metaphysics is essentially disputed, a matter over which people argue interminably; 'infinitely removed from being as evident as the proposition that twice two makes four' (A 733, B 761). Mathematics possesses, indeed, all the immediacy and indubitability of intuition itself, whereas the metaphysical principles, which derive from thought alone, are necessarily contentious. By construing mathematics as an a priori science of intuition Kant thought that he could show why this is so. In mathematics we are dealing with 'a priori intuitions'; this automatically gives a content to our thought which is absent from the abstract employment of the categories. The conclusions of mathematics are arrived at both 'a priori and immediately' (A 732, B 760), whereas those of metaphysics must be derived by laborious argument.

Whether or not we accept Kant's explanation, it is a distinctive feature of his philosophy that he took mathematical truths to be synthetic a priori. At the same time he refused to countenance Plato's explanation of this synthetic a priori status, as deriving from the peculiar nature of mathematical objects: the abstract, immutable numbers and Forms. Kant also disagreed with Hume and Leibniz, both of whom had argued that mathematics is analytic. The question is, therefore, how can mathematics be synthetic a priori, and yet not provide knowledge of some mysterious and unobservable realm? In the *Inaugural Dissertation* Kant argued that the a priori nature of geometry derives from the subject, rather than from the object, of mathematical thought (I 70–2). It is this that led to his mature view that there can be a priori knowledge of space only if space enters into the nature of perception. Hence the theory of space as a 'form' of intuition.

Objective knowledge has, then, a double origin: sensibility and understanding. And just as the first must 'conform to' the second, so must the second 'conform to' the first; otherwise the transcendental synthesis of the two would be impossible. What does it mean to say that the understanding must 'conform to' the sensibility? Since time is the general form of all sensibility, the claim amounts to this: the categories must find their primary application in time, and be 'determined', or limited, accordingly. Thus the concept of substance must have, as its primary instance, not the monads of Leibniz, nor the abstract objects of the Platonic supersphere, but ordinary temporal things, which endure through time, and are subject to change.

If such things are objective, then, by the theory that space is the form of outer sense, they must also be spatial. So to prove the 'objective validity' of the concept of substance is not to prove that the world consists of monads. The world consists rather of ordinary spatio-temporal objects. The philosophical proof of objectivity establishes the existence, not of an abstract, perspectiveless, world, but of the common-sense world of science and everyday perception: the very world which both Humean scepticism and Leibnizian metaphysics had thrown in doubt. It was therefore important to Kant to show, in his proof of objectivity, that the beliefs which he justified corresponded exactly to the laws which Newtonian science had laid down for all perceivable things.

The transcendental unity of apperception

The 'objective' deduction of the categories begins from the premise of self-consciousness, described, in characteristic language, as the 'transcendental unity of apperception'. It is important to understand this phrase which contains in embryo much of Kant's philosophy. 'Apperception' is a term taken from Leibnizian metaphysics; it refers to any experience of which the subject is able to say 'this is mine'. In other words, 'apperception' means 'self-conscious experience'. The unity of apperception consists in the '"I think" which can accompany all my perceptions' (B 131–2), to borrow again Kant's version of Descartes. It consists of my immediate awareness that simultaneous experiences belong to me. I know immediately that this thought, and this perception, are equally *mine*, in the sense of belonging to the unity of consciousness which defines my point of view. Doubt is here impossible: I could never be in the position that Dickens in *Hard Times* attributes to Mrs Gradgrind on her deathbed, knowing that there is a pain in the room somewhere, but not knowing that it is mine. This apprehension of unity is called 'transcendental' because I could never derive it from experience. I could not argue that, because this pain has such a quality, and this thought such another, they must belong to a single consciousness. If I did that, I could make a mistake; I could be in the absurd position of ascribing to myself some pain, thought or perception which belonged, not to me, but to some other consciousness. So the unity that I apprehend in my point of view is not a conclusion from experience, but a presupposition of experience. Its basis 'transcends' anything that experience could establish. As Kant sometimes puts it, the unity of consciousness 'precedes' all the data of intuition (A 107).

The transcendental unity of apperception provides the minimal description of our point of view. I can know at least one thing: that there is a unity of consciousness. To doubt this is to cease to be self-conscious, and so to cease to find significance in doubt. The task is to show that this point of view is possible only in an objective world.

The transcendental deduction

The objective deduction has the same 'transcendental' character as its premise. It is concerned to show that the truth of its conclusion is not a deduction from experience but presupposed in the *existence* of experience. The transcendental unity of apperception is possible only if the subject inhabits the kind of world which the categories describe: an objective world, in which things may be other than they seem. To put the argument in a nutshell: the unity of apperception describes the condition of subjectivity, in which everything is as it seems and seems as it is. But no one can have the point of view of subjectivity who does not have knowledge of objective truths. He must therefore belong to a world of things which can be other than they seem, and which exist independently of his own perspective.

An argument to that effect is hard to find, and it is significant that Kant was so dissatisfied with 'The Transcendental Deduction' that he rewrote it entirely for the second edition of the *Critique*, changing its emphasis from the subjective conclusion given above towards the objective deduction presently under discussion. Even so, the result is very obscure, and a further passage—'The Refutation of Idealism'—was added in order to make the emphasis on objectivity more persuasive. The point of this 'refutation' was to show 'that we have experience, and not merely *imagination*, of outer things' by demonstrating that 'even our inner experience [*Erfahrung*], which for Descartes is indubitable, is possible only on the assumption of outer experience [i.e. experience of an objective world]' (B 275). The flavour of the argument is more apparent than its substance. At least the following three thoughts seem to be involved in it:

(i) Identifying experience. It is a common empiricist assumption that I can know my experience simply by observing it. But this is not so. I do not observe my experience, but only its object. Any knowledge of experience must therefore involve knowledge of its object. But I can have knowledge of the object only if I identify it as continuous. Nothing can have temporal continuity without also having the capacity to exist when unobserved. Its existence is therefore independent of my perception.

(ii) Identity through time. I can identify experience as mine only if I locate it in time. I must therefore ascribe it to a subject who exists in time and endures through time. My unity requires my continuity. But to endure is to be substantial, and nothing can be substantial unless it also enters into causal relations. I endure only if my past explains my future. Otherwise there is no difference between genuine duration and an infinite sequence of momentary selves. If I can be conscious of my experience at all, I can therefore conclude that I belong to a world to which such categories as substance and cause are correctly applied, since they are correctly applied to me. A condition of self-consciousness is, therefore, the existence of just that objective order which my experience suggests to me.

(iii) Ordering in time. I have privileged knowledge of *present* experience. To know my experience is therefore to know it *as* present. This is possible only if I distinguish in experience between *now* and *then*. Hence there is a 'temporal order' inherent in perception, and I must know this order if I am to know myself. But I can know it only if I can make reference to independent objects, and the regularities which govern them. Only then will I be able to describe time as a dimension *in* which experience occurs, rather than as a series of unrelated instants. The reality of time is presupposed in experience. And the reality of time presupposes the reality of an objective sequence. It is only by reference to that sequence, and to the enduring objects that structure it, that I can identify my own perception.

None of those thoughts is clearer in the original than in my brief résumé. It is fair to say that the transcendental deduction has never been considered to provide a satisfactory argument. In all its versions it involves a transition from the *unity* of consciousness to the *identity* of the subject through time. Hume pointed out that the slide from unity to identity is involved in all our claims to objective knowledge; he also thought that it could never be justified. Kant did not find the terms with which to answer Hume. Nevertheless his enterprise has appealed to many subsequent philosophers, and the transcendental deduction has been revived in recent years, most notably by Ludwig Wittgenstein (1889–1951). In the famous 'private language' argument in his *Philosophical Investigations* Wittgenstein argues that there can be no knowledge of experience which does not presuppose reference to a public world. I can know my own experience immediately and incorrigibly, but only because I apply to it concepts which gain their sense from public usage. And public usage describes a reality observable to others besides myself. The publicity of my language guarantees the objectivity of its reference. Wittgenstein's argument—which has seemed persuasive to many—shares the premise and the conclusion of the transcendental deduction. It relies, however, not on metaphysical doctrines about time, but on doctrines about reference and meaning.

If valid, the transcendental deduction achieves a result of immense significance. It established the objectivity of my world while assuming no more than my point of view on it. Descartes, in the proof of the external world offered in his *Meditations*, tried to step outside the point of view of the subject by establishing the existence of an omniscient God: the world is then validated as an object of God's (perspectiveless) awareness. The essence of Kant's 'transcendental' method lies in its egocentricity. All the questions that I can ask I must ask from the standpoint that is mine; therefore they must bear the marks of my perspective, which is the perspective of 'possible experience'. The answer to them is not to be found in the attempt to rise to the standpoint of the reasoning being who knows without experience, but to find, within my experience itself, the response to sceptical enquiry. The transcendental method finds the answer to every philosophical question in the presuppositions of the perspective from which it must be asked.

Principles

Kant argues that every category corresponds to a principle, whose truth is presupposed in its application. Principles are 'rules for the objective employment' of the categories (A 161, B 200). These principles are a priori truths, and they have two aspects. They say how we must think if we are to think at all; and, in their objective aspect, they say how the world must be if it is to be intelligible. Through these principles, the categories 'prescribe laws a priori to appearances, and therefore to nature' (B 163). That is to say, they lay down synthetic a priori truths concerning the world of everyday and scientific observation. They are not a priori truths about 'things-in-themselves'. They do not give knowledge of a world described without reference to our perception. Synthetic a priori knowledge is only of 'things which may be the objects of possible experience' (B 148). In this area, the principles state objective and necessary truths, since the categories 'relate of necessity and a priori to the objects of experience, for the reason that only by means of them can any object of experience be thought' (A 110). The limitation to the 'objects of possible experience' is vital to Kant's philosophy, and he repeatedly emphasises that 'outside the field of possible experience there can be no synthetic a priori principles' (A 248, B 305). We must always bear in mind that Kant wishes to admit a priori knowledge, but also to deny the possibility of the perspectiveless metaphysics of Leibniz.

I have chosen to concentrate on the categories of substance and cause. Kant associated these with a third, that of community, or reciprocal interaction. These concepts had been the principal objects of Hume's sceptical attack. They were also crucial to Leibniz's metaphysics, substance being the idea from which Leibniz began, and the 'Principle of Sufficient Reason', associated by Kant with causality (A 200–1, B 246), being the principle which governed his argument. Kant's discussion of these concepts is of great and lasting interest. He placed them at the heart of the question of objectivity, and expressed, in their analysis, what he took to be the metaphysical foundations of physical science. He derives their associated principles in a section called 'Analogies of Experience', and it is here that Kant makes some of his most revolutionary suggestions concerning the nature of objective knowledge.

Kant's division of all philosophical thought into elements of four and three is obsessive. But there is a special reason, when talking of substance and causality, for his insistence that there should be a third basic concept associated with these; namely, that Kant wished his results to correspond to the three Newtonian laws of motion. Scientific explanation depends upon principles of method: being presupposed in scientific enquiry, these principles cannot be proved through it. Kant believed that such principles would be reflected in basic scientific laws; and it is one of the tasks of metaphysics to provide grounds for their acceptance.

The physical science of Kant's day seemed to assume a priori the existence of universal causation, and of reciprocal interaction. It assumed that it must explain, not the *existence* of matter, but the changes undergone by it. It assumed the need for a law of conservation, according to which, in all changes, some fundamental quantity remains unaltered. It is just such assumptions, Kant thought, that had guided Newton in the formulation of his laws of motion. Kant therefore attempts, in deriving his principles, to establish the 'validity of universal laws of nature as laws of the understanding' (M 74), arguing further that all the fundamental laws of the new astronomy can be seen, on reflection, to rest on principles that are valid a priori (M 83).

The attempt to uphold the Newtonian mechanics is mixed with an attack on Hume's scepticism about causality. Kant tries to show that causal relations are necessary, both in the sense that it is necessary that objects enter into them (there is no event without a cause), and also in the sense that they are themselves a species of necessary connection.

The 'Analogies' contain too many arguments to be treated in detail here. Like other crucial passages of the Analytic, they were substantially rewritten for the second edition, the actual statement of the 'principles' undergoing significant revisions. But two theses deserve singling out on account of their subsequent importance. First, Kant argues that all explanation of change requires the postulation of an unchanging substance, and uses this as proof of the validity of a fundamental 'law of conservation' in science. His arguments provide one of the most important insights into the nature of scientific method since Descartes, and a clear move in the direction of the modern doctrine of the 'unity of science'. According to one version of this doctrine, there is a single law of conservation involved in the explanation of every change, and hence a single stuff (for example, energy), whose laws of transformation govern the whole of nature.

Secondly, Kant defends, in the second Analogy, the important metaphysical doctrine that 'the relation of cause to effect is the condition of the objective validity of our empirical judgements' (A 202, B 247). It is only because we can find causal connections in our world that we can postulate its objectivity. This is a consequence of the connection between objectivity and duration: it is because things endure that I can distinguish their appearance from their reality. But they can endure only if there is a thread of causal connection which unites their temporal parts. This table is as it is *because* it was as it was. The dependence of objectivity on causality is matched by a similar dependence of causality on substance: it is only on the assumption of enduring things that our causal laws gain application. 'Causality leads to the concept of action, this in turn to the concept of force, and thereby to the concept of substance' (A 204). We could put the point briefly by saying that we discover how things really are only by finding causes for how they seem, and we find causes only by postulating a realm of enduring things.

So the thought of an independent object involves thoughts about causality, and causality, Kant argues, is a species of necessity. To know any truth about the world is therefore to have knowledge of necessities: of what must be and of what might have been. This thesis radically contradicts the empiricist view that there are no necessities in nature, and also those modern theories which believe that our basic thoughts about the actual involve mental operations that are simpler than those involved in grasping the necessary and the possible.

All these striking theses emerge from an attempt to give what one might call a fully 'enriched' account of the objectivity of the physical world. Any philosopher who takes Kant's arguments seriously will see how difficult it is to 'reduce' the idea of an objective world to a mere synopsis of experience. Hence he will recognise the implausibility, not only of the scepticism which Kant attacked, but also of the empiricist theory of knowledge from which it began.

Conclusion

The principles are valid a priori, but only in the case of the 'objects of possible experience'. The empiricists were wrong in rejecting the possibility of such a priori principles, but right in their assumption that our own perspective on the world is in some measure a constituent of our knowledge. We can know the world a priori only in so far as it is possible for it to present an appearance to our point of view. It is vain to attempt to rise above that point of view and know the world 'as it is in itself', independently of any possible perception. Thus all attempts to prove Leibniz's Principle of Sufficient Reason 'have, by the universal admission of those concerned, been fruitless' (A 783, B 811). But the 'transcendental' equivalent of the principle, Kant argues, *is* provable: the principle of sufficient reason then becomes the law of causality, the law that every event in the empirical world is bound by causal connections. This is an a priori truth, but only of the 'world of appearance', and therefore only of events in time. Despite Kant's swaggering self-confidence in this matter, many Leibnizians felt that they *had* offered a proof of the Principle of Sufficient Reason— Baumgarten, for one. And one of Baumgarten's disciples, Eberhard, attempted to show that the critical philosophy was no more than a restatement of the Leibnizian system, the Principle of Sufficient Reason being both necessary to Kant's enterprise and provable a priori. This was one of the few criticisms of the *Critique* to which Kant felt obliged to reply (in *On a Discovery*, published in 1790). Kant demonstrates the impossibility of proving the Principle 'without relation to sensible intuition' (K 113), and emphasises the helplessness of pure reason to advance beyond concepts to any substantial truth about the world. The Principle of Sufficient Reason can be established, he argues, only by his 'transcendental' method, which relates the objects of knowledge to the capacities of the knower, and proves a priori only those laws which determine the conditions of experience.

The vain attempt of the Leibnizians to found knowledge in 'pure reason' alone is the topic of the Dialectic. In following the outline of Kant's criticisms we shall be able to see exactly what he meant by 'transcendental idealism', and why he thought it could provide the middle course between empiricism and rationalism.

4 *The logic of illusion*

While the understanding, properly employed, yields genuine, objective, knowledge, it also contains a temptation to illusion. It is this temptation that Kant attempts to diagnose and criticise in his examination of 'pure reason', and once again his argument has a subjective and an objective side. He describes a particular faculty, reason, in its illegitimate employment; he also demolishes all the claims to knowledge which that faculty tempts us to make. His subject-matter in the Dialectic is rationalist metaphysics, and he divides metaphysics into three parts—rational psychology, concerning the nature of the soul, cosmology, concerning the nature of the universe and our status within it, and theology, concerning the existence of God. He then goes on to argue that each proceeds in accordance with its own kind of illusory argument, not towards truth, but towards fallacy. The diagnosis of these errors follows a common pattern. Each attempt by pure reason to establish the metaphysical doctrines towards which it is impelled transgresses the limits of experience, applying concepts in a manner that is 'unconditioned' by the faculty of intuition. Since it is only through the synthesis of concept and intuition that judgement is formed, this attempt cannot produce knowledge. On the contrary, concepts, divorced from their 'empirical conditions', are empty. 'The pure concepts of the understanding can *never* admit of *transcendental* but *always* only of *empirical* employment' (A 246, B 303). At the same time, since concepts contain within themselves this tendency towards 'unconditioned' application, it is an inevitable disease of the understanding that 'pure reason' should usurp its functions, and the categories be transformed from instruments of knowledge into those instruments of illusion which Kant calls 'ideas'.

Here we need to take another look at transcendental idealism, in order to see exactly what it is that Kant regards himself as having established in the Analytic. We find a crucial ambiguity in Kant's doctrines, which persists through the second and third *Critiques*.

Appearance and reality

Kant often describes transcendental idealism as the doctrine that we have a priori knowledge only of 'appearances' and not of 'things as they are in themselves' (or 'things-in-themselves'). His followers and critics disputed heatedly over the 'thing-in-itself'. Moses Mendelssohn thought of it as a distinct entity, so that an appearance is one thing, the thing-in-itself another. Others, under the influence of Kant's pupil J. S. Beck, took the phrase 'thing-in-itself' to refer to a way of describing the very same object which we also know as an appearance. Kant lends support to this second interpretation in his correspondence with Beck, in many passages of the *Critique of Practical Reason*, and in a letter to one of its principal advocates: 'All objects that can be given to us can be conceptualised it two ways: on the one hand, as appearances; on the other hand, as things in themselves' (C 103 n.). But there is no doubt that his mind was not made up about the matter, and this led to a crucial ambiguity in the critical philosophy.

Kant also says that the categories can be applied to 'phenomena', but not to 'noumena'. A phenomenon is an 'object of possible experience', whereas a noumenon is an object knowable to thought alone, and which it does not make sense to describe as the object of experience. It is natural to connect the two distinctions, and to assume that Kant believes appearances, or phenomena, to be knowable through experience, and 'things-in-themselves' to be mere noumena, not knowable at all since nothing is knowable in thought alone. Kant says, for example, that the concept of a 'noumenon' can be used only negatively, to designate the limit of our knowledge, and not positively, to designate things as they are in themselves. So that 'The division of objects into phenomena and noumena, and the world into a world of the senses and a world of the understanding, is . . . quite inadmissible in the positive sense' (A 255, B 311). In which case, the 'thing-in-itself' is not an entity, but a term standing proxy for the unrealisable ideal of perspectiveless knowledge.

The ambiguity in Kant's account is illustrated by the term 'appearance', which is taken sometimes in a transitive, sometimes in an intransitive, sense. Kant sometimes writes as though appearances are 'appearances of' something, whose reality is hidden from us. At other times, he writes as though appearances were independent entities, which derive their name from the fact that we observe and discover their nature. In this second sense, the word 'appearance' corresponds to our idea of a physical object. An appearance can be observed; it is situated in space; it enters into causal relations with other appearances and with the being who observes them. It is governed by scientific laws, and is or can be an object of discovery. It may be as it seems, and also other than it seems. It can have both secondary qualities (qualities which an object possesses only in relation to a particular sensory experience) and primary qualities (qualities which belong to its inner constitution) (A 28–9). In short, appearances possess all the characteristics of physical objects. To say that an appearance is also an appearance *of* something is surely incoherent. For, by Kant's own theory, the 'something' which supposedly underlies appearance could only be a 'noumenon', and about noumena nothing significant can be said. In particular, it makes no sense (or, at least, is devoid of content) to say that a noumenon causes, or stands in any other relation to, an appearance. (Kant's critics—such as Mendelssohn and G. E. Schulze—were quick to seize on this point, and put it forward as the principal weakness of the transcendental philosophy.) Sometimes indeed Kant writes as though every object is an appearance *of* some 'thing-in-itself'. But since this is inconsistent with his theory of knowledge (which allows him neither to know nor even to mean what he purports to say) we must, for the moment, consider the thing-in-itself to be a nonentity. As we shall see, there are counter-vailing reasons which caused Kant to deny his own official theory. But it is impossible to proceed if we allow these reasons, and the rival doctrines which stem from them, to gain precedence at this juncture.

Phenomena and noumena

The first edition of the *Critique* contained a lengthy exposition of the theory of transcendental idealism. This was deleted by Kant from the second edition, perhaps because it gave too much encouragement to the ambiguity described above. Kant also added the section called 'The Refutation of Idealism' (see above, pp. 40–2), which purports to provide a positive proof of objectivity, and a disproof of the 'empirical idealism' attributed to Berkeley. Empirical idealism is the view that 'empirical' objects are nothing but perceptions, and that the world of science has no reality beyond the experience of the observer. All empirical objects become 'ideal' entities, with no reality outside our conception of them. By contrast, Kant argues, transcendental idealism is a form of empirical realism: it implies that empirical objects are real.

Kant's assertion that transcendental idealism entails empirical realism is difficult to interpret. He argues, for example, that space and time are empirically real and *also* transcendentally ideal (A 28, B 44). This could mean that, if we take an empirical perspective, so to speak, then we acknowledge the reality of space and time; while, from the transcendental point of view, these things are 'nothing at all' (ibid.). However, the idea of a transcendental point of view is, as Kant recognises, highly contentious. It is not a point of view that is available to us, and therefore not something of which we can have a positive conception. A simpler reading of Kant's theory is the following: empirical objects are real, whereas transcendental objects are ideal. A transcendental object is not perceivable, and does not belong to the world of space, time and causality. The 'monad' of Leibniz is such an object, and must therefore always remain a mere idea in the mind that conceives it, with no independent reality. But what are empirical objects? The answer that suggests itself is 'whatever objects are discovered or postulated through experience'.

The above states a metaphysical view which exactly corresponds to Kant's theory of knowledge. In the last analysis, it does not matter whether we describe the distinction between the empirical and the transcendental object as a distinction between that which exists and that which does not, or as a distinction between that which is knowable and that which is not. For, to borrow a remark of Wittgenstein's, 'a nothing would do as well as a something about which nothing can be said'. It seems then that the distinction corresponds again to that between phenomena and noumena, the first being knowable, the second unknowable, since the concept of a noumenon can be employed only negatively, in order to mark out the limits of experience. All noumena are transcendental objects, and all transcendental objects, being merely 'intelligible' (i.e. not knowable through experience), are noumena. So it would seem that the three distinctions coincide: phenomenon/noumenon; empirical object/transcendental object; appearance/thing-in-itself. In a lengthy discussion of Leibniz which forms the bridging passage between the Analytic and the Dialectic this is, in effect, what Kant says (especially A 288-9, B 344-6). Many scholars do not accept this interpretation; but it seems to me that, if we do not accept it, we attribute to Kant more inconsistency than his dexterity can sustain.

It is not surprising, therefore, to find that the ambiguity which surrounds Kant's doctrine of 'appearance' attaches also to his concept of the 'phenomenon'. This term is interpreted, sometimes as denoting a real perceivable object which exists independently of the observer, sometimes as denoting a mental 'representation' (or, in modern parlance, 'intentional object'). Under the latter interpretation the phenomenon becomes subjective (it is as it seems, and seems as it is). To establish its existence is to provide no guarantee of objectivity. No significant distinction would then remain between Kant's position (that we can have knowledge of phenomena) and the empirical idealism which he claims to reject. Even Leibniz admitted more objectivity into our 'point of view' than the empirical idealist, since he introduced the notion of the 'well-founded phenomenon' (see above, p. 22), according to which the stability of appearances is sufficient to warrant the distinction between being and seeming. Leibniz's approach to the 'phenomenal world' certainly influenced Kant, more perhaps than he cared to admit. But he wanted to go further in the direction of establishing the objectivity of the world of appearance, not less far.

It is clear from all this that the only acceptable interpretation of the terms 'phenomenon', 'appearance', and 'empirical object' is as denoting items in the physical world. Appearances include tables, chairs, and other such visible things; they also include entities that are observable only through their effects, such as atoms (A 442, B 470) and the most distant stars (A 496, B 524). These 'theoretical' entities also have the reality which comes from existence in space and time, and from the order imposed by the categories. They too are perceivable, in the sense of entering into specific causal relations with the mind which knows them. In other words, any object of scientific investigation is a 'phenomenon', and all phenomena are knowable in principle. But nothing else is knowable. 'Nothing is really given us save perception and the empirical advance [i.e. scientific inference] from this to other possible perceptions' (A 493, B 521). As for the idea of a noumenon, this is 'not the concept of an object' but a 'problem unavoidably bound up with the limitation of our sensibility' (A 287, B 344).

The unconditioned

Kant's intention in the Dialectic is to show that we cannot know the 'world as it is', meaning the world conceived apart from the perspective of the knower. We must not, as Kant puts it, aspire to 'unconditioned' knowledge. At the same time, it seems inevitable that we should do so. Every time we establish something by argument, we assume the truth of the premise. The premise therefore describes the 'condition' under which the conclusion is true. But what about the truth of this condition? That too must be established by argument, and will turn out to possess its truth only 'conditionally'. Hence reason (in its guise as inference) inevitably leads us to search for the 'unconditioned', the ultimate premise whose truth is derived from no other source. This 'idea' of reason contains the source of all metaphysical illusion. For all knowledge that we can legitimately claim is subject to the 'conditions' of possible experience. To aspire to knowledge of the unconditioned is to aspire beyond the conditions which make knowledge possible.

The effort of transcendence is, Kant argues, inevitable. Not only do we seek to transcend the conditions contained in the possibility of experience. We also seek to know the world 'as it is', free from the conditions to which it may be subject by such categories as substance and cause. These enterprises are in fact one and the same; for, as the Analytic shows, the two sets of conditions are identical. In each case the advance of reason towards the 'unconditioned' is the pursuit of knowledge untainted by perspective. Reason always aims to view the world, as Leibniz had viewed it, from no point of view.

'Pure reason'

From the standpoint of Kant's theory of knowledge, reason must be seen as the highest of cognitive faculties, under which all that is distinctive of self-knowledge is subsumed. Apart from its use in understanding (forming judgements), reason can be employed legitimately in two further ways: practically, and in carrying out inferences. Practical reason cannot be regarded as a branch of the understanding since it does not issue in judgements (it makes no claims about the true and the false). Nevertheless its use is legitimate: I can reason what to do, and my action can be a legitimate outcome of this process. Inference, which is the practice of deriving the logical consequences of a judgement, is also legitimate. But, unlike understanding, it employs no concepts of its own (for an inference which, as it were, 'adds a concept' to the premise is for that reason invalid).

It is only when *pure* reason enters our thoughts that the 'logic of illusion' begins to beguile us. Pure reason is distinguished by the fact that it tries to make judgements of its own, using, not concepts, but 'ideas' from which all empirical conditions have been removed. The logic of illusion is 'dialectical': it must inevitably end in fallacy and contradiction. This tendency towards fallacy is not accidental, but intrinsic. There is no way in which reason can set out to know the world through 'ideas' and avoid the errors that lie in wait for it. These errors have already been committed, just as soon as we leave the knowable realms of experience and embark on the journey towards the 'unconditioned' world beyond. At the same time there is no way in which we can avoid the temptation towards this vain journey into the transcendental. Our very possession of a point of view on the world creates the 'idea' of a world seen from no point of view. Thus we strive always 'to find for the conditioned knowledge of the understanding, the unconditioned, whereby its unity might be brought to completion' (A 307, B 364).

Pure reason and metaphysics

I have already drawn attention to Kant's important threefold division of the subject-matter of speculative metaphysics. In 'transcendental psychology' reason generates its doctrines of the soul; in rational cosmology it attempts to describe the world in its 'unconditioned totality'; in theology, it creates the idea of the perfect being who presides over a transcendent world. By a contrivance, Kant reconciles this division with the traditional view, that 'metaphysics has as the proper object of its enquiries three ideas only: *God, freedom* and *immortality*' (B 395n.). The idea of freedom is assigned to cosmology, on the grounds that all the metaphysical problems created by this idea stem from the belief that there is something—the moral agent—which is both in the world of nature and also outside it. This is one of the most important of Kant's doctrines. But I shall postpone discussion of it until the chapter which follows.

Cosmology

The illusions of cosmology are called 'antinomies'. An 'antinomy' is the peculiar fallacy which enables us to derive both a proposition and its negation from the same premise. According to Kant antinomies are not genuine contradictions, since both of the propositions which constitute them are false, being based on a false assumption. He entitles this 'kind of opposition *dialectical*, and that of contradictories *analytical*' (A 504, B 532). He offers various tortuous explanations of how a proposition and its negation can both be false, and it is perhaps unnecessary to be detained by this puzzling piece of logic. Kant's point is that, in deriving each side of an antinomy, the same false assumption must be made. The purpose of his 'critique' is to root out this false assumption and show it to stem from the application of one of reason's 'ideas'. The assumption involved in cosmology is that we can think of the world in its 'unconditioned totality'. This would be possible only by transcending the perspective of 'possible experience' and trying to see all nature as a whole, from a perspective outside of it. The illusory nature of this idea is displayed by the fact that, from the premise of such a transcendent perspective, a 'dialectical' contradiction follows.

Suppose, for example, that I allow myself to entertain the idea of the whole world of nature, as it is situated in space and time. If I now attempt to apply the idea in judgement, I must pass beyond my empirical vision in order to grasp the totality of all objects of experience. I must attempt to envisage the whole of nature, independently of my particular perspective within it. If I could do that, I could ask myself: Is this totality limited or unlimited in space and time? Does it, or does it not, have boundaries? I find myself equally able to prove both conclusions. I can prove, for example, that the world must have a beginning in time (otherwise an infinite sequence of events must have already elapsed, and, Kant argues, a 'completed infinity' is an absurd idea). I can equally prove that it must have no beginning in time (for if it had a beginning, then there must be a reason why it began when it did, which is to suppose, absurdly, that a particular time has a causal property, or a capacity to 'bring into being', independently of the events which occupy it).

A similar contradiction can be derived from the assumption that the world as a whole has an explanation for its existence. From that assumption, I can prove that the world is causally self-dependent, consisting of an infinite chain of causes linking each moment to its predecessor. For the idea of a beginning to this series—the idea of a 'first cause'—is absurd, leading automatically to the question 'What caused the beginning?', to which there is no coherent answer. I can equally prove that the world is causally dependent, deriving its existence from some being which is 'cause of itself', or *causa sui*. For if there were no such being, then none of the causes in the sequence of nature would explain the existence of its effect. In which case, nothing in nature would have an explanation, and it would be impossible to say why anything should exist at all.

Such antinomies result from the attempt to reach beyond the perspective of experience to the absolute vantage-point from which the totality of things (and hence the world 'as it is in itself') can be surveyed. If we suppose nature to be a thing-in-itself—i.e. if we remove from the concept of nature the reference to any possible experience through which it is observed—then the proofs of the antinomies are well-grounded. 'The conflict which results from the propositions thus obtained shows, however, that there is a fallacy in this assumption, and so leads us to the discovery of the true constitution of things, as objects of the senses' (A 507, B 537). The idea of 'absolute totality' holds only of 'things-in-themselves' (A 506, B 534), which is to say, of nothing knowable. For example, the concept of cause, which we can apply *within* the realm of empirical objects in order to designate their relations, becomes empty when lifted out of that realm and applied to the world as a whole. It is then applied beyond the empirical conditions which justify its application, and so leads inevitably to contradiction.

Nevertheless, Kant argues, these antinomies are not to be lightly dismissed as errors no sooner perceived than forgone. The assumption of totality which generates them is both the cause and the effect of all that is most serious in science. Suppose we were to accept the 'big bang' hypothesis concerning the origin of the universe. Only a short-sighted person would think that we have then answered the question how the world began. For what caused the bang? Any answer will suppose that something already existed. So the hypothesis cannot explain the origin of things. The quest for an origin leads us forever backwards into the past. But either it is unsatisfiable—in which case, how does cosmology explain the *existence* of the world?—or it comes to rest in the postulation of a *causa sui*—in which case, we have left the scientific question unanswered and taken refuge in theology. Science itself pushes us towards the antinomy, by forcing us always to the limits of nature. But how can I know those limits if I cannot also transcend them?

Kant engages in an elaborate diagnosis of the antinomies, arguing that the two sides always correspond to rationalism and empiricism respectively, and he takes the opportunity to explore again the various errors of those philosophies. The resulting discussion is exceedingly complex, and has produced as much philosophical commentary as anything in the first *Critique*. Kant's love of system leads him to combine arguments of very different import and quality. But behind the profusion of reasoning lies one of the acutest discussions of scientific method to have issued from the pen of a philosopher. A reading of Kant's discussion inspired men as diverse as Hegel and Einstein, and few can fail to be puzzled by the problems that Kant unearths. How *can* I view the world in its totality? And yet, how can there be explanation if I cannot? How can I explain the existence of anything, if I cannot explain the existence of everything? If I am confined for ever within my own point of view, how can I penetrate the mystery of nature?

Theology

I have discussed the first and fourth of Kant's antinomies. The latter brings us to theology, and to Kant's subsequent suggestion that the idea of a *causa sui* is itself empty, and can be applied in judgement only so as to generate a contradiction. In the chapter entitled 'The Ideal of Reason', Kant reviews the traditional arguments for the existence of God, and imposes upon them a now famous classification. There are, he says, only three kinds of argument for God's existence, the 'cosmological', the 'ontological' and the 'physico-theological'. The first kind comprises all arguments which, proceding from some contingent fact about the world, and from the question '*Why* is it so?', postulate the existence of a necessary being. A version of this is the 'first cause' argument discussed above: only if the series of causes begins in a *causa sui* can any contingent fact be finally explained. Of the second kind are all arguments which, in order to free themselves from contingent premises (which, because they might be false, might also be doubted), attempt to prove the existence of God from the concept of God. Of the third kind are all arguments from 'design', which begin from the premise of some good in nature, and argue by analogy to the perfection of its cause.

Kant says of the argument from design that it 'always deserves to be mentioned with respect. It is the oldest, the clearest, and the most consonant with human reason. It enlivens the study of nature, just as it itself derives its existence and gains ever new strength from that source' (A 623, B 651). In the third *Critique* he explains in more detail why this argument appealed to him. Kant was no atheist, and was perturbed by Hume's posthumous *Dialogues on Natural Religion*, the German version of which appeared as the *Critique* was being prepared for the press. There was time for Kant to wonder about Hume's motives, but not to consider his arguments (A 745, B 773). Hume foreshadows Kant's own critique of rational theology. But he is particularly dismissive of the argument from design, arguing that it proves either nothing at all (since there is no genuine analogy between the perfections of nature and the perfections of art) or, at best, the existence of a being no more perfect than the world of his creation. Kant too was unsatisfied by the argument from design. But although he thought of it as invalid, at the same time he felt it to be the expression of a true presentiment. Hence he tried to provide a wholly novel elucidation of it, from the point of view not of the first but of the third *Critique*.

Considered as an intellectual proof, the argument from design can never be more cogent than the cosmological proof, upon which it depends (A 630, B 658). For it is only on the assumption of ultimate explanation that the argument from design can operate. That assumption carries no weight unless the cosmological proof is valid. We must show that we can step outside nature, in order to postulate the existence of a transcendent, necessary being. But what entitles us to postulate such a being? According to Kant, only the ontological argument will answer that question. For if we ask ourselves how something can be cause of itself, or how it can exist by necessity, the answer must be found in the concept of that thing. The concept of the divine being must explain his existence. This can be true only if the existence of God *follows* from the concept of God, since it is only by logical relations that a concept can explain anything. So, in the end, all three arguments reduce to this single one.

In its traditional forms the ontological argument proves not only the existence, but also the perfection of God. Neither of the other arguments seems able to prove God's absolute perfection: once again, they must rely on the ontological argument to give intellectual grounds for religious sentiment. The ontological argument proceeds as follows. God is an all-perfect being. Among perfections we must count moral goodness, power and freedom. But we must also count existence. For the concept of an existent x is the concept of something more perfect than an x; to take away existence is to take away perfection. So existence is a perfection. Hence it follows from the idea of God, as an all-perfect being, that God exists.

Kant's rebuttal of this argument is famous for its anticipation of a doctrine of modern logic—the doctrine that existence is not a predicate. (When I say that John exists, is bald, and eats oysters, I attribute to John not three properties, but two.) Leibniz, in his discussion of contingency, had already recognised that existence is quite different from ordinary predicates. Nevertheless, he accepted the ontological argument, and did not see the logical consequence of his philosophy. To say that an *x* exists is to add nothing to its concept: it is to say that the concept has an instance. Indeed, there is already a fallacy (Kant even says a contradiction) involved in introducing existence into the concept of a thing (A 597, B 625). For it then becomes empty to assert that the thing exists. The assertion makes no advance from concept to reality. And so it affirms the existence of nothing. The ontological argument says that existence is a perfection. But it cannot be a perfection, since it is not a property. If the argument were valid, Kant thinks, it would follow that the judgement that God exists expresses an analytic truth. The theory that existence is not a predicate implies, however, that all existential propositions are synthetic (A 598, B 626).

The regulative employment of the ideas of reason

Having completed his denunciation of the 'logic of illusion' Kant goes on to argue, at considerable length, and in a relaxed, expansive style appropriate to a writer whose intellectual labour is ended, that there is, after all, a legitimate use for the ideas of reason. Such ideas as that of unconditioned totality, and of the perfect creator who exists of necessity, generate illusions when considered in their 'constitutive' role: that is, when considered as descriptions of reality. The correct way to see them, however, is as 'regulative principles' (A 644, B 672). If we act as if these ideas were true of reality, then we are led to formulate true hypotheses. The ideas of order and totality, for example, lead us to propose ever wider and simpler laws, in terms of which the empirical world becomes ever more intelligible. This 'regulative' employment of the ideas is an employment from within the standpoint of experience. The constitutive employment attempts to transcend that standpoint, into the illusory realm of reason. The contradictions do not stem from the ideas themselves (which are not contradictory but merely empty); they stem from their wrong application.

Thus 'the ideal of a supreme being is nothing but a *regulative principle* of reason, which directs us to look upon all connection in the world as if it originated from an all-sufficient and necessary cause' (A 619, B 647). Considered thus it is the source, not of illusion, but of knowledge. The knowledge that it leads to remains circumscribed by the conditions of possible experience: in other words it conforms to the categories, and does not reach beyond their legitimate territory into a transcendent realm. The idea 'does not show us how an object is constituted, but how, under its guidance, we should *seek* to determine the constitution and connection of the objects of experience' (A 671, B 699). Thus reason is led back from its vain speculations to the empirical world, trading the illusions of metaphysics for the realities of empirical science.

The soul

Kant's discussion of the soul, and of the concept of the 'self' from which it gains its initial description, is among the most subtle parts of his philosophy. The account is given in two complex arguments: the first at the beginning of the Dialectic, in which he attacks the rationalist doctrines of the soul; the second in the third antinomy, and in the *Critique of Practical Reason*, in which he describes the nature of morality.

The 'Paralogisms of Pure Reason', which deal with the rationalist doctrines of the soul, were substantially revised for the second edition, perhaps because this aspect of the critical philosophy forms part of the multi-faceted argument of the transcendental deduction, with which Kant had remained so dissatisfied. Kant's argument in the Analytic had begun by recognising the peculiar reality of self-consciousness. I have a privileged awareness of my states of mind, and this is an 'original' or 'transcendental' act of understanding. The rationalists had sought to deduce from this privileged knowledge a specific theory of its object. They had thought that, because of the immediacy of self-awareness, the self must be a genuine object of consciousness. In the act of self-awareness I am presented with the 'I' which is aware. I can maintain this self-awareness even while doubting every other thing. Moreover, I am necessarily aware of my unity. Finally, I have an intuitive sense of my continuity through time: this cannot be derived from the observation of my body, or from any other external source. It therefore seems natural to conclude that I know myself to be substantial, indivisible, enduring, perhaps even immortal, on the basis of the fact of self-awareness alone. Such, Kant thought, was Descartes' argument. Nor is the conclusion an eccentricity of the 'Cartesian' view of consciousness. Like all the illusions of reason, it is one into which we are tempted just as soon as we begin to reflect on the datum before us. Every rational being must be tempted to think that the peculiar immediacy and inviolability of self-awareness guarantees its content. In the midst of every doubt, I may yet know this thing which is me, and, reason assures me, this intimate acquaintance with my own nature gives grounds for the belief in the immateriality of the soul.

The reasoning is erroneous, since it moves from the purely *formal* unity of apperception to the substantial unity affirmed in the doctrine of the soul. 'The unity of consciousness which underlies the categories is . . . mistaken for an intuition of the subject as object, and the category of substance is then applied to it' (B 421). Although the transcendental unity of apperception assures me that there is a unity in my present consciousness, it tells me nothing else about the kind of thing which bears it. It does not tell me that I am a substance (i.e. an independently existing object) as opposed to an 'accident' or property. (For example it does not refute the view that the mind is a complex property of the body.) It is 'quite impossible, by means of . . . simple self-consciousness to determine the manner in which I exist, whether it be as substance or accident'

(B 420). If I cannot deduce that I am a substance, so much the less can I deduce that I am indivisible, indestructible or immortal. The unity of consciousness does not even assure me that there is something in the empirical world to which the term 'I' applies. For the peculiar features of self-consciousness summarised under the idea of a transcendental unity of apperception are simply features of a 'point of view' on the world. The 'I' as thereby described is not part of the world but a perspective upon it (a way things seem). 'For the I is not a concept but only a designation of the object of inner sense in so far as we know it through no further predicate' (M 98). To study the peculiarities of our self-awareness is, then, to study no item *in* the world. It is rather to explore that limiting point of empirical knowledge. 'The subject of the categories cannot by thinking the categories acquire a concept of itself as an object of the categories' (B 422). It is no more possible for me to make the 'I' into the object of consciousness than it is to observe the limits of my own visual field. 'I' is the expression of my perspective, but denotes no item within it.

The conclusion that Kant draws is this. There is a gap between the premise of 'transcendental psychology'—the transcendental unity of apperception—and its conclusion—the substantiality of the soul. Because the first describes a point of view on the world, and the second an item in the world, it is impossible that reason should take us validly from the one to the other. Whether correct or not, Kant's suggestion has provided the corner-stone of many subsequent philosophies of the self, from that of Schopenhauer to those of Husserl, Heidegger and Wittgenstein.

Sometimes Kant implies that the 'I' of self-awareness refers to a transcendental object. For it might seem that, having proved that the 'I' is not part of the empirical world, Kant has given us reason to refer it to the world of the thing-in-itself which lies beyond experience. This is not a legitimate conclusion from his argument, but, on the contrary, another, more subtle reiteration of the fallacy that it was designed to expose. Nevertheless it is a conclusion which Kant was inclined to countenance, since, without it, he thought, morality would not be possible. Kant sought for a positive doctrine of the soul, not through pure reason, but through practical reason (B 430–1). In order to understand this idea we must therefore explore his description of the moral life of the rational agent.

5 *The categorical imperative*

Kant's *Critique of Practical Reason* was preceded by a brilliant résumé of his moral viewpoint, the *Foundations of the Metaphysic of Morals*. These works treat of 'practical reason': in using this expression Kant was consciously reviving the ancient contrast between theoretical and practical knowledge. All rational beings recognise the distinction between knowing the truth and knowing what to do about it. Judgements and decisions may each be based on, and amended through, reason, but only the first can be true or false. Hence there must be an employment of our rational faculties which does not have truth, but something else, as its aim. What is this something else? Aristotle said happiness; Kant says duty. It is in the analysis of the idea of duty that Kant's distinctive moral vision is expressed.

Suppose we establish the objectivity of judgement, and provide the necessary metaphysical grounding to those scientific principles which underlie the process of discovery. There remains another problem of objectivity, raised by practical, rather than theoretical, knowledge. Can we know what to do objectively, or must we simply rely on our subjective inclination to guide us? It is to this problem that Kant addressed himself, producing the most metaphysical and abstract basis that has ever been given for the common intuitions of morality.

The antinomy of freedom

The starting-point of Kant's ethics is the concept of freedom. According to his famous maxim that 'ought implies can', the right action must always be possible: which is to say, I must always be free to perform it. The moral agent 'judges that he can do a certain thing because he is conscious that he ought, and he recognises that he is free, a fact which, but for the moral law, he would never have known' (P 165). In other words, the practice of morality forces the idea of freedom upon us. But, Kant argues, this idea, viewed theoretically, contains a contradiction, and he displays this contradiction in the third antinomy of the first *Critique*.

Every change which occurs in the order of nature has a cause: this is an 'established principle' of the Analytic, and 'allows of no exception' (A 536, B 564). If this is so, then every event in nature is bound in chains of ineluctable necessity. At the same time I think of myself as the originator of my actions, giving rise to them spontaneously, under the influence of no external constraint. If my action is part of nature, this seems to contradict the view that every event in nature is bound by causal necessity. If it is not part of nature, then it falls outside the realm of causal connection, and my will is the originator of nothing in the natural world.

There is only a contradiction here if I really *am* free. Kant is sometimes content to argue merely that I must *think* of myself as free. It is a presupposition of all action in the world—and hence of reasoned decisions—that the agent is the originator of what he does. And, Kant suggests, I cannot forsake this idea without losing the sense of myself as agent. The very perspective of reason which sees the world as bound in chains of necessity also sees it as containing freedom. Occasionally Kant goes further, and argues for the 'primacy' of practical reason (P 313f.), meaning that *all* thought is an exercise of freedom, so that, if practical reason were impossible, we could not think coherently. In which case the certainty of my freedom is as great as the certainty of anything. (This argument occurs, in more rhetorical form, in the writings of Sartre, whose existentialist theory of the moral life owes much to Kant.) If this is true, then of course the antinomy of freedom becomes acute: we are compelled by practical reason to accept that we are free, and by understanding to deny it.

Kant felt that there must be a solution to this antinomy, since in the practical sphere the employment of reason is legitimate. It is indeed practical reason which tells me what I am. The illusory progress of *pure* reason towards self-contradiction ought not to forbid *practical* reason, through which the antinomy must therefore be resolved. Pure reason leaves, as it were, a 'vacant place' in its account of the world, where the moral agent should be. 'This vacant place is filled by pure practical reason with a definite law of causality in an intelligible world . . . namely, the moral law' (P 195). This new 'law of causality' is called 'transcendental freedom', and it defines the condition of the moral agent. The law of cause and effect operates only in the realm of nature (the empirical realm). Freedom, however, belongs, not to nature, but precisely to that 'intelligible' or transcendental realm to which categories like causality do not apply. I exist in the world of nature, as one 'appearance' among others. But I also exist as a 'thing-in-itself', bound not by causality, but by the laws of practical reason. It is not that I am *two* things, but rather one thing, conceived under two contrasting aspects. Thus 'there is not the smallest contradiction in saying that a *thing in appearance* (belonging to the world of sense) is subject to certain laws, from which the very same as a *thing in itself* is independent'. Moreover the moral agent must always 'conceive and think of himself in this twofold way' (F 112). Freedom, then, is a transcendental 'idea', without application in the empirical world. And in knowing ourselves to be free we know ourselves at the same time as part of nature and as members of a transcendental world.

The transcendental self

The doctrine of transcendental freedom is both puzzling and appealing. Its appeal lies in its promise of access to the transcendental; its puzzling quality comes from Kant's previous proof that such access is impossible. By Kant's own argument, there is nothing to be known, and nothing meaningfully to be said, about the transcendental world. Kant recognises the difficulty, and admits that the 'demand to regard oneself *qua* subject of freedom as a noumenon, and at the same time from the point of view of physical nature as a phenomenon in one's own empirical consciousness' is 'paradoxical' (P 130). And he even goes so far as to say that, while we do not comprehend the fact of moral freedom, 'we yet comprehend its *incomprehensibility*, and this is all that can fairly be demanded of a philosophy which strives to carry its principles to the very limit of human reason' (F 122).

We can go some say towards explaining Kant's doctrine if we relate the 'transcendental freedom' that underlies practical reason to the 'transcendental unity of apperception' which underlies our knowledge of nature. Our perspective on the world contains two distinct aspects; and neither the unity of consciousness, nor transcendental freedom, can be deduced from our knowledge of the empirical world. But they are each guaranteed a priori as preconditions of the knowledge which we have. The first is the starting-point for all our knowledge of truths, the second the starting-point for all deliberation. They are transcendental, not in the positive sense of involving knowledge of a transcendental object, but in the negative sense of lying at the limit of what can be known. Freedom, being a perspective *on* the empirical world, cannot also be part of it. The knowledge of our own freedom is therefore a part of the 'apperception' which defines our perspective. (Authority for this interpretation can be found in the first *Critique*, notably A 546–7, B 574–5.)

Pure reason attempts to know the transcendental world through concepts. In other words, it attempts to form a positive conception of noumena. This attempt is doomed to failure. Practical reason, however, not being concerned in the discovery of truths, imposes no concepts on its objects. It will never, therefore, lead us into the error of forming a positive conception of the transcendental self. We know this self only practically, through the exercise of freedom. While we cannot translate this knowledge into judgements about our nature, we can translate it into some other thing. This other thing is given by the laws of practical reason, which are the synthetic a priori principles of action. Just as there are a priori laws of nature that can be derived from the unity of consciousness, so too are there a priori laws of reason which can be derived from the perspective of transcendental freedom. These will not be laws about the true and the false: they will have no part to play in description, prediction and explanation. They will be practical laws, concerning what to do. The free agent will be bound by them in all his practical reasoning, since acceptance of them is a presupposition of the freedom without which practical reason is impossible.

It is true that Kant wavers between the doctrine that the transcendental self is a kind of perspective, and the doctrine that it is a distinct noumenal thing. He even attempts to resuscitate through practical reason all those theoretical conclusions concerning God, the soul and immortality that had been dismissed as illusions of pure reason. I shall not, for the present, follow Kant into these mysterious regions. But the reader should bear in mind that I have only postponed the deep metaphysical problem which Kant's ethical doctrine creates.

The problem of practical reason

Kant's idea of freedom becomes clearer when seen in the context of the problem that it was supposed to solve. Rational beings exist not only as self-conscious centres of knowledge, but also as agents. Their reason is not detached from their agency, but forms a constitutive part of it; which is to say that, for a rational being there is not only action, but also the *question* of action (the question 'What shall I do?'), and this question demands a reasoned answer. My rationality is expressed in the fact that some of my actions are intentional (they issue, to use Kant's term, from my 'will'). Of all such actions the question can be asked: Why do that? This question asks, not for a cause or explanation, but for a reason. Suppose someone asks me why I struck an old man in the street. The answer: 'Because electrical impulses from my brain precipitated muscular contractions, and this resulted in my hand making contact with his head' would be absurd and impertinent, however accurate as a causal explanation. The answer: 'Because he annoyed me' may be inadequate, in that it gives no good reason, but it is certainly not absurd. Reasons are designed to justify action, and not primarily to explain it. They refer to the grounds of an action, the premises from which an agent may conclude what to do.

Practical reasons concern either ends or means. If I have an end in view then I may deliberate over the means to achieve it. All philosophers agree that such reasoning exists; but many of them think that it shows no special 'practical' employment of the rational faculties. It is merely theoretical reason, put to use. Kant himself is of this view, arguing that 'precepts of skill' (how to find the means to one's ends) are merely theoretical principles (P 157). Sceptical philosophers go further, and argue, with Hume, that there is no other use for reason in practical matters. All reasoning concerns means. Reason can neither generate, nor justify, the ends of our activity, since, in Hume's words, 'reason is, and ought to be, the slave of the passions'. It is from the 'passions' that our ends are drawn, since it is passion, and passion only, that provides the ultimate motive to act. Reason can persuade us to act only when we are already motivated to obey it. If that is the case, then, Kant held, there can be no objective practical knowledge. For there can be no way in which reason will settle the question what to do.

Kant held that practical reason is possible. He affirmed the (common-sense) belief that reason may constrain and justify not only the choice of means, but also the choice of ends upon which it depends. In which case there may be an objective exercise of practical reason. It would be objective because based in reason alone, recommending ends of action to any rational being, irrespective of his passions, interests and desires. For this to be possible, however, reason must, as Hume argued, not only justify but also motivate our actions. If reason did not also *prompt* me to act, then reason would play no part in the process of decision-making. So it would not be practical. Now, if reason generates only judgements about the world and inferences therefrom, it is hard to see how it *can* be a motive to act. That such and such a judgement is true or false may prompt me to all kinds of action, depending upon my ends. If these ends stem from the 'passions' then reason has no part in determining them. The only way in which reason can become practical, therefore, is by issuing not in judgements but in imperatives. An imperative does not describe the world; it addresses itself to an agent, and, if he accepts it, determines what he does. If, therefore, there are imperatives which arise simply from the exercise of reason, then reason alone can move us to action. 'Reason, with its practical law, determines the will immediately' (P 156).

Autonomy of the will

Kant's moral philosophy emerges from the amalgamation of the idea of transcendental freedom with that of an imperative of reason. He believes that reasoning about ends must always suppose just the kind of transcendental freedom that his metaphysics claims to be possible. Freedom is the power to will an end of action for myself. Any derivation of my ends from an external source is at the same time subjection of myself to that source. And any natural process which governs my action confers on me the unfreedom of its cause. I then become the passive channel through which natural forces find their enactment. If my action is called unfree it is because there is a sense in which it is not truly *mine*.

An action that originates in me can be attributed *only* to me, and is therefore in a real sense mine. In respect of such an action I am free. I act freely whenever *I* act, and unfreely whenever some other agency acts through me. This raises the question what am *I*? The obvious answer is 'a transcendental self'; since that explains my freedom from the causality of nature. But Kant now supplements this answer with a theory of the will. An action originates in me whenever I decide on the action, simply on the basis of considering *it*. I do not consult my desires, interest or any other 'empirical condition', since that is to subject myself to the causality of nature. I simply reflect on the action, and choose it for its own sake, as an end in itself. This is the paradigm of a free action: one that is brought into being by reason alone. Such an action can be attributed, Kant thought, to no 'natural' force, no chain of 'empirical' causality. It arises spontaneously out of the rational processes which constitute my will.

Freedom, then, is the ability to be governed by reason. The imperatives of reason discussed in the last section are 'laws of freedom': principles whereby reason determines action. So that there is a 'causality of freedom' in addition to the 'causality of nature', and freedom is nothing more than obedience to the first, perhaps in defiance of the second. This ability to be motivated by reason alone Kant called the autonomy of the will, and he contrasted it with the 'heteronomy' of the agent whose will is subject to external causes. Kant designates as external any cause which belongs to the 'causality of nature'—that is, any cause which is not founded in reason alone. An action which springs from desire, emotion or interest is therefore 'heteronomous'.

Kant now develops his conception of the autonomous *agent*. This is an agent who is able to overcome the promptings of all heteronomous counsels, such as those of self-interest and desire, should they be in conflict with reason. Such a being postulates himself as a 'transcendental being', in that he defies the causality of nature and refers the grounds of his actions always to the 'causality of freedom'. Only an autonomous being has genuine ends of action (as opposed to mere objects of desire), and only such a being deserves our esteem, as the embodiment of rational choice. The autonomy of the will, Kant goes on to argue, 'is the sole principle of all moral laws, and of all duties which conform to them; on the other hand, heteronomy of the will not only cannot be the basis of any obligation, but is, on the contrary, opposed to the principle thereof, and to the morality of will' (P 169). Because autonomy is manifest only in the obedience to reason, and because reason must guide action always through imperatives, autonomy is described as 'that property of the will whereby it is a law to itself' (F 85).

Metaphysical difficulties

We must now return to the metaphysical problem of transcendental freedom. Two difficulties in particular stand out, since they correspond to difficulties which Kant himself had discovered in the rationalist metaphysics of Leibniz. First, how is the transcendental self to be individuated? What makes *this* self *me*? If the essential feature is reason and the agency which springs from it, then, since the laws of reason are universal, how am I to be distinguished from any other being who is subject to them? If the essential feature is my 'point of view' on the world, how is Kant to avoid the Leibnizian view of the self as a monad, defined by its point of view, but existing outside the world that it 'represents' thereby, incapable of entering into real relation with anything contained in it?

Secondly (or rather to continue the objection), how is the transcendental self related to the empirical world? In particular, how is it related to its own action, which is either an event in the empirical world or else totally ineffective? I must exist, as Kant acknowledges, both as an 'empirical self', within the realm of nature, and as a transcendental self, outside it. But since the category of cause applies only to nature, the transcendental self remains for ever ineffective. In which case, why is its freedom so valuable? Kant relies on the view that the category of cause denotes a relation in time (of before and after); whereas the relation of a reason to that which springs from it is not temporal at all (P 269). His tortuous discussion of this in the first *Critique* (A 538–41, B 566–9) fails to make clear how a reason offered to the transcendental self can motivate (and so explain) an event in the empirical world.

Kant's preferred stance towards these difficulties is summarised in the assertion that the idea of ourselves as members of a purely 'intelligible' realm to which categories do not apply 'remains always a useful and legitimate idea for the purpose of rational belief, although all knowledge stops at its threshold' (F 121). At the same time, Kant continued to regard the paradox of human freedom as unavoidable: we could never solve it through theoretical reason, while practical reason assured us only that it *has* a solution. However, we must acknowledge 'the right of pure reason in its practical use to an extension which is not possible in its speculative use' (P 197). Hence we can accept the verdict of practical reason on trust. Of course, we can always raise the question of freedom anew: it then becomes 'How is practical reason possible?' We know that it *is* possible, for without it our perspective on the world would vanish. But 'how pure reason can be practical—to explain this is beyond the power of human reason' (F 119).

Kant is able to derive, with compelling logic, an entire system of common-sense morality from the premise of transcendental freedom. Since the paradox of freedom remains unsolved at the end of this derivation, Kant may not be wholly wrong in his suggestion that we shall never be able to comprehend it.

Hypothetical and categorical imperatives

There is a division in practical thought between hypothetical and categorical imperatives. The first typically begin with an 'If . . .', as in 'If you want to stay, be polite!' Here the end is hypothetical, and the imperative states the means to it. The validity of all such imperatives can be established in accordance with the 'supreme principle' that 'whoever wills the end, wills the means'. This principle, Kant argues, is analytic (it derives its truth from concepts alone). But, although hypothetical imperatives may be valid, they can never be objective, since they are always *conditional*. They give a reason only to the person who has the end mentioned in the antecedent (in the example given above, the person who wants to stay), and are binding on no one whose desires conflict with it. This is true even of the 'counsels of prudence', which tell us what to do in order to be happy. For the concept of happiness is merely a label

for whatever a rational being desires; the hypothetical imperatives which refer us to our happiness apply universally only
because they specify nothing determinate. One man's happiness may be another's pain, and the imperative accepted by one
may not recommend itself to the other. It seems then that all
hypothetical imperatives remain subjective, conditional on the
individual's desires, and none of them corresponds to a true
'command of reason'.

Categorical imperatives do not typically contain an 'if'. They
tell you what to do *unconditionally*. They may nevertheless be
defended by reasons. If I say 'Shut the door!' then my command
is arbitrary unless I can answer the question 'Why?' If I answer
it to your satisfaction, then the imperative binds you. If the
answer refers to some independent interest of yours, however,
the imperative also ceases to be categorical, as in 'If you want to
avoid punishment, shut the door.' Only if the answer represents
the action *itself* as an end do we have a non-arbitrary categorical imperative. The signal of this is the presence of an 'ought':
'You ought to shut the door'. In the categorical 'ought' we have
the true imperative of reason.

It is not implausible to follow Kant in aligning this familiar
distinction between hypothetical and categorical imperatives
with the distinction between reasoning over means and reasoning over ends. The problem of practical reason then becomes
'How are categorical imperatives possible?' Furthermore, Kant
argues, morality can be expressed only in categorical imperatives. 'If duty is a conception that is to have any import and real
legislative authority for our actions, it can only be expressed in
categorical imperatives and not at all in hypothetical imperatives' (F 60). Obedience to a hypothetical imperative is always
obedience to the condition expressed in its antecedent. It therefore always involves heteronomy of the will. Obedience to a
categorical imperative, however, since it springs from reason
alone, must always be autonomous. Thus Kant also aligns the
distinction between the two kinds of imperatives with that
between heteronomy and autonomy, and thereby associates the
problem of the categorical imperatives with that of transcen-

dental freedom: 'what makes categorical imperatives possible is this, that the idea of freedom makes me a member of an intelligible world' (F 107).

But if categorical imperatives are to be possible, they too require a supreme principle, which will show how reason discovers them. Hence practical reason is faced with a problem as general as the problem of theoretical reason, and requiring the same kind of answer. We must show how synthetic a priori *practical* knowledge is possible. The supreme principle of hypothetical imperatives is, as we have seen, analytic. Hence hypothetical imperatives make no real demands on the agent, but simply relate his ends to the means needed to secure them. Categorical imperatives, however, make real and unconditional demands; they are, in this sense, synthetic. Moreover, since their foundation lies in reason alone, they must be based a priori. The very form of a categorical imperative prevents it from deriving authority from any other source—for example, from a desire, need or interest, or any other 'empirical condition' of the agent. In particular, there is no way in which categorical imperatives can be deduced from 'the particular attributes of human nature' (F 61). Thus Kant rejects all the usual systems of ethics of his day, arguing that they are unable to explain, what alone upholds the objectivity of moral judgement, the 'unconditional necessity' which attaches to the moral law. This necessity is explained only by a theory with an a priori basis. Hence all reference to empirical conditions—even to the most established facts of human nature—must be excluded from the grounds of morality (F 64).

The categorical imperative

The supreme principle of categorical imperatives is called *the* categorical imperative, on the assumption that there is, or ought to be, only one such principle (perhaps to avoid the possibility of conflicting duties (L 20)). In fact the principle is restated in five variant forms, two of which involve new conceptions. It is therefore normal to consider the categorical imperative as a composite law of reason, with three separate parts. The law is derived, in its first and most famous formulation, as follows.

If we are to find an imperative that recommends itself on the basis of reason alone, then we must abstract from all the distinctions between rational agents, discounting their interests, desires and ambitions, and all the 'empirical conditions' which circumscribe their actions. Only then will we base our law in practical reason alone, since we will have abstracted from any other ground. By this process of abstraction I arrive at the 'point of view of a member of an intelligible world' (F 108). This is a point of view outside my own experience, which could therefore be adopted by any rational being, whatever his circumstances. The law that I formulate will then be an imperative that applies universally, to all rational beings. When deciding on my action as an end, I will be constrained by reason to 'act only on that maxim which I can at the same time will as a universal law' (my paraphrase from F 38). (The term 'maxim' means both 'principle' and 'motive': a categorical imperative always commands, and always lays down a law.) The principle is in one sense 'formal': that is, it commands nothing specific. At the same time it is synthetic, since it legislates among all the possible ends of action, allowing some, and forbidding others. For example, it forbids the breaking of promises, for to will the universal breaking of promises is to will the abolition of promising, hence to will the abolition of the advantage which accrues to breaking promises, and so to will the abolition of my motive. Such forbidden ends of action are shown, by their confrontation with the supreme moral law, to involve the agent in a contradiction.

Kant regarded this first formulation of the categorical imperative as the philosophical basis of the famous golden rule, that we should do as we would be done by. It is a priori in that it is based in what can recommend itself to reason alone. This explains its right to a 'universal' form, and to the kind of necessity embodied in the categorical 'ought'.

The categorical imperative finds the ends of action by abstracting from everything but the fact of rational agency. Rational agency must therefore provide its own ends. The autonomous being is both the agent and the repository of all value, and exists, as Kant puts it (F 65), 'as an end in himself'. If we are to have values at all, we must value (respect) the existence and endeavours of rational beings. In this way autonomy prescribes its own limit. The constraint on our freedom is that we must respect the freedom of all: how else can our freedom issue in *universal* laws? It follows that we must never use another without regard to his autonomy; we must never treat him as a means. This brings us to the second major formulation of the categorical imperative, as the law that I must 'so act as to treat humanity, whether in my own self or in that of another, always as an end, and never as a means only' (my paraphrase from F 47). 'Humanity' here covers all rational beings, and the distinction between those beings which can and those which cannot be regarded as mere means, is what we are referring to in distinguishing *things* from *persons*. This distinction is the foundation of the concept of a 'right'. If someone asks whether an animal, a child or an inanimate object has rights, he is asking whether the categorical imperative applies to it, in this second, most powerful, form.

We cannot, then, treat rational agents merely as the means through which external forces find enactment: to do so is to deny the autonomy which alone commands our respect. In abstracting towards the moral law, I am always respecting the sovereignty of reason. So while the form of my law is universal (the first imperative), its content must derive from its application to rational beings as ends in themselves (the second imperative). Hence I must always think of the moral law as a piece of universal legislation, which binds rational beings equally. I am thereby led to the idea of 'the will of every rational being as a universally legislative will' (F 70). This conception in turn leads to another, that of a 'kingdom of ends', in which the universal legislation to which we all willingly bow when acting autonomously has become a law of nature. So 'every rational being must so act as if he were by his maxims in every case a legislating member of the universal kingdom of ends' (my para-phrase from F 49–50). This third imperative suggests that all speculation about ends is also the postulation of an ideal world, in which things are as they ought to be and ought to be as they are. In this kingdom nothing conflicts with reason, and the rational being is both subject and sovereign of the law which there obtains.

Moral intuitions

Kant believes that the various formulations of the categorical imperative can be derived by reflection on the single idea of autonomy, and that this alone is sufficient to recommend them to every rational being. He also thinks that they lend support to ordinary moral thought, just as the synthetic a priori principles of the understanding uphold our common scientific knowledge. It is a singular merit of Kant's moral system that it imposes order on an intuitive vision of morality. This vision is not the property of one man only, but (as Kant and many others have thought) of all people everywhere. Kant had been much influenced by the third Lord Shaftesbury (1671–1713) and his follow-ers—the so-called 'British Moralists'—who had argued that certain fundamental moral principles were not matters of indi-vidual preference, but rather, when reduced to their true basis in the human soul, universally acceptable, recording the unspo-ken agreement of rational beings everywhere. Kant accepted that view. But he attempted to free it from the study of our 'niggardly stepmother', nature (F 10). It was of the greatest importance to him, therefore, that his theory should generate the axioms of an intuitive morality. 'We have simply showed by the development of the universally received notion of moral-ity that an autonomy of the will is inevitably connected with it' (F 92). It is instructive to list some of the common intuitions which Kant's theory explains.

(i) The content of morality. Common morality enjoins re-spect for others and for oneself; it forbids exceptions in one's own favour; it regards all people as equal before the moral law.

These are immediate consequences of the categorical imperative. In its second formulation, moreover, the imperative lends support to quite specific, and universally accepted, laws. It forbids murder, rape, theft, fraud and dishonesty, along with all forms of arbitrary compulsion. It imposes a universal duty to respect the rights and interests of others, and a rational requirement to abstract from personal involvement towards the viewpoint of the impartial judge. Thus it encapsulates fundamental intuitions about justice, together with a specific and intuitively acceptable moral code.

(ii) The force of morality. On Kant's view, the motive of morality is quite different from that of interest or desire. It rules us absolutely and necessarily, we feel its power even when we are most defying it. It is not one consideration to be balanced against others, but rather a compelling dictate which can be ignored but never refuted. This accords, he thinks, with common intuition. If a man is told that he can satisfy the greatest of his lusts, only on condition that he will afterwards be hanged, then he is sure to refuse the offer. But if he is told that he must betray his friend, bear false witness, kill an innocent, or else be hanged, then his interest in his own life counts for nothing in determining what he ought to do. He may bow to the threat; but only with a consciousness of doing wrong; and the moral law itself, unlike any motive of desire, propels him onward to destruction.

(iii) The good will. In the moral judgement of action we refer the consequences produced to the agent who produced them. Unlike the intentional or the negligent the unforeseeable and unintended is never blamed. Moral judgement is directed, not to the effects of an action, but to the good or bad intention that it shows. Hence, in Kant's famous words, 'nothing can possibly be conceived in the world, or even out of it, which can be called good without qualification, except a good will' (F 11). Kant's theory accords exactly with this common intuition. All virtue is contained in autonomy, all vice in its absence, and all morality is summarised in the imperatives that guide the will.

(iv) The moral agent. Underlying intuitive morality is a view of the moral agent. The moral agent is differently motivated and differently constituted from the agencies of nature. His actions have not only causes, but also reasons. He makes decisions for the future, and so distinguishes his intentions from his desires. He does not suffer his desires always to overcome him, but sometimes resists and subdues them. In everything he is both active and passive, and stands as legislator among his own emotions. The moral agent is an object not only of affection and love (which we may extend to all of nature) but also of esteem, and he commands our esteem to the extent that the moral law is manifest in him. In all these intuitive distinctions—between reason and cause, intention and desire, action and passion, esteem and affection—we find aspects of the vital distinction which underlies them, that between person and thing. Only a person has rights, duties and obligations; only a person acts for reasons in addition to causes; only a person merits our esteem. The philosophy of the categorical imperative explains this distinction and all those which reflect it. It also explains why the 'respect for persons' lies embedded in every moral code.

(v) The role of law. Someone may act as the good man acts, but this casts no credit on him if his motive is self-interest. We distinguish action *according to* duty from action *from* duty, and confine our praise to the second. 'The former (*legality*) is possible even if inclinations have been the determining principles of the will; but the latter (*morality*) has moral value, which can be placed only in this: that the action is done out of duty . . .' (P 248). This is a clear and intuitively acceptable consequence of Kant's theory. So too is the more theoretical proposition, that the fundamental concept in moral thought is not goodness, but obligation (P 217).

(vi) Reason and the passions. We recognise in all our moral efforts that there may be a conflict between duty and desire. There thus arises, in every moral being, the idea of conscience as an independent motive, able to legislate among desires and so to forbid or permit them. Kant distinguishes the 'good will'

of the moral agent from the 'holy will' that acts always without resistance from desire. The 'holy will' needs no imperative (P 168) since it bends automatically in the direction of duty, whereas the ordinary agent stands always in need of principles, since his inclination is to thwart them. This sense of the conflict between reason and the passions is a widespread intuition. Kant takes it, however, to somewhat counter-intuitive extremes. He believes that the motive of benevolence, so dear to empiricist morality, is a species of mere inclination, and therefore morally neutral. 'It is a very beautiful thing to do good to men from love to them and from sympathetic goodwill, or to be just from love of order, but this is not the true moral maxim' (P 249). Kant seems to have more praise for the misanthropy which does good against every inclination, than for the expressions of cheerful benevolence. It is in his ability to *resist* inclination that the worth of the moral agent resides. When, for example, a man who desires death goes on living out of a duty of self-preservation, only then, and for the first time, does self-preservation, in ceasing to be an instinct, become a sign of moral worth.

Morality and the self

Those intuitions already lead us, Kant thinks, towards the doctrine of a transcendental freedom. If that doctrine is nonsense, then so is all our moral and practical thought. For if we examine the intuitions systematically, we see that they distinguish the moral agent from his desires, and the free, reason-governed, autonomous nature of the person, from the unfree, passive (or, in Kant's term, 'pathological') nature of the animal. Surely, then, we must face up to the paradox of freedom. For we do think of ourselves both as empirical beings, bound by the laws of causality, and as transcendental beings, obedient to imperatives of reason alone.

We must remind ourselves again of the methodological character of the 'transcendental object'. This phrase designates, not an object of knowledge, but a limit to knowledge, defined by the perspective of practical reason. I am constrained by reason to view the world as a 'field of action', and hence to postulate the freedom of my will. Only from that postulate can I deliberate at all. From this perspective of practical reason I arrive inexorably at the categorical imperatives which compel my action. On one interpretation the doctrine of the self and its agency is not a doctrine of how things *are* in a transcendental world, but of how things *seem* in the empirical world. 'The conception of an intelligible world is then only a *point of view* which reason finds itself compelled to take outside appearances, *in order to conceive itself as practical*' (F 114). The rational agent requires, then, a special perspective on the world: he sees his actions under the aspect of freedom, and while what he sees is the same as what he sees when studying the world scientifically, his practical knowledge cannot be expressed in scientific terms. He seeks not causes but reasons, not mechanisms but rational ends, not descriptive laws but imperatives. Thus Kant answers in the affirmative the question posed in the first *Critique*: 'is it possible to regard one and the same event as being in one aspect merely an effect of nature and in another aspect due to freedom?' (A 543, B 571). But the answer, referring as it does to a transcendental perspective, is such that we can comprehend only its incomprehensibility (F 122).

The objectivity of morals

If my freedom and the laws which guide it are constituted by a particular way things seem, how can I consider the commands of morality to be objectively valid? Reason alone, Kant argues, compels me to accept the categorical imperative; hence it has 'objective necessity'. It does not matter that this compulsion issues from a point of view. For the same is true of the compulsion to accept the a priori laws of science. If reason is both a motive to action, and also impelled by its nature towards definite precepts, what more can be demanded by way of objectivity? When someone asks 'Why should I be moral?' he is asking for a reason. An answer that refers to his interest binds him only 'conditionally'. But the perspective of practical reason is able to rise above all 'conditions', and this is part of what is implied in its 'transcendental' nature. It generates imperatives which bind unconditionally. In which case it answers the question 'Why be moral?' for all rational agents, irrespective of their desires. The person with evil desires can no more escape the force of reason's answer than the person who desires what is right.

So conceived, the task of proving the objectivity of morality is less great than that of proving the objectivity of science, despite popular prejudice to the contrary. For the faculty of the understanding requires two 'deductions', one to show what we must believe, the other to show what is true. Practical reason, which makes no claims to truth, does not stand in need of this second, 'objective', deduction. It is enough that reason compels us to think according to the categorical imperative. There is nothing further to be proved about an independent world. If sometimes we speak of moral truth, and moral reality, this is but another way of referring to the constraints which reason places on our conduct.

The moral life

The moral nature of the rational being resides in his ability to impregnate all his judgements, motives and affections with the universal demands of practical reason. Even in our most private and intimate encounters, reason covertly abstracts from the immediate circumstances and reminds us of the moral law. Those philosophers—such as Shaftesbury, Hutcheson and Hume—who had stressed the importance to morality of the emotions, were not wrong, except in their faulty concept of emotion. The moral life involves the exercise of anger, remorse, indignation, pride, esteem and respect. And these are all emotions, since they are not subject to the will. '*Respect* is a *tribute* which we cannot refuse to merit, whether we will or not; we may indeed outwardly withhold it, but we cannot help feeling it inwardly' (P 241). But at the heart of such emotions is a respect for the moral law, and an abstraction from present and immediate conditions. It is this which justifies their place in the moral life of rational beings. Kant's discussion of pride and self-respect (L 120–7) is remarkably acute. By emphasising the element of reason that lies embedded in human emotion, he is able to rebut the charge that 'moral feeling' plays no part in the motivation of the rational man (L 139). But any theory which pays attention to the complexity of moral feeling must emphasise the imperative which lies at its heart.

The process of abstraction leads us, Kant thought, in a metaphysical direction. The moral life imposes an intimation of transcendental reality; we feel compelled towards the belief in God, in immortality, and in a divine ordinance in nature. These 'postulates of practical reason' are as ineluctable a product of moral thought as the imperative which guides us. Pure reason falls over itself in the attempt to prove the existence of God and the immortality of the soul. But 'from the practical point of view the *possibility* [of these doctrines] must be assumed, although we cannot theoretically know and understand it' (P 127). This obscure concession to the claims of theology is hard to accept. But some light is cast on Kant's intention by the third of his *Critiques*, to the examination of which we now must turn.

6 *Beauty and design*

It is not God's command that binds us to morality, but morality that points to the possibility of a 'holy will'. Kant warns against the 'fanaticism, indeed the impiety, of abandoning the guidance of a morally legislative reason in the right conduct of our lives, in order to derive guidance directly from the idea of the Supreme Being' (A 819, B 847). Kant's writings on religion exhibit one of the first attempts at the systematic demystification of theology. He criticises all forms of anthropomorphism, and expounds, in his *Religion Within the Limits of Reason Alone* (1793), a 'hermeneutical rule' of 'moral interpretation'. All scripture and religious doctrine that conflicts with reason must be interpreted allegorically, so as to express moral insights which gain vivacity, rather than validity, from their religious expression. The attempt to make the idea of God intelligible through images, and so to subsume God under the categories of the empirical world, is self-contradictory. If God is a transcendental being, then there is nothing to be said of him from our point of view except that he transcends it. If he is not a transcendental being, then he no more deserves our respect than any other work of nature. Under the first interpretation we can respect him only because we respect the moral law which points towards his existence. On the second interpretation, we could respect him only as a subject of the moral law which governs his activity.

Kant's demythologised religion was not uncommon among his contemporaries. He differed, however, in appropriating the images of traditional religion for the veneration of morality. The worship due to God becomes reverence and devotion for the moral law. The faith which transcends belief becomes the certainty of practical reason which surpasses understanding. The object of esteem is not the Supreme Being, but the supreme attribute of rationality. The moral world is described as the 'realm of grace' (A 815, B 844), the actual community of rational beings as the 'mystical body' in the world of nature (A 808, B 836), and the Kingdom of God to which mortals aspire is transmuted into the Kingdom of Ends which they make real through their self-legislation. It is not surprising to learn from one of Jachmann's letters that 'many evangelists went forth [from Kant's lectures on theology] and preached the gospel of the Kingdom of Reason'.

Nevertheless, Kant accepted the traditional claims of theology, and even tried to resuscitate them under the obscure doctrine of the 'postulates of practical reason'. Moreover, he felt that one of the traditional arguments for God's existence, the argument from design, contains a vital clue to the nature of creation. It is in the third *Critique*, at the end of an account of aesthetic experience, that Kant attempts to reveal his meaning.

The third critique

The *Critique of Judgement* is a disorganised and repetitious work, which gains little from Kant's struggle to impose on its somewhat diffuse subject-matter the structure of the transcendental philosophy. A contemporary who attended Kant's lectures on aesthetics recorded that 'the principal thoughts of his *Critique of Judgement* [were] given as easily, clearly, and entertainingly as can be imagined'. Kant was seventy-one when he came to write the work, however, and there seems little doubt that his mastery of argument and of the written word were beginning to desert him. Nevertheless, the third *Critique* is one of the most important works of aesthetics to have been composed in modern times; indeed, it could fairly be said that, were it not for this work, aesthetics would not exist in its modern form. Kant's most feeble arguments were here used to present some of his most original conclusions.

Kant felt the need to explore in the *Critique of Judgement* certain questions left over from the first two *Critiques*. Moreover he wished to provide for aesthetics its own 'faculty', corresponding to understanding and practical reason. The faculty of judgement 'mediates' between the other two. It enables us to see the empirical world as conforming to the ends of practical reason, and practical reason as adapted to our knowledge of the empirical world. Kant believed that 'judgement' has both a subjective and an objective aspect, and divided his *Critique* accordingly. The first part, concerned with the subjective experience of 'purposiveness' or 'finality', is devoted to aesthetic judgement. The second, concerned with the objective 'finality' of nature, is devoted to the natural manifestation of design. I shall concentrate on the first, which suffices in itself to bring the critical system to its conclusion.

The eighteenth century saw the birth of modern aesthetics. Shaftesbury and his followers made penetrating observations on the experience of beauty; Burke presented his famous distinction between the beautiful and the sublime; Batteux in France and Lessing and Winckelmann in Germany attempted to provide universal principles for the classification and judgement of works of art. The Leibnizians also made their contribution, and the modern use of the term 'aesthetic' is due to Kant's mentor A. G. Baumgarten. Nevertheless, no philosopher since Plato had given to aesthetic experience the central role in philosophy that Kant was to give to it. Nor had Kant's predecessors perceived, as he perceived, that both metaphysics and ethics must remain incomplete without a theory of the aesthetic. Only a rational being can experience beauty; and without the experience of beauty, rationality is unfulfilled. It is only in the aesthetic experience of nature, Kant suggests, that we grasp the relation of our faculties to the world, and so understand both our own limitations, and the possibility of transcending them. Aesthetic experience intimates to us that our point of view is, after all, only *our* point of view, and that we are no more creators of nature than we are creators of the point of view from which we observe and act on it. Momentarily we stand outside that point of view, not so as to have knowledge of a transcendent world, but so as to perceive the harmony that exists between our faculties and the objects in relation to which they are employed. At the same time we sense the divine order that makes this harmony possible.

The problem of beauty

Kant's aesthetics is based on a fundamental problem, which he expresses in many different forms, eventually giving to it the structure of an 'antinomy'. According to the 'antinomy of taste' aesthetic judgement seems to be in conflict with itself: it cannot be at the same time aesthetic (an expression of subjective experience) and also a judgement (claiming universal assent). And yet all rational beings, simply in virtue of their rationality, seem disposed to make these judgements. On the one hand, they feel pleasure in an object, and this pleasure is immediate, not based in any conceptualisation of the object, or in any inquiry into cause, purpose or constitution. On the other hand, they express their pleasure in the form of a judgement, speaking 'as if beauty were a quality of the object' (J 51), thus representing their pleasure as objectively valid. But how can this be so? The pleasure is immediate, based in no reasoning or analysis; so what permits this demand for universal agreement?

However we approach the idea of beauty we find this paradox emerging. Our attitudes, feelings and judgements are called aesthetic precisely because of their direct relation to experience. Hence no one can judge the beauty of an object that he has never heard or seen. Scientific judgements, like practical principles, can be received 'at second hand'. I can take you as my authority for the truths of physics, or for the utility of trains. But I cannot take you as my authority for the merits of Leonardo, or for the beauties of Mozart, if I have seen no work by the one or heard none by the other. It would seem to follow from this that there can be no rules or principles of aesthetic judgement. 'A principle of taste would mean a fundamental premise under the condition of which one might subsume the concept of an object, and then, by a syllogism, draw the inference that it is beautiful. That, however, is absolutely impossible. For I must feel the pleasure immediately in the perception of the object, and I cannot be talked into it by any grounds of proof' (J 141). It seems that it is always experience, and never conceptual thought, that gives the right to aesthetic judgement, so that anything which alters the experience of an object alters its aesthetic significance (which is why poetry cannot be translated). As Kant puts it, aesthetic judgement is 'free from concepts', and beauty itself is not a concept. Hence we arrive at the first proposition of the antinomy of taste: 'The judgement of taste is not based on concepts; for, if it were, it would be open to dispute (decision by means of proofs)' (J 198).

However, such a conclusion seems to be inconsistent with the fact that aesthetic judgement is a form of *judgement*. When I describe something as beautiful I do not mean merely that it pleases *me*: I am speaking about it, not about myself, and if challenged I try to find reasons for my view. I do not *explain* my feeling, but give *grounds* for it, by pointing to features of its object. And any search for reasons has the universal character of rationality. I am in effect saying that others, in so far as they are rational, ought to feel just the same delight as I feel. This points to the second proposition of Kant's antinomy: 'the judgement of taste is based on concepts; for otherwise . . . there could be no room even for contention in the matter, or for the claim to the necessary agreement of others' (J 198).

The synthetic a priori grounds of taste

Kant says that the judgement of beauty is grounded not in concepts but in a feeling of pleasure; at the same time this pleasure is postulated as universally valid, and even 'necessary'. The aesthetic judgement contains an 'ought': others ought to feel as I do, and to the extent that they do not, either they or I am wrong. It is this which leads us to seek reasons for our judgements. The terms 'universality' and 'necessity' refer us to the defining properties of the a priori. It is clear that the postulate that others ought to feel as I do is not derived from experience: it is, on the contrary, a presupposition of aesthetic pleasure. Nor is it analytic. Hence its status must be synthetic a priori.

The argument is very slippery. The 'necessity' of the judgement of taste has little to do with the necessity of the a priori laws of the understanding, nor does its universality issue in a definite principle. Kant sometimes recognises this, and speaks of aesthetic *pleasure* rather than aesthetic judgement as universally valid, and so a priori (J 146). Nevertheless, he was convinced that aesthetics raises precisely the same problem as all philosophy. 'The problem of the critique of judgement ... is part of the general problem of transcendental philosophy: How are synthetic a priori judgements possible?' (J 145).

Kant offers a 'transcendental deduction' in answer. It is only fifteen lines long, and wholly inadequate. He lamely says: 'what makes this deduction so easy is that it is spared the necessity of having to justify the objective [application] of a concept' (J 147). In fact, however, he argues independently for an a priori component in the judgement of taste, and for the legitimacy of its 'universal' postulate.

Objectivity and contemplation

Kant's concern is, as always, with objectivity. Aesthetic judgements claim validity. In what way can this claim be upheld? While the objectivity of theoretical judgements required a proof that the world is as the understanding represents it to be, no such proof was necessary for practical reason. It was enough to show that reason constrained each agent towards a set of basic principles. In aesthetic judgement the requirement is weaker still. We are not asked to establish principles that will compel the agreement of every rational being. It is sufficient to show how the thought of universal validity is possible. In aesthetic judgement we are only 'suitors for agreement' (J 82). It is not that there are valid rules of taste, but rather that we must *think* of our pleasure as made valid by its object.

Kant distinguishes sensory from contemplative pleasures. The pleasure in the beautiful, although it is 'immediate' (arising from no conceptual thought), nevertheless involves a reflective contemplation of its object. The pure judgement of taste 'combines delight or aversion immediately with the bare contemplation of the object . . .' (J 87). Aesthetic pleasure must therefore be distinguished from the purely sensuous pleasures of food and drink. It can be obtained only through those senses that also permit contemplation (which is to say, through sight and hearing).

This act of contemplation involves attending to the object not as an instance of a universal (or concept) but as the particular thing that it is. The individual object is isolated in aesthetic judgement and considered 'for its own sake'. But contemplation does not rest with this act of isolation. It embarks on a process of abstraction which exactly parallels the process whereby practical reason arrives at the categorical imperative. Aesthetic judgement abstracts from every 'interest' of the observer. He does not regard the object as a means to his ends, but as an end in itself (although not a moral end). The observer's desires, aims and ambitions are held in abeyance in the act of contemplation, and the object regarded 'apart from any interest' (J 50). This act of abstraction is conducted while focusing on the individual object in its 'singularity' (J 55). Hence, unlike the abstraction that generates the categorical imperative, it leads to no universal rule. Nevertheless, it underlies the 'universality' of the subsequent judgement. It is this which enables me to 'play the part of judge in matters of taste' (J 43). Having abstracted from all my interests and desires, I have, in effect, removed from my judgement all reference to the 'empirical conditions' which distinguish me, and referred my experience to reason alone, just as I refer the ends of action when acting morally. 'Since the delight is not based on any inclination of the subject (or on any other deliberate interest) . . . he can find as reason for his delight no personal conditions to which his own subjective self might alone be party' (J 50–1). In which case, it seems, the subject of aesthetic judgement must feel compelled, and also entitled, to legislate his pleasure for all rational beings.

Imagination and freedom

What aspect of rationality is involved in aesthetic contemplation? In the 'subjective deduction' of the first *Critique* (see p. 33 above), Kant had argued for the central role of imagination in the 'synthesis' of concept and intuition. Imagination transforms intuition into datum; we exercise imagination whenever we attribute to our experience a 'content' which represents the world. When I see the man outside my window, the concept 'man' is present in my perception. This work of impregnating experience with concepts is the work of imagination.

Kant thought that imagination could also be 'freed from' concepts (that is, from the rules of the understanding). It is this 'free play' of the imagination that characterises aesthetic judgement. In the free play of imagination concepts are either wholly indeterminate, or if determinate not applied. An example of the first is the imaginative 'synthesis' involved in seeing a set of marks as a pattern. Here there is no determinate concept. There is nothing to a pattern except an experienced order, and no concept applied in the experience apart from that indeterminate idea. An example of the second is the 'synthesis' involved in seeing a picture as a face. Here the concept 'face' enters the imaginative synthesis, but it is not applied to the object. I do not judge that this, before me, is a face, but only that I have imaginative permission so to see it. The second kind of 'free play' is at the root of our understanding of artistic representation. Kant was more interested in the first kind, and this led him to a formalistic conception of the beautiful in art.

The free play of the imagination enables me to bring concepts to bear on an experience that is, in itself, 'free from concepts'. Hence, even though there are no rules of taste, I can still give grounds for my aesthetic judgement. I can give reasons for my pleasure, while focusing on the 'singularity' which is its cause.

Harmony and common sense

Kant valued art less than nature, and music least among the arts, 'since it plays merely with sensations' (J 195). Nevertheless the example of music provides a good illustration of Kant's theory. When I hear music I hear a certain organisation. Something begins, develops, and maintains a unity among its parts. This unity is not indeed *there* in the notes before me. It is a product of my perception. I hear it only because my imagination, in its 'free play', brings my perception under the indeterminate idea of unity. Only beings with imagination (a faculty of reason) can hear musical unity, since only they can carry out this indeterminate synthesis. So the unity is a perception of mine. But this perception is not arbitrary, since it is compelled by my rational nature. I perceive the organisation in my experience as objective. The experience of unity brings pleasure, and this too belongs to the exercise of reason. I suppose the pleasure, like the melody, to be the property of all who are constituted like me. So I represent my pleasure in the music as due to the workings of a 'common sense' (J 153), which is to say, a disposition that is at once based in experience, and common to all rational beings.

But how is it that the experience of unity is mixed with pleasure? When I hear the formal unity of music, the ground of my experience consists in a kind of compatibility between what I hear and the faculty of imagination through which it is organised. Although the unity has its origin in me, it is attributed to an independent object. In experiencing the unity I also sense a harmony between my rational faculties and the object (the sounds) to which they are applied. This sense of harmony between myself and the world is both the origin of my pleasure and also the ground of its universality.

. . . one who feels pleasure in simple reflection on the form of an object, without having any concept in mind, rightly lays claim to the agreement of everyone, although this judgement is empirical and a singular judgement. For the ground of this pleasure is found in the universal, though subjective, condition of reflective judgements, namely the final harmony of an object . . . with the mutual relation of the faculties of cognition (imagination and understanding), which are requisite for every empirical cognition. (J 32)

Form and purposiveness

It seems, then, that our pleasure in beauty has its origin in a capacity, due to the free play of imagination, first to experience the harmonious working of our own rational faculties, and secondly to project that harmony outwards on to the empirical world. We see in objects the formal unity that we discover in ourselves. This is the origin of our pleasure, and the basis of our 'common sense' of beauty. And it is 'only under the presupposition . . . of such a common sense that we are able to lay down a judgement of taste' (J 83).

Kant distinguishes 'free' from 'dependent' beauty, the first being perceived wholly without the aid of conceptual thought, the second requiring prior conceptualisation of the object. When I perceive a representational picture, or a building, I can have no impression of beauty until I have first brought the object under concepts, referring in one case to the content expressed, in the other to the function performed (J 73). The judgement of such 'dependent' beauty is less pure than the judgement of 'free' beauty, and would only become pure for the person who had no conception of the meaning or function of what he saw (J 74). The purest examples of beauty are therefore 'free'. Only in the contemplation of such examples are our faculties able to relax entirely from the burdens of common scientific and practical thought, and enter into that free play which is the ground of aesthetic pleasure. Examples of this free beauty abound in nature, but not in art.

The unity that we perceive in the free beauties of nature comes to us purified of all interests: it is a unity that makes reference to no definite purpose. But it reflects back to us an order that has its origin in ourselves, as purposive beings. Hence it bears the indeterminate marks of purpose. As Kant put it, aesthetic unity displays 'purposiveness without purpose'. Aesthetic experience, which leads us to see each object as an end in itself, also leads us to a sense of the purposiveness of nature.

The perception of 'purposiveness', like the regulative ideas of reason (see p. 60 above), is not a perception of what is, but a perception 'as if'. However, it is an inescapable 'as if': we *must* see the world in this way if we are to find our proper place in it, both as knowing and as acting creatures. Aesthetic judgement, which delivers to us the pure experience of design in nature, frees us both for theoretical insight and for the endeavours of the moral life. It also permits the transition from the theoretical to the practical: finding design in nature, we recognise that our own ends might be enacted there (J 38). Moreover, and again like the ideas of reason, the concept of purposiveness is 'supersensible': it is the idea of a transcendental design, the purpose of which we cannot know.

Aesthetic experience is the vehicle of many such 'aesthetic ideas'. These are ideas of reason which transcend the limits of possible experience, while trying to represent, in 'sensible' form, the inexpressible character of the world beyond (J 175–6). There is no true beauty without aesthetic ideas; they are presented to us both by art and by nature. The aesthetic idea imprints on our senses an intimation of a transcendental realm. The poet, even if he deals with empirical phenomena, 'tries by means of the imagination . . . to go beyond the limits of experience and to present [these things] to sense with a completeness of which there is no example in nature' (J 176–7). This is how Kant explains the effect of aesthetic condensation. For example, when Milton expresses the vengeful feelings of Satan, his smouldering words transport us. We feel that we are listening not to this or that, as one might say, 'contingent' emotion, but to the very essence of revenge. We seem to transcend the limitations contained in every natural example and to be made aware of something indescribable which they palely reflect.

When Wagner expresses through the music of *Tristan* the unassuageable longing of erotic love, it is again as though we had risen above our own circumscribed passions and glimpsed a completion to which they aspire. No concept can allow us to rise so far: yet the aesthetic *experience*, which involves a perpetual striving to pass beyond the limits of our point of view, seems to 'embody' what cannot be thought.

Teleology and the divine

Kant attempts, then, to move from his philosophy of beauty to an account of our relation to the world which will be free of that limitation to our own perspective which he had argued, in the first *Critique*, to be a necessary condition of self-consciousness. In aesthetic experience we view ourselves in relation to a transcendental, or supersensible, reality which lies beyond the reach of thought. We become aware of our own limitations, of the grandeur of the world, and of the inexpressible good order that permits us to know and act on it. Kant has recourse to Burke's distinction between the beautiful and the sublime. Sometimes, when we sense the harmony between nature and our faculties, we are impressed by the purposiveness and intelligibility of everything that surrounds us. This is the sentiment of beauty. At other times, overcome by the infinite greatness of the world, we renounce the attempt to understand and control it. This is the sentiment of the sublime. In confronting the sublime, the mind is 'incited to abandon sensibility' (J 92).

Kant's remarks about the sublime are obscure, but they reinforce the interpretation of his aesthetics as a kind of 'premonition' of theology. He defines the sublime as 'that, the mere capacity of thinking which, evidences a faculty of mind transcending every standard of taste' (J 98). It is the judgement of the sublime that most engages our moral nature. It thereby points to yet another justification of the 'universality' of taste, by showing that, in demanding agreement, we are asking complicity in a moral sentiment (J 116). In judging of the sublime, we demand a universal recognition of the immanence of a supersensible realm. A man who can feel neither the solemnity nor the awesomeness of nature, lacks in our eyes the necessary sense of his own limitations. He has not taken that 'transcendental' viewpoint on himself from which all true morality springs.

It is from the presentiment of the sublime that Kant seems to extract his faith in a Supreme Being. The second part of the *Critique of Judgement* is devoted to 'teleology': the understanding of the ends of things. Here Kant expresses, in a manner that has proved unsatisfactory to many commentators, his ultimate sympathy for the standpoint of theology. Our sentiments of the sublime and of the beautiful combine to present an inescapable picture of nature as created. In beauty we discover the purposiveness of nature; in the sublime we have intimations of its transcendent origins. In neither case can we translate our sentiments into a reasoned argument: all we know is that we know nothing of the transcendental. But that is not all we *feel*. The argument from design is not a theoretical proof, but a moral intimation, made vivid to us by our sentiments towards nature, and realised in our rational acts. It is realised in the sense that the true end of creation is intimated through our moral actions: but it is seen that this intimation is of an ideal, not of an actual, world. So we prove the divine teleology in all our moral actions, without being able to show that it is true of the world in which we act. The final end of nature is known to us, not theoretically, but practically. It lies in reverence for the pure practical reason that 'legislates for itself alone'. When we relate this reverence to our experience of the sublime, we have a sense, however fleeting, of the transcendental (T 113).

Thus it is that aesthetic judgement directs us towards the apprehension of a transcendent world, while practical reason gives content to that apprehension, and affirms that this intimation of a perspectiveless vision of things is indeed an intimation of God. This is what Kant tries to convey both in the doctrine of the aesthetic ideas and in that of the sublime. In each case we are confronted with an 'employment of the imagination in the interests of mind's supersensible province' and a compulsion to 'think nature itself in its totality as a presentation of something supersensible, without our being able to put this presentation forward as objective' (J 119). The supersensible is the transcendental. It cannot be thought through concepts, and the attempt to think it through 'ideas' is fraught with self-contradiction. Yet the ideas of reason—God, freedom, immortality—are resurgent in our consciousness, now under the guise of imperatives of action, now transformed by imagination into sensuous and aesthetic form. We cannot rid ourselves of these ideas. To do so would be to say that our point of view on the world is all that the world consists in, and so to make ourselves into gods. Practical reason and aesthetic experience humble us. They remind us that the world in its totality, conceived from no finite perspective, is not ours to know. This humility of reason is also the true object of esteem. Only this is to be reverenced in the rational being, that he feels and acts as a member of a transcendental realm, while recognising that he can know only the world of nature. Aesthetic experience and practical reason are two aspects of the moral: and it is through morality that we sense both the transcendence and the immanence of God.

7 Transcendental philosophy

Kant was regarded by his immediate successors as having irreversibly changed the course of philosophy. But already in Kant's lifetime the intellectual world was torn by controversy over the meaning of his critical system. Was Kant really a Leibnizian after all, as Eberhard had accused him of being (K 107)? Did he believe that the world of nature is nothing but a 'well-founded phenomenon', reality itself consisting in timeless, spaceless, noumenal substances whose attributes are derived from reason alone? Is the 'thing-in-itself' the underlying substance which sustains appearances? In a series of letters to the ageing Kant, his pupil Jakob Beck rehearsed this interpretation, and sought to demonstrate its untenability. But if the transcendental philosophy is not a version of Leibnizian rationalism, why is it not, then, a repetition of the sceptical empiricism of Hume? Kant's philosophy is very much clearer in its negative than in its positive aspect, and in his day he had been called (by J. G. Hamann) 'the Prussian Hume'. In the long peroration that concludes the 'Antinomy' of the first *Critique*, Kant emphasises this negative aspect, and writes with pride of the method that has enabled him to rise above all pre-existing argument in order to show that certain conclusions are not just undemonstrated, but indemonstrable.

Neither the Leibnizian nor the Humean interpretation is really tenable. It is true that Kant sometimes speaks of concepts as 'rules' for organising our perceptions (e.g. A 126), a conclusion that is reminiscent of Hume. It is also true that he is tempted by the 'transcendental hypothesis' of a realm of 'things as they are' (e.g. A 780, B 808), a conclusion that would align him with Leibniz. But these remarks are aberrations. Kant's true critical philosophy can be assimilated to neither of its antecedents, since it removes the grounds from both.

The first important school of thought to arise out of Kantian philosophy was the 'subjective idealism' of Fichte (1762–1814), Schelling (1775–1854) and Hegel (1770–1831). According to these philosophers, the critical philosophy, in arguing away the 'thing-in-itself', had shown that reality is to be conceived in mental terms. Knowledge of an object is construed as 'positing' (*setzen*), rather than 'receiving'. For Fichte, Kant's great achievement was to have shown that the mind has knowledge only through its own activity; in an important sense, the objects of knowledge are a *product* of that activity. Thus Fichte wrote to a friend: 'I suppose I am more strictly a transcendental idealist than Kant; for he still admits a manifold of appearance, but I assert in plain terms that even this is produced by us, by means of a creative power.' The mind is identified with the 'transcendental self', construed as the one noumenal object with which we are acquainted. But who, once again, are we? In Fichte's philosophy the transcendental self becomes a kind of universal spirit by which the separate empirical selves are constructed, along with the 'world of appearance' in which they expend their energies, the whole depending on an unknowable synthesis which generates nature from the inexhaustible reservoir of the 'thing-in-itself'.

Schopenhauer too (1788–1860) was influenced by this interpretation, believing that Kant had rightly identified the 'transcendental self' with the will (which is therefore the true 'substance' behind appearances). For Schopenhauer scientific concepts like space, time, object and cause apply only in appearance, imposing order on the world of appearance (or the 'veil of Maya'—the term Schopenhauer borrowed from oriental mysticism). Behind this veil the will takes its endless, unknowable and unsatisfiable course. Hegel, by contrast, developed Fichte's idea of the known as 'posited' by the knower. He tried to show that the objective reference justified in the transcendental deduction is but the first stage in an expanding process of self-knowledge. Mind (*Geist*) comes to know itself through the positing of an ever more complex world. Hegel described this process as 'dialectical', meaning not to bury but to praise it. He believed that Kant's first *Critique* had displayed, not the errors of pure reason, but the dynamic process of conjecture and refutation whereby reason constantly negates its own advances, achieving from the ruin of partial knowledge an ever more complete, more 'absolute', picture of reality.

Kant would have rejected that return to the Leibnizian vision. 'The light dove,' he wrote, 'cleaving the air in her free flight, and feeling its resistance, might imagine that flight would be still easier in empty space' (A 5, B 8). Thus he dismissed as insubstantial any pretence to an absolute form of knowledge, which seeks to soar above the resistant medium of experience. The notion of a transcendental object is misunderstood when considered as referring to a real thing. The idea is posited only as a 'point of view' (A 681, B 710), in order to make clear that 'the principles of pure understanding can apply only to objects of the senses . . . never to things in general without regard to the mode in which we are able to apprehend them' (A 246, B 303). There is no description of the world that can free itself from the reference to experience. Although the world that we know is not our creation, nor merely a synopsis of our perspective, it cannot be known except from the point of view which is ours. All attempts to break through the limits imposed by experience end in self-contradiction, and although we may have intimations of a 'transcendental' knowledge, that knowledge can never be ours. These intimations are confined to moral life and aesthetic experience, and while they tell us, in a sense, what we really are, they can be translated into words only to speak unintelligibly. Philosophy, which describes the limits of knowledge, is always tempted to transcend them. But Kant's final advice to it is that given in the last sentence of Wittgenstein's *Tractatus Logico-Philosophicus*: That whereof we cannot speak, we must consign to silence.

Further reading

Writings by Kant

There is no adequate selection in English from Kant's voluminous writings. The student cannot avoid jumping in at the deep end, with the *Critique of Pure Reason*. The standard English edition by Norman Kemp-Smith (1929) contains texts of and page references to both editions. The writings on ethics are available in several editions: my references are to the translation by T. K. Abbott, *Kant's Critique of Practical Reason and other works on the theory of Ethics* (London, 1879), which contains both major works, together with an interesting memoir of Kant. *Foundations of the Metaphysic of Morals* is also available in a useful edition (1959), edited and translated by L. W. Beck. The standard English edition of the *Critique of Judgement* (including both the *Critique of Aesthetic Judgement* and the *Critique of Teleological Judgement*) is translated by J. C. Meredith (Oxford, 1928). Other writings are listed at the beginning of this work.

Writings about Kant

The few biographies of Kant make unexciting reading. The fullest, although not the most accurate, is that of J. H. W. Stuckenberg, *The Life of Immanuel Kant* (London, 1882).

Commentaries are legion. A growing interest in Kant among English-speaking philosophers has led to many works of high quality and lucidity. The best of these is P. F. Strawson's *The Bounds of Sense* (London, 1966), which contains a thorough exposition, and partial defence, of the argument of the first *Critique*, in its 'objective' interpretation. The 'subjective' rejoinder from Ralph Walker (*Kant*, in the series 'Arguments of the Philosophers', London, 1979), is clear and scholarly, although rather less persuasive. Those interested in a vigorous empiricist interpretation will enjoy Jonathan Bennett's two commentaries, *Kant's Analytic* (Cambridge, 1966) and *Kant's Dialectic* (Cambridge, 1974). The best short introduction in English remains that of A. C. Ewing (London, 1938) entitled *A Short Commentary on Kant's Critique of Pure*

Reason. Neither the second nor the third *Critique* has received commentary of the same quality. The best that I know in English is H. J. Paton's *The Categorical Imperative* (London, 1974) on the ethics, and Donald W. Crawford's *Kant's Aesthetic Theory* (Wisconsin, 1974) on the aesthetics.

Hegel

Peter Singer

In memory of my father, Ernest Singer

Preface

No philosopher of the nineteenth or twentieth centuries has had as great an impact on the world as Hegel. The only possible exception to this sweeping statement would be Karl Marx—and Marx himself was heavily influenced by Hegel. Without Hegel, neither the intellectual nor the political developments of the last 150 years would have taken the path they did.

Hegel's impact alone makes it important to understand him; but Hegel's philosophy is in any case worth studying for its own sake. His profound ideas led him to some conclusions that strike the modern reader as bizarre, even absurd. Whatever one thinks of his conclusions, however, there are arguments and insights in his work that retain their force to the present day. The effort required to understand Hegel is repaid by them, and also by the satisfaction of having mastered the challenge to our comprehension that Hegel represents.

That Hegel does present a challenge is undeniable. Commentaries on Hegel are studded with references to the 'Himalayan severity' of his prose, to his 'repulsive terminology' and to the 'extreme obscurity' of his thought. To illustrate the nature of the problem I have just now picked up my copy of what many consider to be his greatest work, *The Phenomenology of Mind*, and opened it at random. The first complete sentence on the page on which it opened (p. 596) reads: 'It is merely the restless shifting change of those moments, of which one is indeed being-returned-into-itself, but merely as being-for-itself, i.e. as abstract moment, appearing on one side over against the others.' Admittedly, I have wrenched the sentence from its context; even so, it indicates some of the difficulties one has in making sense of Hegel. Equally formidable sentences can be found on every one of the *Phenomenology*'s 750 pages.

To explain the work of such a philosopher in a short book intended for an audience with no prior knowledge of his work is no easy task. To make the task a little more manageable, I have done two things. The first is to limit the scope. I have not attempted to give an account of all of Hegel's thought. So the reader will find here no account of what Hegel said in his *Lectures on Aesthetics*, nor of his *Lectures on the History of Philosophy*, nor of his *Lectures on the Philosophy of Religion*, nor of anything in his *Encyclopedia of the Philosophical Sciences*, except where these works overlap with other works that are discussed. (In the case of the *Encyclopedia* the overlap is considerable, the major section not covered elsewhere being that on the philosophy of nature.) These omissions are significant, of course, but I console myself with the thought that Hegel himself would not have considered them absolutely central to his philosophical system. More serious, however, is the absence of any detailed account of Hegel's *Science of Logic*, which he undoubtedly did consider a key work. I have tried to give something of the aim, method and flavour of it, but the *Logic* is so very long and so very abstract that an adequate account is, in my view, beyond the scope of any 100-page introduction to Hegel.

The second part of my strategy for making the lofty heights of Hegel's thought accessible to novices is to select the gentlest possible approach route. Accordingly I begin with the most concrete, least abstract, part of Hegel's thought, his philosophy of history. From there, still remaining on the social and political level, we move upwards to his views of freedom and the rational organisation of society. Only then do we attempt the rocky pinnacles of the *Phenomenology*, after which our ascent a short way up the *Logic* will take little extra effort.

Hegel scholars may object to the selection of works I have chosen to discuss, or to the order in which I discuss them. I have already indicated that the order is not intended to suggest anything about how Hegel himself would have chosen to present his ideas. As for the selection, I do not pretend that Hegel thought his *Lectures on the Philosophy of History* any more important than, say, the section of his *Encyclopedia* on the philosophy of nature. All I know is that I do not have space to discuss them both, and I am certain that Hegel's philosophy of history has been more important to the development of modern thought, and remains to this day far more interesting to the general reader, than his philosophy of nature. (Don't be misled by the title: Hegel's philosophy of nature does not contain his musings upon the value and beauty of forests and mountains. It is Hegel's attempt to show how the findings of the natural sciences—physics, chemistry, biology etc.—conform to his logical categories. Much of what Hegel said has since been rendered obsolete: for example his view that nature cannot develop is falsified by our knowledge of evolution.) My selection has therefore been influenced by three separate factors: what is central to Hegel's thought, what can be rendered intelligible to the general reader within the length of this volume, and what remains interesting and important to people living in the late twentieth century.

For the view of Hegel expressed in the following pages I am indebted to many people. At Oxford I was fortunate to be able to attend two remarkable series of classes offered by J. L. H. Thomas, who forced his students to probe passages of the *Phenomenology* sentence by sentence, until they yielded their meaning. The detailed work we did in those classes was admirably complemented by the broader brushwork of Patrick Gardiner's lectures on German Idealism. My other debts are to the authors of books from which I have freely plundered their best (I hope) ideas. Most prominent among these are Richard Norman's *Hegel's Phenomenology*, Ivan Soll's *An Introduction to Hegel's Metaphysics*, and two books entitled *Hegel*, one by Walter Kaufmann and the other by Charles Taylor. Bob Solomon read the typescript and suggested some improvements, as did Henry Hardy, Keith Thomas and an anonymous OUP reader.

It remains only to thank Jean Archer for her excellent typing, and Ruth, Marion and Esther for allowing me some time to work during their summer holidays.

PETER SINGER

Melbourne, Australia
March 1982

Contents

1 *Hegel's times and life*

Hegel's times

George Wilhelm Friedrich Hegel was born in Stuttgart in 1770. His father was a minor civil servant at the court of the Duchy of Württemberg. Other relatives were teachers or Lutheran ministers. There is nothing particularly extraordinary to relate about his life, but the times in which he lived were momentous, politically, culturally and philosophically.

In 1789 news of the fall of the Bastille reverberated around Europe. It is of this moment that Wordsworth wrote:

> Bliss was it in that dawn to be alive,
> But to be young was very heaven!

Hegel was just short of his nineteenth birthday. He too was later to call the French Revolution a 'glorious dawn' and to add: 'All thinking beings shared in the jubilation of this epoch.' Sharing in it himself one Sunday morning in spring, he went out with some fellow students to plant a liberty tree, a symbol of the hopes sown by the Revolution.

By the time Hegel was twenty-one, the Revolutionary Wars had begun, and Germany was soon to be invaded by the revolutionary armies. The area we now know as Germany then consisted of more than 300 States, duchies and free cities, loosely linked together as the Holy Roman Empire under the leadership of Francis I of Austria. Napoleon put an end to this thousand-year-old empire when he trounced the Austrians at Ulm and Austerlitz, and then in 1806 crushed the armies of the next most powerful German State, Prussia, at the battle of Jena. Hegel was living in Jena at the time. One might have expected his sympathies to have been with the defeated German State, but a letter he wrote the day after Jena was occupied by the French shows only admiration for Napoleon: 'The Emperor—this world soul—I saw riding through the city to review his troops; it is indeed a wonderful feeling to see such an individual who, here concentrated into a single point, sitting on a horse, reaches out over the world and dominates it.'

This admiration remained throughout the period in which Napoleon ruled over Europe; and when in 1814 Napoleon was defeated, Hegel referred to this as a tragic thing, the spectacle of an immense genius destroyed by mediocrity.

The period of French power, between 1806 and 1814, was a period of reform in Germany. In Prussia, von Stein, a liberal, was appointed chief adviser to the king, and immediately abolished serfdom and reorganised the system of government. He was followed by von Hardenberg, who promised to give Prussia a representative constitution; but after Napoleon's defeat these hopes were dashed. The Prussian king, Frederick William III, lost interest in reform and in 1823, after years of delay, set up only provisional 'estates' which could do no more than advise, and in any case were completely dominated by landowners. Moreover in 1819, at a meeting at Carlsbad, all the German States agreed to censor newspapers and periodicals and to adopt repressive measures against those who advocated revolutionary ideas.

From a cultural point of view, Hegel lived in the golden age of German literature. Twenty years younger than Goethe and ten years younger than Schiller, he was nevertheless old enough to appreciate all of their mature works as they appeared. He was a close friend of the poet Hölderlin, and a contemporary of the leaders of the German Romantic movement, including Novalis, Herder, Schleiermacher and the Schlegel brothers. Goethe and Schiller were major influences on Hegel, and he was obviously taken with some of the Romantic movement's ideas, though he rejected most of what the Romantics stood for.

Most significant of all for Hegel's development was the state of German philosophy in the period in which he worked. To appreciate the background to Hegel's own thought, we need to begin this story with Kant, and briefly sketch what happened thereafter.

Immanuel Kant published the *Critique of Pure Reason* in 1781. This is now regarded as one of the greatest philosophical works of all time. Kant set out to establish what our reason or intellect can or cannot achieve in the way of knowledge. He concluded that our mind is no merely passive receiver of information obtained by our eyes, ears and other senses. Knowledge is only possible because our mind plays an active role, organising and systematising what we experience. We know the world within a framework of space, time and substance; but space, time and substance are not objective realities that exist 'out there', independently of us. They are creations of our intuition or reason without which we could not comprehend the world. What, then, one might naturally ask, is the world really like, independently of the framework within which we grasp it? This question, Kant says, can never be answered. Independent reality—Kant called it the world of the 'thing-in-itself'—is for ever beyond our knowledge.

During Kant's lifetime it was not simply the *Critique of Pure Reason* that built his towering reputation. There were also two other critiques, the *Critique of Practical Reason*, on ethics, and the *Critique of Judgement*, a large part of which is on aesthetics. In the former, Kant pictured man as a being capable of following a rational moral law, but also liable to be swayed from it by the non-rational desires which have their origin in our physical nature. To act morally is thus always a struggle. Victory is to be won by the suppression of all desires except the feeling of reverence for the moral law, which leads us to do our duty for its own sake. In contrast to this view of morality as based only on the reasoning aspects of human nature, in the *Critique of Judgement* Kant pictured aesthetic appreciation as involving a harmonious union of our understanding and our imagination.

In the closing words of the *Critique of Pure Reason*, Kant expressed the hope that by following the path of critical philosophy that he had trodden, it might be possible 'before the present century runs out' to attain what many centuries before had been unable to achieve, namely 'to give human reason complete satisfaction about that which has always engaged its curiosity, but so far in vain'. So impressive was Kant's achievement that for a time it did indeed seem, not just to Kant but also to his readers, as if there were only a few more details to be filled in, and then all philosophy would be complete. Gradually, however, dissatisfaction with Kant began to be expressed.

The first source of dissatisfaction was Kant's view of the 'thing-in-itself'. That something should exist and yet be completely unknowable seemed an unsatisfactory limitation on the powers of human reason. And was not Kant contradicting himself when he said that we could know nothing of it, and yet claimed to know that it exists and is a 'thing'? It was Johann Fichte who took the bold step of denying the existence of the thing-in-itself, thus being more true to Kant's philosophy, he asserted, than Kant was himself. The whole world, in Fichte's view, was to be seen as something constituted by our active minds. What mind cannot know, does not exist.

The second source of dissatisfaction was the division of human nature implied by Kant's moral philosophy. Here it was Schiller who began the attack, in his *Lectures on the Aesthetic Education of Man*. He too saw himself as using Kant to improve upon Kant, for he borrowed from the *Critique of Judgement* the model of aesthetic judgement as a unity of understanding and imagination. Surely, said Schiller, all our life should be similarly harmonious. To portray human nature as for ever divided between reason and passion, and our moral life as an eternal struggle between the two, is degrading and defeatist. Perhaps, Schiller suggested, Kant was accurately describing the sorry state of human life today, but it was not always so and it need not always be so. In ancient Greece, so much admired for the purity of its artistic forms, there had been a harmonious unity between reason and passion. To serve as a basis of a restoration of that long-lost harmony in human nature, Schiller therefore urged the revival of the sense of the aesthetic in every aspect of life.

Hegel was later to write that Kant's philosophy 'constitutes the basis and point of departure for modern German philosophy'. We could add that Fichte and Schiller, in their different ways, showed the directions these departures were to take. The unknowable thing-in-itself and the conception of human nature divided against itself were both, for Kant's successors, problems in need of solutions.

In an early essay, Hegel expressed his admiration for Schiller's objections to Kant's view of human nature, and especially for the point that this disharmony was not an eternal truth about human nature, but a problem to be overcome. He could not accept, however, the idea that aesthetic education was the way to overcome it. Instead he regarded the task as one for philosophy.

Hegel's life

After doing unusually well at school, Hegel won a scholarship to a well-known seminary at Tübingen, where he studied philosophy and theology. Here he became friendly with the poet Hölderlin and with a younger, very talented student of philosophy named Friedrich Schelling. Schelling was to achieve a national reputation as a philosopher before anyone had heard of Hegel; later, when his reputation had been eclipsed by that of Hegel, he was to complain that his former friend had taken over his own ideas. Though Schelling is little read nowadays, the parallels between his views and Hegel's are sufficiently close to lend the complaint some plausibility, provided we overlook how much more Hegel made of the points on which the two concurred.

After completing his studies at Tübingen, Hegel accepted a post as family tutor with a wealthy family in Switzerland. This was followed by a similar position in Frankfurt. During this period Hegel continued to read and think about philosophical questions. He wrote essays on religion, not for publication but to clarify his thoughts. The essays show him to have been thinking along radical lines. Jesus is compared with Socrates, and emerges from the comparison as decidedly the inferior teacher of ethics. Orthodox religion is, in Hegel's eyes, a barrier to the goal of restoring man to a state of harmony, for it makes man subordinate his own powers of thought to an external authority. For the rest of his life, Hegel retained something of this attitude to orthodox religion; yet his radicalism ebbed to the extent that, later on, he could consider himself a Lutheran Christian and regularly attend Lutheran church services.

When his father died in 1799 Hegel found himself with a modest inheritance. He gave up tutoring and joined his friend Schelling at the University of Jena, in the small state of Weimar. Schiller and Fichte had been at Jena, and Schelling was now also well-known; Hegel, on the other hand, had published virtually nothing and had to be content to lecture privately, supplementing his capital only by the small fees he collected from the few students (eleven in 1801, thirty by 1804) who came to hear him.

At Jena, Hegel published a long pamphlet on the differences between the philosophies of Fichte and Schelling: in every case, in his opinion, Schelling's view was to be preferred. For a time he worked with Schelling on a *Critical Journal of Philosophy*, for which he wrote several essays. In 1803 Schelling left Jena, and Hegel began to prepare his first major work, *The Phenomenology of Mind*. His inheritance now exhausted, he was badly in need of money. He accepted a publisher's contract which provided him with a cash advance but contained draconian penalty clauses if he should fail to post the manuscript by the due date of 13 October 1806. This turned out to be the day Jena was occupied by the French following their victory over the Prussians. Hegel had to rush the final sections of the book in order to meet his deadline, and then to his consternation found that he had no alternative but to send off the manuscript—his only copy—amidst all the confusion caused by the arrival of the warring armies outside Jena. Luckily the manuscript travelled undisturbed and the work appeared early in 1807.

The initial reaction was respectful, if hardly enthusiastic. Schelling was understandably perturbed to find that the preface contained a polemical attack on what seemed to be his views. In a letter Hegel explained that he intended to criticise not Schelling but only his unworthy imitators. Schelling replied that this distinction was not made in the preface itself, and refused to be mollified. Their friendship was at an end.

Life at Jena had been disrupted by the French occupation. Now that the university had closed down, Hegel worked for a year as a newspaper editor, and then accepted the headmastership of the academic high school at Nuremberg. He remained in this post for nine years, and made a success of it. In addition to the more usual subjects, he taught his schoolboys philosophy. What they made of his lectures is not known.

In Nuremberg Hegel's domestic life became settled. At Jena he had fathered an illegitimate son, the mother being his landlady, who is recorded as having had two previous illegitimate children by other lovers. In 1811, aged forty-one, Hegel married the daughter of an old Nuremberg family. She was scarcely half his age, but the marriage was, as far as one can tell, a happy one. They had two sons, and after the death of the mother of Hegel's first child, his wife was sufficiently tolerant to take his illegitimate son into her household as well.

During these years Hegel published his lengthy *Science of Logic*, which appeared in three volumes in 1812, 1813 and 1816. His works were now gaining wider appreciation, and in 1816 he was invited to take the post of Professor of Philosophy at the University of Heidelberg. Here he wrote the *Encyclopedia of the Philosophical Sciences*, which is a relatively brief statement of his entire philosophical system. Much of the material in it is also contained, in amplified form, in his other works.

Hegel's reputation was now so high that the Prussian Minister of Education asked him to take up the prestigious chair of philosophy at the University of Berlin. The Prussian educational system had benefited from the reforms of von Stein and von Hardenberg, and Berlin was becoming the intellectual centre of all the German States. Hegel accepted the offer with alacrity, and taught at Berlin from 1818 until he died in 1831.

In every respect this final period was the climax of Hegel's life. He wrote and published his *Philosophy of Right* and lectured on the philosophy of history, the philosophy of religion, aesthetics and the history of philosophy. He was not a good lecturer in the conventional sense, but he clearly captivated his students. Here is a description by one of them:

I was unable at first to find my way into either the manner of his delivery or the train of his thought. Exhausted, morose, he sat there as if collapsed into himself, his head bent down, and while speaking kept turning pages and searching in his folio notebooks, forward and backward, high and low. His constant clearing of his throat and coughing interrupted any flow of speech. Every sentence stood alone and came out with effort, cut in pieces and jumbled ...Eloquence that flows along smoothly presupposes that the speaker is finished with the subject inside and out and has it by heart ... this man, however, had to raise up the most powerful thoughts from the deepest ground of things ... a more vivid representation of these difficulties and this immense trouble than was accomplished by the manner of his delivery would be inconceivable.

Hegel was now attracting large audiences. People came to hear him from all over the German-speaking world, and many of the brightest became his disciples. After his death they were to edit and publish his lecture notebooks, supplemented by additions from their own notes of what he had said. It is in this way that several of Hegel's works—the *Lectures on the Philosophy of History*, the *Lectures on Aesthetics*, the *Lectures on the Philosophy of Religion* and the *Lectures on the History of Philosophy*—have come down to us.

In 1830, in recognition of his status, Hegel was elected Rector of the University. The following year, at the age of sixty-one, he suddenly fell ill and the next day died in his sleep. 'What an awful void!' wrote one of his colleagues: 'He was the cornerstone of our university.'

2 *History with a purpose*

Hegel took history seriously. In contrast to Kant, who thought he could say on purely philosophical grounds what human nature is and always must be, Hegel accepted Schiller's suggestion that the very foundations of the human condition could change from one historical era to another. This notion of change, of development throughout history, is fundamental to Hegel's view of the world. Friedrich Engels, looking back on Hegel's importance to himself and to his colleague Karl Marx, wrote:

What distinguished Hegel's mode of thinking from that of all other philosophers was the exceptional historical sense underlying it. However abstract and idealist the form employed, the development of his ideas runs always parallel to the development of world history, and the latter is indeed supposed to be only the proof of the former.

We need not yet concern ourselves about the meaning of Engels's last clause—the reference to the development of world history as the 'proof' of Hegel's system of ideas—for the undoubted parallel between the development of Hegel's ideas and the development of world history to which Engels draws attention is sufficient justification for using Hegel's understanding of world history as our way into his system of ideas.

The other point to be drawn from what Engels says is simply that in assessing the importance of Hegel's influence on Marx and himself, he gives first place to Hegel's historical sense. So in beginning our introduction with Hegel's *Philosophy of History*, we are beginning with a topic that is central not only to Hegel's system, but also to the enduring influence of his ideas.

What is philosophy of history?

It is first necessary to understand what a 'philosophy of history' is, in Hegel's sense of the term. Hegel's *Philosophy of History* contains a good deal of historical information. One can find in it a kind of outline of world history, from the early civilisations of China, India and Persia, through ancient Greece to Roman times, and then tracing the path of European history from feudalism to the Reformation and on to the Enlightenment and the French Revolution. Yet Hegel obviously did not think of his *Philosophy of History* as merely a historical outline. His work is a work of philosophy because it takes the bare facts of history as its raw material, and attempts to go beyond these facts. Hegel himself said that 'the philosophy of history means nothing but the thoughtful consideration of it'. While this may be his own definition, however, it conveys a less than adequate idea of what Hegel is up to in his *Philosophy of History*. What Hegel's definition leaves out is his intention that the 'thoughtful consideration' of history should seek to present its raw material as part of a rational process of development, thus revealing the meaning and significance of world history.

Here, already, we have one of Hegel's central beliefs—the belief that history has some meaning and significance. Had Hegel viewed history along the lines of Macbeth's bleak vision of life, that is, as 'a tale told by an idiot, full of sound and fury, signifying nothing', he would never have attempted to write the *Philosophy of History* and his life's work would have been unrecognisably different. The modern scientific view is, of course, much like Macbeth's. It tells us that our planet is just one tiny speck in a universe of unimaginable size; and that on this planet life began from a chance combination of gases and then evolved by the blind forces of natural selection. Consistently with this view of the origin of our species, most modern thought refuses to assume that history has any ultimate purpose beyond the myriad individual purposes of the countless human beings who make history. In Hegel's day there was nothing unusual about his confident belief that human history is not a meaningless jumble of events—indeed, it is not really out of the ordinary even now, for religious thought has traditionally seen meaning and significance in the course taken by human history, even if it has significance only as a prelude to a better world still to come.

There are many different ways in which the claim that history is meaningful may be understood. It may be taken as a claim that history is the working out of the purposes of some Creator who set the whole process in motion; or, more mysteriously, it may be intended to suggest that the universe itself can somehow have purposes. The assertion that history has a meaning can also be shorn of all religious or mystical connotations and understood simply as the more limited claim that reflection on our past enables us to discern the direction history is taking, and the destination it will ultimately reach; this destination, for some fortunate reason, being a desirable one and hence one we can accept as the goal of our own strivings.

It is possible to interpret Hegel's *Philosophy of History* in different ways, corresponding to these different ways of understanding the claim that there is a meaning to history. In accordance with our general strategy of coming to grips with Hegel, we shall begin with those elements of the work that endow history with a meaning in the third, and least mysterious, of the various ways of understanding the claim.

In his own introduction to the *Philosophy of History*, Hegel clearly states his view of the direction and destination of all human history:'The history of the world is none other than the progress of the consciousness of freedom.' This sentence sets the theme for the entire work. (One might even say that it sums up the theme of *all* of Hegel's thought—but more of that later.) Now we must see how Hegel elaborates upon his theme.

He begins with an account of what he calls 'The Oriental World'—by which he means China, India and the ancient empire of Persia. China and India Hegel regards as 'stationary' civilisations, societies that have reached a certain point of their development and then somehow stuck fast. He describes them as 'outside the World's History', in other words not part of the overall process of development that is the basis of his philosophy of history. True history begins with the Persian Empire, 'the first Empire', says Hegel, 'that passed away'.

Hegel's discussion of the Oriental world contains many points of detail, all related to the idea that in oriental society only one person—the ruler—is a free individual. All others are totally lacking in freedom, because they must subordinate their will to that of the Patriarch, Lama, Emperor, Pharaoh, or whatever else the despot may be called. This lack of freedom goes very deep. It is not simply that the subjects of the despot know that the despot can punish them cruelly for disobeying his will. This would imply that they have wills of their own, that they can and do think about whether it is prudent or right to obey the despot. The truth is, says Hegel, that the oriental subject has no will of his own in the modern sense. In the Orient not only law, but even morality itself, is a matter of external regulation. Our concept of individual conscience is lacking. Hence there is no sense of the possibility of individuals forming their own moral judgements about right and wrong. For the inhabitants of the Orient—other than the ruler—opinions on these matters come from outside; they are facts about the world, and no more to be questioned than the existence of the mountains and the seas.

This lack of personal independence takes different forms in different oriental cultures, according to Hegel, but the result is always the same. The Chinese State, Hegel tells us, is organised on the principle of the family. Government is based on the paternal management of the Emperor, and all others see themselves as children of the State. It is for this reason that Chinese society places such strong emphasis on the honour and obedience one owes to one's parents. India, in contrast, has no concept of individual freedom because the basic institution of society—the caste system which allocates to each his or her occupation in life—is not seen as a political institution, but as something natural and hence unchangeable. The governing power in India is therefore not a human despot, but the despotism of nature.

Persia is different. Although at first glance the Persian Emperor seems to be an absolute ruler in much the same sense as the Emperor of China, the basis of the Persian Empire is not merely natural family obedience extended to the entire State, but a general principle, a Law which regulates the rules as well as the subject. For Persia was a theocratic monarchy, based on the religion of Zoroaster, which involved the worship of Light. Hegel makes much of the idea of light as something pure and universal, something which, like the sun, shines on all and confers equal benefits on all. Of course this does not mean that Persia was egalitarian. The Emperor was still an absolute ruler and hence the only free man in the Empire; yet the fact that his rule was based on a general principle and was not seen as a natural fact meant that development was possible. The idea of rule based on an intellectual or spiritual principle signifies the beginning of the growth of the consciousness of freedom that Hegel intends to trace. Hence it is the beginning of 'true history'.

The Greek world

In the Persian Empire the potential for growth in the consciousness of freedom existed; but this potential could not be realised within the structure of the Empire. In its efforts to expand, however, the Persian Empire came into contact with Athens, Sparta and the other city-states of ancient Greece. The Persian Emperor asked the Greeks to acknowledge his supremacy. They refused. The Emperor assembled an enormous army and a vast fleet of ships. The Persian fleet and the Greek fleet met at Salamis. This epic battle, Hegel says, was a contest between an oriental despot who sought a world united under one lord and sovereign, and separate States that recognised the principle of 'free individuality'. The Greek victory meant that the tide of world history passed from the despotic oriental world to the world of the Greek city-states.

While Hegel sees the Greek world as animated by the idea of free individuality, it is his view that the freedom of the individual is by no means fully developed at this stage of history. He has two different reasons for regarding the Greek idea of freedom as a limited one. One of these reasons is straightforward and the other is more complex.

The straightforward reason is that the Greek idea of freedom allows slavery. Indeed, 'allows' is too weak a term, for in Hegel's view the Greek form of democracy positively required slavery if it was to function at all. If, as was the case in Athens, every citizen has the right and duty to take part in the public assembly that is the supreme decision-making body of the city-state, then who is there to do the daily work of providing the necessities of life? There must be a category of workers who lack the rights and duties of citizens—in other words, there must be slaves.

In the oriental world only *one*—the ruler—is free. The existence of slavery means that the Greek world has progressed to a stage at which *some*—not all—are free. But even those who are free citizens of a Greek city-state are only free, Hegel believes, in an incomplete way. His reason for saying this is not so easy to grasp. He claims that the Greeks had no concept of individual conscience. This concept, as we have seen, Hegel thought to be lacking in the oriental world too; but whereas in the Orient people simply obeyed, without reflection, a moral code that was handed down to them from on high, with the Greeks the motivation came from inside themselves. They had, according to Hegel, the habit of living for their country, without further reflection. This habit did not derive from the acceptance of some abstract principle, such as the idea that everyone should act for the sake of his or her country. Rather the Greeks habitually thought of themselves as so indissolubly linked with their own particular city-state that they did not distinguish between their own interests and the interests of the community in which they lived. They could not conceive of themselves as living apart from, or in opposition to, this community, with all its customs and forms of social life.

All this means that the readiness of the Greeks to do what is best for the community as a whole comes from within. This would suggest that the Greeks were free in a way in which the Orientals were not. They did as they themselves wished to do, not as some external decree required them to do. Yet Hegel says that this is an incomplete form of freedom just because the motivation comes so naturally. Whatever is the result of the habits and customs in which one was brought up is not the result of the use of one's reason. If I do something from habit, I have not deliberately chosen to do it. My actions, it might be said, are still governed by forces external to my will— the social forces that gave me my habits—even though there is no despot telling me what to do, and the motivation for the action appears to come from within.

As a symptom of this dependence on external forces Hegel refers to the Greek tendency to consult an oracle for guidance before any important venture is undertaken. The advice of the oracle might be based on the state of the intestines of a sacrificed animal, or on some other natural event quite independent of my own thought. Genuinely free people would not allow their most important decisions to be determined by such events; they would make their own decisions, using their capacity to reason. Reason lifts free people above the chance events of the natural world, and enables them to reflect critically upon their situation and the forces that influence them. Hence freedom cannot be fully achieved without critical thought and reflection.

Critical thought and reflection, then, is the key to further progress in the development of freedom. The command attributed to the Greek god Apollo urged the Greeks along this path: 'Man, know thyself.' This summons to free enquiry, untrammelled by customary beliefs, was taken up by the Greek philosophers, and especially by Socrates. Socrates typically expresses his own views in the form of a dialogue with some worthy Athenian who thinks that he knows well what is good or just. This 'knowledge' turns out to be merely the ability to echo some common saying about goodness or justice, and Socrates has no difficulty in showing that this customary conception of morality cannot be the full story. For example, against the common idea that justice consists in giving to each what is owed to him, Socrates poses the case of a friend who has lent you a weapon, but has since become deranged. You may owe him the weapon, but is it really just to return it? Thus Socrates leads his audience to critical reflection upon the customary morality they have always accepted. This critical reflection makes reason, not social custom, the final judge of right and wrong.

Hegel sees the principle exemplified by Socrates as a revolutionary force against the Athenian State. Thus he judges the death sentence passed upon Socrates as unimpeachably correct: the Athenian people were condemning the deadliest foe of the customary morality on which their communal existence was based. Yet the principle of independent thought was too firmly rooted in Athens to be extirpated by the death of one individual; and so in time the accusers of Socrates were condemned and Socrates himself posthumously exonerated. This principle of independent thought was, none the less, the ultimate cause of the downfall of Athens and marks the beginning of the end of the world-historical role played by the Greek civilisation.

The Roman world

In contrast to the unreflective customary unity which formed the basis of the Greek city-states, Hegel pictures the Roman Empire as built up from a collection of diverse peoples, lacking all natural patriarchal or other customary bonds, and hence requiring the most severe discipline, backed by force, to hold it together. This makes the dominance of Rome in the next stage of world history appear something of a reversion to the despotic oriental model, as typified in the Persian Empire. But while the course of world history, as Hegel presents it, is certainly not a smooth and steady progression, it does not go backwards either. The gains made in a previous epoch are never lost entirely. So Hegel carefully distinguishes between the underlying principles of the Persian and the Roman Empires. The idea of individuality, of the private capacity for judgement, that was born in the Greek era has not disappeared. Indeed, the Roman State rests upon a political constitution and a legal system which has individual right as one of its most fundamental notions. Thus the Roman State recognises individual freedom in a way that the Persian Empire never could; the catch is, of course, that this recognition of individual freedom is a purely legal or formal matter—Hegel calls it 'abstract freedom of the individual'. The real freedom that allows individuals to develop a diversity of ideas and ways of living—'concrete individuality' in Hegel's terminology—is ruthlessly crushed by the brute power of Rome.

The real difference between the Persian and the Roman Empires, then, is that whereas in the former the principle of oriental despotism held unbridled sway, in the latter there is a constant tension between the absolute power of the State and the ideal of individuality. This tension was lacking in the Persian Empire because the ideal of individuality was yet to be developed; it was lacking in the Greek world because, while the idea of individuality had come to the fore, political power was not so ruthlessly centralised in opposition to it.

The Roman world, as Hegel paints it, is not a happy place. The joyous, spontaneous free spirit of the Greek world has been broken. In the face of the demands of the State for outward conformity, freedom can only be found by retreating into oneself, by taking refuge in a philosophy such as Stoicism, Epicureanism or Scepticism. The details of these opposing philosophical schools need not concern us here; what is important is their common tendency to pooh-pooh everything that the real world has to offer—riches, political power, worldly glory—and to substiute an ideal of living which makes the adherent absolutely indifferent to anything the outside world can do.

The spread of these philosophical schools was, according to Hegel, a result of the helplessness that the individual, who sees himself as a free being, must feel in the face of a domineering power he is unable to influence. The retreat into philosophy is, however, a negative response to this situation; it is a counsel of despair in the face of a hostile world. There was a need for a more positive solution. This solution was provided by Christianity.

To understand why Hegel sees Christianity in this way, we must appreciate that for Hegel human beings are not just very clever animals. Humans live in the natural world, as animals do, but they are also spiritual beings. Until they recognise themselves as spiritual beings, humans are trapped in the natural world, the world of material forces. When the natural world is implacably resistant to their aspiration for freedom, as the Roman world was, there is no escape *within* the natural world, apart from the already mentioned retreat into a philosophy based on a purely negative attitude towards the natural world. Once humans recognise themselves as spiritual beings, however, the hostility of the natural world ceases to be all-important; it can be transcended in a positive manner because there is something positive beyond the natural world.

The Christian religion is special, according to Hegel, because Jesus Christ was both a human being and the Son of God. This teaches humans that, though limited in some respects, they are at the same time made in the image of God and have within themselves an infinite value and an eternal destiny. The result is the development of what Hegel calls 'religious self-consciousness': a recognition that it is the spiritual world, not the natural world, that is our true home. To achieve this awareness humans have to break the hold that natural desires, and indeed the whole of natural existence, has over them.

It is the role of the Christian religion to achieve this awareness that the spiritual nature of human beings is what is essential to them. This does not, however, happen all at once; for it is not mere inner piety that is required. The change that takes place in the pious heart of the Christian believer must transform the real external world into something that satisfies the requirements of humans as spiritual beings. As we shall see, it takes the whole of the Christian era up to Hegel's own time for humanity to become capable of achieving this.

What does happen rather sooner is that the limitations on

freedom characteristic of the Greek era are abolished. First, Christianity opposes slavery, for each unit of mankind has the same essential infinite value. Secondly, the dependence on oracles ceases, for oracles represent the dominance of the chance happenings of the natural world over the free choice of spiritual beings. Thirdly, and for much the same reason, the customary morality of Greek society is replaced by a morality based on the spiritual idea of love.

Christianity comes to the fore under the Roman Empire and becomes the official religion of the Empire under Constantine. Though the western half of the Empire falls to the barbarian invasions, the Byzantine Empire remains Christian for more than a thousand years. Yet this is, in Hegel's view, a stagnant, decadent Christianity, for it was an attempt to put a Christian veneer over structures that were already rotten to the core. It takes a new people to carry the Christian principle to its ultimate destiny.

The Germanic world

It may seem strange that Hegel should refer to the entire period of history from the fall of the Roman Empire up to modern times as 'The Germanic World'. He uses the term 'Germanische'—'Germanic' rather than simply 'German'—and he includes not only Germany proper, but also Scandinavia, the Netherlands, and even Britain. Nor, as we shall see, are developments in Italy and France ignored, though here he lacks the excuse of linguistic and racial affinities for stretching the term 'Germanic' to include these countries. One might suspect a certain amount of ethnocentrism in Hegel's designation of this era as 'The Germanic World'; but his chief reason for doing so is that he takes the Reformation as the single key event of history since Roman times.

Hegel paints a gloomy picture of Europe during the thousand years that passed after the fall of Rome. During that time the Church, in his view, became a perversion of the true religious spirit, inserting itself between man and the spiritual world, and insisting on blind obedience from its followers. The Middle Ages is, in Hegel's words, 'a long, eventful and terrible night'; a night which is ended by the Renaissance, 'that blush of dawn which after long storms first betokens the return of a bright and glorious day'. It is the Reformation, however, and not the Renaissance which Hegel describes as 'the all-enlightening Sun' of the bright day that is our modern time.

The Reformation resulted from the corruption of the Church, a corruption that was in Hegel's view not an accidental development but a necessary consequence of the fact that the Church does not treat the Deity as a purely spiritual thing, but instead embodies it in the material world. Ceremonial observances, rituals and other outward forms are its basis; and compliance with them is what it takes as essential to the religious life. Thus the spiritual element in human beings is fettered to mere material objects. The ultimate expression of this deep-seated corruption is the practice of selling, for that most worldly of objects, money, something that concerns man's deepest and inmost nature—the spiritual peace brought by the remission of sins. Hegel is of course referring to the practice of selling 'indulgences' which started Luther's protest.

Hegel sees the Reformation as an achievement of the Germanic people, arising from 'the honest truth and simplicity of its heart'. 'Simplicity' and 'heart' are for Hegel the keynotes of the Reformation, which was begun by the simple German monk, Luther, and took root only in the Germanic nations. Its result was to do away with the pomp and circumstance of the Roman Catholic Church and to substitute the idea that each individual human being has, in his own heart, a direct spiritual relationship to Christ.

It would be quite contrary to Hegel's view of the Reformation, however, to present it as an event within some isolated sphere of life labelled 'religion'. For one thing, Hegel always stresses the interrelatedness of different aspects of our historical development. For another, as we have already seen, for humans to fulfil their spiritual nature it is not enough for them to perfect their religious life; they must also make the world in which they live something suitable for free spiritual beings. Thus Hegel sees the Reformation as much more than an attack on the old Church, and the replacement of Roman Catholicism by Protestantism. The Reformation proclaims that every human being can recognise the truth of his or her own spiritual nature, and can achieve his or her own salvation. No outside authority is needed to interpret the scriptures, or to perform rituals. The individual conscience is the ultimate judge of truth and goodness. In asserting this, the Reformation unfurls 'the banner of Free Spirit' and proclaims as its essential principle: 'Man is in his very nature destined to be free.'

Since the Reformation, the role of history has been nothing but the transforming of the world in accordance with this essential principle. This is no small task, for if every human being is freely able to use his powers of reasoning to judge truth and goodness, the world can only receive universal assent when it conforms with rational standards. Therefore all social institutions—including law, property, social morality, government, constitutions and so on—must be made to conform to general principles of reason. Only then will individuals freely choose to accept and support these institutions. Only then will law, morality and government cease to be arbitrary rules and powers which free agents must be compelled to obey. Only then will human beings be free and yet fully reconciled with the world in which they live.

This notion of making all social institutions conform to general principles of reason has about it the ring of the Enlightenment. To subject everything to the clear cold light of reason, rejecting all that has its basis in superstition or hereditary privilege, was the doctrine of French thinkers of the eighteenth century like Voltaire and Diderot. The Enlightenment and its sequel, the French Revolution, are indeed the next—and almost the last—events in Hegel's account of world history; but Hegel's attitude towards it is not quite what his remarks about the essence of the Reformation might lead one to expect.

Hegel accepts the view that the French Revolution was the result of the criticisms of the existing order made by French philosophers. France before the Revolution had a nobility without real power, but with a confused mass of privileges which had no rational basis. Against this utterly irrational state of affairs the philosophers' conception of the Rights of Man asserted itself, and triumphed. Hegel leaves us in no doubt as to his view of the significance of this event.

Never since the sun has stood in the firmament and the planets revolved around it had it been perceived that man's existence centres in his head, i.e. in thought, inspired by which he builds up the world of reality ... not until now had man advanced to the recognition of the principle that thought ought to govern spiritual reality. This was accordingly a glorious mental dawn. All thinking beings shared in the jubilation of this epoch.

Yet the immediate result of this 'glorious mental dawn' was the Revolutionary Terror, a form of tyranny which exercised its power without legal formalities and inflicted as its punishment the quick death of the guillotine. What had gone wrong? The mistake was to attempt to put into practice purely abstract philosophical principles, without regard to the disposition of the people. This attempt was based upon a misunderstanding of the role of reason, which must not be applied in isolation from the existing community and the people that make it up.

The French Revolution itself was thus a failure. Its world-historical significance, however, lies in the principles it passed on to other nations, and particularly to Germany. The short-lived victories of Napoleon were sufficient to bring about within Germany a code of rights, to establish freedom of the person and freedom of property, to open the offices of the State to the most talented citizens and to abolish feudal obligations. The monarch remains as the apex of government and his personal decision is final; yet because of the firmly established laws and settled organisation of the State, what is left to the personal decision of the monarch is, says Hegel, 'in point of substance, no great matter'.

Hegel's account of world history has now reached his own times, and so it comes to an end. He concludes by repeating (in slightly different words) the theme he introduced at the start of it all—'the history of the world is nothing but the development of the idea of freedom'—and suggesting that the progress of the idea of freedom has now reached its consummation. What was required was both that individuals should govern themselves according to their own conscience and convictions, and also that the objective world, that is the real world with all its social and political institutions, should be rationally organised. It would not be sufficient to have individuals governing themselves according to their own conscience and convictions. This would be only 'subjective freedom'. As long as the objective world was not rationally organised, individuals acting in accordance with their own conscience would come into conflict with its law and morality. Existing law and morality would therefore be something opposed to them, and a limit upon their freedom. Once the objective world is rationally organised, on the other hand, individuals following their consciences will freely choose to act in accordance with the law and morality of the objective world. Then freedom will exist on both the subjective and the objective level. There will be no restrictions on freedom, for there will be perfect harmony between the free choices of individuals and the needs of society as a whole. The idea of freedom will have become a reality and the history of the world will have achieved its goal.

This is a climactic ending indeed; but it leaves an obvious question dangling. What would a rational organisation of morality, law and other social institutions be like? What is a truly rational State? In the *Philosophy of History* Hegel has very little to say on this subject. His rosy description of the Germany of his own day, coupled with his statement that the progress of the idea of freedom has now reached its consummation, can only mean that he believes his own country, in his own times, to have achieved the status of a rationally organised society. He refrains from saying this explicitly, though, and his description of modern Germany is too brief to allow us to see clearly why the particular arrangements he describes should be more rational than all previous forms of government.

The reason for this brevity may simply be that the *Philosophy of History* was written as a course of lectures, and university lecturers, as we all know, frequently find themselves short of time near the end of the course; but it is equally possible that Hegel deliberately said little about this subject in the *Philosophy of History*, because it is the chief focus of his *Philosophy of Right*. It is to this work that we must turn for a more complete picture of what Hegel takes to be a rationally organised and hence genuinely free community.

3 Freedom and community

A puzzle

We have seen that Hegel believes all the events of the past to have been leading up to the goal of freedom. At the conclusion of the *Philosophy of History* there was an indication that this goal might have been reached; but Hegel provided few indications why Prussia (or any of the other German States existing at that time) should be regarded as the glorious result for which three thousand years of world history had been striving. When Hegel gave his lectures on the philosophy of history, Prussia's period of liberal reform under von Stein and von Hardenberg was over. Prussia was dominated by the King and a few other powerful families. It lacked a parliament of any importance, denied the overwhelming majority of its citizens any say in the running of the State, and imposed a strict censorship. How could Hegel have regarded such a society as the pinnacle of human freedom? Is it any wonder that the German philosopher Arthur Schopenhauer should have said, with Hegel in mind: 'Governments make of philosophy a means of serving their State interests, and scholars make of it a trade'? Or that Karl Popper should believe that Hegel had one aim, 'to fight against the open society, and thus to serve his employer, Frederick William of Prussia'?

In this chapter I shall try to explain Hegel's concept of freedom. If I succeed, I will have shown that whatever his motivation, Hegel's thinking on this subject has to be taken seriously because it cuts deeply into assumptions we frequently make when we say that one society is free and another is not.

We have seen that in the introduction to the *Philosophy of History* Hegel says that world history is nothing but the progress of consciousness of freedom. He adds, a few lines further on, that this term 'freedom' is 'an indefinite, and incalculably ambiguous term . . . liable to an infinity of misunderstandings, confusions and errors'. Unfortunately he declines to give a further definition, saying that instead the essential nature of freedom 'is to be displayed' in the process of interpreting the history of the world. This is not entirely satisfactory. Our examination of the *Philosophy of History* may have given us a glimmering of what Hegel takes freedom to be; but if so, it is a glimmering that urgently requires the further illumination of Hegel's more explicit comments in the *Philosophy of Right*.

First, a word about the title. To an English-speaking reader, 'Philosophy of Right' suggests a work about right and wrong, in other words a study of ethics. Ethics does figure prominently in Hegel's *Philosophy of Right*, but its subject is closer to political philosophy. The German word in Hegel's title which is translated as 'Right' is *Recht*. This can mean 'right', but has wider associations, including that of 'law', in the sense in which we refer to 'the Law' as a whole rather than to one particular law. So the *Philosophy of Right* expresses Hegel's philosophical ideas about ethics, jurisprudence, society and the state. Since freedom is always central to Hegel's concerns, the *Philosophy of Right* contains Hegel's most detailed discussion of freedom in the social and political sphere. Naturally, it contains discussions of other topics as well, but I shall pass over them in the interest of pursuing the crucial concept of freedom.

Abstract freedom

It will be best to begin with something familiar. Consider what might be called the classical liberal conception of freedom. Liberals generally see freedom as the absence of restrictions. I am free if others do not interfere with me and do not force me to do what I do not want to do. I am free when I can do as I please. I am free when I am left alone. This is the concept of freedom that Isaiah Berlin, in his celebrated essay 'Two Concepts of Liberty', called 'negative freedom'.

Hegel was familiar with this concept of freedom but, unlike Berlin and many other contemporary liberals and libertarians who regard it as the most desirable form of freedom, he refers to it as formal or abstract freedom, meaning that it has the form of freedom, but not the substance. He writes; 'If we hear it said that the definition of freedom is ability to do what we please, such an idea can only be taken to reveal an utter immaturity of thought, for it contains not even an inkling of the absolutely free will, of right, ethical life, and so forth.' Hegel's objection to this notion of freedom is that it takes the choices of the individual as the basis from which freedom must begin—how and why these choices are made is a question that those who hold this conception of freedom do not ask. Hegel does ask it, and his answer is that the individual choice, considered in isolation from everything else, is the outcome of arbitrary circumstances. Hence it is not genuinely free.

This seems high-handed. How dare Hegel tell us that our choices are arbitrary—while his, presumably, are genuinely free? Is this anything more than a blatant attempt to impose his values on us?

Maybe. But we may become a little more sympathetic to what Hegel is trying to say if we consider an analogous contemporary debate. Some economists believe that the proper test of how well an economic system works is the extent to which it enables people to satisfy their preferences. These economists take individual preferences as the basis from which assessment must begin. They do not ask how these preferences come about. To select among preferences and give some preferences more weight than others (apart from the differing weights given to their preferences by the individuals who hold them) would be, these economists say, a blatant attempt to impose one's own values on others by denying them the capacity to decide what they really want out of life.

I shall call these economists 'liberal economists'. The liberal economists have their critics, whom I shall call 'radical economists'. The radical economists ask some questions about how individual preferences are formed before they agree to take such preferences as the sole basis for judging how well an economic system works. They bring up examples of the following kind: suppose that at a certain time people in our society take the normal human body odours for granted. That humans sweat and that it is possible to smell a sweaty person are things they barely notice, and in so far as they do notice them, they do not consider them unpleasant. Then someone discovers a product which has the effect of inhibiting sweat and the odour it gives off. That is an interesting discovery, but, in the society described, interest in the product will be very limited. Our inventor, however, does not give up easily. He launches a clever advertising campaign designed to make people anxious about whether they sweat more than other people, and whether their friends might find their body odour offensive. His advertising is successful. People develop a preference for using the new product; and because the product is widely available at a price within their means, they can satisfy this preference. From the standpoint of the liberal economists, all this is fine. That the economy works in this way provides them with no basis for rating it less favourably than they otherwise would have. The radical economists think this is manifestly absurd. To avoid such absurdities, they say, economists must face the difficult task of enquiring into the basis of preferences, and must judge economic systems by their ability to satisfy not just any preferences, but those preferences that are based on genuine human needs or contribute to genuine human welfare. The radical economists concede that if we adopt their method, we cannot claim that our assessment is value-free; but they add that no method of assessing an economic system can be value-free. The method of assessment used by the liberal economists simply took the satisfaction of existing preferences as its sole value. A value-judgement is therefore implicit in the use of this method, though disguised under a cloak of objectivity. The liberal economists effectively give their blessing to whatever circumstances happen to influence what people prefer.

There is a clear parallel between this debate and Hegel's debate with those who define freedom as the ability to do what we please. This negative concept of freedom is like the liberal economist's conception of a good economic system: it refuses to ask what influences form the 'pleasings' that we act upon when we are free to do as we please. Those who hold this conception of freedom assert that to ask such a question, and to use the answers as a basis for sorting out genuinely free choices from those that are free only in form and not in substance, would be to write one's own values into the conception of freedom. Hegel's retort, like that of the radical economists, would be that the negative conception of freedom is already based on a value, the value of action based on choice, no matter how that choice is reached or how arbitrary it may be. The negative conception of freedom, in other words, gives its blessing to whatever circumstances happen to be influencing the way people choose.

If you agree that it is absurd to see no objection to an economic system that artificially creates new preferences so that some may profit by satisfying them, you must agree that the radical economists have a point. Admittedly it will be difficult to sort out the preferences which contribute to genuine human welfare from those that do not. It may prove impossible to reach agreement on this. Nevertheless, the difficulty of the task is no reason for taking all preferences at face value.

If you agree that the radical economists have a point, it is only a small step to agreeing that Hegel has a point. Indeed, it is really no step at all; for Hegel anticipated the central point of the radical economists' position, a point that has been popularised in the twentieth century by J. K. Galbraith, Vance Packard and a host of other critics of the modern industrial economy. Here is Hegel, writing at the very infancy of the consumer society, but perceptive enough to pick up the way it was going:

What the English call 'comfort' is something inexhaustible and illimitable. Others can reveal to you that what you take to be comfort at any stage is discomfort, and these discoveries never come to an end. Hence the need for greater comfort does not exactly arise within you directly; it is suggested to you by those who hope to make a profit from its creation.

This remark occurs in a section of the *Philosophy of Right* that examines what Hegel calls 'The System of Needs'; it follows hard upon a reference to the great figures in classical liberal economic theory, Adam Smith, J. B. Say and David Ricardo. Hegel's criticism of this 'system of needs' shows that the ground of his opposition to the liberal economic view of society was essentially that taken by radical economists today. Behind it lies Hegel's steady historical perspective. He never loses sight of the fact that our wants and desires are shaped by the society in which we live, and that this society in turn is a stage in a historical process. Hence abstract freedom, the freedom to do as we please, is effectively the freedom to be pushed to and fro by the social and historical forces of our times.

As a criticism of the negative concept of freedom, Hegel's view should by now seem reasonable enough. What, however, does he intend to put in its place? We all must live in a particular society at a particular period of history. We will all be shaped by the society and times in which we live. How then can freedom be anything more than the freedom to act as we are led to act by social and historical forces?

Freedom and duty

Some of our desires are the product of our nature—like the desire for food, we were born with them, or like sexual desires, we were born with the potential to develop them. Many of our other desires were formed by our upbringing, our education, the society in which we live, our environment generally. Biological or social as the origins of these desires might be, it is true in either case that we did not choose them. Since we did not choose our desires, we are not free when we act from desire.

This argument is reminiscent of Kant rather than Hegel, but Hegel goes along with it up to a point. Let us follow it a little further. If we are not free when we act from desire, it seems that the only possible path to freedom is to purge oneself of all desires. But what would then be left? Kant's answer is: reason. Motivation to action can come from desires, or from reason. Do away with the desires, and we are left with pure practical reason.

Action based on reason alone—the idea is not easy to grasp. We can talk readily enough of a person's actions being rational or irrational, but we normally do so in relation to the ultimate ends or goals that person has, and these ends will be based on desires. For example, knowing that Mohammed Ali desires to retain his reputation as a great boxer, I may say that it is irrational for him to attempt yet another come-back at the age of thirty-seven; but if I am asked whether I consider it rational of Ali to desire to retain his reputation, what can I say? Only that this kind of desire is too basic to be either rational or irrational: it is just a brute fact about the man. Can there be judgements of rationality or irrationality which are not based on basic desires of this kind?

Kant says there can be. When we take away all particular desires, even the most basic ones, we are left with the bare, formal element of rationality, and this bare formal element is the universal form of the moral law itself. This is Kant's famous 'categorical imperative', which he puts thus: 'Act only so that the maxim of your action can be willed as a universal law.'

The most puzzling step in this is the move from bare formal rationality to the idea of something universal. Kant holds—and Hegel obviously agrees—that reason is implicitly universal. If we know that all men are mortal and that Socrates was a man, then a law of reasoning tells us that Socrates was mortal. The law of reasoning that tells us this is a universal law—it holds not just for Greeks or for philosophers or even for Earthlings, but for all rational beings. In practical reasoning—that is, reasoning about what to do—this universal element is often concealed by the fact that we start from particular desires which are anything but universal. Consider this piece of practical reasoning: 'I want to be rich; I can defraud my employer of a million dollars without being detected; therefore I should defraud my employer.' Here the reasoning starts from my desire to be rich. There is nothing universal about this desire. (Don't be misled by the fact that many people desire to be rich; the desire from which I begin this reasoning is the desire that I, Peter Singer, should be rich. Very, very few people share this desire.) Because there is nothing universal about the starting-point of this piece of reasoning, there is nothing universal about its conclusion, which certainly does not hold for all rational beings. If we were to reason about what to do *without* starting from any particular desire, however, there would be nothing to prevent our reasoning from holding for all rational beings. Pure practical reasoning, independently of particular desires, could only embody the universal element in reasoning. It would therefore, Kant contends, take the form prescribed by the categorical imperative.

If Kant is right, the only kind of action that is not the result of our innate or socially conditioned desires is action in accordance with the categorical imperative. Only action in accordance with the categorical imperative, therefore, can be free. Since only free action can have genuine moral worth, the categorical imperative must be not only the supreme imperative of reason, but also the supreme law of morality.

One final point is needed to complete the picture. If my action is free, my motivation for acting in accordance with the categorical imperative cannot be any particular desire I might happen to have. It cannot, therefore, be my desire to go to heaven, or to win the esteem of my friends; nor can it be my benevolent desire to do good to others. My motivation must simply be to act in accord with the universal law of reason and morality, for its own sake. I must do my duty because it is my duty—the Kantian ethic is sometimes summed up in the slogan: 'Duty for duty's sake.' It does indeed follow from what Kant said that we are free when we do our duty for its own sake, and not otherwise.

So we have arrived at the conclusion that freedom consists in doing one's duty. To the modern reader this conclusion is paradoxical. The term 'duty' has come to be associated with obedience to the conventional rules of institutions like the army and the family. When we speak of doing our duty we often mean that we are doing what we would much rather not be doing, but feel ourselves constrained to do by customary rules we are reluctant to defy. 'Duty' in this sense is the very opposite of freedom.

If this is the basis of the paradoxical air of the conclusion that freedom consists in doing our duty, we should put it aside. Kant's conclusion was that freedom consists in doing what we really see as our duty in the broadest sense of the term. To put his point in a way that modern readers might be readier to accept: freedom consists in following one's conscience. This accurately captures Kant's meaning, as long as we remember that 'conscience' here does not mean whatever socially conditioned 'inner voice' I may happen to have; it means a conscience based on a rational acceptance of the categorical imperative as the supreme moral law. Put this way, the conclusion we have reached so far may still stretch credulity, but it should no longer appear paradoxical. Freedom of conscience is, after all, widely recognised as an essential part of what we take freedom to be, even if it is not the whole of it.

It is time to return to Hegel. Much of what I have been describing as a Kantian position is also Hegelian. That we are not free when we act from particular innate or socially conditioned desires; that reason is essentially universal; that freedom is to be found in what is universal—all of this Hegel takes from Kant and makes his own. Moreover in the *Philosophy of History*, as we have seen, Hegel takes the Reformation as the dawning of the new age of freedom, because it proclaims the rights of the individual conscience. Thus Hegel, like Kant, sees a connection between freedom and the development of the individual conscience. Nor does Hegel dissent from the idea that freedom consists in doing one's duty. Duty, he says, appears as a restriction on our natural or arbitrary desires, but the truth is that 'in duty the individual finds his liberation ... from mere natural impulse ... In duty the individual acquires his substantive freedom.' Commenting directly on Kant, Hegel said: 'In doing my duty I am by myself and free. To have emphasised this meaning of duty has constituted the merit of Kant's philosophy and its loftiness of outlook.'

For Hegel, then, doing our duty for its own sake is a notable advance on the negative idea of freedom as doing what we please. Yet Hegel is not satisfied with Kant's position. He sees its positive elements, but he is at the same time one of its most trenchant critics. Part II of the *Philosophy of Right*, entitled 'Morality', is in large part an attack on Kant's ethical theory.

Hegel has two main objections. The first is that Kant's theory never gets down to specifics about what we ought to do. This is not because Kant himself lacked interest in such practical questions, but because his entire theory insists that morality must be based on pure practical reasoning, free from any particular motives. As a result, the theory can yield only the bare, universal form of the moral law; it cannot tell us what our specific duties are. This universal form is, Hegel says, simply a principle of consistency or non-contradiction. If we have no point to start from, it cannot get us anywhere. For example, if we accept the validity of property, theft is inconsistent; but we can deny that property gives rise to any rights and be perfectly consistent thieves. If the directive 'Act so as not to contradict yourself!' is the *only* thing we have to move us to act, we may find ourselves doing nothing at all.

This objection to Kant's categorical imperative will be familiar not only to students of Kant, but also to those who have an interest in contemporary moral philosophy. The importance of the requirement that moral principles be universal in form is still widely insisted upon—for example, by R. M. Hare, author of *Freedom and Reason* and *Moral Thinking*—and the objection that this requirement is an empty formalism that tells us nothing is still frequently made. In defence of Kant it has been suggested that we should interpret him as allowing us to start from our desires, but requiring that we act upon them only if we are able to put them into a universal form, that is, to accept them as a suitable basis of action for anyone in a similar situation. Hegel anticipates this interpretation, claiming that any desire can be put into a universal form, and hence, once the introduction of particular desires is allowed, the requirement of universal form is powerless to prevent us justifying whatever immoral conduct takes our fancy.

Hegel's second major objection to Kant is that the Kantian position divides man against himself, locks reason into an eternal conflict with desire, and denies the natural side of man any right to satisfaction. Our natural desires are merely something to be suppressed, and Kant gives to reason the arduous, if not impossible, task of suppressing them. In this objection, as we have seen, Hegel was following the lead given by Schiller in his *Lectures on the Aesthetic Education of Man*; but Hegel made his own use of Schiller's criticism.

We can put the point in terms of another familiar problem of modern ethics. For Hegel the second major objection to Kant's ethics is that it offers no solution to the opposition between morality and self-interest. Kant leaves unanswered, and for ever unanswerable, the question: 'Why should I be moral?' We are told that we should do our duty for its own sake, and that to ask for any other reason is to depart from the pure and free motivation morality demands; but this is no answer at all, just a refusal to allow the question to be raised.

In his *Aesthetic Education of Man*, Schiller had pointed back to a time when the question had simply not arisen, when morality had not been split off into something separate from customary ideals of the good life, when there was no Kantian conception of duty. Hegel saw that once the question had been asked, a return to customary morality was impossible. In any case, Hegel regarded the Kantian conception of duty as an advance that is not to be regretted, for it helps to make modern man free in a way the Greeks, embedded in their narrow customary horizons, never could be. What Hegel sought to do was to answer the question in a way that united the natural satisfaction of the Greek form of life with the free conscience of the

Kantian idea of morality. His answer would at the same time provide a remedy for the other chief defect of the Kantian theory, its total lack of content.

The organic community

Hegel finds the unity of individual satisfaction and freedom in conformity to the social ethos of an organic community. What sort of community did he have in mind?

Towards the end of the nineteenth century Hegel's idea of an organic community was adopted by the British philosopher F. H. Bradley, who may not have equalled Hegel as an original thinker, but definitely surpassed him as a prose stylist. I shall therefore let Bradley's presentation of the basis of the harmony between private interest and communal values speak for Hegel. Bradley is describing the development of the child growing up in a community:

The child . . . is born . . . into a living world . . . He does not even think of his separate self; he grows with his world, his mind fills and orders itself; and when he can separate himself from that world, and know himself apart from it, then by that time his self, the object of his self-consciousness, is penetrated, infected, characterized by the existence of others. Its content implies in every fibre relations of community. He learns, or already perhaps has learnt, to speak, and here he appropriates the common heritage of his race, the tongue that he makes his own is his country's language, it is . . . the same that others speak, and it carries into his mind the ideas and sentiments of the race . . . and stamps them in indelibly. He grows up in an atmosphere of example and general custom . . . The soul within him is saturated, is filled, is qualified by, it has assimilated, has got its substance, has built itself up from, it *is* one and the same life with the universal life, and if he turns against this he turns against himself.

Bradley's point—and Hegel's—is that because our needs and desires are shaped by society, an organic community fosters those desires that most benefit the community. Moreover it so imbues its members with the sense that their own identity consists in being a part of the community that they will no more think of going off in pursuit of their own private interests than one part of the organism that is my body—say, my left arm—would think of hiving off from my shoulder to find something better to do than stuff my mouth with food. Nor should we forget that the relationship between an organism and its parts is reciprocal. I need my left arm and my left arm needs me. The organic community will no more disregard the interests of its members than I would disregard an injury to my left arm.

If we can accept this organic model of a community, we shall grant that it would end the ancient conflict between the interests of the individual and the interests of the community; but how does it preserve freedom? Does it not display mere small-minded conformity to custom? Where does it differ from the Greek communities which Hegel regarded as lacking the essential principle of human freedom brought forward in the Reformation and captured, if one-sidedly, in Kant's notion of duty?

The citizens of Hegel's community differ from those of the Greek city-states precisely because they belong to a different historical era and have the achievements of Rome, Christianity and the Reformation as part of their intellectual heritage. They are aware of their capacity for freedom and their ability to make their own decisions in accordance with their conscience. A customary morality, which demands conformity to its rules simply because it is the custom to conform to them, cannot command the obedience of free thinking beings. (We saw how the questioning of Socrates was a mortal threat to the basis of the Athenian community.) Free thinking beings can only give their allegiance to institutions that they recognise as conforming to rational principles. Therefore the modern organic community, unlike the ancient ones, must be based on principles of reason.

In the *Philosophy of History* we saw that happened when people first ventured to strike down irrational institutions and build a new State based on purely rational principles. The leaders of the French Revolution understood reason in a purely abstract and universal sense which would not tolerate the natural dispositions of the community. The Revolution was the political embodiment of the mistake Kant made in his purely abstract and universal conception of duty, which would not tolerate the natural side of human beings. In keeping with this pure rationalism the monarchy was abolished, and all other degrees of nobility as well. Christianity was replaced by the cult of Reason, and the old system of weights and measures abolished to make way for the more rational metric system. Even the calendar was reformed. The result was the Terror, in which the bare universal comes into conflict with the individual and negates him—or, to put it in less Hegelian terms, the State sees individuals as its enemies and puts them to death.

Disastrous as the failure of the French Revolution was for those who suffered by it, there is a crucial lesson to be learnt from it, namely that to build a State on a truly rational basis we must not raze everything to the ground and attempt to start again completely from scratch. We must search for what is rational in the existing world and allow that rational element to have its fullest expression. In this manner we can build on the reason and virtue that already exists in a community.

Here is a modern parable that may illustrate why Hegel regards the French Revolution as a glorious failure, and what he would have us learn from it. When people first began to live in towns, no one thought of town planning. They just put up their houses, shops and factories wherever seemed most convenient, and the cities grew higgledy-piggledy. Then along came someone who said: 'This is no good! We are not thinking about how we want our towns to look. Our lives are being ruled by chance! We need someone to plan our towns, to make them conform to our ideals of beauty and good living.' So along came the town planners, who bulldozed the old neighbourhoods and erected streamlined high-rise apartment buildings, surrounded by swathes of green lawns. Roads were widened and straightened, shopping centres were put up in the midst of generous parking areas, and factories were carefully isolated from residential zones. Then the town planners sat back and waited for the people to thank them. But the people complained that from their high-rise apartments they could not watch their children as they played on the lawns ten floors below. They complained that they missed the local corner shops, and that it was too far to walk across all those green lawns and parking spaces to the shopping centres. They complained that since everyone now had to drive to work, even those new wide straight roads were choked with traffic. Worst of all, they complained that, now no one was walking, the streets had become unsafe and those lovely green lawns were dangerous to cross after dark. So the old town planners were fired, and a new generation of town planners grew up, who had learnt from the mistakes of their predecessors. The first thing the new town planners did was to put a stop to the demolition of old neighbourhoods. Instead they began to notice the positive features of the old, unplanned towns. They admired the varied vistas of the narrow, crooked streets, and noticed how convenient it was to have shops and residences and even small factories mixed up together. They remarked on how these streets kept traffic to a minimum, encouraged people to walk, and made the town centre both lively and safe. Not that their admiration for the old unplanned towns was totally unreserved; there were a few things that needed to be tidied up, some particularly offensive industries were moved away from where people lived, and many old buildings had to be restored or else replaced with buildings in keeping with the surroundings. What the new town planners had discovered, however, was that the old cities *worked*; and it was this that had to be preserved, whatever tinkering might still be desirable.

The old, unplanned cities are like the ancient communities that grew up with custom as their basis; the first town planners resemble the French revolutionaries in their fervour to impose rationality on reality; while the second generation of planners are the true Hegelians, made wiser by the past and ready to find rationality in a world that is the result of practical adaptation rather than deliberate planning.

Now we can see why the free citizens of the modern era give their allegiance to a community which, at first glance, does not differ greatly from the custom-based communities of the ancient world. These free citizens understand the rational principles on which their community is based, and so they freely choose to serve it.

There are, of course, some differences between the modern rational community and the communities of ancient Greece. Because the modern era knows that all human beings are free, slavery has been abolished. Without slavery, Hegel believes, the time-consuming form of democracy practised in Athens is unworkable. Nor does Hegel think much of representative democracy with universal suffrage, partly because he thinks individuals cannot be represented (he says only 'the essential spheres of society and its large-scale interests' are suitable for representation) and partly because with universal suffrage each individual vote has so little significance that there is widespread apathy, and power falls into the hands of a small caucus of particular interests.

The rational community is, Hegel says, a constitutional monarchy. A monarchy is required because somewhere there must be the power of ultimate decision, and in a free community this power should be expressed by the free decision of a person. (Compare the Greek communities, which often consulted an oracle—a force external to the community—for the final resolution of difficult issues.) On the other hand, Hegel says, if the constitution is stable the monarch often has nothing to do but sign his name. Hence his personal make-up is unimportant, and his sovereignty is not the capricious rule of an oriental despot. The other elements of the constitutional monarchy are the executive and the legislature. The executive consists of civil servants. The only objective qualification for office is proof of ability; but where there are several eligible candidates and their relative abilities cannot be determined with precision, a subjective condition enters which it is the task of the monarch to decide. Hence the monarch retains the right to appoint the executive. The legislature, in keeping with Hegel's ideas of representation, has two houses of parliament, the upper consisting of the landed class and the lower of the business class. It is, however, 'large-scale interests' such as corporations and professional guilds that are represented in the lower house, not individual citizens as such.

I have dealt swiftly with these details of Hegel's rational community because to readers living in the twentieth century his preferences can only seem quaint, and his arguments for them have often—though not always—been shown by subsequent experience to be erroneous. So far as Hegel's conception of freedom is concerned, the particular institutional arrangements he prefers are not crucial. It should by now be clear that Hegel is not talking about freedom in the political sense in which popular sovereignty is an essential element of a free society. He is interested in freedom in a deeper, more metaphysical sense. Hegel's concern is with freedom in the sense in which we are free when we are able to choose without being coerced either by other human beings or by our natural desires, or by social circumstances. As we have seen, Hegel believes such freedom can exist only when we choose rationally, and we choose rationally only when we choose in accordance with universal principles. If these choices are to bring us the satisfaction which is our due, the universal principles must be embodied in an organic community organised along rational lines. In such a community individual interests and the interests of the whole are in harmony. In choosing to do my duty I choose freely because I choose rationally, and I achieve my own fulfilment in serving the objective form of the universal, namely the State. Moreover—and here is the remedy for the second great defect in Kantian ethics—because the universal law is embodied in the concrete institutions of the State, it ceases to be abstract and empty. It prescribes to me the specific duties of my station and role in the community.

We may well reject Hegel's description of a rationally organised community. Our rejection will not affect the validity of his conception of freedom. Hegel was seeking to describe a community in which individual interests and the interests of the whole are in harmony. If he failed, others can continue the search. If none succeeds, if we finally accept that no one ever will succeed, we will have to acknowledge that freedom, in Hegel's sense, cannot exist. Even that would not invalidate Hegel's claim to have described the only genuine form of freedom, and this form of freedom could still serve as an ideal.

Liberal? Conservative? Totalitarian?

We began this chapter with a puzzle. How could Hegel, who stresses freedom to the point of making it the goal of history, suggest that freedom had been achieved in the autocratic German society of his own time? Was he a servile toady who wished to endear himself to his rulers by twisting the meaning of the term into its very opposite? Worse still, was he the intellectual grandfather of the type of totalitarian State that emerged in Germany a hundred years after his death?

The first step to clearing up this puzzle is to ask a question of fact: Is the ideally rational State that Hegel describes merely a description of the Prussian State at the time he was writing? It is not. There are strong similarities, but there are also significant differences. I shall mention four. Probably the most important is that Hegel's constitutional monarch ideally had little to do except sign his name, whereas Frederick William III of Prussia was much more of an absolute monarch than that. A second difference is that there was no functioning parliament at all in Prussia; Hegel's legislature, though relatively powerless, did provide an outlet for the expression of public opinion. Thirdly, Hegel was, if within very definite limits, a supporter of freedom of expression. Admittedly, by today's standards he appears most illiberal on this issue, for he excluded from this freedom anything that amounted to slander, abuse or 'contemptuous caricature' of the government and its ministers. We are not now seeking to judge him by today's standards, however, but to compare his proposals with the state of affairs in Prussia at the time he was writing; and since the *Philosophy of Right* appeared only eighteen months after the strict censorship imposed by the Carlsbad decrees of 1819, Hegel was certainly arguing for greater freedom of speech than was allowed at the time. Fourthly, Hegel advocated trial by jury as a way of involving citizens in the legal process; but there was no right to trial by jury in Prussia at the time.

These differences are sufficient to acquit Hegel of the charge of having drawn up his philosophy entirely in order to please the Prussian monarchy. They do not, however, make Hegel any kind of liberal in the modern sense. His rejection of the right to vote and his restrictions on freedom of speech are enough to show this. His dislike of anything smacking of popular representation went so far that he wrote an essay opposing the English Reform Bill, which when finally passed in 1832 ended notorious inequalities and abuses in the election of members of the House of Commons (while still excluding the majority of adult males—let alone females—from the electoral roll).

After what we have seen of Hegel's ideas of freedom, however, this should come as no surprise. Hegel would have thought that popular suffrage would amount to people voting in accordance with their material interests or with the capricious and even whimsical likes and dislikes they may form for one candidate rather than another. Had he been able to witness an election in a modern democracy, he would not have had to change his mind. Those who defend democracy today could scarcely disagree with Hegel over the manner in which most voters decide whom to favour with their votes; they would differ with Hegel in regarding the elections as an essential element in a free society, no matter how impulsive or arbitrary the majority of the electors may be. Hegel would have emphatically rejected this, on the grounds that an impulsive or arbitrary choice is not a free act. We are free only when our choice is based on reason. To make the entire direction of the State dependent on such arbitrary choices would, in his view, amount to handing over the destiny of the community to chance.

Does this mean that Hegel is indeed a defender of the totalitarian State? This is Karl Popper's view, in his widely read *The*

Open Society and Its Enemies, and he backs up the claim with quotations bound to raise the hackles of any modern liberal reader. Here are some examples: 'The State is the Divine Idea as it exists on earth . . . We must therefore worship the State as the manifestation of the Divine on earth . . . The State is the march of God through the world . . . The State . . . exists for its own sake.' These quotations are, Popper thinks, enough to show Hegel's insistence upon 'the absolute moral authority of the state, which overrules all personal morality, all conscience', and to give Hegel an important role in the development of modern totalitarianism.

Hegel's emphasis on rationality as the essential element in freedom lends further credence to this reading. For who is to decide what is rational? Armed with the doctrine that only rational choices are free, any ruler can justify the suppression of all opposed to his own rational plans for the future of the State. For if his plans are rational, those who oppose them must be motivated not by reason but by selfish desires or irrational whims. Their choices, not being rationally based, cannot be free. To suppress their newspapers and leaflets is thus not to restrict free speech, to arrest their leaders is not to interfere with their freedom of action, and to close down their churches and set up new, more rational forms of worship does not interfere with their freedom of religion. Only when these poor misguided people are led by these methods to appreciate the rationality of their leader's plans will they be truly free! If this is Hegel's concept of freedom, did ever a philosopher provide a better example of the Orwellian double-speak that Hitler and Stalin used so effectively to implement their totalitarian designs?

Popper's case is not as strong as it seems. First, his quotations nearly all come not from Hegel's own writings, but from notes of his lectures taken by students and published only after his death, by an editor who explained in his preface that he had done a certain amount of rewriting. Second, at least one of these resonant utterances is a mistranslation. Where Popper quotes 'The State is the march of God through the world', a more accurate translation would be: 'It is the way of God with the world, that the State exists.' This amounts to no more than the claim that the existence of States is in some sense part of a divine plan. Third, for Hegel 'State' does not mean simply 'the government' but refers to all social life. Thus he is not glorifying the government against the people, but referring to the community as a whole. Fourth, these quotations need to be balanced by others, for Hegel frequently presents one aspect of a subject in an extreme form before balancing it against another. Thus Hegel's remarks on the State follow upon earlier passages in which he says: 'the right of subjective freedom is the pivot and centre of the difference between antiquity and modern times' and goes on to say that this right 'in its infinity' has become 'the universal effective principle' of the new form of civilisation. Later, we find him saying: 'What is of the utmost importance is that the law of reason should be shot through and through by the law of particular freedom . . .'. Moreover Hegel insists that, 'in view of the right of self-consciousness', laws can have no binding force unless they are universally known. To hang the laws so high that no citizen can read them, as Dionysius the Tyrant is said to have done, or to bury them in learned tomes no ordinary citizen can read, is injustice. Along similar lines is Hegel's searing attack on the reactionary writer von Haller, who defended a doctrine of 'might makes right' that would have suited Hitler well. Of this author Hegel says: 'The hatred of law, of right made determinate in law, is the shibboleth whereby fanaticism, flabby-mindedness and the hypocrisy of good intentions are clearly and infallibly recognised for what they are, disguise themselves as they may.' So strong a defence of the rule of law is an awkward base from which to construct a totalitarian State, with its secret police and dictatorial power.

That the extravagant language Hegel used to describe the State, and his idea that true freedom is to be found in rational choices, are both wide open to misuse and distortion in the service of totalitarianism is undeniable; but that it *is* a misuse is equally undeniable. We have seen enough of his views about constitutional monarchy, freedom of expression, the rule of law, and trial by jury to make this plain. The problem is that Hegel was serious about reason, to an extent that few of us are now. When someone tells us how the affairs of the State can most rationally be conducted, we take him to be expressing his personal preferences. Others, we assume, will have different preferences and as for what is most 'rational', well, since none of us can really tell, we may as well forget about it and settle for what we like best. So when Hegel writes of 'worshipping' the State, or of freedom being realised in a rational State, we are inclined to apply these remarks to whatever type of State takes our fancy—a reading utterly contrary to Hegel's intentions. By a 'rational State' Hegel himself meant something quite objective and quite specific. It had to be a State that individuals really did choose to obey and support, because they genuinely agreed with its principles and truly found their individual satisfaction in being part of it. For Hegel, no rational State could ever deal with its citizens as the Nazi and Stalinist States dealt with theirs. The idea is a contradiction in terms. Similarly, the threat of the interests of the State coming into conflict with and ruthlessly crushing the rights of the individual loses its grip once we realise that in Hegel's rational State the interests of the individual and of the collective are in harmony.

To all this a modern reader will probably react with a 'Yes, but . . .'. 'Yes' to indicate that Hegel was not himself advocating totalitarianism; 'but' to suggest that on this interpretation Hegel was extraordinarily optimistic about the possibilities of harmony between humans, and even more extraordinarily at odds with reality if he believed that the harmony would exist in the kind of State he described.

The latter criticism I believe to be unanswerable. If Hegel's remarks about the State are to be defensible, the rational State he has in mind must be very different from any State that existed in his day (or has existed since, for that matter). Yet the State he described, while it may have differed *significantly*, certainly did not differ *radically* from States existing in his own day. The most likely explanation is that Hegel was too conservative, or else too cautious, to advocate a radical departure from the political system under which he lived and taught. To say that Hegel's 'one aim' was to please the King of Prussia is clearly wrong; but it may be fair to say that in order to avoid the wrath of the King of Prussia (and of all the other German rulers) Hegel muted the radical thrust of his underlying philosophical theory.

There is, however, one more thing that needs to be said about Hegel's vision of harmony between humans. His political philosophy is only a part of a much larger philosophical system, in which unity between individual human beings has a metaphysical basis. In the last two chapters we have given the historical and political sides of Hegel's thought more than their fair allocation of space, considering their place in Hegel's work as a whole, and so it is in any case time to move on to the larger philosophical system. We shall soon see that to turn to the other side of Hegel's thought is equally desirable for a deeper understanding of both his philosophy of history and his political philosophy.

4 *The odyssey of mind*

Mind or spirit?

It is time to confess: I have been cheating. My account of Hegel's philosophy so far has carefully omitted all mention of something that Hegel himself refers to repeatedly and regards as crucial: the idea of *Geist*. So crucial is this idea that Hegel actually says that the whole object of the *Philosophy of History* is to become acquainted with *Geist* in its guiding role in history. Without some knowledge of this idea, therefore, one can have only a partial grasp of Hegel's view of history. In the *Philosophy of Right*, too, the concept of *Geist* is never far away. Hegel refers to the State, for instance, as 'objectified *Geist*'. So the preceding chapters were deliberately misleading; my only excuse is that I misled in a good cause, the cause of easing the reader gently into the strange and often obscure world of Hegel's ideas.

For the English-speaking reader, the difficulties of Hegel's concept of *Geist* begin with its translation. In German the word is common enough, but it has two distinct, though related meanings. It is the standard word used to mean 'mind', in the sense in which our mind is distinct from our body. For example, 'mental illness' is *Geisteskrankheit*—literally, 'mind-sickness'. *Geist* can, however, also mean 'spirit' in the varied senses of that English word. Thus 'the spirit of the times' is *der Zeitgeist*, while the third element of the Christian Trinity of Father, Son and Holy Ghost (or Holy Spirit) is *der Heilige Geist*. The translator's task is made doubly difficult by the fact that in some passages Hegel seems to use the word much as we would use 'mind', in other contexts he uses it as we would use 'spirit', and in others still his usage has elements of both meanings.

In this impossible situation, the translator has three options: to use 'mind' throughout; to use 'spirit' throughout; or to use whichever seems most appropriate in the context. I have rejected the third option, because it is obviously important to Hegel that what he calls *Geist* is one and the same thing, notwithstanding the different aspects of it that emerge in his various writings. When I began work on this book, my presumption was that I would use 'spirit', for this has been the choice of virtually all the recent translators of Hegel. Yet as I began to get more deeply into the attempt to present Hegel in a form that would be understandable to readers who are not already Hegel scholars, I became convinced that to use 'spirit' is to prejudge, for the English-speaking reader, the whole question of what *Geist* really means for Hegel. In English, apart from special usages like 'spirit of the age' and 'team spirit', the word 'spirit' has an inescapably religious or mystical flavour. A spirit taps out the message on the Ouija board, or haunts the deserted Gothic mansion. A spirit is a ghostly, disembodied being, the sort of thing you believe in if you are a bit superstitious, but not if you take a cool, clear scientific view of the world.

Now it may be that at some point in our examination of Hegel we shall have to say that his philosophy is based on this somewhat superstitious view of the world, and his concept of *Geist* is intended to refer to just such a ghostly, disembodied being. We must not, however, assume this from the start. Hegel is a philosopher working in the Western philosophical tradition. Philosophers in this tradition have always been much concerned with the nature of mind, or consciousness, and its relation to the physical world. Descartes began the modern philosophical era by asking what he could know with complete certainty; and he answered by saying that while he might be dreaming, or deceived by an evil demon and hence mistaken in almost all his beliefs, the one thing he could know with certainty is: 'I think, therefore I exist.' I cannot be deceived about that, for to be deceived, I must still exist. What, though, is this 'I'? It is not my physical body—about that I could be deceived. The 'I' that I know with certainty is simply a thing that thinks:

in other words, a mind. From this argument arose the central preoccupations of subsequent Western philosophy. How are my thoughts and feelings connected to my body? Are there both mental objects, such as thoughts, and material objects, such as bodies? If so, in what way can two such different kinds of thing interact? My brain is a material thing; how can matter be conscious? This nest of issues is known among philosophers as 'the mind—body problem'. Another set of issues, also traceable to Descartes, focuses on problems of knowledge: How can we know what the world is like? Can we be sure that our thoughts are in any way a reflection of some 'real' world that is 'out there', as we tend to assume? If all my conscious experiences, including the sensations of colour and shape and texture that I rely upon for simple beliefs like that in the existence of the sheet of paper in front of me now, are always in my mind, how can I ever know anything at all of the world outside my own consciousness?

The point of this digression into the problems of the Western philosophical tradition is simply this: it is entirely to be expected that a philosopher like Hegel should write about mind. That he does so should not suggest that he believes in the existence of disembodied spirits or of anything else in which you and I, cool, clear-thinking adherents of the scientific world-view that we may be, do not also believe. Therefore we should at least start our discussion of what Hegel is saying by taking his references to *Geist* not as talk about some peculiar mystical being, but as a contribution to the long-standing philosophical debate about the nature of mind. Accordingly in this book I return to the practice of an earlier generation of translators of Hegel and render *Geist* as 'mind'. We shall see as we go along in just what sense of that word Hegel's concept is to be understood.

The task of the Phenomenology

That my presentation of Hegel's views up to this point has been seriously incomplete can be seen by returning to a question I brushed aside early in the discussion of Hegel's philosophy of history. *Why* is the history of the world nothing but the progress of the consciousness of freedom? The question cries out for an answer. Hegel explicitly denies—and it would in any case be quite out of keeping with his whole line of thought—that the direction of history is some kind of fortunate accident. Hegel asserts that what happens in history happens *necessarily*. What does this mean? How can it be true? Hegel's answer is that history is nothing but the progress of the consciousness of freedom because history is the development of mind. In the *Philosophy of History* Hegel did not set out to explain this notion, because he had already published a very long and very dense volume intended to demonstrate the necessity of mind developing as it does. That volume is *The Phenomenology of Mind*. Karl Marx called it 'the true birthplace and secret of Hegel's philosophy'. Others, defeated by its 750 pages of bewildering and tortuous prose, have been content to let whatever secrets it might contain rest undisturbed. No account of Hegel, however, can decently overlook it.

The obvious place to start is with the title. The *Oxford English Dictionary* tells us that 'phenomenology' means 'the science of phenomena, as distinct from that of being'. That is all very well if we are familiar with the distinction between 'phenomena' and 'being'. For those that are not, the same dictionary obligingly tells us that 'phenomenon' means, in its philosophical use, 'that of which the senses or the mind directly takes note; an immediate object of perception (as distinguished from substance, or a thing in itself)'. The distinction being made here can be illustrated by considering the difference between the moon as it appears in my vision, and the moon as it really is. In my vision it appeared last night as a silvery crescent no bigger than a tennis-ball; it really is, of course, a sphere of rock with a diameter of several thousand kilometres. The silvery crescent is the phenomenon. Phenomenology, then, is the study of the way in which things appear to us.

If phenomenology is the study of the way in which things appear to us, a 'phenomenology of mind', we might guess, will be a study of the way in which mind appears to us. Such a guess would be correct, but there is a characteristically Hegelian twist to add. When we study how our mind appears to us, we can only be studying how it appears to our minds. Thus a phenomenology of mind is really a study of how mind appears to itself. Accordingly, Hegel's *Phenomenology of Mind* traces different forms of consciousness, viewing each one from inside, as it were, and showing how more limited forms of consciousness necessarily developed into more adequate ones. Hegel himself describes his project as 'the exposition of knowledge as a phenomenon' because he sees the development of consciousness as a development toward forms of consciousness that more fully grasp reality, culminating in 'absolute knowledge'.

In his introduction to the *Phenomenology*, Hegel explains why he believes it necessary to carry out this kind of study. He begins with the problem of knowledge. The aim of philosophy, he says, is the 'actual knowledge of what truly is' or, as he somewhat mysteriously characterises it, 'the absolute'. Before we start to pronounce upon 'what truly is', however, hadn't we better pause to reflect upon knowledge itself, that is, on how we come to know reality? In our attempts to gain knowledge we are attempting to grasp reality. Hence knowledge, Hegel says, is often likened to an instrument by which we grasp truth; if our instrument is faulty we may end up holding nothing but error.

So we begin with an enquiry into knowing. Immediately we are beset by sceptical worries. If trying to know reality is like using some kind of instrument for grasping reality, isn't there a danger that applying our instrument to reality will alter it, so that we grasp something very different from undisturbed reality? (Compare the way modern physicists find it impossible to pin down the speed and location of subatomic particles, because whatever instrument they use to observe them will also interfere with them.) Even if we abandon the 'instrument' metaphor, Hegel says, and regard knowledge as a more passive medium through which we observe reality, we are still observing reality-through-the-medium, not reality itself.

If an instrument or a medium through which we are looking has a distorting effect, one way of coming to know the true state of affairs is to discover the nature of the distortion and subtract the difference it makes. For example, if I look at a stick half in the water and half out, the part in the water appears bent. Is the stick really bent? I can calculate this if I know the law of refraction and thus the difference that looking at it through water makes. Subtracting this difference, I will discover what the stick is really like. Can we perhaps do the same with the distorting effect of the instrument or medium of knowledge, and thus come to know reality as it is?

No, Hegel says, this escape from our puzzle is not open to us. Knowing is not like seeing. For in the case of knowing, what is one to subtract? It would be like subtracting not the difference the water makes to the ray of light, but the ray of light itself. Without knowledge we would not know the stick at all; to subtract our act of knowing, therefore, would be to leave us knowing nothing.

So our instrument cannot guarantee us an image of undisturbed reality, nor can we come closer to reality by making allowances for the disturbance caused by our instrument. Should we therefore embrace the sceptical position that there is nothing we can truly know? But such scepticism, Hegel says, is self-refuting. If we are to doubt everything, why not doubt the claim that we can know nothing? Moreover the sceptical argument we have been considering has its own presuppositions, which it claims to know. It starts with the idea that there is such a thing as reality, and that knowledge is some kind of instrument or medium by which we grasp reality. In so doing, it presupposes a distinction between ourselves and reality, or the absolute. Worse still, it takes for granted that our knowledge and reality are cut off from one another, but at the same time still treats our knowledge as something real, that is, as a part of reality. Thus scepticism will not do either.

Hegel has neatly set up a certain view of knowing, and then shown that it leads into a hole from which we cannot escape, and in which we cannot remain. We must, he now says, abandon all these 'useless ideas and expressions' about knowledge as an instrument or medium, all of which divide knowledge from reality as it is.

In all of this argument there is no mention of any philosopher who has held the view of knowledge that Hegel now says we must reject. To some extent he is criticising assumptions common to the whole school of empiricist philosophers—Locke, Berkeley, Hume and many others. It would, however, have been obvious to all his readers that his main target is Kant. Kant argued that we can never see reality as it is; for we can only comprehend our experiences within the frameworks of space, time and causation. Space, time and causation are not part of reality, but the necessary forms in which we grasp it; therefore we can never know things as they are independently of our knowledge.

In another work, the *Lesser Logic,* Hegel does name his opponent and mounts a similar attack against him (though as if to display his intellectual fertility, he presses home his point with a slightly different argument). The passage is worth quoting, because it concludes with an analogy that suggests the way forward:

We ought, says Kant, to become acquainted with the instrument, before we undertake the work for which it is to be employed; for if the instrument be insufficient, all our trouble will be spent in vain ... But the examination of knowledge can only be carried out by an act of knowledge. To examine this so-called instrument is the same thing as to know it. But to seek to know before we know is as absurd as the wise resolution of Scholasticus, not to venture into the water until he had learned to swim.

The lesson taught by the folly of Scholasticus is clear. To learn to swim we must plunge boldly into the stream; and to obtain knowledge of reality, we must plunge boldly into the stream of consciousness that is the starting-point of all we know. The only possible approach to knowledge is an examination of consciousness from the inside as it appears to itself—in other words, a phenomenology of mind. We shall not start with sophisticated doubts, but with a simple form of consciousness that takes itself to be genuine knowledge. This simple form of consciousness will, however, prove itself to be something less than genuine knowledge, and so will develop into another form of consciousness; and this in turn will also prove inadequate, and develop into something else, and so the process will continue until we reach true knowledge.

The Phenomenology of Mind is the tracing of this process in detail: as Hegel puts it, 'the detailed history of the process of training and educating consciousness itself up to the level of science'. Part of this training and educating is in fact the development of ideas that has occurred throughout history; thus Hegel's *Phenomenology* is in part an anticipation of the material covered in the *Philosophy of History*. This time, however, the same events are treated in a different manner, for Hegel's aim is to exhibit the process of the development of consciousness as a *necessary* one. Each form of consciousness, in revealing itself to be less than genuine knowledge, leads us to what Hegel calls 'a determinate negation'. This is not the empty scepticism defended by philosophers who find fault with our ordinary methods of knowing; from that empty scepticism there would be no way forward. A determinate negation, on the other hand, is itself something. (Think of the negation sign in mathematics: it produces not zero, but a definite negative number.) The 'something' that is the result of the discovery that a form of consciousness is inadequate, is itself a new form of consciousness, namely, consciousness aware of the inadequacies of the previous form and forced to adopt a different approach in order to surmount them. Thus we shall be compelled to move from one form of consciousness to the next in a restless searching for true knowledge.

The *Phenomenology* will therefore provide an answer to the question raised earlier, as to *why* the history of the world is nothing but the development of the consciousness of the idea of freedom, and why what happens in history happens necessarily. Yet, incredibly, the answer given to this monumental question is merely a by-product of the principal aim of the work, which is to demonstrate the possibility of genuine knowledge, and thus to serve as a foundation for philosophy's aim of providing, as Hegel put it, 'actual knowledge of what truly is'.

The goal of the process to be traced in the *Phenomenology* is true knowledge, or 'the absolute'. How will we know that we have reached it? Will not sceptical doubts still be possible? No, says Hegel, because 'the terminus is at that point where knowledge is no longer compelled to go beyond itself . . .'. In other words, whereas previously consciousness has been forced to admit that its own knowledge is inadequate, and to strive for more adequate knowledge that is beyond its grasp—to seek to know the 'thing-in-itself'—at the end of the process, reality will no longer be an unknowable 'beyond'. Consciousness will know reality directly, and be at one with it. There will be nothing further to reach for, and the restless compulsion to attain more adequate knowledge will at last be satisfied.

Hegel has set himself an extraordinary task. Beginning with a powerful critique of the approach to knowledge taken by Kant (and not only by Kant, but by all philosophers who start off by assuming a division between one who knows and the thing that is known—which means virtually all philosophers from Plato onwards), Hegel sets out to develop a new method. His method is to trace the development of all the possible forms of consciousness to the final goal of genuine knowledge, which must not be knowledge of the appearance of reality, but knowledge of reality itself. We must now see how he carries out this task.

Knowledge without concepts?

Hegel starts with the most primitive form of consciousness, which he calls 'certainty at the level of sense-experience' or, more briefly, 'sense-certainty'. He has in mind a form of consciousness which does nothing but grasp what is in front of it at any given moment. Sense-certainty simply records the data received by our senses. It is knowledge of the particular thing present to our senses. Sense-certainty makes no attempt to order or classify the raw information obtained by the senses. Thus when this form of consciousness has in front of it what we would describe as a ripe tomato, it cannot describe its experience as a tomato, for that would be to classify what it sees. It cannot even describe the experience as one of seeing something round and red, for these terms too presuppose some form of classification. Sense-certainty is aware only of what is now present to it; as Hegel puts it, it is the certainty of the 'this', or of the 'here' and 'now'.

Sense-certainty seems to have a strong claim to being genuine knowledge, for it is directly aware of the 'this', without imposing on it the distorting filters of a conceptual scheme involving space, time or any other categories. Sense-certainty is simple awareness of the object exactly as it is. Yet, as Hegel shows, the claim that sense-certainty is knowledge does not stand up to further investigation. As soon as sense-certainty attempts to utter its knowledge, it becomes incoherent. What is the 'this'? It can be broken down into the 'here' and the 'now', but these terms cannot convey truth. If, late one night, we are asked what is the 'now', we may reply 'Now it is night-time.' Suppose we write that down—a truth cannot lose anything by being written down, Hegel says, nor by being preserved. So the next day at noon we take out the truth we have written down, only to find that, as Hegel puts it, 'it has turned stale'. Similarly I say 'Here is a tree', but another sense-certainty can just as well say 'Here is a house.'

Hegel's argument seems to be based on a perverse misunderstanding of the language used to convey the knowledge of sense-certainty. Surely it is possible to restate the knowledge of sense-certainty in a manner that is immune to such cheap tricks? Yet the trick is not as easy to get around as one might imagine. From the standpoint of sense-certainty it is not possible to say, for example, 'At midnight it is night' or 'There is a tree in the park.' These utterances presuppose a general ordering of things, including our concepts of time and space.

How then can the knowledge of self-certainty be expressed? Hegel's point is that it cannot be expressed in language at all, because sense-certainty is knowledge of the pure particular, while language always involves bringing something under some more general or universal label. 'Tomato' is a universal term that picks out a whole class of objects, not a single particular object—and the same is true of every other term. Hegel's attack on the truthfulness of 'Now it is night-time' is intended to show that to use terms like 'now', 'here' and 'this' is no way to express knowledge of the pure particular. These terms are also universals, for there is more than one 'now' and more than one 'here'. Thus sense-certainty, in seeking to express its knowledge of the pure particular, has got sucked into the necessity of the universal term.

Hegel believes that he has established the impossibility of knowledge without universal concepts. Two possible objections to his argument are worth brief mention. The first points out an obvious exception to the rule that every term picks out a class of objects rather than a particular object: proper names. 'John D. Rockefeller', 'Rosa Luxemburg', 'The Sydney Opera House' and other proper names do pick out particular objects. Could not sense-certainty describe its experience by giving every 'this' a proper name?

In the *Phenomenology* Hegel ignores the fact that proper names are an exception to his view of language; but we can make a fair guess at what his reply would be, for in his *Logic* he asserts that proper names are meaningless, precisely because they lack reference to anything beyond the name itself, that is, to anything universal. For the particular knowledge of sense-certainty to be expressed by proper names, we can imagine him saying, would be merely to stick meaningless labels on every 'this' of which one was aware. Such labels would convey nothing.

This brings us to the second possible objection, which grants that the knowledge of sense-certainty may be impossible to put into language and convey to others, but contends that it is none the less knowledge. Why should we assume that all knowledge can be put into words? Mystics have often asserted that the truths of mystical experiences are impossible to put into words, and yet are the deepest truths of all. 'A truth cannot lose anything by being written down,' Hegel said; but perhaps this simple claim was the first step down the path away from truth. Should we not have stopped Hegel right there, and insisted on the validity of knowledge too pure for words?

To this objection Hegel must reply, for it threatens the heart of his enterprise. He does not deny that there is something which cannot be reached by language, but he asserts that this is 'nothing else than what is untrue, irrational, something barely and simply believed'. I may well think that I know what I mean, even if I cannot put it into words, but in fact this is not knowledge, it is purely subjective, a personal opinion. Opinion is not knowledge. It can only become knowledge by being brought out into the open.

Hegel makes his point by playing on the multiple meanings of the German 'meinen', to believe or to intend, and its associated noun, 'Meinung', which means 'opinion'. If we disregard this way of doing philosophy by punning, we are left with an assertion rather than an argument. Nevertheless the assertion—that something which is in principle incommunicable cannot possibly be knowledge—is plausible enough.

We can now take stock of our analysis of the claim that this primitive form of consciousness represents genuine knowledge. An attempt was made to state what sort of knowledge could be possessed by a consciousness that does nothing more than grasp what is in front of it at any given moment. The attempt failed, because the truths reached by that form of consciousness proved to be either palpable falsehoods, or something purely personal that can never be expressed. In neither case could these alleged truths be accepted as knowledge.

Thus sense-certainty proved itself inadequate. The result was achieved, as Hegel promised us in his introduction, from within—that is, all that was necessary to show the inadequacy of sense-certainty was to take its claims at face value and try to make them more precise. Sense-certainty did not succumb to a rival form of consciousness; it collapsed through its own incoherence. At the same time, and again as we were promised in the introduction, this outcome was not only a negative result. We were led to appreciate the impossibility of knowledge of pure particulars, and thus the necessity of bringing particular sense-experiences under some form of conceptual scheme, a scheme that classifies what we experience under a universal aspect, and so makes it possible to communicate our experience through language. If we are to achieve knowledge, we cannot passively experience; we must allow our mind to play a more active role in ordering the information received by our senses. The next form of consciousness Hegel examines, therefore, is one in which consciousness actively attempts to create some unity and coherence out of the raw data of sense-experience.

The emergence of self-consciousness

From the naïve form of consciousness discussed in the preceding section, Hegel traces the development of consciousness through two further stages which he calls 'perception' and 'understanding'. In each stage consciousness plays a more active role than it did in the preceding stage. At the level of perception, consciousness classifies objects according to their universal properties; this proves inadequate, and so at the level of understanding, consciousness imposes its own laws on reality. The laws Hegel has in mind are Newton's laws of physics, and the view of the universe that came to be based on them. Although these laws are commonly regarded as a part of reality that Newton and other scientists have discovered, Hegel sees them as no more than an extension of the classification by consciousness of the raw data of sense-experience. Just as bringing these data under universal categories essential to language made it possible to communicate, so the laws of physics are a way of making the data more coherent and predictable. The concepts employed in this process—notions like 'gravity' and 'force'—are not things we see existing in reality, but constructs made by our understanding to help us grasp reality.

Consciousness at the level of understanding does not see these constructs for what they are; it takes them as objects to be understood. We who trace the process of the development of consciousness can see that consciousness is, in effect, trying to understand its own creations. It has itself for its object. This means that consciousness has reached the point at which it can reflect upon itself. It is latent self-consciousness. With this conclusion Hegel brings the first part of the *Phenomenology*—the part headed 'Consciousness'—to a close. In the following part, under the general title 'Self-consciousness', he drops the direct investigation of the problem of knowledge that provided the focus of the first part, switching his attention to the development of latent self-consciousness into fully explicit self-consciousness. (This is still, of course, part of the development of mind towards the stage of absolute knowledge.)

The desiring mind

Hegel's notion of self-consciousness is important; in different ways, it has influenced both Marxist and existentialist thinkers. Self-consciousness, he maintains, cannot exist in isolation. If consciousness is to form a proper picture of itself, it needs some contrast. It requires an object from which to differentiate itself. I can only become aware of myself if I am also aware of something that is not myself. Self-consciousness is not simply a consciousness contemplating its own navel.

Although self-consciousness needs an object outside itself, this external object is also something foreign to it, and a form of opposition to it. There is therefore a peculiar kind of love–hate relationship between self-consciousness and the external object. This relationship, in the best tradition of love–hate relationships, comes to the surface in the form of desire. To desire something is to wish to possess it—and thus not to destroy it altogether—but also to transform it into something that is yours, and thus to strip it of its foreignness.

The introduction of this notion of desire marks the switch in Hegel's concern from theoretical problems of discovering truth to practical problems of changing the world. We have here a foreshadowing of the 'unity of theory and practice' of which Marxists make so much. Truth is to be obtained not through contemplation alone, but by working on the world and changing it. On Marx's tombstone are engraved the words of his famous Eleventh Thesis on Feuerbach: 'The philosophers have only interpreted the world in various ways; the point, however, is to change it.' Marx certainly had Hegel in mind as one of 'the philosophers', and it is undeniable that Marx wished to change the world far more radically than Hegel did; Hegel could none the less have pointed out that the underlying idea of Marx's words can be found in the *Phenomenology*, at the point where the self-conscious being finds that to realise itself fully it must set about changing the external world and making it its own.

Desire appeared as the expression of the fact that self-consciousness needs an external object, and yet finds itself limited by anything that is outside itself. But to desire something is to be unsatisfied; so desire is—to make a typically Hegelian play on words—an unsatisfactory state for self-consciousness. Worse still, self-consciousness seems doomed to be permanently unsatisfied, for if the object of desire is done away with as an independent object, self-consciousness will have destroyed what it needed for its own existence.

Hegel's solution to this dilemma is to make the object of self-consciousness *another* self-consciousness. In this manner each self-conscious being has another object with which to contrast itself, yet the other 'object' turns out to be not a simple object which must be possessed and thereby 'negated' as an external object, but another self-consciousness which can possess itself, and thereby can do away with itself as an external object.

If this seems obscure, don't worry. It is even more obscure in Hegel's text. One commentator, Ivan Soll, remarks on the 'extreme opacity' of Hegel's argument at this point; another, Richard Norman, deals swiftly with this section, saying: 'since I find large parts of it unintelligible, I shall say little about it'. Hegel's central point is that self-consciousness demands not simply any external object, but another self-consciousness. One way of explaining this is to say that to see oneself, one needs a mirror. To be aware of oneself as a self-conscious being, one needs to be able to observe another self-conscious being, to see what self-consciousness is like. An alternative explanation is that self-consciousness can only develop in a context of social interaction. A child growing up in total isolation from all other self-conscious beings would never develop mentally beyond the level of mere consciousness, for self-consciousness grows out of a social life. Each of these explanations is plausible enough. Unfortunately it is difficult to relate either of them to the words Hegel uses. One or both of them may nevertheless resemble what he had in mind.

Master and slave

We pass now to the most admired section of the entire *Phenomenology*. The two self-consciousnesses are on stage. For ease of exposition, let us refer to self-conscious beings as *persons*. (Hegel, of course, does not deign to make the exposition easier.) Each person, then, needs the other to establish his own awareness of himself. What precisely is it that each requires from the other? Hegel suggests that it is acknowledgement or recognition. To understand his point we need to note that the German word for self-consciousness, *'Selbstbewusstsein'*, also has the sense of 'being self-assured' (unlike the English word, which is associated with embarrassment and hesitation). It is this sense of the German word that gives support to Hegel's idea that my self-consciousness is threatened by the existence of another person who fails to acknowledge me as a person. As Richard Norman has suggested, we can take the work of existential psychiatrists like R. D. Laing as an elaboration of this idea. If the worth of one person is systematically denied recognition by all those on whom he or she depends—as can happen in a family in which one member has become a scapegoat for everyone's problems—that person's sense of identity can be utterly destroyed. (The result of this lack of acknowledgement, according to Laing, is schizophrenia.)

If this notion of the need for acknowledgement or recognition is still obscure, consider the analogy of a nation achieving diplomatic recognition. That diplomatic recognition is important to States is obvious from the efforts that some States, like East Germany and China, have made to obtain it—and from the efforts that others have made to prevent them obtaining it. Until a nation has been recognised by others, it is not a full-fledged State. Diplomatic recognition is peculiar in that on the one hand it apparently does no more than recognise something that is already in existence, and yet on the other hand it makes something less than a State into a complete State. The same peculiarity belongs to Hegel's conception of recognition.

The demand for recognition is mutual. One might think, therefore, that people could peacefully recognise each other and be done with it. Instead Hegel tells us that self-consciousness seeks to become pure, and to do this it must show that it is not attached to mere material objects. In fact self-consciousness is doubly attached to material objects: it is attached to its own living body, and to the living body of the other person from whom it requires acknowledgement. The way to prove that one is not attached to either of these material objects is to engage in a life-and-death struggle with the other person: by seeking to kill the other, one shows that one is not dependent on the body of the other, and by risking one's own life, one shows that one is not attached to one's own body either. Hence the initial relationship of the two individuals is not peaceful mutual re-cognition, but combat.

It is difficult to know what to make of this. Hegel seems to be saying that violent combat is not an accidental occurrence in human affairs, but a necessary element in the process of prov-ing oneself a person. Can he really mean to say, though, that people who have not risked their lives are not really, or fully, persons? Perhaps it would be better—certainly it is more chari-table—to regard the process of 'proving' as one that merely makes explicit what was already implicit. (For example, when we prove a theorem, we do not thereby make it true; we only show that it was true all along.) On this interpretation, some-one who has never risked his life can still be a person, although his existence as a person has not been demonstrated. Being more charitable still, we might interpret Hegel as holding only that it is necessary, somewhere along the line, that some people stake their lives to prove their independence of their bodies; the proof does not have to be repeated for each person.

To return to the conflict. The original idea was that each individual was intent upon the death of the other. A moment's thought shows, however, that this outcome suits nobody—not the defeated, who will be dead, nor the victor, who will then have destroyed the source of recognition he needs to confirm his sense of himself as a person. So the victor realises that the other person is essential to him, and spares his life; but the original equality of two independent people has been replaced by an unequal situation in which the victor is independent and the loser is dependent. The former is the master, the latter the slave.

In this way Hegel accounts for the division between ruler and ruled. Once again, though, this situation is not stable. The reason Hegel gives for its instability is strikingly original.

At first it seems that the master has everything. He sets the slave to work in the material world, and sits back to enjoy both the subservience of the slave and the fruits of the slave's labours. But consider now the master's need for acknowledgement. He has the acknowledgement of the slave, to be sure, but in the eyes of the master the slave is merely a thing, not an independent consciousness at all. The master has, after all, failed to achieve the acknowledgement he requires.

Nor is the situation of the slave as it first appeared to be. The slave lacks adequate acknowledgement, of course, for to the master he is a mere thing. On the other hand, the slave works on the external world. In contrast to his master, who receives the temporary satisfactions of consumption, the slave shapes and fashions the material objects on which he works. In doing so he makes his own ideas into something permanent, an external object. (For example, if he carves a log of wood into a chair, his conception of a chair, his design and his efforts, remain a part of the world.) Through this process the slave becomes more aware of his own consciousness, for he sees it in front of him as something objective. In labour, even labour under the direction of another, hostile mind, the slave discovers that he has a mind of his own.

Some forty years later Karl Marx developed his own notion of *alienated labour*. Like Hegel, Marx regarded labour as a process in which the worker puts his own thoughts and efforts—in fact all that is best in himself—into the object of his labours. The worker thereby *objectifies* himself, or externalises himself. Marx then made much of a point that is implicit in what Hegel says: if the object of labour is the property of another, especially an alien, hostile other, the worker has lost his own objectified essence. This is what happens to the labour of the slave; but, as Marx insisted, it also happens under capitalism. The chair, shoes, cloth or whatever it is that the worker has produced belong to the capitalist. They enable the capitalist to profit, and thereby to increase his capital and strengthen his dominance over the workers. So the objectified essence of the worker is not merely lost to him; it actually turns into a hostile force that oppresses him. This is alienated labour, the key idea of Marx's early writings and the forerunner of the notion of surplus value which is the basis of the Marxist critique of capitalist economics.

Philosophy and religion

For Marx the solution to the problem of alienated labour was the abolition of private property and of the division of mankind into the rulers and the ruled. Hegel, on the other hand, saw himself as tracing a path that consciousness had already travelled. So there could be no question of leaping off at this point into some future classless society. In fact, it is precisely at this point that the *Phenomenology* becomes more historical, edging closer to the material Hegel was later to deal with more concretely in his *Philosophy of History*. The section on master and slave is followed by a discussion of Stoicism, a philosophical school that became important under the Roman Empire and included among its leading writers both Marcus Aurelius, the Emperor, and Epictetus, a slave. Stoicism therefore bridges the gulf between master and slave. In Stoicism the repressed slave who has come to full self-awareness through work can find a type of freedom; for Stoicism teaches withdrawal from the external world—in which the slave remains a slave—and retreat into one's own consciousness. As Hegel says: 'In thinking I am free, because I am not in another, but remain simply and solely in touch with myself; and the object which for me is my essential reality is ... my own existence.' And again: 'The essence of this consciousness is to be free, on the throne or in chains ...'. The Stoic in chains is still free because chains do not matter to him. He detaches himself from his body and finds his consolation in his mind, where no tyrant can touch him.

The weakness of Stoicism is that thought, cut off from the real world, lacks all determinate content. Its edifying ideas are barren of substance and soon get tedious. Stoicism is then succeeded by another philosophical attitude, scepticism, and from scepticism we progress to what Hegel calls 'the unhappy consciousness', a notion which I shall briefly discuss because of the importance it had to some of Hegel's successors.

'The unhappy consciousness' is clearly a form of consciousness that existed under Christianity. Hegel also refers to it as 'the alienated soul', and this expression provides a better clue to what Hegel has in mind. In the alienated soul, the dualism of master and slave is concentrated into one consciousness, but the two elements are not unified. The unhappy consciousness aspires to be independent of the material world, to resemble God and be eternal and purely spiritual; yet at the same time it recognises that it is a part of the material world, that its physical desires and its pains and pleasures are real and inescapable. As a result the unhappy consciousness is divided against itself. This conception should be familiar from the discussion of Hegel's attitude to Kant's ethics in the preceding chapter; on this occasion, it is Christianity rather than Kant that Hegel has in mind. Recall St Paul's 'The good which I want to do I fail to do; but what I do is the wrong which is against my will', and St Augustine's plea: 'Give me chastity and continence, but do not give it yet.'

Hegel's target is any religion which divides human nature against itself—and he asserts that this is the upshot of any religion which separates man from God, putting God in a 'beyond' outside the human world. This conception of God, he maintains, is really a projection of one aspect of human nature. What the unhappy consciousness does not realise is that the spiritual qualities of God which it worships are in fact qualities of *its own self*. It is in this sense that the unhappy consciousness is an alienated soul: it has projected its own essential nature into a place for ever out of its reach, and one which makes the real world in which it lives seem, by contrast, miserable and insignificant.

Reading Hegel's treatment of the unhappy consciousness in isolation from his other writings, one could well take him to be attacking all religion, or at the very least Judaism, Christianity and other religions based on a conception of God as a being distinct from the human world. He appears to be denying the existence of any such God, and explaining our belief in God as a projection of our own essential attributes. Only pantheism, or a humanism which takes humanity itself as divine, would be immune from this condemnation. Yet Hegel was, as we have seen, a member of the Lutheran Church, and in several of his other writings, including the *Philosophy of History*, and even in a later section of the *Phenomenology* itself, Protestant Christianity is viewed in a much more positive light. Did Hegel, in his later writings and his personal behaviour, compromise the radical thrust of his views about religion, as he appears to have compromised the radical thrust of his view of the State? After Hegel's death, a group of young radicals took this view of Hegel's philosophy. They saw themselves as following the true, uncompromised essence of his thought, and placed special emphasis on his discussion of the unhappy consciousness. We shall follow this sequel in the final chapter of this book.

Mind's goal

We shall now pass over a huge chunk of the *Phenomenology*. Some of what we are missing is tedious and obscure; other sections come close to equalling in interest and importance those we have just discussed. Sometimes the topics are just what one would expect to find in a philosophical work. There are discussions of the metaphysical ideas of Fichte and Kant. There is a critique of hedonism, or the pursuit of pleasure. There is a discussion of Kant's ethics, making objections similar to those we have already encountered in discussing the *Philosophy of Right*. Moral sentimentality of the type made popular in Hegel's time by the Romantic movement also comes in for critical analysis.

Other topics are more unusual. There is, for instance, a long section on physiognomy and phrenology—the pseudo-sciences based on the idea that one can tell people's character from (in the case of physiognomy) the shape of their faces or (according to phrenology) the bumps on their skulls. Hegel opposes these ideas, not because he has evidence of their inaccuracy, or any reason as mundane as that, but for the philosophical reason that mind is not to be tied to anything as material as a face or a skull.

Another unusual section is an analysis of a society built upon the *laissez-faire* economic theory of Adam Smith and his school, according to which each works to accumulate wealth for himself, but in fact contributes by his labours to the prosperity of the whole. Hegel's objection here—a point later to be taken up and made much of by both Marxist and non-Marxist critics of free-enterprise economics—is that by encouraging individuals to seek their own private interests, this economic system prevents individuals from seeing themselves as part of a larger community.

These diverse topics, along with many others, are woven into Hegel's conception of the path mind must travel in order to reach absolute knowledge. We have seen how he maintained that there could be no adequate knowledge without a self-conscious mind, and how self-consciousness was developed by working on the world and changing it. From that point on, Hegel sees all of human history as the development of mind. Historical periods such as Ancient Greece, the Roman Empire, the Enlightenment and the French Revolution have much the same significance as they do in the *Philosophy of History*. They are stages in the progress of mind towards freedom. So too are many of the elements of the organic community that Hegel described in the *Philosophy of Right*. Despite these broad similarities, there are some differences between the way Hegel treats this material in the *Phenomenology* and his later treatment in the *Philosophy of History* and the *Philosophy of Right*. I shall mention three.

The difference that strikes the reader at once is that in the *Phenomenology* no specific countries, periods, dates, events or people are named. While the references to specific periods and events are usually obvious enough—especially to the reader familiar with the *Philosophy of History*—everything is dealt with as if it were an instance of a general process that mind is forced to pass through by the inner necessity of its drive to self-realisation. It is as if references to specific people, times or places would somehow suggest that things might have turned out differently if the people or circumstances had been different. Hegel manages to give the impression that the process he is describing would have occurred if the development of mind had taken place on Mars. Indeed, so abstract is the tone of the *Phenomenology*, so devoid of a sense of time and place, that if mind *had* developed on Mars, Hegel would not have had to change anything.

A second difference is that whereas both the *Philosophy of History* and the *Philosophy of Right* culminate in the achievement of a State resembling the Prussian form of monarchy, this type of State is not even mentioned in the *Phenomenology*. The sections that parallel the *Philosophy of History* end with the French Revolution. The French Revolution is a climax to history in the sense that it represents mind in a state of absolute freedom, aware of its ability to change the world and to mould political and social life according to its own will. For reasons similar to those offered in the *Philosophy of History*, Hegel portrays the abstract freedom of the French Revolution as leading inevitably to its opposite, the negation of the free self that is terror and death; but there is no further political development in the *Phenomenology*. Instead the path of mind moves to more rarefied levels, first to the moral view of the world advanced by Kant, Fichte and the Romantics, then to the religious state of mind, and finally to absolute knowledge itself, which is achieved by philosophy.

There is an obvious explanation for the absence of references to the Prussian State in the *Phenomenology*. When Hegel wrote it he was teaching not in Prussia, but at Jena. Moreover he wrote during the period of the Napoleonic wars, when France was the dominant power in Europe, and the future of the German States was unpredictable. So Hegel would have had to be remarkably prescient to anticipate the resurgence of the Prussian State and to make it the culmination of his political history. The understandable absence of references to some such State has naturally made the *Phenomenology* popular with those who believe that in his later works Hegel compromised his true views in order to please his political masters.

The third major difference between the *Phenomenology* and the later works is that in the *Philosophy of History* Hegel describes the course of history as nothing but the progress of the consciousness of the idea of freedom, whereas in the *Phenomenology* the emphasis is, as we have seen, on development towards absolute knowledge. Taking these terms in their ordinary senses, it would seem that in the two works Hegel takes different and incompatible views. Surely one can be knowledgeable while languishing in a tyrant's cell; and one can live in total freedom on a tropical island in blissful ignorance of all science, politics and philosophy. But by now we should know enough about Hegel to beware of taking his terms in their ordinary senses. For Hegel, absolute knowledge and true freedom are inseparable. Our final task, so far as the *Phenomenology* is concerned, is to understand what he means by absolute knowledge. To do this we first need to understand why the progress of the consciousness of the idea of freedom is also the progress of mind towards absolute knowledge.

Our earlier examination of Hegel's conception of freedom revealed that for him we are free when we are able to choose uncoerced by other people, by social circumstances, or by natural desires. That examination concluded with the promise that a better understanding of this view would emerge once we knew a little about his system of ideas as a whole. We have now learnt from the *Phenomenology* that Hegel sees all human history as the necessary path of the development of mind. The fact that he takes mind as the driving force of history indicates why he insists that our own desires, whether natural or socially conditioned, are a restriction on freedom. Freedom for Hegel is not freedom to do as we please: it consists in having a free mind. Mind must be in control of everything else, and must know that it is in control. This does not mean (as it did for Kant) that the non-intellectual side of nature is simply to be suppressed. Hegel gives our natural and socially conditioned desires their place, as he gives traditional political institutions their place; but it is always a place within a hierarchy ordered and controlled by mind.

The kind of freedom Hegel believes to be genuine is to be found, as we saw, in rational choice. Reason is the essential nature of the intellect. A free mind, unimpeded by coercion of any sort, will follow reason as easily as a river unimpeded by mountains or hills would flow directly to the sea. Anything that is an obstacle to reason is a limitation on the freedom of mind. Mind controls everything when everything is rationally ordered.

We also saw that Hegel regards reason as inherently universal. If reason is the essential medium of mind, it follows that mind is inherently universal. The particular minds of individual human beings are linked because they share a common universal reason. Hegel would put this even more strongly: the particular minds of individual human beings are aspects of something inherently universal, namely mind itself. The greatest obstacle to the rational ordering of the world is simply that individual human beings do not realise that their minds are part of this universal mind. Mind progresses towards freedom by chipping away at this obstacle. Remember how at the very beginning of the *Phenomenology* consciousness was limited to knowledge of the bare particular 'this', and was compelled to accept the universal terms implicit in language. From that point on, every step has been a step along a winding road that leads towards a mind closer to conceiving of itself as something both rational and universal. This is the road to freedom, because individual human minds cannot find freedom in rational choice when they are locked into conceptions of themselves that do not acknowledge the power of reason or its inherently universal nature.

Once this is understood, it is not difficult to see a connection between freedom and knowledge. All that needs to be said is that for human beings to be free, they must be fully aware of the rational and hence universal nature of their intellect. This self-awareness is absolute knowledge. As Hegel wrote in the *Philosophy of History*:

That the mind of the Egyptians presented itself to their consciousness in the form of a *problem* is evident from the celebrated inscription in the sanctuary of the Goddess Neith: '*I am that which is, that which was, and that which will be; no one has lifted my veil.*' ... In the Egyptian Neith, truth is still a problem. The Greek God Apollo is its solution; his utterance is: '*Man, know thyself.*' In this dictum is not intended a self-recognition that regards the specialities of one's own weaknesses and defects: it is not the individual that is admonished to become acquainted with his idiosyncrasy, but humanity *in general* is summoned to self-knowledge.

Humanity in general, Hegel could well have added, is at the same time summoned to freedom.

Absolute knowledge

We have seen that the goal of the *Phenomenology* is absolute knowledge, and that this is linked with the goal of history being the consciousness of freedom. Self-knowledge is both a form of knowledge and the basis of Hegel's conception of freedom. Why, though, does Hegel describe self-knowledge as 'absolute knowledge'? Should we not say that self-knowledge is part of knowledge, but by no means the whole of it? Psychology, after all, is only one science among many; and even if we add to it anthropology, biology, history, evolutionary theory, sociology and all the other sciences that can contribute to our knowledge of ourselves, there will be many areas of knowledge entirely outside this category or at best very remotely linked to it: geology, physics, astronomy and so on. Are these not also part of absolute knowledge?

There are two misconceptions in this objection. One is easy to clear up. By 'absolute knowledge' Hegel does not mean knowledge of everything. Absolute knowledge is knowledge of the world as it really is, in contrast to knowledge of mere appearances. To gain absolute knowledge we do not have to know all the facts it is possible to know. It is the job of scientists to learn more and more about the universe. Hegel's aim was the philosophical goal of showing how real knowledge is possible, not the scientist's aim of increasing the knowledge we have.

The second misconception can only be eliminated by an explanation of Hegel's position on the nature of ultimate reality. Hegel described himself as an 'absolute idealist'. 'Idealism' in philosophy does not mean what it means in ordinary language: it has nothing to do with having lofty ideals or striving to be morally perfect. The philosophical term should really be 'ideaism' rather than 'ideal-ism', for its sense is that it is *ideas*, or more broadly our minds, our thoughts, our consciousness, that constitute ultimate reality. The opposed view is materialism, which contends that ultimate reality is material, not mental. (Dualists believe that both mind and matter are real.)

Hegel believes, then, that the ultimate reality is mind, not matter. He also believes that the *Phenomenology* has led to this conclusion. From the stage of sense-certainty onwards, every attempt to gain knowledge of an objective reality independent of mind failed. The raw information received by the senses proved meaningless until it was brought under a conceptual system produced by consciousness. Consciousness had to shape the world intellectually, to classify and order it, before knowledge was possible. So-called 'material objects' turned out to be not things existing quite independently of consciousness, but constructs of consciousness, involving concepts like 'property' and 'substance'. At the level of self-consciousness, consciousness became aware of the laws of science as laws of its own creation, and so for the first time mind had itself as the object of its scrutiny. It was also at this stage that consciousness began to shape the world practically as well as intellectually, by taking material objects and working on them, fashioning them in accordance with its own images of how they should be. Self-consciousness then began to shape its social world too, a process culminating in the discovery that reason is sovereign over everything. In other words, although we set out merely to trace the path of mind as it comes to *know* reality, at the end of the road we find that we have been watching mind as it *constructs* reality.

Only on this conception of reality as the creation of mind can Hegel fulfil the undertaking he made in the introduction to the *Phenomenology*, to show that we can have genuine knowledge of reality. Remember how he poured scorn on all conceptions of knowledge as some kind of instrument for grasping reality, or as a medium through which we view reality. All these conceptions, he said, divide knowledge from reality. Kant, with his notion of the 'thing-in-itself' as for ever beyond knowledge, was obviously one of the targets of this criticism. In contrast, Hegel promised that the *Phenomenology* would reach a point 'where knowledge is no longer compelled to go beyond itself', where reality will no longer be an unknowable 'beyond', but instead mind will know reality directly and be at one with it. Now we can understand what all this meant: absolute knowledge is reached when mind realises that *what it seeks to know is itself.*

This point is the key to understanding the *Phenomenology*

as a whole. It is probably the most profound of all the ideas of Hegel that I am attempting to convey in this book, so let us go over it again.

Reality is constituted by mind. At first mind does not realise this. It sees reality as something independent of it, even as something hostile or alien to it. During this period mind is estranged or alienated from its own creation. It tries to obtain knowledge of reality, but this knowledge is not genuine knowledge because mind does not recognise reality for what it is, and so regards it as a mysterious thing beyond its grasp. Only when mind awakens to the fact that reality is its own creation can it give up this reaching after the 'beyond'. Then it understands that there is nothing beyond itself. Then it knows reality as directly and immediately as it knows itself. It is at one with it. As Hegel puts it in the concluding section of the *Phenomenology*, absolute knowledge is 'mind knowing itself in the shape of mind'.

Hegel has thus brought his gigantic work to a bold and brilliant conclusion. He has produced a startling solution to the fundamental problem of philosophy, and at the same time shown why history had to move along the paths it has in fact travelled. Whether his vast edifice stands solidly is another question; but even if it crumbles before our eyes, we cannot help admiring the breadth and originality of the design.

There is one feature of the design that your guide cannot resist pointing out. Ask yourself *when* absolute knowledge is achieved. The answer is, of course, that it is achieved as soon as mind understands that reality is its own creation and there is no 'beyond' for it to know. And when does this occur? Well, since this conception of reality is the upshot of Hegel's *Phenomenology*, it must occur when Hegel's own mind grasps the nature of the universe. On Hegel's view, mind comes to its final resting-place when he, Hegel, understands the nature of reality. There can scarcely be a more momentous conclusion to a work of philosophy. The closing pages of *The Phenomenology of Mind* are no mere *description* of the culmination of all human history: they *are* that culmination.

Two questions

So magnificent is Hegel's philosophical cheek that to question it seems petty. Nevertheless there are many questions that virtually ask themselves. I shall briefly consider two central ones.

The first concerns Hegel's idealism. We may admit that there can be no knowledge without an intellect that structures the raw information received by the senses. We may grant that human beings shape their world practically, as well as theoretically, by working on it. But even when all this and more is taken into account, there remains the stubborn conviction that there must still be *something* 'out there' independently of our experience of it. After all, to say that mind imposes its categories on the raw information it receives from the senses—on the 'this' that is immediately present to consciousness at the level of sense-certainty—is to presuppose that there is raw information coming from somewhere. Hegel can deny that this raw information amounts to knowledge, but he cannot deny that it suggests the existence of something outside mind itself. The same point holds even more obviously for the view that mind shapes the world practically by working upon it. Michelangelo may have thought of David, taken a lump of marble, and turned it into a statue that accorded with his thoughts; but he would not have got far if there had been no marble in the first place.

This line of thought (in the theoretical rather than the practical sphere) led Kant to postulate his unknowable 'thing-in-itself'. Hegel has made some acute criticisms of this idea, but has he really shown that we can do without it?

The second question also flows from Hegel's idealism. Some idealists are subjectivists. They maintain that what is ultimately real are one's *own* thoughts and sensations. Different minds may have different thoughts and sensations, and if they do, there is no possible way of judging the contents of one mind to be true and those of the other false—indeed on this view such classifications are meaningless, for they erroneously presuppose an objective reality beyond the thoughts and sensations of individual minds. Hegel rejects the view that there are countless different 'realities' corresponding to the countless different minds that exist. He calls his form of idealism *absolute idealism* to distinguish it from subjective idealism. For Hegel there is only one reality, because, ultimately, there is only one mind.

Now we have returned to the question with which our investigation of the *Phenomenology* began. If Hegel believes that there is only one mind, what on earth can he mean by 'mind'? He must mean some kind of collective or universal mind. In that case, would not 'spirit', with all its religious connotations, have been a better translation all along? Is not the idea of a collective mind fundamentally a religious idea? Should we not regard it as Hegel's conception of God?

Perhaps; but if we are in the end forced to this view, it will be with a better understanding of the ambiguities and uncertainties of Hegel's position than we would have had if we had opted for that translation from the start.

That there remain uncertainties about Hegel's conception of mind is undeniable. On the one hand, he needs the conception of a collective or universal mind not only to avoid a subjective form of idealism, but also to make good his vision of mind coming to see all of reality as its own creation. If there are millions of distinct individual minds, no single mind will be able to see much of reality as its own practical creation, for a large part of reality will consist of the practical creations of other minds. The manner in which mind conceives of the world before it has achieved absolute knowledge—as something independent of it and even hostile to it—will often prove to be no deception, but the literal truth. All this seems to force upon us an interpretation of Hegel that would understand his term 'mind' as some kind of cosmic consciousness; not, of course, a traditional conception of God as a being separate from the universe, but rather as something more akin to those Eastern philosophies which insist that All is One.

On the other hand Hegel regarded himself as a thorough-going defender of reason. Can we reconcile this with what he says, and needs to say, about mind? One way of doing so might be to take very seriously the extent to which Hegel believes consciousness to be necessarily social. From the first section of the *Phenomenology*, Hegel insists that knowledge is only knowledge if it can be communicated. The necessity of language rules out the idea of an entirely independent consciousness. As consciousness develops into self-consciousness, too, it must interact with other consciousnesses if it is to develop. In the end mind can only find freedom and self-understanding in a rationally organised community. So minds are not separate atoms, linked together by the accidents of association. Individual minds exist together, or they do not exist at all.

Hegel's social theory of mind is important, particularly for its influence on later thought, but it may not be enough to allow us to make sense of his idea of knowledge as mind at one with itself. There is still a second element to be drawn into service, however, and this is his idea of the universal nature of reason. We have already seen how Hegel regards reason as the essential principle of mind, and sees reason as essentially universal. He could therefore say: in so far as individual minds are truly mind—and not selfish or capricious desire—they really would all think and act in harmony with each other, they really would all recognise each other as having one and the same essential nature. This essential nature—this 'universal mind'—is neither an individual mind, nor a collective mind, but simply rational consciousness.

This may be an extreme and one-sided view of the nature of reason and of mind. It may be based, as I suggested his political philosophy might be based, on a misguided optimism about the possibility of harmony between human minds. It is not, however, a retreat into the mystical unity of a cosmic consciousness. Whether it is an accurate interpretation of the central message of the *Phenomenology* is another question.

5 *Logic and dialectics*

As I said in my preface, it is not my intention to give an exposition of Hegel's *Science of Logic*. On the other hand I do not wish to leave the reader with the mistaken impression that *the Logic* is an unimportant or peripheral work in the overall structure of Hegel's philosophy. I shall therefore say something about what Hegel set out to achieve in the *Logic*. In so doing I shall take the opportunity to explain that aspect of logic so frequently said to be Hegel's greatest discovery, the dialectical method.

Hegel's conception of logic

The goal of logic, Hegel tells us in the introduction to his *Science of Logic*, is truth. That is all very well, but what sort of truth? Hegel begins by referring to the traditional view of the subject, which begins with a separation between *form* and *content* and takes logic to be the study of the form of true or valid thought, irrespective of its content. Logic as usually conceived studies forms of argument like:

> Everything that is A is B
> *x* is A
> Therefore *x is* B

Here we have a form without content. We could write 'human', 'mortal' and 'Socrates' for A, B and *x* respectively; or we could write 'four-legged animal', 'furry' and 'my pet tortoise'. The argument is valid in either case, though where there is a false premise, the conclusion may also be false. Validity is a matter of form, not content. To the logician the content is of no interest.

It follows from this separation of form and content that logic tells us nothing about the actual world. The forms of argument which logic describes would be exactly as they are if humans were immortal, or if tortoises were furry. They would not change if there were no humans or tortoises at all.

If we recall how in the *Phenomenology* Hegel began to investigate the problem of knowledge by challenging the commonly assumed distinction between the knower and what is known, it should come as no surprise to learn that Hegel mentions this traditional distinction between form and content only in order to deny it. Logic, he says, is the study of thought; but in his *Phenomenology of Mind* he has already shown that there is no objective reality independent of thought. Thought is objective reality, and objective reality is thought. Therefore when logic studies thought, it must also be studying reality. 'If we wish still to employ the word *matter*', he says, rubbing the point home, the content of logic is 'the true genuine matter'. He goes on to provide us with some images of the subject-matter of logic. It is, he says, 'the truth as it is, without husk in and for itself', or, to put it another way: 'this content shows forth God as he is in his eternal essence before the creation of nature and of a finite mind'.

Walter Kaufmann calls this 'perhaps the maddest image in all of Hegel's writings', but what it suggests is not entirely unrelated to the traditional view that logic tells us nothing about the world. In saying that Logic is not about the world of nature and of finite minds, Hegel accepts part of the traditional view. The part he is most anxious to reject is the idea that reality, or truth, is to be found *only* in the world of nature and people. On the contrary, it follows from his absolute idealism that ultimate reality is to be found in what is mental or intellectual, not in what is material. It is to be found, to be specific, in rational thought. Logic is therefore the study of this ultimate reality in its pure form, abstracted from the particular forms it takes in the finite minds of human beings or in the natural world.

Hegel's view of mind as ultimate reality has a further consequence for the importance of logic. Since mind shapes the world, a study of rational thought will reveal the principles on which the world had been shaped. To put it in terms of Hegel's own image: to understand God's eternal essence before the creation of the world is to understand the basis on which the world was created.

The dialectical method

While working on a draft of *Capital* Marx wrote to Engels:

In the *method* of treatment the fact that by mere accident I again glanced through Hegel's *Logic* has been of great service to me . . . If there should ever be time for such work again, I would greatly like to make accessible to the ordinary human intelligence, in two or three printer's sheets, what is *rational* in the method which Hegel discovered but at the same time enveloped in mysticism . . .

The method Marx is referring to is of course the dialectical method, which Hegel describes as 'the only true method' of scholarly and scientific exposition. It is the method he uses in the *Logic* to uncover the form of pure thought.

Marx never found the time to write his explanation of what is rational in the dialectical method. Many others did, however, and they were by no means as brief as Marx had intended to be. Some of these commentators build up dialectics into an alternative to all previous forms of logic, something that supersedes such ordinary reasoning as the simple syllogistic form of argument set out on the first page of this chapter. There is nothing in Hegel to justify such extravagant claims for the dialectical method. Nor is there any need to treat the dialectical method, as others do, as something deep and mysterious. It is, Hegel says, a method with a 'simple rhythm'; to dance to it takes no great skill.

In our exposition of the *Phenomenology* we have in fact already been doing the dialectical two-step, for that work is, as Hegel tells us, 'an example of this method as applied to a more concrete object, namely consciousness'. No one but Hegel could think of consciousness as portrayed in the *Phenomenology* as a relatively concrete object. But more concrete examples of the dialectic are available in Hegel's later works, so for ease of exposition let us begin with an instance from the *Philosophy of History*.

In the *Philosophy of History*, one immense dialectical movement dominates world history from the Greek world to the present. Greece was a society based on customary morality, a harmonious society in which citizens identified themselves with the community and had no thought of acting in opposition to it. This customary community forms the starting-point of the dialectical movement, known in the jargon as the *thesis*.

The next stage is for this thesis to show itself to be inadequate or inconsistent. In the case of the community of ancient Greece, this inadequacy is revealed through the questioning of Socrates. The Greeks could not do without independent thought, but the independent thinker is the deadly foe of customary morality. The community based on custom thus collapses in the face of the principle of independent thought. It is now the turn of this principle to develop, which it does under Christianity. The Reformation brings acceptance of the supreme right of individual conscience. The harmony of the Greek community has been lost, but freedom is triumphant. This is the second stage of the dialectical movement. It is the opposite or negation of the first stage, and hence is known as the *antithesis*.

The second stage then also shows itself to be inadequate. Freedom, taken by itself, turns out to be too abstract and barren to serve as the basis for a society. Put into practice, the principle of absolute freedom turns into the Terror of the French Revolution. We can then see that both customary harmony and abstract freedom of the individual are one-sided. They must be brought together, unified in a manner that preserves them, and avoids their different forms of one-sidedness. This results in a third and more adequate stage, the *synthesis*. In the *Philosophy of History*, the synthesis in the overall dialectical movement is the German society of Hegel's time, which he saw as harmonious because it is an organic community, yet preserving individual freedom because it is rationally organised.

Every dialectical movement terminates with a synthesis, but not every synthesis brings the dialectical process to a stop in the way that Hegel thought the organic community of his own time brought the dialectical movement of history to an end. Often the synthesis, though adequately reconciling the previous thesis and antithesis, will turn out to be one-sided in some other respect. It will then serve as the thesis for a new dialectical movement, and so the process will continue. We saw this happen more than once in the *Phenomenology*. For example the section on consciousness concluded with the emergence of self-consciousness. Taking this as the thesis, we saw that self-consciousness needed some object from which to differentiate itself. The external object can be taken as the antithesis. This was unsatisfactory because the external object is something foreign or hostile to self-consciousness. The synthesis of these was desire, in which self-consciousness retains the external object, but makes it its own. The state of desire in turn proved (literally) unsatisfactory, and so we moved to an external object which was itself a self-consciousness. The second self-consciousness might be regarded as the antithesis of the first, and the synthesis of these two was a situation in which master was dominant over slave, thereby obtaining acknowledgement. This new synthesis proved no more lasting than its predecessors, for the slave ends up more independent and self-aware than the master. This antithesis found its synthesis in Stoicism, the philosophy of both master and slave . . . and so on.

In the *Logic* this same method is applied to the abstract categories in which we think. Hegel starts with the most indeterminate, contentless concept of all: being, or bare existence. Pure being, he says, is pure indeterminateness and vacuity. Pure being has in it no object for thought to grasp. It is entirely empty. In fact, it is nothing.

From this breathtaking beginning the dialectic of the *Logic* moves forward. The first thesis, *being*, has turned into its antithesis, *nothing*. Being and nothing are both opposites and the same; their truth, therefore, is this movement into and apart from each other—in other words, it is *becoming*.

So the dialectic leads on; but we shall not follow. We have seen enough to grasp the idea of the dialectical method. For Hegel it is a method of exposition, but it is a method that, Hegel says, 'is in no way different from its object and content—for it is the content in itself, *the dialectic which it has in itself*, that moves it on'. In the categories of our thought, in the development of consciousness, and in the progress of history, there are opposing elements which lead to the disintegration of what seemed stable, and the emergence of something new which reconciles the previously opposing elements but in turn develops its own internal tensions. This process is a necessary one, because neither thought nor consciousness can spring into existence in an adequate form. They can achieve adequacy only by the process of dialectical development. According to Hegel, the dialectic works as a method of exposition because the world works dialectically.

The absolute idea

Hegel's overriding aim in the *Logic* is straightforward: to demonstrate the necessity of absolute idealism. He seeks to do this by starting, as we have seen, from the bare concept of being, and showing that this concept leads by dialectical necessity to other concepts which more precisely and truly capture the nature of reality; and these other concepts in turn prove inadequate and require others, until finally we reach 'the absolute idea', of which Hegel says: 'Everything else is error and gloom, opinion, striving, caprice and transitoriness; the absolute idea alone is being, imperishable life, self-knowing truth, and the whole of truth.' The *Logic* thus parallels the *Phenomenology*, except that it moves in the realm of concepts instead of in the realm of consciousness. Accordingly it has as its goal not absolute knowledge, but the absolute idea itself. Whether it is successful in proving the necessity of absolute idealism is something I shall not consider here, but one would have to search hard to find a philosopher alive today who believes that Hegel succeeds.

So what is 'the absolute idea'? That is not an easy question to answer. Perhaps the best answer is: everything. That, however, is not tremendously enlightening, so I shall try to be more specific.

Hegel says that the absolute idea 'contains every determinateness'. By that he means that it includes within itself every determinate or distinct thing—every human being, every tree, every star, every mountain, every grain of sand. Nature and mind, he says, are different ways in which its existence is manifested: they are different forms of the absolute idea. Art and religion are different ways of comprehending the absolute idea; or, to put it exactly as Hegel does, art and religion are different ways in which the absolute idea comprehends *itself*. (That it is self-comprehension that is involved follows from the fact that human beings are part of the absolute idea.) Philosophy, too, is a way of comprehending the absolute idea, but it is a higher form than art or religion because it grasps it conceptually, and consequently understands not only its own form of comprehension, but the aesthetic and religious forms as well.

It is of the essence of the absolute idea to manifest itself in distinct, limited forms, and then to return to itself. Self-comprehension is the form in which it returns to itself. This is the process we observed in the *Philosophy of History* and the *Phenomenology*, and now observe in the *Logic*. Self-comprehension becomes an objective social form in the ideal State described in the *Philosophy of Right*. In the *Lectures on Aesthetics* and the *Lectures on the Philosophy of Religion*, Hegel assesses the adequacy of various forms of art and religion as modes of comprehending the absolute idea. On the surface or lurking beneath, the self-comprehension of the absolute is the dominant theme of all Hegel's philosophy.

I have said that for Hegel the absolute is everything. I have also said that it seeks to comprehend itself. So we return again to the question we left unresolved at the conclusion of our discussion of the *Phenomenology*: does Hegel really believe that the universe as a whole, and everything in it, forms some kind of conscious entity? Is the absolute idea God?

It is clear that Hegel, notwithstanding his Lutheranism, was no orthodox Christian theist. The message of the section of the *Phenomenology* on 'the unhappy consciousness' is frequently repeated elsewhere in his works. To regard God as something apart from the world is to alienate the soul of man. If God exists, he is in the world, and human beings partake of his nature.

Then is Hegel a pantheist, one who asserts that God is simply identical with the world? This interpretation would be consistent with some of the things he says, but in the *Lectures on the Philosophy of Religion* Hegel explicitly rejects it, denying even that anyone has ever claimed that 'all is God'. Certainly Hegel does not think that particular things and finite human beings are literally God.

Could Hegel be an atheist, perhaps? We have seen that he places philosophy above religion as a means of comprehending the absolute idea. The Italian philosopher Benedetto Croce described Hegel's philosophy as 'radically irreligious, because it is not content to oppose itself to religion or to range it alongside of itself, but it resolves religion into itself and substitutes itself for it'. Croce was right to point to this sense in which Hegel's philosophy, in refusing to yield pride of place to religion, is deeply irreligious; yet there is so much else in Hegel's thought that is recognisably in the religious mould. There are his images and metaphors, like the one he used to describe the nature of the *Logic*. There is his philosophy of history, which is intended to illustrate how history works towards its goal under the direction of mind. There is also his view of ultimate reality as being able to comprehend itself, which suggests that ultimate reality is personal. To portray Hegel as an atheist is to go against some of his most central ideas.

Not an orthodox theist, not a pantheist, not an atheist—what else is left? Some years ago a Hegel scholar named Robert

Whittemore argued that Hegel was a panentheist. The term comes from Greek words meaning 'all in God'; it describes the view that everything in the universe is part of God, but—and here it differs from pantheism—God is more than the universe, because he is the whole, and the whole is greater than the sum of all its parts. Just as a person is more than all the cells that make up his or her body—although the person is nothing separate from the body—so on this view God is more than all the parts of the universe, but not separate from it. Equally, just as no single cells amount to a person, so no individual parts of the universe amount to God.

Whittemore's interpretation is plausible, not only because it is consistent with what Hegel says specifically about God, but also because it makes sense of the dominant theme of his philosophy. If God is the absolute idea, the ultimate reality of the universe, the whole of its parts, we can understand why the absolute idea must manifest itself in the world, and there progress to self-comprehension. God needs the universe in the same way as a person needs a body.

The idea that God can lack anything is repugnant to most religious believers. That Hegel might be saying such a thing is, in their eyes, a reason for interpreting his philosophy as irreligious; but that is, I believe, a mistake. For Hegel sees God not as eternal and immutable, but as an essence that needs to manifest itself in the world, and, having made itself manifest, to perfect the world in order to perfect itself. It is a strange vision, but a powerful one. It is a vision that places immense weight on the necessity of progress: for the onward movement of history is the path God must take to achieve perfection. Therein may lie the secret of the immense influence that Hegel, for all his outward conservatism, has had on radical and revolutionary thinkers.

6 Aftermath

After Hegel's death, those who considered themselves his followers split into two camps. The orthodox or Right Hegelians followed in the style of Hegel's later years. They reconciled his religious views with Protestant Christianity, and accepted the generally positive view of the Prussian State expressed in the *Philosophy of Right*. This conservative school of Hegelianism produced no major thinkers, and after having for some years the status of a semi-official philosophy in Berlin, it went into so steep a decline that by the 1860s Hegel's philosophy was totally out of fashion in Germany.

The other camp was very different. It consisted of a group of young men with radical leanings. Their attitude to Hegel was like Hegel's attitude to Kant. Just as Hegel had seen Kant's doctrine of the thing-in-itself as a failure to carry through the radical implications of his philosophy, so these students of Hegel saw his acceptance of Christianity, the Prussian State, and the general conditions of their time as Hegel's failure to carry through the radical implications of *his* philosophy. This group became known as the Young Hegelians, or Left Hegelians. The future lay with them.

The Young Hegelians saw Hegel's philosophy as a demand for a better world, a world in which the opposition between individual and society would be overcome, a rationally organised world, a world of genuine freedom, in short a world fashioned to reflect the absolute supremacy of the human mind and its powers of reason. This better world was not, for the Young Hegelians, simply a Utopian ideal drawn up in a fanciful moment. It was the culmination of the historical and philosophical arguments of the Hegelian system. It was a dialectical necessity, a synthesis that would have to emerge to reconcile the conflicting elements of the world in which they lived.

Scorning the idea that Germany in the 1830s could be the fulfilment of the promise of Hegel's philosophy, the Young Hegelians set about finding ways of achieving their radical vision. At first they seized on religion as the crucial obstacle to a society that would allow human powers to reach their full potential. Developing the hints in the section of the *Phenomenology* on 'the unhappy consciousness', they argued that religion is a form of alienation. Man creates God, and then imagines that God has created him. Man puts into his image of God all that is best in himself: knowledge, goodness and power. Then man bows down before this image of his own making and sees himself, by comparison, as ignorant, sinful and weak. To restore human beings to their full powers, all that is needed is to make them realise that it is human beings who are truly the highest form of divinity.

To this end two Young Hegelians wrote books that had a tremendous impact on nineteenth-century thought about religion. David Friedrich Strauss wrote a brilliant *Life of Jesus* which, by treating the Gospels as source-materials open to historical criticism, set a model for all future study of the historical Jesus. Ludwig Feuerbach's *The Essence of Christianity* portrayed all traditional religion as man's projection of his own attributes into another sphere. It was thus the first modern attempt to develop a psychology of religious belief. Translated into English by Marian Evans (who also helped to translate Strauss, and is better known by her pseudonym George Eliot), the book had a world-wide impact at a time when Hegel's own writings were little known outside Germany.

The Young Hegelians then moved beyond religion. In a still more radical manner, Feuerbach turned Hegel's ideas against their author. He accused Hegel of having presented truths about the world in a mystified manner. Believing that mind is ultimately real, Hegel had seen the problem of disharmony in the world as a problem in the realm of thought, and so had believed that philosophy could solve it. Now Feuerbach inverted Hegel.

Being is not to be derived from thought, but thought from being. Man does not have his true basis in mind: mind has its true basis in man. Hegel's philosophy is itself a form of alienation, for it takes the essence of real, living people to be something—'mind itself'—outside themselves. We need neither theology nor philosophy, Feuerbach said, but a science which studies real people in their actual lives.

From here it is not far to the Young Hegelian through whose work elements of Hegel's thought were to have a lasting impact on the history of the world. Karl Marx came to the University of Berlin some six years after Hegel's death. He soon attached himself to the Young Hegelians and joined in the prevailing criticism of religion. When Feuerbach proclaimed the need to go beyond the realm of thought, Marx responded eagerly to the call. In his *Economic and Philosophical Manuscripts of 1844* Marx praised Hegel's *Phenomenology* for its account of alienation and of the importance of labour. He then developed his own view of labour under the capitalist system as the key form of alienation. To bring about the liberation of humanity, alienated labour must be abolished. To abolish alienated labour, Marx said, it is necessary to abolish private property and the wage system that goes with it: in other words, to institute communism.

In these youthful *Manuscripts* Marx describes communism in terms that all Hegelians would have found familiar:

Communism . . . is the genuine resolution of the antagonism between man and nature and between man and man; it is the true resolution of the conflict between existence and essence, objectification and self-affirmation, freedom and necessity, individual and species. It is the riddle of history solved and knows itself as this solution.

As he grew older Marx used less Hegelian terminology, but he never abandoned the vision of communism he had reached through his transformation of Hegel's philosophy.

It is entertaining, if fruitless, to speculate on what thinkers long dead would say if they could return to life and see what has happened to their ideas. Few of them could be as startled as Hegel would have been to see that the historical culmination of his philosophy has not been comprehension of the absolute idea, but a vision of a communist society that for more than a hundred years has inspired revolutionary movements around the world.

Notes on sources

Each chapter of this book, apart from the first and the last, deals with one of Hegel's works. Here I shall provide references for passages I have quoted from these works, and from other sources. In every case the edition used is the one cited in the list of further reading which follows these notes. Where I have used several quotations from a single passage, only the first is identified; the others will then have been taken from the same or a closely following page. I have provided references for summaries and paraphrases only if the original passage is likely to prove difficult to locate.

Chapter 1: Hegel's times and life

Page 115. Hegel's comments on the French Revolution are from his *Philosophy of History*, p. 447.

Page 119. Hegel's estimate of Kant's importance comes from the *Science of Logic*, vol. I, p. 44.

Page 122. The description of Hegel lecturing is by H. G. Hotho and can be found in Walter Kaufmann, *Hegel*, pp. 350–1. Kaufmann's book also contains other documentation for the details of Hegel's life.

Chapter 2: History with a purpose

Page 123. Engels praised Hegel's sense of history in the course of a review of Marx's *Contribution to the Critique of Political Economy*, available in K. Marx and F. Engels, *Selected Works* (Foreign Languages Publishing House, Moscow, 1951), vol. I, pp. 337–8.

Page 125. The famous sentence setting out the goal of history occurs on p. 19 of the *Philosophy of History*. China and India are said to be 'outside' history on p. 116, and Persia is put at the beginning of true history on p. 173.

Page 129. Hegel's discussion of Socrates is on pp. 269–70.

Page 130. The distinction between the Persian and Roman Empires is set out on p. 278.

Page 132. For Hegel's account of the special nature of Christianity, see p. 333.

Page 134. 'a long, eventful and terrible night' is on p. 411.

Page 134. The essential principle of the Reformation is on pp. 416–17.

Page 136. The passage on the French Revolution is from p. 447.

Chapter 3: Freedom and community

Page 139. Schopenhauer attacked Hegel in the preface to the second edition of his major work, *The World as Will and Idea*. The passage is quoted by Popper in *The Open Society and Its Enemies*, vol. II, p. 33. Popper's own estimate of Hegel's aim is on the preceding page.

Pages 140–1. Isaiah Berlin's 'Two Concepts of Liberty' is in his *Four Essays on Liberty* (Oxford University Press, London, 1969).

Page 141. Hegel's objection to the negative concept of freedom is in paragraph 15 of *The Philosophy of Right*.

Pages 143–4. The comments on 'comfort' are from an 'addition'—that is, remarks added to the text by Hegel's editors, using notes taken by students at Hegel's lectures—to paragraph 191.

Page 148. The remark on duty is from paragraph 149; the one on Kant is from the addition to paragraph 133.

Page 150. Bradley's description is to be found in his *Ethical Studies* (first published 1876; republished by Oxford University Press, Oxford, 1962), pp. 171–2. The passage is quoted by Richard Norman, *Hegel's Phenomenology*, pp. 84–5, and I have used his condensation of it.

Pages 152–3. For the view of town planning used here to illustrate Hegel's idea of rationality, see Jane Jacobs, *The Death and Life of Great American Cities* (Random House, New York, 1961).

Page 154. Hegel sets out the constitutional arrangements of his rational State in paragraphs 291–2.

Pages 156–7. For Hegel's views on freedom of expression, see paragraph 319; and on the jury system, 228. On the whole issue of the similarity between Hegel's State and the Prussian State of his time, see T. M. Knox, 'Hegel and Prussianism', in Walter Kaufmann (ed.), *Hegel's Political Philosophy*. This volume also contains a reply by E. F. Carritt.

Pages 157–8. Popper marshals his quotations from Hegel on p. 31 of *The Open Society and Its Enemies*, vol. II. This method of presenting Hegel's ideas is attacked by Walter Kaufmann in 'The Hegel Myth and Its Method', available in *Hegel's Political Philosophy* and in Alasdair MacIntyre (ed.), *Hegel*. Kaufmann also points out the mistranslation of the sentence about the State. The German reads: 'es ist der Gang Gottes in der Welt, dass der Staat ist'. The sentence occurs in the addition to paragraph 258.

Page 159. 'the right of subjective freedom . . .' is from paragraph 124, and 'What is of the utmost importance . . .' from the addition to 265. In paragraph 215 Hegel insists that laws are not binding unless universally known.

Page 159. His attack on von Haller is the subject of a lengthy footnote to paragraph 258.

Chapter 4: The odyssey of mind

Page 165. Marx's reference to the *Phenomenology* is in his *Economic and Philosophical Manuscripts of 1844*, in D. McLellan (ed.), *Karl Marx: Selected Writings* (Oxford University Press, Oxford, 1977), p. 98.

Pages 165–6. The passages quoted here are from Hegel's introduction to *The Phenomenology of Mind*, pp. 131ff.

Page 168. The passage on Kant is from the section of the *Encyclopedia* on logic, published in English under the title *The Logic of Hegel*, paragraph 10. The passage is quoted by Norman, *Hegel's Phenomenology*, p. 11.

Pages 171–2. For Hegel's view of proper names, see his *Science of Logic*, vol. I, pp. 104–5. The view is referred to by Ivan Soll, *An Introduction to Hegel's Metaphysics*, p. 97.

Page 172. The statement that what cannot be reached by language is untrue is from the *Phenomenology*, p. 160. For the various meanings of 'meinen', which I have translated as 'believed' in the sentence quoted, see Soll, *An Introduction to Hegel's Metaphysics*, p. 102.

Page 180. For Marx's theory of alienated labour, see the section so titled in the *Economic and Philosophical Manuscripts of 1844*.

Page 181. 'In thinking I am free . . .' is on p. 243 of the *Phenomenology*.

Page 187. The passage quoted is from p. 220 of the *Philosophy of History*.

Page 190. 'Mind knowing itself . . .' is from the *Phenomenology*, p. 798.

Chapter 5: Logic and dialectics

Page 195. The metaphorical descriptions of the subject-matter of *The Science of Logic* are from that work, vol. I, p. 60. Kaufmann refers to Hegel's image on p. 195 of his *Hegel*.

Page 196. Marx's acknowledgement of the usefulness of the method of the *Logic* is quoted from a letter he wrote to Engels in 1858, reprinted in D. McLellan, *The Thought of Karl Marx* (Macmillan, London, 1971), p. 135. See also Marx's comments in the 'Afterword' to the second German edition of *Capital*: K. Marx, *Capital*, vol. I (Foreign Languages Publishing House, Moscow, 1961), pp. 19–20. A 'simple rhythm' is from the *Science of Logic*, vol. I, p. 65.

Page 201. Hegel's rejection of pantheism is to be found on p. 97 of the first volume of the *Lecture on the Philosophy of Religion*.

Page 201. Benedetto Croce's description of Hegel as 'radically irreligious' is from *What is Living and What is Dead in the Philosophy of Hegel?*, pp. 70–1. Robert Whittemore's 'Hegel as Pantheist' appeared in *Tulane Studies in Philosophy*, vol. IX (1960), pp. 134–64.

Further reading

Hegel's works

The standard German edition of Hegel's collected works is the twenty-volume Jubilee Edition, edited by H. Glockner and published in Stuttgart from 1927–30. For the English-speaking reader wondering where to begin reading Hegel's own works, I would recommend following the order of the works discussed in this book. English translations of these works are:

Lectures on the Philosophy of History, tr. J. Sibree (Dover, New York, 1956). The Introduction to these lectures is available separately, as *Reason in History: A General Introduction to the Philosophy of History*, tr. R. S. Hartman (Library of Liberal Arts, New York, 1953), and as *Lectures on the Philosophy of World History, Introduction: Reason in History*, tr. H. B. Nisbet (Cambridge University Press, Cambridge, 1975). The latter edition contains additional scholarly material.

Hegel's Philosophy of Right, tr. T. M. Knox (Oxford University Press, London, 1967).

The Phenomenology of Mind, tr. J. B. Baillie (Harper & Row, New York, 1967). There is also a more recent and, in the view of many, more reliable translation by A. V. Miller, entitled *Hegel's Phenomenology of Spirit* (Oxford University Press, Oxford, 1977).

Hegel's Science of Logic, tr. W. H. Johnston and L. G. Struthers in two volumes (Allen & Unwin, London, 1929); also more recently translated by A. V. Miller (Allen & Unwin, London, 1969).

Probably the most important of Hegel's other works is his *Encyclopedia of the Philosophical Sciences*. This work has been published in English in its separate components. The section on logic, sometimes called the 'Lesser Logic', was translated by W. Wallace and published under the confusing title *The Logic of Hegel* (Clarendon Press, Oxford, 1874). There is now a new edition, with a foreword by J. N. Findlay (Clarendon Press, Oxford, 1975). The second part is available as *Hegel's Philosophy of Nature*, tr. A. V. Miller

(Clarendon Press, Oxford, 1970) and also in a translation by M. J. Petry (Allen & Unwin, London, 1970). Wallace's original translation of *Hegel's Philosophy of Mind* (Clarendon Press, Oxford, 1894) has been republished, together with additional material translated by A. V. Miller (Clarendon Press, Oxford, 1971).

English translations of Hegel's other writings are:

Early Theological Writings, tr. T. M. Knox (University of Chicago Press, Chicago, 1948). This volume contains the earliest of Hegel's surviving works.

Hegel's Political Writings, tr. T. M. Knox (Clarendon Press, Oxford, 1964). Hegel's occasional political essays, such as that on the English Reform Bill, are collected here.

Lectures on the Philosophy of Religion, tr. E. B. Speirs and J. B. Sanderson, in three volumes (Routledge & Kegan Paul, London, 1968).

Hegel's Aesthetics, tr. T. M. Knox, in two volumes (Clarendon Press, Oxford, 1975).

Lectures on the History of Philosophy, tr. E. S. Haldane and F. H. Simson, in three volumes (Routledge & Kegan Paul, London, 1955).

Books about Hegel

For readers wishing for further guidance I would recommend Richard Norman's slim and stimulating volume, *Hegel's Phenomenology: A Philosophical Introduction* (Sussex University Press, Brighton, 1976). Next could come Ivan Soll, *An Introduction to Hegel's Metaphysics* (University of Chicago Press, Chicago, 1969). After that one might move on to the shorter of Charles Taylor's two books on Hegel, *Hegel and Modern Society* (Cambridge University Press, Cambridge, 1979), or, if one is ready for it, to the much longer and more difficult *Hegel* (Cambridge University Press, Cambridge, 1975). For a detailed study of Hegel's *Phenomenology*, see Robert Solomon, *In the Spirit of Hegel: A Study of Hegel's Phenomenology* (Oxford University Press, New York, 1983).

Older, but still useful works are: Edward Caird, *Hegel* (Blackwood, Edinburgh, 1901); Benedetto Croce, *What is Living and What is Dead in the Philosophy of Hegel?*, tr. D. Ainslie

(Russell & Russell, New York, 1969); W. T. Stace, *The Philosophy of Hegel* (Dover, New York, 1955); and J. N. Findlay, *Hegel: A Re-examination* (Allen & Unwin, London, 1958).

Information on Hegel's life, together with translations of many letters and other documents, can be found in Walter Kaufmann, *Hegel* (Weidenfeld & Nicolson, London, 1965). *Hegel's Development* by H. S. Harris (Clarendon Press, Oxford, 1972) is the best study of Hegel's early years. The influential work by George Lukacs, *The Young Hegel*, is now available in an English translation by R. Livingstone (Merlin Press, London, 1975).

Several interesting books have been written specifically on Hegel's social and political ideas. These include: Herbert Marcuse, *Reason and Revolution* (Humanities Press, New York, 1954); Shlomo Avineri, *Hegel's Theory of the Modern State* (Cambridge University Press, Cambridge, 1972); Raymond Plant, *Hegel* (Allen & Unwin, London, 1973); and Judith Shklar, *Freedom and Independence: a Study of the Political Ideas of Hegel's 'Phenomenology of Mind'* (Cambridge University Press, Cambridge, 1976). Some heated exchanges over the extent to which Hegel's philosophy supports the authoritarian State have been collected by Walter Kaufmann in a volume entitled *Hegel's Political Philosophy* (Atherton Press, New York, 1970). There is also a collection of articles edited by Z. Pelczynski, entitled *Hegel's Political Philosophy* (Cambridge University Press, Cambridge, 1971). Together with this one might read—though with considerable caution—Karl Popper's provocative attempt to find the origins of totalitarianism in Hegel's thought: see *The Open Society and Its Enemies*, vol. II, chapter 12 (Routledge & Kegan Paul, London, 1966).

For further study of the religious aspect of Hegel's thought, see Emil Fackenheim, *The Religious Dimension of Hegel's Thought* (Indiana University Press, Bloomington, 1967), and Bernard Reardon, *Hegel's Philosophy of Religion* (Macmillan, London, 1977). See also Robert C. Whittemore's article, 'Hegel as Panentheist' in *Tulane Studies in Philosophy*, vol. IX (1960), pp. 134–64. This volume is a special issue on Hegel.

There are innumerable scholarly articles on Hegel in the philosophical journals. Some of the best have been collected in Alasdair MacIntyre (ed.), *Hegel: A Collection of Critical Essays* (Anchor, New York, 1972).

Finally, the various transformations of Hegel's thought by the Young Hegelians are well described in Sidney Hook, *From Hegel to Marx* (Humanities Press, New York, 1958), and also in David McLellan, *The Young Hegelians and Karl Marx* (Macmillan, London, 1969).

Schopenhauer

Christopher Janaway

Preface

The status of Schopenhauer's work is somewhat enigmatic. He is recognized as a profound and erudite thinker, but he is not what one would call a philosopher's philosopher. Philosophical specialists may enjoy his marvellous style and find his ideas provocative, but they do not usually model themselves on him: to someone schooled on Kant or Aristotle, he is apt to come over as too wayward and too 'literary'. Yet philosophy is what he is doing, with few concessions, and many readers he has inspired have regarded him as the paradigm of the deep, difficult metaphysician. It is a pity if the general or literary reader rejects him because he is too philosophical; and if the philosopher rejects him because he does not appeal only to philosophers, that is simply foolish. Although the chief drawback with Schopenhauer is that his 'system' seems to collapse under even the gentlest analytical probing, our loss is great if we let that blind us to his strengths. At his best, Schopenhauer displays a gift for cogent and lucid debate, and for exposing the flaws of his predecessors. But what should also earn our respect is Schopenhauer's lack of complacency. He does not play safe, but risks confrontation with problems that ought to make us feel insecure. He asks what the self is, and can give no easy reply. He presses on into the greatest insecurity, asking what value one's existence may have—and his conclusion here is even less comfortable. Within the classical restraint of his prose, he faces up to these concerns both as a philosopher and with all the resources of his personality. If we can bring back into a single focus the genuine, probing philosopher and the imagination that excited Wagner, Hardy, and Proust, along with many others, then we shall be seeing Schopenhauer in his true light.

I would like to thank John Atwell, David Berman, Anthony Grayling, and Fiona Janaway for their helpful comments on an earlier draft of this book, many of which I have heeded. Thanks also to Catherine Clarke and a reader for Oxford University Press for their assistance with the final version.

C. J.

Contents

Abbreviations and works cited

Schopenhauer's works are referred to as follows, in translations by E. F. J. Payne, unless otherwise stated. Some very minor changes are made to some quoted passages.

B	*On the Basis of Morality* (1841; Indianapolis/New York, 1965).
F	*On the Freedom of the Will* (1841), trans. K. Kolenda (Oxford, 1985).
M1–M4	*Manuscript Remains*, vols. 1–4, ed. A. Hübscher (Oxford/New York/Hamburg, 1988–90).
N	*On the Will in Nature* (1836; New York/Oxford, 1992).
P1, P2	*Parerga and Paralipomena*, vols. 1 & 2 (1851; Oxford, 1974).
R	*The Fourfold Root of the Principle of Sufficient Reason* (1813, 1847; La Salle, Illinois, 1974).
W1, W2	*The World as Will and Representation*, vols. 1 & 2 (1819, 1844; New York, 1969).

1   *Schopenhauer's life and works*

Arthur Schopenhauer was born in 1788 in Danzig, and died in Frankfurt am Main in 1860. There are a number of photographs taken during the last decade of his life, from which we derive our most immediate sense of the man. He looks unconventional and grimly determined, but the sparkle in his eye is that of someone vigilant, incisive, and capable of mischief—not altogether different from the persona which emerges from his writings. At the end of his life Schopenhauer was just beginning to enjoy a measure of fame. His philosophy, however, is not a product of old or middle age. Although most of the words which he published were written after he settled in Frankfurt at the age of 45, it was in the years between 1810 and 1818 that he had produced the entire philosophical system for which he became celebrated. As Nietzsche later wrote, we should remember that it was the creative, rebellious energy of a man in his twenties which produced *The World as Will and Representation*. The mature Schopenhauer occupied himself in consolidating and supplementing the position he had presented in this masterpiece, which was, until very near the end of his life, neglected by the intellectual world.

Independence of spirit is the trait most characteristic of Schopenhauer. He writes fearlessly with little respect for authority, and detests the hollow conformism which he finds in the German academic establishment. But behind this is the significant fact that he was also financially independent. When he came of age in 1809, he inherited wealth which, with astute management, was sufficient to see him through the rest of his life. His father, Heinrich Floris Schopenhauer, had been one of the wealthiest businessmen in Danzig at the time of Arthur's birth. A cosmopolitan man, committed to the liberal values of the Enlightenment and to republicanism, he left Danzig when it was annexed by Prussia, and moved to the free city of Hamburg. Arthur had in common with his father a love of French and English culture and a horror of Prussian nationalism. The name 'Arthur' was chosen because it was shared by several European languages—though the intention here was chiefly to fit the infant for his envisaged career in pan-European commerce. Later Arthur felt he had also inherited his father's intense, obsessive personality. His father's death in 1805, probably by suicide, was a great blow to him.

Schopenhauer received a broad and enriching education in school, enhanced by the travel and social contacts that his wealthy family made possible. Sent to France at the age of 9 when his sister was born, he acquired fluent French. After some years of schooling, at the age of 15 he embarked with his parents on a two-year trip to Holland, England, France, Switzerland, and Austria. He saw many of the famous sights of the day, and at times was deeply affected by the poverty and suffering he witnessed. While his parents toured Britain, however, he was consigned to a boarding-school in Wimbledon, whose narrow, disciplinarian, religious outlook (a marked contrast to the education he had hitherto received) made a negative impression that was to last. This episode says much about Schopenhauer's character and upbringing. He was a seething, belligerent pupil who would not submit to the stultifying practices that surrounded him, and he seems quite isolated in his defiance. His parents wrote to him, his father niggling about his handwriting, his mother gushing about the wonderful time they were having and pleading with him to take a more reasonable attitude, but neither showed much inclination to see things from his point of view. It is tempting to view the situation as a microcosm of his later life. As his life progressed, it became clearer that it would not be constructed around close relationships with others. He began to see company as like a fire 'at which the prudent man warms himself at a distance' (M1, 123), and resolved to be lonely even when with others, for fear of losing his own integrity. He later wrote that five-sixths of human beings were worth only contempt, but equally saw that there were inner obstacles to human contact: 'Nature has done more than is necessary to isolate my heart, in that she endowed it with suspicion, sensitiveness, vehemence and pride' (*M4*, 506). He was prone to depression, and confessed 'I always have an anxious concern that causes me to see and look for dangers where none exist' (*M4*, 507).

Some writers on Schopenhauer's personality have looked to his relationships with his parents, and what they have found is not surprising. His father was an anxious, exacting, and formidable man, very ambitious for his son. Johanna Schopenhauer, née Trosiener, also from a successful business family in Danzig, was quite different. A lively, sociable person, she had literary aspirations which culminated in a career as a romantic novelist, making her during her lifetime more famous than her son. She was a significant force in his life, but relations between them were never warm. In her marriage too, as she herself wrote, she saw no need to 'feign ardent love' for her husband, adding that he did not expect it. After Heinrich Schopenhauer died, the independently minded Johanna was free to embark on her own career, and moved to Weimar, where she established an artistic and intellectual salon frequented by many of the luminaries of the day. Arthur benefited from some of the relationships he established in this circle, notably with Goethe, and with the oriental scholar Friedrich Majer, who stimulated in him a life-long interest in Indian thought. However, his relationship with his mother became stormy, and in 1814 she threw him out for good, never to see him again.

By the time this happened Schopenhauer had abandoned the career in business which his father had projected for him, and had found his way into the life of learning. In 1809 he went to the University at Göttingen, from where he was to move on to Berlin two years later. He attended lectures on a variety of scientific subjects, having originally intended to study medicine; but he soon gravitated towards philosophy. The Göttingen philosopher G. E. Schulze played a decisive role in

Schopenhauer's career when he advised him to begin by reading the works of Plato and Kant. Though Schopenhauer was, by any standards, a widely read and scholarly thinker, it is fair to say that his reading of these two philosophers provoked in him the fundamental ideas that shaped his philosophy from then on. The Hindu Upanishads, which he learned of through Friedrich Majer, were the third ingredient which he later blended with Platonic and Kantian elements to make something quite original in *The World as Will and Representation*.

When he moved to Berlin, Schopenhauer heard lectures by Schleiermacher and Fichte, two of the philosophical heavyweights of the day, though, true to form, he was fairly contemptuous of them, and certainly did not seem to think he was there to absorb what they had to say. His lecture notes and marginal annotations to the books he was reading (preserved in the *Manuscript Remains*) show him keen to object and debate, and, for a young student, he reacts with an almost uncanny sureness of his own position. This too is a pattern that was not to vary greatly. Schopenhauer did not learn in association with others, by exchanging ideas and submitting himself to scrutiny. He learned, and wrote, by relying on his own judgement and treating other people's ideas as raw material to be hammered into the shape he wanted. What he could not use he sometimes decried as rubbish, with a witty style of mockery that usually succeeds in keeping the reader on his side. Schopenhauer would have made far less of himself without such single-minded determination, but the same feature has its compensating weakness: it can be a virtue for a philosopher to exhibit more give and take, more sense of dialogue and self-criticism, than Schopenhauer sometimes does.

When Schopenhauer was ready to write his doctoral thesis, in 1813, war broke out. Schopenhauer had an aversion to fighting, and even more of an aversion to fighting on the Prussian side against the French. He fled south to Rudolstadt near Weimar and there completed his first work, *On the Fourfold Root of the Principle of Sufficient Reason*, which gained him his doctorate at Jena, and was published in an edition of 500 copies in the same year. The book takes a stock academic topic, the principle of sufficient reason (which says that, for everything that is, there must be a ground or reason why it is), lays out concisely the ways in which it has been dealt with in the history of philosophy, then proceeds to a four-part explanation of the different kinds of reason. The systematic framework is derived from Kant, whose thought Schopenhauer has clearly assimilated, though not uncritically. There are enough twists to make this the beginning of something new, and more than a hint of what is to come in his major work. Schopenhauer always considered *The Fourfold Root* essential to understanding his thought, and undertook a revision of it for re-publication in 1847.

Another early publication is the essay *On Vision and Colours*, of 1816. This short book is a product of his involvement with Goethe, whose anti-Newtonian theory of colours had been published at the beginning of the decade. In discussing this theory, Schopenhauer and Goethe came to know each other quite well. Schopenhauer did not regard it as a central project of his own, but understandably did not turn down the invitation to work with one of the greatest men he was ever likely to meet. Goethe, forty years his senior, recognized the rigour of Schopenhauer's mind, and regarded him as someone with great potential, but was less concerned to foster his talent than to receive help in his own intellectual endeavours. The brief period in which they worked together is the one exceptional collaboration in Schopenhauer's career—but still he did not have it in him to become anyone's disciple. His own work *On Vision and Colours* diverged somewhat from Goethe's thinking, and he did not disguise the fact that he thought it superior. The partnership tailed off, Schopenhauer disappointed, though not crushed, by Goethe's lukewarm response. He later sent Goethe a copy of *The World as Will and Representation*, and had an apparently cordial meeting with him in 1819. But by now the two had parted company. As Goethe was to say, they were like two people who eventually shook hands, one turning to go south, the other north.

Schopenhauer's true destination is revealed in Volume I of *The World as Will and Representation*, which he completed in Dresden and published in 1818, although 1819 is the date that stands on the title-page. The dispassionate, Kantian exercise which Schopenhauer carried out in *The Fourfold Root* of 1813 did not reveal the driving force of his philosophy. It did not address questions concerning suffering and salvation, ethics and art, sexuality, death, and the meaning of life, but it was in these areas that his preoccupations already lay. The collected *Manuscript Remains* show Schopenhauer's greatest book in a process of composition over a period of almost ten years. Adapting the thought of both Plato and Kant, he had become convinced that there was a split between ordinary consciousness and a higher or 'better' state in which the human mind could pierce beyond mere appearances to a knowledge of something more real. The thought had aesthetic and religious overtones: Schopenhauer wrote of both the artist and the 'saint' as possessing this 'better consciousness'—though it should be said straightaway that his philosophical system is atheist through and through. He also struck one of the keynotes of pessimism, saying that the life of ordinary experience, in which we strive and desire and suffer, is something from which to be liberated. Such thoughts were well established in Schopenhauer's mind by 1813.

The idea which allowed his monumental book to take shape was his conception of the will. In the finished work, as its title indicates, Schopenhauer presents the world as having two sides, that of *Vorstellung* (representation), or the way things present themselves to us in experience, and that of *Wille* (will), which is, he argues, what the world is *in itself*, beyond the mere appearances to which human knowledge is limited. The will is not easy to define. It is, to begin with, easier to say what it is not. It is not any kind of mind or consciousness, nor does it direct things to any rational purpose (otherwise 'will' would be another name for God). Schopenhauer's world is purposeless. His notion of will is probably best captured by the notion of *striving towards* something, provided one remembers that the will is fundamentally 'blind', and found in forces of nature which are without consciousness at all. Most importantly, the human psyche can be seen as split: comprising not only capacities for understanding and rational thought, but at a deeper level an essentially 'blind' process of striving, which governs, but can also conflict with, the conscious portions of our nature. Humanity is poised between the life of an organism driven to survival and reproduction, and that of a pure intellect that can rebel against its nature and aspire to a timeless contemplation of a 'higher' reality. Though he does still envisage a kind of resigned 'salvation', Schopenhauer thinks ordinary existence must involve the dual miseries of pain and boredom, insisting that it is in the very essence of humanity, indeed of the world as a whole, that it should be so.

Many have found Schopenhauer's philosophy impossible to accept as a single, consistent metaphysical scheme. But it does have great strength and coherence as a narrative and in the dynamic interplay between its different conceptions of the world and the self. What is set down at the beginning should be treated not so much as a foundation for everything that is to come, but as a first idea which will be revealed as inadequate by a second that seems to undermine it, only to re-assert itself in transformed guise later on. There is a superficial resemblance here to the method of his contemporary Hegel, though everything to do with Hegel was anathema to Schopenhauer, and in other respects they could hardly differ more as writers. Thomas Mann likened Schopenhauer's book to a great symphony in four movements, and it is helpful to approach it in something of this spirit, seeking contrasts of mood and unities of theme amid a wealth of variations. Certainly there have been few philosophers who have equalled Schopenhauer's grasp of literary architecture and pacing, and few whose prose style is so eloquent.

For all this, the great work went virtually unnoticed for many years after its publication. Schopenhauer was embittered, but he was not one to think that the world was right and he was wrong; he continued throughout his life to believe in the supreme value of his work. In 1820 he was awarded the right to lecture at the University in Berlin, after speaking before a gathering of the faculty chaired by Hegel, the professor of philosophy. Schopenhauer duly presented himself to lecture, under the stunning title 'The whole of philosophy, i.e. the theory of the essence of the world and of the human mind.' But he had chosen to speak at the same time as Hegel. Two hundred attended the lecture of the professor, who was at the peak of his career, and the unknown Schopenhauer was left with a pitiful few. His name was on the lecture-schedule in later years, but he never returned to repeat the experience, and this was the end of his lecturing career. Hegel was the epitome of everything that Schopenhauer disliked in philosophy. He was a career academic, who made use of the institutional authority which Schopenhauer held in contempt. He upheld the Church and the State, for which Schopenhauer, an atheist and an individualist, had no time. Although thoroughly conservative himself, Schopenhauer regarded the political state merely as a convenient means for protecting property and curbing the excesses of egoism; he could not stomach Hegel's representation of the state as 'the whole aim of human existence' (*P1*, 147). Hegel was also an appalling stylist, who seemed to build abstraction upon abstraction without the breath of fresh air provided by common-sense experience, and Schopenhauer—not alone in this—found his writing pompous and obscurantist, even dishonest. The emblem at the head of Hegelian university philosophy, he says, should be 'a cuttle-fish creating a cloud of obscurity around itself so that no one sees what it is, with the legend, *mea caligine tutus* (fortified by my own obscurity)' (*N*, 24). It is not true to say that Schopenhauer's philosophy was based on opposition to Hegel—Hegel was far from his mind as he created his major work—but Hegel's triumphant success, coupled with his own continuing lack of recognition, nevertheless produced in him a rancour which dominated much of his subsequent career.

During the 1820s Schopenhauer was at his least productive. He travelled to Italy, suffered during and after his return journey from serious illness and depression, and continued an affair with Caroline Richter, a chorus girl at the National Theatre in Berlin. He planned a number of writing projects, such as translations of Hume's works on religion and of Sterne's *Tristram Shandy,* but nothing came of them. His notebooks were full, sometimes with invective against Hegelianism which he reworked for inclusion in later works, but he completed no more publications while in Berlin. It is especially sad that the English publisher he approached about translating Kant's *Critique of Pure Reason* and other works should have turned him down. Schopenhauer's English was good, his feel for literary form superb, and his knowledge of Kant's work intimate. One can only speculate how the history of ideas would have been affected had he succeeded in making Kant more accessible to the English-speaking world at this comparatively early date. (By contrast, a result of his scholarship to which we are indebted is the rediscovery of the first edition of the *Critique,* which was re-published in 1838 partly thanks to his efforts.)

In 1831 cholera reached Berlin, apparently claiming Hegel among its victims, and Schopenhauer left the city. After some indecision he settled in Frankfurt, where he was to continue living an outwardly uneventful life, balanced between writing and recreation—theatre, opera, walking, playing the flute, dining out, and reading *The Times* in the town's library. Now he was able to produce more books. In 1836 he published *On the Will in Nature,* which was designed to support his doctrine of the will by putting forward corroborative scientific evidence from independent sources. It is still a work of interest, although arguably it does not stand very well on its own apart from *The World as Will and Representation.* However, in 1838 and 1839 Schopenhauer entered for two essay competitions set by the Norwegian Royal Scientific Society and its Danish counterpart, and the two occasions produced a pair of fine self-standing essays, *On the Freedom of the Will* and *On the Basis of Morality,* which were published together in 1841 under the title *The Two Fundamental Problems of Ethics.* In terms of doctrine these pieces are not radical departures from his earlier work, but both are well-constructed and persuasive pieces in which local parts of the grand design are presented with clarity. They can readily be recommended to a student of ethics today. In the essay on freedom Schopenhauer presents a convincing case for determinism, only to say, as some more recent philosophers have, that the deeper issues of freedom and responsibility are scarcely resolved thereby. This essay was rewarded with a gold medal by the Norwegians.

The second essay, part of which is a thorough criticism of Kant's ethics, suffered a different fate in Denmark: despite its being the only entry, the Royal Society refused to award it a prize. It had not, they judged, successfully answered the question set—and they took exception to the 'unseemly' manner in which a number of recent philosophers of distinction had been referred to. Who did they mean, asked Schopenhauer in his Preface to the essays: Fichte and Hegel! Are these men the *summi philosophi* one is not allowed to insult? It is true that Schopenhauer had not been playing the conventional game of academic politeness, but now he seizes the chance to let rip with all the means at his command. He produces an escalating series of allegations about the emptiness and confusion of Hegel's philosophy, throwing in a picturesque quote from Homer about the chimaera which is a compound of many beasts, and ending

Further, if I were to say that this *summus philosophus* of the Danish Academy scribbled nonsense quite unlike any mortal before him, so that whoever could read his most eulogized work, the so-called *Phenomenology of Mind*, without feeling as if he were in a madhouse, would qualify as an inmate for Bedlam, I should be no less right. (*B*, 16)

In 1844 a second volume of *The World as Will and Representation* was published along with a new edition of the first volume. Schopenhauer was wise in not trying to re-write his youthful work. What he provides instead is a substantial elaboration of the original, clarifying and extending it with the benefit of mature reflection. The second volume is actually longer than the first, and the two combine well to produce a single work. They were published together again in a third edition in 1859, the year before he died. Schopenhauer's final new publication was another two-volume book, entitled *Parerga and Paralipomena*, which appeared in 1851. The imposing title means 'complementary works and matters omitted', and the contents range from extended philosophical essays to the more popular 'Aphorisms on the Wisdom of Life' which have often been published separately. Somewhat strangely, it was this late work, which was reviewed favourably first in England, that led to Schopenhauer's becoming well known. There was demand for new editions of his writings, and he even became a topic for German university courses. He received many visitors, and much correspondence, including the complete libretto of the *Ring of the Nibelung* from an ardent fan, Richard Wagner, of whose music, incidentally, he did not think very highly. In the first fifty years after his death Schopenhauer was to become one of the most influential writers of Europe. Though he made no claim to be a poet, the verses which came to stand at the very end of *Parerga and Paralipomena* (*P2*, 658) are no doubt an honest reflection of what he felt in his last years:

1856

Finale

> I now stand weary at the end of the road;
> The jaded brow can hardly bear the laurel.
> And yet I gladly see what I have done,
> Ever undaunted by what others say.

2 *Within and beyond appearance*

Appearance and thing in itself

Schopenhauer's philosophical thinking is easiest to grasp if one first sees the backbone that runs right through it. This is the distinction, which he found in Kant, between appearance and thing in itself. The world of appearance consists of things as we know them by the ordinary means of sense experience and scientific investigation, in other words, the empirical world. Appearance is not to be understood as straightforward illusion; the things that meet us in our empirical knowledge are not hallucinations, but, to use the Greek word for appearances, they are the phenomena that make up the world. However, there is still the question whether the whole world consists only of these phenomena. Should we regard 'what there is' as being exhausted by our empirical knowledge? We can at least conceive of a reality independent of what we could experience, and this is what Kant meant by talking of things 'in themselves'.

Kant's achievement was to show that knowledge was limited: we could never know how the world was in itself, only how it could appear to us, as scientists or ordinary perceivers. The pretensions of traditional metaphysicians to know about God, the immortality of the soul, or a supernatural order pervading the whole universe, were therefore doomed. According to Schopenhauer's assessment (in his 'Critique of the Kantian Philosophy' (Appendix to *W1*, 417–25)), Kant had added to this destructive achievement two others that were more positive. The first was the idea that the world of appearance had fundamental and necessary organizing principles which could be discovered. The second was the view that ethics could be separated off from the sphere of appearance, and was not knowledge in the way that science was: when considering ourselves as beings who must act and judge things to be right or wrong, we were not dealing with how matters lay in the empirical world.

First, let us take the idea that appearance, the world as we know it, has a necessary structure. Kant thought that the world of appearance must occupy space and time. It is obviously hard to imagine there not being space or time, but Kant went further and argued that without them there could not be a knowable world at all. A similar point applies to cause and effect, and to the principle that things can endure unchanged through time. The rules of the empirical world are that it must contain enduring things, arranged in space and time, and having systematic effects upon one another. Nothing else, Kant argued, could ever count as an empirical world that we could know. However, his most startling claim is that all these rules are not present in the world as it is in itself. They are all rules simply about how the world must be *if* we are to be able to experience it. So space and time, cause and effect, relate only to the way in which things have to appear to us. Take away the experiencing subject, and none of the world's structure would remain.

The second positive point from Kant concerns our view of ourselves. As well as trying to understand the world, we are called upon to act and make decisions and these will ultimately be governed by questions of morality. Kant argues that morality can work only if each of us conceives himself or herself purely as a rational being, who is constrained by duty, and has freedom to choose the principles on which he or she will act. No kind of empirical investigation could reveal us to be such purely rational, free beings: if you like, there are no such things in the physical world. Nevertheless, it is a conception of ourselves which we must have. So, even though my knowledge is limited to the empirical world, I cannot ever believe that what I am is limited in the same way. Kant's idea, simply put, is that I must think that *in myself*, beyond appearances, I am a free and purely rational agent.

Now when Schopenhauer came across the Kantian philosophy as a student at Göttingen, he found it convincing, but incomplete. He embraced the distinction between appearance and thing in itself. On the appearance side, he wanted to modify Kant's views, but was happy to agree that the empirical world did not exist in itself, and was given its structure by rules of space, time, and causality imposed by us. It was, however on the side of the thing in itself that he felt Kant had fudged his account. What *is* the world really, in itself? And what am I? This was the double riddle which Kant had left by distinguishing appearance from thing in itself, and claiming that it was only of appearances that one could have knowledge. The conception of the thing in itself gave rise to other philosophical problems which had been much discussed in the German academic world. Both Schopenhauer's first teacher, Schulze, and Fichte, whose lectures he heard in Berlin, were prominent in the debate. In presenting his solution to the riddle, claiming that the thing in itself, both in the world and in the microcosm of the human being, was *will*, Schopenhauer was addressing a burning problem of the day, and to some extent trading on a familiar post-Kantian idea.

The better consciousness

At the beginning, the young Schopenhauer was reading not only Kant, but also Plato, and here he encountered another way of understanding the difference between what appears and what 'really is'. What 'really is' for Plato is a set of unchanging entities called Ideas or Forms. Individual things are imperfect, they come and go, but this does not affect the fundamental order in the universe which is constituted by absolute and eternal Forms. Plato thought that the greatest achievement for humanity would be to gain an understanding of these eternal Forms, such as Justice itself, Goodness itself, and Beauty itself. The human soul would be elevated to a plane where it transcended the limitations of mere opinion and mortal appetite, gained an apprehension of absolute standards of value, and achieved a release from conflict and suffering. At a crucial phase in his development Schopenhauer succumbed to this vision. Even though the Kantian thing in itself was supposed to be beyond the limits of human knowledge, while Plato's Ideas were the objects of knowledge *par excellence*, Schopenhauer conflated what the two were saying, and formed a Platonic view about what an insight into the thing in itself beyond appearance would be like. For many years he thought he had made an important discovery: '*Plato's Ideas* and *Kant's thing-in*-itself . . . that these two are one and the same is as unheard of as it is sure and certain' (*M1*, 377). Although he did come to see that the positions of the two great philosophers were in fact distinct, the fusion created in his mind had acquired an energy of its own. He believed that empirical consciousness, limited as it was to the phenomena of space, time, and causality, was something inferior which we should aspire to escape from, if possible. Only if there was a 'better' consciousness could human beings find anything that was of true value.

The term 'better consciousness' appears only in Schopenhauer's earliest unpublished manuscripts. It was not a very well-focused concept, and he abandoned it. But his later ideas about the value of art and about resigned detachment from life are continuous with his early view. In 1813, for example, he wrote the following in his notebooks:

As soon as we *objectively consider, i.e. contemplate* the things of the world, then for the moment *subjectivity* and thus the source of all misery has vanished. We are free and the consciousness of the material world of the senses stands before us as something strange and foreign which no longer wears us down. Also we are no longer involved in considering the nexus of space, time and causality (useful for our individuality), but see the Platonic Idea of the object. . . . This liberation from temporal consciousness leaves the better eternal consciousness behind. (*M1*, 50)

Ordinary consciousness is seen as something to which 'misery' attaches; if only we can break the Kantian rules that limit knowledge to appearance, we shall enter into a realm in which both we ourselves and the objects of our direct 'contemplation' are timeless. This 'liberation' Schopenhauer thinks may be found in art, and in the attitude to the world which he calls that of the 'saint'. Both the artistic genius and the saint supposedly contemplate reality from a standpoint which transcends ordinary empirical understanding. Many recent commentators have played down the influence of Plato, and treated Schopenhauer as a rather unorthodox Kantian. But the 'better consciousness' is dramatically un-Kantian; Schopenhauer's own assessment that Kant and Plato were united in his philosophy is nearer the mark, even if the two make themselves felt in quite different ways.

In fact, Schopenhauer was prone to cite three influences: 'I do not believe my doctrine could have come about before the Upanishads, Plato and Kant could cast their rays simultaneously into the mind of one man' (M1, 467). What of the third influence? Schopenhauer's knowledge of Plato and Kant, and his notion of the 'better consciousness', were already formed when he encountered the Upanishads, the sacred Hindu writings which he acquired in 1814 (in a Latin version taken from the Persian and entitled *Oupnek'hat*) and which he described in his late years as 'the consolation of my life' (P2, 397). We may note two principal ideas which impressed Schopenhauer in the Hindu writings he studied: one is *Mâyâ* or illusion, the other the identity of the individual with the world as a whole, embodied in the powerful Sanskrit saying *'Tat tvam asi'* ('This art thou'). Schopenhauer often refers to our ordinary experience as not penetrating the 'veil of *Mâyâ*'. This is not the common sceptical thought that we cannot trust our senses to tell us about the material world, but rather the idea that the material world of our experience is not something eternal, and not something we should ultimately put our trust in. Schopenhauer thinks that the world of material things which we experience and can investigate in science must be cast aside as of no genuine worth by comparison with the timeless vision open to artists and saints. The suspension, or denial, of one's complete differentiation from the rest of the world ('This art Thou') will be a feature of that timeless vision. Schopenhauer had to work out how one's understanding of both the world and the self would be transformed on abandoning ordinary empirical consciousness, and what came to play a central role here was the notion of losing the sense of oneself as a separate individual. Some of his ideas have a kinship with Buddhism which he later emphasized, though the relationship here was one of convergence rather than influence (W2, 169).

The Fourfold Root

While all these thoughts began to form, Schopenhauer set himself to write his doctoral dissertation, *On the Fourfold Root of the Principle of Sufficient Reason*. In it he makes no mention of the 'better consciousness', and deals simply with the principles governing ordinary experience and reasoning. He was obviously satisfied with the answers he reached, since he later retained them substantially unchanged, and frequently refers back to the dissertation. The fact that he produced an expanded version of the dissertation in 1847 confirms his statement that it is to be considered part of his complete system of thought. The text of *The Fourfold Root* we usually read today is this later version.

Schopenhauer begins *The Fourfold Root* with the single principle of sufficient reason which was the stock-in-trade of the eighteenth-century academic tradition associated with Leibniz and Christian Wolff. The principle states simply: 'Nothing is without a ground or reason why it is' (R, 6). Nothing is self-standing; everything is in relation to something else which is the reason for its being, or the explanation of it. However, there are, according to Schopenhauer, four distinct ways in which something may relate to a ground or reason, associated with four different kinds of explanation, which, he claims, none of his predecessors has clearly distinguished. The most familiar kind are causal or physical explanations, where we explain one event or state in terms of its relation to another which caused it. Then there are cases where we explain why some judgement is true by relating it to the grounds for its truth, such as an empirical observation or another truth from which it can be inferred. Thirdly, there are mathematical explanations—in which we explain, for example, why a triangle has the properties it does. Finally, there is explanation of what people do. We explain actions by relation to motives, which are their reasons, or causes, or both. In all these cases we are dealing with relations imposed by the mind, Schopenhauer thinks, and in each case the relation is one of necessity. Hence, in his terms, there are physical necessity, logical necessity, mathematical necessity, and moral necessity. Once we understand what the mind is doing when it operates with these relationships, we will have understood the forms that all explanation takes, and hence the true significance of the principle of sufficient reason. Let us deal with the four kinds of relation in turn.

By far the most substantial section of *The Fourfold Root* is devoted to the principle of causal explanation. An obvious class of objects the mind can grasp is that of the particular perceptible things that occupy space and time, and make up empirical reality. Space and time, as we saw, provide the basic structure of empirical reality. But space and time are not perceivable; what we can perceive is what fills space and time, and that, for Schopenhauer, is simply matter (R, 46). Were there not both time and space, there could be neither distinct material things, nor change, and so nothing for causality to apply to. Now the principle of causality states that every change in the world of material things must have a cause, or, as Schopenhauer puts it, 'every state that appears must have ensued or resulted from a change that preceded it' (R, 53). The principle allows of no exceptions: what we usually call the cause of some event is merely a particular change that preceded it, but that change must itself have ensued from some previous changes, and so on. By ensuing, Schopenhauer means following regularly, or 'as often as the first state exists'. Cause and effect are related in such a way that, if the first occurs, the second cannot but occur. This relation is seen as one of necessity.

Schopenhauer has a simple, uncluttered view about the nature of empirical reality. Individual material things exist in space and time. A material thing is something capable of interacting causally with other material things. And every change that occurs to a material thing is the necessary result of some preceding change that occurs to a material thing. One complication, however, is that Schopenhauer is not a realist about material things, but an idealist: that is, material things would not exist, for him, without the mind. He holds, with Kant, that the whole structure we have just described exists only as something presented to us as subjects, not in itself. When Schopenhauer says that empirical things in space and time are objects, he means that they are *objects for a subject*. 'Object' in his parlance means something met with in experience, or in the subject's consciousness. Space and time are the fundamental forms brought to experience by us. So the material occupants of space and time would not exist if it were not for the subject, and the causal connections which obtain between the states of material things are connections which we, as subjects, impose.

In Schopenhauer's account of perception, the human intellect 'creates' the world of ordinary material things (*R*, 75), and does so by applying the principle of cause and effect to sensations received by our bodily senses. We apprehend some change in our bodily state. The intellect then applies the principle of causality, and projects as cause of the sensation a material object 'outside' in space—and this projection is the object which we say we perceive. Thus the principle of causality is doubly important to Schopenhauer: it not only governs all interaction between material things, but is responsible for our construction of those very material things in the first place. The account has a certain ingenuity, but is troubling. For one thing, where do bodily sensations come from? They must surely be originally caused in the body by something prior to the operation of the intellect, but Schopenhauer does not discuss what that prior cause might be. Secondly, how do we apprehend the initial sensation? It cannot be that the mind perceives the sensation as a change in a material thing (the body), and yet if it does not do so, why is the principle of causality, which governs changes of material things, called into operation at all?

Schopenhauer's second class of objects for the mind is made up of *concepts*. Concepts are, for Schopenhauer, mental representations which are by nature secondary: he calls them 'representations of representations'. The basic representations are experiences of things in the material world, such as a particular tree; the concept *tree* is, by contrast, a general representation formed to stand for many such objects, by leaving out the detailed elements of what is experienced in each case. Schopenhauer is fond of emphasizing that concepts are always at least one step removed from direct experience, for which he uses the Kantian term *Anschauung* (intuition or perception). He thinks that a concept, to be of much use to us, must always be capable of being cashed out in terms of experience. Concepts such as *being*, *essence*, or *thing*, have the least cash value in these terms (R, 147, 155). As we shall see, Schopenhauer also takes the view that in some areas, such as art and ethics, abstract conceptual thinking can actually stand in the way of genuine insight.

Nevertheless, possession of concepts is a distinctively human characteristic for Schopenhauer, raising us above the consciousness of which other animals are capable. Other creatures, in his view, can have a perception of material things existing in space and time, much as we do—in a remarkable passage he laments the fact that 'in the West where [man's] skin has turned white' we have ceased to acknowledge our kinship with animals whom we demean as 'beasts or brutes' (R, 146). But the other animals do lack conceptual representations, and so lack the ability to make judgements, to reason, to have a language, or an understanding of past and future. Thinking, or making judgements, is the fundamental function of concepts. Schopenhauer calls a judgement a combination or relationship of concepts, though he is not very clear about what this relationship involves. He is more interested in the idea that a judgement can express knowledge, and it is here that the principle of sufficient reason comes in again. 'If a judgement is to express a piece of *knowledge*, it must have a sufficient ground or reason; by virtue of this quality, it then receives the predicate *true*. *Truth* is therefore the reference of a judgement to something different therefrom' (*R*, 156). It is a familiar thought that a judgement amounts to knowledge if it is true and sufficiently grounded in something outside itself. Schopenhauer's brief remarks appear to make no distinction between a judgement's having a sufficient ground and its being true. Whether he would accept a notion of truth as correspondence with the way things are, independently of grounds for judging them to be so, remains obscure.

What Schopenhauer succeeds in establishing is that true judgements may be grounded in quite different ways. They may be grounded in another judgement, as when we argue, conclude, or infer (*R*, 157–8) from one truth to another. They may, on the other hand, be 'empirical truths', grounded not in another judgement, but in experience. For example, our judgement 'There is snow on the trees' may have its justification in the evidence of our senses. On the other hand in the syllogism: 'There is snow on the trees, Snow is a white substance, Therefore, there is a white substance on the trees,' the truth of the final judgement is grounded simply in the truths of the two premises. Schopenhauer calls this a 'logical' or 'formal' truth, meaning simply one whose ground is based on deduction, rather than observation. There are two other kinds of truth in his account, which he calls transcendental truth and metalogical truth. These occur respectively when a judgement is founded on the conditions of experience or on the conditions of thought in general. A notable transcendental truth is 'Nothing happens without a cause', which is neither grounded in observation nor on deduction from any other truths, but is an underlying principle on which all experience is based. (Schopenhauer is here following Kant closely). Metalogical truths are supposedly a kind of judgements where, if we try to go against them, we cease to be able to think properly at all.

One example Schophenhauer gives is 'No predicate can be simultaneously attributed and denied to a subject': we cannot think, for example, 'Snow is and is not white'. The principle of sufficient reason itself is a truth of this kind, Schopenhauer claims, though in some of its guises, especially the principle of causality, it appears as a transcendental truth (*R*, 162).

Schopenhauer's third class of objects in *The Fourfold Root* is made up simply of space and time. Once again, we are close to Kant, who thought that we can have knowledge not only of the particular things that fill space and time, but of the basic properties of space and time as such. Geometry and arithmetic, on this view, are bodies of knowledge concerning position in space and succession in time, but they are neither scientific empirical knowledge, nor a matter of mere logical deduction. With this view of geometry and arithmetic, which would now be disputed, Kant arrived at the idea that we must be able to grasp space and time in a pure, non-empirical way in our minds. Schopenhauer follows suit, and produces his third form of the principle of sufficient reason. The relation between a triangle's having three sides and its having three angles, for example, is that the one is grounded in, is a sufficient reason for, the other. But, Schopenhauer argues, this relation is not that between cause and effect, and is not that between a piece of knowledge and its justification either. We must distinguish not only the ground of becoming (change grounded in causes) and the ground of knowing (knowledge-claims grounded in justifications), but also the ground of being. If we say that a triangle has three angles because it has three sides, the ground we are referring to is simply the way that space, or one facet of it, is.

The final form of the principle of sufficient reason has application to only a single object for each subject. Each of us can be aware of himself or herself as a subject of will. We experience our own states of wanting and making decisions, and can always ask Why? (*R*, 212). Our willing, we assume , is preceded by something which is its ground, and which explains our action or decision. This prior something is what Schopenhauer calls a *motive*, and the principle in operation is what he terms the 'law of motivation', or the principle of the sufficient reason of act-ing. It states simply that every act of will can be explained as ensuing from some motive. The connection between motive and act of will is one of cause and effect, the same as holds universally for changes in the material world. Motivation is thus, as Schopenhäuer puts it, 'causality seen from within' (R, 214).

The limits of sufficient reason

The Fourfold Root is a remarkable sustained attempt to sepa-rate different forms of explanation which the tradition before Schopenhauer had not always distinguished. We may certainly sympathize with his request that henceforth 'every philoso-pher, who in his speculations bases a conclusion on the princi-ple of sufficient reason or ground, or indeed speaks of a ground at all, should be required to state what kind of ground he means' (R, 233). However, clarifying the framework which governs our experience and reasoning was only one part of Schopenhauer's task. He remarks in the enlarged edition of 1847 that none of the relationships he has dealt with applies beyond the phenomena out of which our experience is com-posed: the principle of sufficient reason would not apply in any of its forms to the world considered as thing in itself (R, 232–3). He also reminds us that 'the sublime Plato' degrades phenom-enal reality to what is 'always only arising and passing away, but never really and truly existing' (R, 232).

In his 1813 notebooks Schopenhauer returned to his task of revealing what lay beyond all these subject-imposed modes of connection. Now something of great iportance occurred: as he proceeded in his investigations, it became clear that revealing the nature of the thing in itself and clarifying the 'better' Platonic consciousness were two distinct enterprises. The thing in itself was a hidden essence working away underneath the order we imposed on the objects of our experience. It was also his own inner nature, something in him that drove him on—it was the world, as it were, surging up within him. To this hidden nature he gave the name *will*, and with it he now associated the 'misery' which ordinary life has to offer. By contrast, if only he could cease *being* this will, and cease imposing all subjective forms of connection, the same world would take on a wholly different aspect, revealing itself spread out before him in timeless objective glory as a panoply of Platonic Ideas. Schopenhauer's philosophy really took shape once he attained this distinction between thing in itself (will) and Platonic Ideas: the first the murky reality underlying the empirical world in which the individual toils and tries to understand the connections of things, the other an exceptional vision to aspire to, of all connections undone and a brighter reality contemplated without striving and pain.

3 *The world as will and representation*

Schopenhauer's greatest work, *The World as Will and Representation*, is divided into four books, with a long appendix on Kant's philosophy in Volume I. Each of the four books sets out a distinct movement of thought. The first presents the world as representation, or as it is for our experience. The second book adds that this same world (and we ourselves within it) must be viewed under another aspect, as will. We called the appearance/thing in itself distinction the backbone of Schopenhauer's philosophy: now 'the world as representation' is what falls on the 'appearance' side of this line, while 'the world as will' is the thing in itself. But then in Book 3 aesthetic contemplation emerges as a cessation of willing in the individual, which transforms the world of objects into a timeless reality of Ideas, and finally Book 4 intensifies Schopenhauer's pessimistic view of the ordinary life of desire and action, and advocates an abolition of the will within oneself as the path to what is ethically good, and ultimately to a kind of resigned mystical salvation.

Representation

In its first aspect, then, the world is representation. The world, in other words, is what presents itself in a subject's experience. (A more old-fashioned translation of the German *Vorstellung* gives us 'the world as idea'—but to retain this could be misleading because of Schopenhauer's use of *Idee* for a Platonic Idea elsewhere in the system.) Schopenhauer begins by expounding an idealist position. This is the view that the material objects which we experience depend for their order and their existence on the knowing subject. He calls his position transcendental idealism, which is Kant's term, but he also emphasizes his continuity with Berkeley, as he sees in the latter's doctrine that 'to be is to be perceived' the initial glimmer of the truth in idealism—Kant's contribution being to explain how what is perceived constitutes a world of objects when it is governed by the necessary rules of space, time, and causality. Schopenhauer's account of the world of empirical things is what it was in *The Fourfold Root*: empirical things consist of matter, which fills distinct portions of space and time, and which is in causal interaction with other such portions. But his idealism says that without the subject of experience, all such objects would not exist.

To be more specific, it is *individual* things that would not exist without the experiencing subject. What we experience in the ordinary course of our lives are distinct things. One table is an individual distinct from another, one animal or person likewise. But what is the principle on which this division of the world into individual things works? Schopenhauer has a very clear and plausible answer: location in space and time. Two tables are distinct individuals because they occupy distinct portions of space, or of time, or of both. Now if you take this view, and also think, with Kant, that the organizing of things under the structure of space and time stems from the subject, and applies only to the world of phenomena, not to the world as it is in itself, then you will conclude that individuals do not exist in the world as it is in itself. The world would not be broken up into individual things, if it were not for the space and time which we, as subjects, impose. Here then are two important tenets of Schopenhauer's philosophy. Space and time are the principle of individuation, or in his favoured Latin version, the *principium individuationis*; and there can be no individuals on the 'in itself' side of the line.

Schopenhauer has four main arguments for idealism. One alleges that we cannot imagine anything which exists outside our own minds, because 'what we are imagining at that moment is . . . nothing but just the process in the intellect of a knowing being' (*W2*, 5). This is reminiscent of a controversial argument attempted by Berkeley, who thought that an unperceived tree could not be imagined. Schopenhauer's use of the argument is not very convincing, however, because even though *my imagining* a world independent of my mind does presuppose my own mind, the existence of a world independent of my mind does not. A second argument is the claim that idealism is the only viable alternative to scepticism. Scepticism maintains that we can have no certain knowledge about the existence or nature of material things, because all that we can be certain of is what falls within our own consciousness. If you deny idealism (the argument runs) and think that the world of material things has to exist wholly outside a subject's consciousness, then you will have to admit that scepticism wins the day, and that we can never have certain knowledge about a world of material things. If we wish to preserve our entitlement to *knowledge* concerning the world of things that occupy space and time and follow causal laws, the solution is to accept that they do not lie outside our consciousness.

Schopenhauer's third argument adds to this by suggesting that realism—the alternative to idealism—saddles itself with two 'worlds', one of which is redundant:

According to realism, the world is supposed to exist, as we know it, independently of this knowledge. Now let us once remove from it all knowing beings, and thus leave behind only inorganic and vegetable nature. Rock, tree, and brook are there, and the blue sky . . . But then let us subsequently put into the world a knowing being. That world then presents itself *once more* in his brain . . . Thus to the *first* world a *second* has been added, which, although completely separated from the first, resembles it to a nicety. . . . All this proves absurd enough, and thus leads to the conviction that that absolutely *objective* world outside the head, independent of it and *prior* to all knowledge, which we at first imagined we had conceived, was already no other than the second world already known *subjectively*, the world of the representation, and that it is this alone which we are actually capable of conceiving. (*W2*, 9–10)

Schopenhauer is here in a territory littered both before and after him with debates of some complexity. The three arguments so far discussed can be found already in Berkeley. They are, however, not decisive for quite simple reasons. The realist may reply to the 'scepticism' argument by saying that if the choice is between scepticism and idealism, then scepticism is the better option. The idea that material things depend on the subject for their existence may seem too high a price to pay for a guarantee of knowledge. Also the argument only says that *if* we can have any certain knowledge, idealism must be preferred. One might settle for not having certain knowledge, and insist that the empirical world must nevertheless be conceived as existing independently of the subject's consciousness. To the third argument, that the world of things existing outside consciousness is redundant, the realist can reply simply that this world outside consciousness would be *the* world. It is only the idealist who wants to say that the *picture* of material things which we have in consciousness is already a world of material things. The realist does not accept this, and makes a clear distinction between the one world existing independently of us, and our picture of it. However, Schopenhauer's points correspond to familiar parts of the debate, and are valuable against some opponents. A realism which said both that we can be certain only about what lies within consciousness, and that the world outside consciousness exactly resembles the picture we have built of it, would be threatened by his criticisms.

The fourth argument for idealism is the one which Schopenhauer most relies on. It rests on the concepts *subject* and *object*. The subject is that which knows or experiences, the object that which is known or experienced. The world of representation, for Schopenhauer, requires both. He makes two large claims: first, that nothing can be both object and subject, secondly that there can never be a subject without an object, or an object without a subject. It is the last point which he takes to establish idealism, and indeed to make it something obvious. Nothing can be an object for experience without there being a subject to experience it or think about it. But why must we think of material objects in space and time in this way? Schopenhauer would argue that the point of calling them objects is to indicate that they can and do fall within our experience. But then he also requires us to believe that whatever we can experience must exist only in relation to our experiencing it. This simple principle is central to Schopenhauer's position. Because of it, he does not think that idealism can be seriously doubted, once one properly understands it. But it is surely a questionable principle.

A fair proportion of Book I of *The World as Will and Representation* is devoted to the distinction between perception and conceptual reasoning. As we saw in the previous chapter, Schopenhauer thinks that we share our perceptual abilities with other animals, but that concepts and reasoning are what mark us out from them. Perceiving the world is the business of what he calls intellect or understanding, and he suggests that conceptual thinking and judgement play no part in this. On the other hand, manipulating concepts to form judgements, relating judgements to one another as premiss and conclusion, and so on, is the business of what he calls reason. By playing down the significance of reason and treating concepts as more or less faint abstractions out of direct experience or intuition, Schopenhauer paves the way for a close assimilation between the human mind and that of other living creatures.

Will

As we cross from the First Book into the Second, a sudden reversal takes place. In the world as representation, what am I? The world spreads out before me, containing individual material things in space and time which change according to causal laws—but I myself am just the subject which is distinct from every object that it experiences, including that object which I call my body. Something is missing. I seem to be 'a winged cherub without a body' (*W1*, 99), the world confronting me as something alien to which I do not belong.

For the purely knowing subject as such, this body is a representation like any other, an object among objects. Its movements and actions are so far known to him in just the same way as the changes of all other objects of perception; and they would be equally strange and incomprehensible to him, if their meaning were not unravelled for him in an entirely different way. Otherwise, he would see his conduct follow on presented motives with the constancy of a law of nature, just as the changes of other objects follow upon causes, stimuli, and motives. But he would be no nearer to understanding the influence of the motives than he is to understanding the connexion with its cause of any other effect that appears before him. (*W1*, 99–100)

Schopenhauer is generating a puzzlement in order to make us receptive to the central idea of the whole book, which is now unveiled:

All this, however, is not the case; on the contrary, the answer to the riddle is given to the subject of knowledge appearing as an individual, and this answer is given in the word *will*. This and this alone gives him the key to his own phenomenon, reveals to him the significance and shows him the inner mechanism of his being, his actions, his movements. To the subject of knowing, who appears as an individual only through his identity with the body, this body is given in two entirely different ways. It is given in perception of the intellect as representation, as an object among objects, liable to the laws of these objects. But it is also given in a quite different way, namely as what is known immediately to everyone, and is denoted by the word *will*. (*W1*, 100)

What Schopenhauer means is that when I act (when I do something) my body moves; and my awareness of its movement is unlike my awareness of other events that I perceive. I am 'outside' other objects, or they are 'outside' me—but my own body is mine in a uniquely intimate way. This can be expressed by saying that other events are merely observed to happen, whereas movements of my body are expressions of *my will*. Schopenhauer's account of acts of will is anti-dualist. A dualist would maintain that the mental realm and the bodily realm are distinct, and that *willing* (or volition) was an event in the mental realm, while the movement of the body was something distinct that occurred in the physical realm. Schopenhauer denies this:

The act of will and the action of the body are not two different states objectively known, connected by the bond of causality; they do not stand in the relation of cause and effect, but are one and the same thing, though given in two entirely different ways, first quite directly, and then in perception for the understanding. (ibid.)

Wanting, striving, and trying are to be seen as things that we do with our bodies, not as events that occur in detachment from our bodies. They manifest themselves in physical reality, but also retain an 'inner' aspect, because each of us knows what he or she strives for, in a direct, non-observational way. Thus what Schopenhauer calls the 'action of the body' is neither in a wholly mental or a wholly physical realm, but is one single occurrence which presents two aspects: we each have 'inner' awareness of something that is also part of the ordinary empirical world, and can be observed as such.

This account of acts of will is a decisive step for Schopenhauer, since it places the human subject firmly within the material world. If striving towards ends is setting the body in motion, then, while we will, we are rooted in the world of objects. Schopenhauer thus cannot conceive of a subject of will as being anything other than bodily. He also makes the converse claim that our bodily existence is nothing other than willing. Whenever we undergo feelings of fear or desire, attraction or repulsion, whenever the body itself behaves according to the various unconscious functions of nourishment, reproduction, or survival, Schopenhauer discerns *will* manifesting itself—but in a new and extended sense. What he wants to show is that ordinary conscious willing is no different in its basic nature from the many other processes which set the body, or parts of it, in motion. Admittedly, willing to act involves conscious thinking—it involves the body's being caused to move by motives in the intellect—but it is, for Schopenhauer, not different in principle from the beating of the heart, the activation of the saliva glands, or the arousal of the sexual organs. All can be seen as an individual organism manifesting will, in Schopenhauer's sense. The body itself is will; more specifically, it is a manifestation of will to life (*Wille zum Leben*), a kind of blind striving, at a level beneath that of conscious thought and action, which is directed towards the preservation of life, and towards engendering life anew.

This interesting idea is wrapped up in the much wider claim that the whole world in itself is will. Just as my body's movements have an inner aspect not revealed in objective experience, so does the rest of the world. Schopenhauer seeks an account which makes all fundamental forces in nature homogeneous, and thinks that science is inherently unsatisfying because it always tails off without explaining the essence or hidden inner character of the phenomena whose behaviour it accounts for. His unifying account of nature is that all natural processes are a manifestation of will. This is likely at first sight to be dismissed as fanciful—but we should heed Schopenhauer's warning that he is vastly extending the concept 'will':

hitherto the identity of the inner essence of any striving and operating force in nature with the will has not been recognized, and therefore the many kinds of phenomena that are only different species of the same genus were not regarded as such . . . Consequently, no word could exist to denote the concept of this genus. I therefore name the genus after its most important species, the direct knowledge of which lies nearest to us, and leads to the indirect knowledge of all the others. But anyone who is incapable of carrying out the required extension of the concept will remain involved in a permanent misunderstanding. (*W1*, 111)

So we must not transfer 'will' simple-mindedly from human actions to the whole of nature. It serves only as the most convenient term where none yet exists. Nevertheless, this aspect of Schopenhauer's philosophy is puzzling. What is the 'required extension' of the concept? Perhaps it is an extension of sense: if 'will' is now to have a new meaning, this might save

Schopenhauer from claiming something ridiculous. But this line should not be taken too far. Schopenhauer insists that 'will' is not interchangeable with 'force', for example (*W1*, 111–12), and that the issue is not a mere 'dispute about words'. In saying that all processes are will, 'we have in fact referred something more unknown to something infinitely better known, indeed to the one thing really known to us immediately and completely' (*W1*, 112). To subsume willing under force (or energy, which has also been suggested) is not Schopenhauer's intention. The global doctrine of will can tell us something informative only because we have some grasp of what willing is from our own actions. An alternative interpretation is that Schopenhauer is keeping the sense of 'will' fixed, and simply widening the range of phenomena that it refers to. He does say that in mechanics '*seeking* shows itself as gravitation, . . . *fleeing* as reception of motion' and similar things (*W2*, 298); he is prepared to speak in remarkable terms of 'the powerful, irresistible impulse with which masses of water rush downwards, the persistence and determination with which the magnet always turns back to the North Pole, the keen desire with which iron flies to the magnet' (*W1*, 117–18). How are we to take this? If meant literally, it is merely embarrassing. But perhaps he is doing something more subtle here, and attempting to teach us our own kinship with nature by rhetorical means: the behaviour of the inorganic world is to an extent '*like* the vehemence of human desires' and so 'it will not cost us a great effort of the imagination to recognize once more our own inner nature, even at so great a distance'. This is not to say that iron really desires anything, or that water rushes because it wants to.

What we usually call willing is supposed to be a clear guide to the way the world is. So 'will' must still be understood in terms of its application to human actions; however, we must enlarge its sense at least far enough to avoid the barbarity of thinking that every process in the world has a mind, a consciousness, or a purpose behind it. For the most part, Schopenhauer assures us, the world operates blindly and 'in a dull, one-sided, and unalterable manner'—and the same is even true of many manifestations of the will within each human individual. The following passage states Schopenhauer's view as clearly as any:

only the *will* is *thing in itself* . . . It is that of which all representa-tion, all object, is the phenomenon, the visibility, the *objectivity*. It is the innermost essence, the kernel, of every particular thing and also of the whole. It appears in every blindly acting force of nature, and also in the deliberate conduct of man, and the great difference between the two concerns only the degree of the manifestation, not the inner nature of what is manifested. (*W1*, 110)

This surely means that every force in nature, those that involve conscious purpose and those that do not, must be understood as some form of striving or end-seeking, even if in highly attenu-ated form.

Two more peculiarities of this doctrine should be noted. First, if the will is the thing in itself, it is not something occupying space and time. Space and time are merely the subject-imposed structure of the world as representation, and the thing in itself is what remains when the world as represen-tation is thought away. Given Schopenhauer's idea that space and time are the principle of individuation, the thing in itself cannot be split up into separate individuals. Beyond representa-tion, space, and time, it is simply the world as a whole that is to be conceived as will. Secondly, there can be no causal inter-action between the will, as thing in itself, and events in the ordinary empirical world. Causality too is something which operates only at the level of empirical changes occurring to individual material things, not at the level of the thing in itself. Kant seemed to require that the thing in itself could impinge upon us causally, rather like some empirical object, and Schopenhauer was well aware that this claim was the stum-bling-block of Kantianism for many of his contemporaries. Schopenhauer himself avoids the problem, and never claims that the will as thing in itself is a cause. But then what is the relationship between the world in itself and the things and events that lie within our empirical knowledge? Schopenhauer talks sometimes of the will's 'manifestation' in empirical reality, but his preferred term is 'objectification'. This means just that the world shows to us the side of it which we can experience. We have to think of the single will and its objectification in a multitude of phenomena as two sides of a coin, two aspects of the same world.

A big problem here concerns the knowability of the thing in itself. Schopenhauer's doctrine of the will is metaphysical. Metaphysics, for him, gives an account of the fundamental nature of reality, but uses the data of experience as the only possible guide: 'the solution to the riddle of the world must come from an understanding of the world itself . . . the task of metaphysics is not to pass over experience in which the world exists, but to understand it thoroughly, since inner and outer experience are certainly the principal source of all knowledge' (W1, 428). Strictly speaking, our knowledge reaches only as far as the phenomena of inner and outer experience. So we do not— cannot—know the bare thing in itself. When I am conscious of my own willing in action, what I know is a phenomenal manifestation of the will, not the thing in itself. Nevertheless, it is this knowledge of my own willing which is to provide the key to knowing the nature of the whole world in itself. How?

As we saw, Schopenhauer sets up a contrast between experience of the world of material objects, and 'immediate' awareness of one's own willing. Sometimes he writes as if the latter amounted to knowledge of the thing in itself directly: 'my body is the only object of which I know not merely the one side, that of the representation, but also the other, that is called *will*' (W1, 125); 'Everyone finds himself to be this will, in which the inner nature of the world consists' (W1, 162); 'a way *from within* stands open to us to that real inner nature of things to which we cannot penetrate *from without*' (W2, 195). This may suggest direct cognitive contact with the thing in itself inside us, and a further inference that everything in the world has a similar inner nature. But we must wonder how this can be achieved, if the thing in itself is strictly unknowable. When he is being more careful, Schopenhauer says that even the act of will which we know 'immediately' is an event in time, and is therefore part of our representation, rather than the thing in itself. Still, he says, the thing in itself, though it 'does not appear quite naked', has 'to a great extent cast off its veils' in our 'inner' awareness of action (*W2*, 197). In consciousness of our own willing we are still on this side of the divide between representation and thing in itself, but we can say that we come closer to knowledge of the thing in itself. This is still troubling, however. If knowledge of our acts of will is the nearest we get to the thing in itself, and if even here we do not know it directly, what grounds do we really have for claiming to know what it is?

As an exercise in metaphysics, Schopenhauer's doctrine of the will as thing in itself is so obviously flawed that some people have doubted whether he really means it—perhaps *will* is just a concept which explains a wide range of phenomena, and is not supposed to extend to the unknowable thing in itself? On the other hand, if that were the whole of his position, he could offer no 'solution to the riddle' in the way that he clearly intends. Given such problems, it is perhaps not surprising that his metaphysics has had few followers. Nevertheless, to stop there would be short-sighted. Schopenhauer's more restricted notion of the *will to life*, which characterizes observable aspects of human and animal behaviour, is an interesting and powerful idea. His conception of will expressing itself within humanity, and the polarity he discovers between our being governed by the will and our escaping it, enables him, as we shall see, to present large tracts of our lives in a new light. It enables him to explain thought-processes as having an organic, survival-directed function, to show the influence of unconscious drives and feelings on the intellect, to suggest that our picture of ourselves as rational individual thinkers is in some sense an illusion, to place sexuality at the core of human psychology, to account for the power of music and the value of aesthetic experience, to argue that ordinary life is inevitably unfulfilled, and to advocate the renunciation of individual desires as the route to reconciliation with our existence. It has been these applications, rather than the bald metaphysical statement that the thing in itself is will, that have had the most influence on philosophers, psychologists, and artists of later generations.

Will, body, and the self

Unity of body and will

Schopenhauer's claim 'My body and my will are one' (*W1*, 102) has a number of different aspects to it. The first, as we saw, is the idea that *acts* of will are movements of the body. Schopenhauer takes a robust line on this, saying that 'every true, genuine, immediate act of the will is also at once and directly a manifest act of the body' (*W1*, 101). This would suggest, somewhat perversely, that there can be no such thing as a willing which goes unfulfilled because one's muscles or nerves do not function in the right way. (Would Schopenhauer say that stroke victims have not 'genuinely' willed, if their bodies fail to move as they want them to?) But Schopenhauer is trying to oust the traditional division between mental and physical, and to supplant it with a division between will on the one hand, and intellect and reason on the other. Perception, judgement, and reasoning are all functions of what he has called representation. We observe the way a state of affairs is in the world of objects, judge that it should be altered or preserved, and form the intention to act. Schopenhauer's chief point is that none of this is yet *willing*. The operations of perception, thought, and intention are quite separate preparatory events which may trigger the will—the body, that is—into action. He plays down the gap between willing and the movements one carries out with one's body, concentrating instead on the gulf between representing the world of objects, and being in goal-seeking motion within it.

Schopenhauer's other evidence for the unity of will and the body is that almost everything that impinges on the body sets off some reaction of the will, and that conversely, when the will is aroused, there are always bodily manifestations. The list of mental states included under the heading of the will is extensive:

all desiring, striving, wishing, demanding, longing, hoping, loving, rejoicing, jubilation, and the like, no less than not willing or resisting, all abhorring, fleeing, fearing, being angry, hating, mourning, suffering pains—in short, all emotions and passions. For these emotions and passions are weaker or stronger, violent and stormy or else quiet impulses of one's own will, which is either restrained or unleashed, satisfied or unsatisfied. In their many variations they relate to the successful or frustrated attainment of that which is willed, to the endurance or the overcoming of that which is abhorred. Consequently, they are explicit affections of the same will which is active in decisions and actions. (F, 11)

Sometimes, Schopenhauer admits, when the bodily senses are affected our reaction is neutral, and does not rouse the will in any of these ways—but only rarely. For the most part, such an occurrence is to some degree painful or pleasant, welcome or irritating. Similarly, when we are in one of the mental states on Schopenhauer's list, there is usually a characteristic bodily accompaniment: the heart beats faster, the blood drains from our face or suffuses it. Thus 'every vehement and excessive movement of the will, in other words, every emotion, agitates the body and its inner workings directly and immediately' (W1, 101). For Schopenhauer these considerations tend to show the identity of the body with the will. They do at least suggest a close affinity between bodily existence and the empirical manifestations of willing in Schopenhauer's broader sense.

A representation in the conscious mind which causes the body to move in action is what Schopenhauer calls a *motive*. We share some kinds of motive with other animals that perceive the world. For example, behaviour in a cat which is caused by perceiving a predator or some food, would be classed by Schopenhauer as willing brought about by a motive. Humans, on the other hand, are distinctive in being able to act not just on perceptual motives, but also on rational ones: representing matters conceptually, we reason ourselves to a conclusion about what to do, and this process plays a causal role in setting us into action. A cat may eat because it senses food and is hungry, a human being because doing so is judged the best course of action. But willing manifests itself in the body's movements in the same way in both cases. Different kinds of willing really differ, for Schopenhauer, only in the causes that precede them. He makes a basic distinction between three kinds of cause. They are motive, stimulus, and cause pure and simple (as found in mechanical and chemical changes).

So far 'willing' has stood for a range of mental states which have bodily manifestations, including active striving, the emotions, and feelings of pleasure and pain. But some manifestations of the will in the body are not what we should call mental states at all, and are of a kind which we share even with lowlier parts of nature. Plants behave in certain ways in reaction to light, moisture, gravity, and so on. They do not perform actions, and their movements and modifications are not caused by motives, for the simple reason that they have no minds with which to perceive. The plant's turning towards the sun is caused by a *stimulus*, rather than by a motive. Nevertheless, Schopenhauer is prepared to call such plant-behaviour a manifestation of will, because he thinks it can only be understood as goal-directed, even if there is no mind present to entertain the goal. Having located will in bodily movement, and distinguished it from representation, he sees an affinity between the plant's movement in response to stimuli and those of the cat and the human brought about by motives. It is clear that human beings and animals also respond to stimuli—the involuntary contraction of the pupil of the eye provides but one example. This occurrence, for Schopenhauer, is equally a manifestation of the will—though not an *act* of will, because it is not caused by a conscious representation of the world.

Will to life

Schopenhauer's conception of the will is not restricted to the body's episodic reactions to motives and stimuli, for he claims that 'the whole body is nothing but the objectified will' (*W1*, 100), meaning that the way in which the body grows and develops, and the way in which its parts are organized, reveal a principle of striving towards ends which is 'blindly' at work:

Teeth, gullet, and intestinal canal are objectified hunger; the genitals are objectified sexual impulse; grasping hands and nimble feet correspond to the more indirect strivings of the will which they represent. (*W1*, 108)

What underlies and explains the body's functioning, indeed its very existence, is its being directed towards life—or what Schopenhauer calls *will to life*. (The usual translation of *Wille zum Leben* as 'will to live' is linguistically correct, but what Schopenhauer has in mind is more inclusive; it is a striving not just to live, but also to engender life and to protect offspring. (See *W2*, 484–5.) In other words, *life*, rather than *living*, is the common end of all *Wille zum Leben*.) Schopenhauer is boldly seeking a single hypothesis to explain the ways in which all life-forms grow, function, and behave.

It is easy to think that the idea of the 'will to life' is wrongly fixated on the idea that there are purposes in nature. However, although Schopenhauer speaks of 'purposes' or 'ends' being fulfilled by behaviour patterns and the workings of particular organs, he clearly does not think that organisms entertain any conscious purposes—for the will works 'blindly':

we see at once from the instinct and mechanical skill of animals that the will is also active where it is not guided by any knowledge. ... The one-year-old bird has no notion of the eggs for which it builds a nest; the young spider has no idea of the prey for which it spins a web; the ant-lion has no notion of the ant for which it digs a cavity for the first time. ... Even in us the same will in many ways acts blindly; as in all those functions of our body which are not guided by knowledge, in all its vital and vegetative processes, digestion, circulation, secretion, growth, and reproduction. (*W1*, 114–15)

So, despite superficial appearances, Schopenhauer does not simply wish to understand nature in anthropomorphic terms. Although he asks us to interpret the world using concepts applied first to ourselves, the notion of the will to life has the effect of demoting humanity from any special status separate from the rest of nature. First, in our bodies, the same 'blind' force operates as throughout nature: we are organized to live and to propagate life not by any conscious act of will. Secondly, there is a close continuity between even the conscious, purposive willing of human action and the life-preserving functions and instincts at work elsewhere. In our seeking of mates and providing for offspring, we are driven by the same instincts as other animals. And Schopenhauer sees the human capacities for perception, rationality, and action as an offshoot of the same wider principle which leads insects to build nests, feathers to grow, and cells to divide. In this respect, the will to life can seem quite a forward-looking notion. Another crucial feature is Schopenhauer's steadfast opposition to anything approaching an external or divine purpose for nature. Even though it is 'a single will' which expressed itself throughout the multiplicity of phenomena, this means only that all behaviour is of the same striving or goal-directed kind. All life-forms strive towards life; but there is no co-ordinated purpose to nature, rather the kind of purposelessness and conflict which are usually associated with Darwinism. Schopenhauer derides those 'pantheists' and 'Spinozists' who think the world divine, but have not 'the remotest idea why the whole tragi-comedy exists' (*W2*, 357).

On the other hand, Schopenhauer does believe that the various species of animate and inanimate things in the world are eternal and static. There are not only individuals which we happen to classify as ants, or oak trees, or magnetic fields. Rather, each individual is of a *kind*, and the kinds that can exist are fixed. Thus, while individual things come and go over time, *the ant* or *the oak tree*, as a kind, is a permanent feature of empirical reality. Schopenhauer has two ways of expressing this point, which he frequently repeats. One is to say that the will (the thing in itself) manifests or objectifies itself in a series of *grades*. The other is to say that *the ant* and *the oak tree* as such are Ideas, or as he often puts it '(Platonic) Ideas'. The most adequately objective knowledge we could have would be of the nature of these abiding forms 'fixed in the nature of things'. Such objective knowledge would not consist in knowing the thing in itself in its naked form, which is impossible, but in knowing the timeless patterns of the things that are experienceable by us.

The following passage shows quite well how Schopenhauer uses his doctrine of the will to life and his notion of the order of Ideas in nature:

everywhere in nature we see contest, struggle, and the fluctuation of victory . . . Every grade of the will's objectification fights for the matter, the space, and the time of another. . . . This universal conflict is to be seen most clearly in the animal kingdom. Animals have the vegetable kingdom for their nourishment, and within the animal kingdom again every animal is the prey and food of some other. This means that the matter in which an animal's Idea manifests itself must stand aside for the manifestation of another Idea, since every animal can maintain its own existence only by the incessant elimination of another's. Thus the will to life generally feasts on itself, and is in different forms its own nourishment, till finally the human race, because it subdues all the others, regards nature as manufactured for its own use. (W1, 146–7)

Intellect as an outgrowth of will

Now we come to a step in Schopenhauer's argument whose importance cannot be overestimated. He claims that all our knowledge of the empirical world is the product of the kind of organism we are. The structure of knowledge and of its objects depends on the kind of manifestation of will to life which its subject happens to be. Everything the reader was told at the outset about the world of representation, the forms of space, time, and causality which govern the objects of our experience, and the concepts and judgements which we can obtain from them by abstraction—all of this is merely a surface beneath which lurks the driving force of our nature, the will. We grow into creatures who can perceive, judge, and reason, in order to fulfil the ends of life: survival, nourishment, and reproduction. In Schopenhauer's narrative this is a marked change of fortune for the human subject. The capacity for knowledge on which we pride ourselves suddenly appears as merely a way in which a particular species manipulates the environment that impinges on it, so as to foster its well-being:

[the intellect] is designed for comprehending those ends on the attainment of which depend individual life and its propagation. But such an intellect is by no means destined to interpret the inner essence-in-itself of things and of the world, which exists independently of the knower. (*W2*, 284)

To establish this picture, Schopenhauer has to claim not only that all biological functions are manifestations of will to life, but also that knowledge, perception, and reasoning are biological functions. This he does by espousing a particularly blunt form of materialism: states of mind are states of the brain. If, instead of regarding our processes of thought and perception from the point of view of self-consciousness, we take an 'objective' view of them, we must conclude them to be 'nothing more than the physiological function of an internal organ, the brain' (*W2*, 273). The whole world of individual objects in space and time consists only of our representations, and representations are brain-functions. So the brain, the 'pulpy mass in the skull', supports the whole world of objects—Schopenhauer's materialist account of mental states combines with his idealism to produce the claim that the empirical world of individual things is a product of the brain's functioning. For fear of saying such things, people in the past invented the notion of an immaterial soul, but Schopenhauer will have none of that:

We say fearlessly that this pulpy mass, like every vegetable or animal part, is also an organic structure, like all its humbler relations in the inferior dwelling-place of our irrational brothers' heads, down to the humblest that scarcely apprehends. (*W2*, 273).

Finally, the brain is a biological organ, and so it cannot be exempt from Schopenhauer's doctrine of the will to life:

the *will-to-know*, objectively perceived, is the brain, just as the *will-to-walk*, objectively perceived, is the foot; the *will-to-grasp*, the hand; the *will-to-digest*, the stomach; the *will-to-procreate*, the genitals, and so on. (*W2*, 259)

So the position is this: our capacity for knowledge of empirical objects resides in the functioning of the brain, the brain is an organ of the body, and all organs of the body have developed in order to propagate life. Our much-vaunted knowledge is thus a derivative feature of what we are; the primary element in us is the will that manifests itself in the body as a whole. Conscious actions, caused by perception of the world and reasoning about it, are merely one way in which this will in our bodies is set into motion. The individual human subject is different from other kinds of striving thing in the world only by virtue of the fact that the particular organization of his or her brain gives rise to self-consciousness and reasoning. But these capacities are only the tip of an iceberg, whose bulk is the will. Our predicament is to be driven by this will, whether we like it or not, into conflict, pain, and frustration. Schopenhauer still holds out the hope of rising above this predicament, but, as we shall see, the will within us must be suspended or turn against itself before we can exploit the capacities of our intellects to their full potential. Knowledge must eventually 'throw off its yoke, and, free from all the aims of the will, exist purely for itself, simply as a clear mirror of the world' (*W1*, 152). But for that to happen is very much an exception.

The self

What am I? Schopenhauer can say that I am an individual item in the world, a living, bodily thing of a certain species, which is capable of self-conscious thought and action. But he makes it something of a puzzle how I can think of myself in this way. In his philosophy the self is seen successively as a subject of experience and knowledge, a subject of will and action, a bodily manifestation of will to life, and a pure mirror of timeless reality. Sometimes it is as if a struggle for dominance is being waged between these different conceptions. The dichotomy between *subject* and *object*, which is the starting-point for the whole of *The World as Will and Representation*, is especially important here. As we saw, he explains that the subject is that which knows, the object that which is known by it. But this must leave us in some doubt about what a subject is.

A subject of representation is, for Schopenhauer, a single consciousness in which many diverse experiences of objects are united. Material things and conceptual thoughts are representations for the subject. But the subject itself is the 'I' that thinks and perceives, as opposed to the things thought and the things perceived. It is vital to understand that Schopenhauer's subject of representations is not any part of the world of objects. It is not a thing at all. It is not in space or time, does not interact causally with objects, is not visible, not identified with the body, or even with the individual human being. His favourite metaphorical images for it are the eye that looks out on the world but cannot see itself, and the extensionless point at which light-rays focus in a concave mirror. The subject is where experiences all converge, but it is never itself an object of experience: 'We never know it, but it is precisely that which knows wherever there is knowledge' (*W1*, 5). Schopenhauer is not alone in having such a view of the subject. It is recognizable as a version of Kant's conception of the pure 'I' of self-consciousness (apperception); moreover, says Schopenhauer, 'the fine passage from the sacred *Upanishad* applies: "It is not to be seen: it sees everything; it is not to be heard: it hears everything; it is not to be recognized: it recognizes everything"' (*R*, 208). Wittgenstein later borrowed Schopenhauer's image of the eye that cannot see itself and the idea that the subject was not part of the world.

Schopenhauer's attitude to this pure subject of representation is ambivalent. On the one hand, he says that 'Everyone finds himself as this subject' (*W1*, 5). We are conscious not only of what we think and perceive, but of *being* that which thinks and perceives; moreover, he suggests, we cannot avoid the idea that that which thinks and perceives is distinct from every object of which it is conscious—even the body, which is 'an object among objects'. At the same time, however, each of us is an individual distinct from others. Each of us is closely associated with one particular part of the material world, and, as a subject of action or will, each of us must be a bodily thing. We seem to be two kinds of subject at once: subject of willing, which is essentially embodied, and subject of knowledge, which knows everything objectively, including its own body and acts of will, and hovers outside the world of individual things altogether. Our conception of ourselves ought, perhaps, to be split. Yet we think of the 'I' that thinks and perceives and the 'I' that acts as one and the same. Schopenhauer calls this a 'miracle *par excellence*', saying that 'the identity of the subject of willing with that of knowing by virtue whereof . . . the word "I" includes and indicates both, is the knot of the world, and hence inexplicable' (*R*, 211–12).

One may think that Schopenhauer inadvertently refutes his own conception of the pure subject which is not an object. For he admits that it provides at best an incomplete and perplexing way of thinking of oneself, says that it is inexplicable how 'I' could refer both to this pure subject and to the acting, material body, and even has to invoke the notion of a 'miracle' to get round the problem. We may also not be convinced that we do 'find ourselves' as the pure knowing subject, or that this is a conception which a philosophical account of self-consciousness needs to use at all. However, Schopenhauer's difficulties are not simply a matter of ineptness on his part—they go deep into an area of enduring perplexity. Each of us is not *merely* an object in the world; some account needs to be given of one's awareness of being oneself, of being 'inside' one's experience and seeming to be distinct from the rest of the world. Schopenhauer is not a dualist: he eschews any notion that souls, spirits, or immaterial substances constitute part of reality. Reality is material, and what each of us refers to using 'I' is, partly, an active, material thing in the world. But he is surely right in saying that that cannot be the end of the story. It seems true that I somehow 'find myself as a subject', however precisely we account for that. Some philosophers more recently have suggested that there is a fundamental, perhaps insuperable problem in trying to square 'subjective' and 'objective' views of ourselves. The underlying difficulty which Schopenhauer reveals is a substantial philosophical issue.

The struggle between competing views of the self is made even more intense by Schopenhauer's materialist account of the workings of the intellect as brain-functions, and his doctrine that the individual's body is an expression of will-to-life.

That which in self-consciousness, and hence subjectively, is the intellect, presents itself in the consciousness of other things, and hence objectively, as the brain; and that which in self-consciousness, and hence subjectively, is the will, presents itself in the consciousness of other things, and hence objectively, as the entire organism (W2, 245).

That focus of brain-activity (or the subject of knowledge) is indeed, as an indivisible point, simple, yet it is not on that account a substance (soul), but a mere condition or state. . . . This *knowing* and conscious *ego* is related to the will, which is the basis of its phenomenal appearance, as the image in the focus of the concave mirror is to that mirror itself; and, like that image, it has only a conditioned, in fact, properly speaking, a merely apparent reality. Far from being the absolutely first thing (as Fichte taught, for example), it is at bottom tertiary, since it presupposes the organism, and the organism presupposes the will. (W2, 278)

We need to tease out two distinct elements here. One is Schopenhauer's materialism, the other his view that the will is our essence.

We can consider ourselves both subjectively and objectively. If we are considering ourselves objectively, as things occurring in the empirical world, then materialism is the most plausible and consistent position to take, according to Schopenhauer. To be a materialist pure and simple would be 'one-sided' (W2, 13), because materialism can never give a proper account of what it is to be a subject who experiences and understands the world: 'materialism is the philosophy of the subject that forgets to take account of itself'. But one side of the truth is an objective account of ourselves as things inhabiting the empirical world, and the only choice here is to conceive of ourselves as material occupants of space and time, falling under causal laws. So what from one viewpoint we call thought and perception are, from the other viewpoint, processes of the material brain and nervous system. From this objective point of view, the subject which we take ourselves to be is—in Schopenhauer's most extreme claim about it—'merely apparent'.

But even this unsettled combination of subjective and objective views about oneself is not the complete predicament which Schopenhauer places us in. For brain and organism are not merely part of an inert, material reality. They are expressions of the blind will in nature, enabling life to exist and propagate itself. The will is primary, and lies beneath the division between subject and object altogether. The larger contrast between will and representation re-asserts itself here. The subject that represents and the object that is represented are both, in a sense, illusory, because in the world in itself the division between subject and object does not exist. Even if I the subject disappeared, and along with me all the individual objects that make up my experience, the will would still be there in itself, continuing to strive and throw up new life-forms. And the most fundamental point about the self, for Schopenhauer, is that this same will is exactly what now strives away within the bodily organism that has produced me the subject.

5 Character, sex, and the unconscious

Will and intellect

For Schopenhauer, the primary element in human beings is the will. The intellect is only secondary; Schopenhauer explains it as a particular manifestation of the will to life in the brain and nervous system, and 'a mere tool in the service of the will' (*W2*, 205). Schopenhauer invents many images for the relationship between intellect and will, but his favourite is that of the sighted, lame man who is carried on the shoulders of the strong, blind man. The intellect is conscious, and is our window on the world, but the driving force which takes us where we are going is deeper down inside the psyche, inside the body or organism which we also are. The doctrine of the primacy of the will has many applications which are broadly psychological or ethical. Schopenhauer is in some respects a forerunner of twentieth-century views about the unconscious mind and the influence of sexuality on our behaviour, both of which emerge from his considerations of the opposition between intellect and will. His ethics also depends on the idea that the core of each individual, which makes them the person they are, is not the intellect, but the enduring, underlying will.

Once again we find that the individual's sense of his or her identity is something of a precarious affair. The self is a kind of compound between the will and the intellect. Although objectively the intellect is an expression of will as well, in our own self-consciousness we can distinguish the intellect as that part of us which is occupied with conscious perception and thought. The subjective symptoms of this split are various kinds of conflict and domination of which we may be aware: a 'strange interplay within us' between the intellect and the will (W2, 207). For example, the will is a comparatively primitive part of us, and not sophisticated enough to react to imaginary ideas in a different way from genuine beliefs:

If . . . we are alone, and think over our personal affairs, and then vividly picture to ourselves, say, the menace of an actually present danger, and the possibility of an unfortunate outcome, anxiety at once compresses the heart, and the blood ceases to flow. But if the intellect then passes to the possibility of the opposite outcome, and allows the imagination to picture the happiness long hoped-for as thereby attained, all the pulses at once quicken with joy, and the heart feels as light as a feather, until the intellect wakes up from its dream . . . We see that the intellect strikes up the tune, and the will must dance to it; in fact, the intellect causes it to play the part of a child whom its nurse at her pleasure puts into the most different moods by chatter and tales alternating between pleasant and melancholy things. (W2, 207–8)

On the other hand, our ordinary experience of the world is suffused with the positive or negative significance that comes from the will:

In the immediate perception of the world and of life, we consider things as a rule merely in their relations . . . we regard houses, ships, machines, and the like with the idea of their purpose and their suitability therefor. . . . Let us picture to ourselves how much every emotion or passion obscures and falsifies knowledge, in fact how every inclination or disinclination twists, colours, and distorts not merely the judgement, but even the original perception of things. Let us recall how, when we are delighted by a successful outcome, the whole world at once assumes a bright colour and a smiling aspect, and on the other hand looks dark and gloomy when care and sorrow weigh on us. Let us then see how even an inanimate thing, which is yet to become the instrument for some event we abhor, appears to have a hideous physiognomy; for example the scaffold, the fortress to which we are taken, the surgeon's case of instruments, the travelling coach of loved ones, and so on. (W2, 372–3)

We tend not to use the intellect in a 'pure' fashion. The way we confront the world of objects in experience and thought is driven by the will—further evidence for Schopenhauer that the will is primary in us. He has many more examples of the bias the will exerts:

Our *advantage*, of whatever kind it may be, exercises a similar secret power over our judgement; what is in agreement with it at once seems to us fair, just, and reasonable.... A hypothesis, conceived and formed, makes us lynx-eyed for everything that confirms it, and blind to everything that contradicts it. What is opposed to our party, our plan, our wish, or our hope often cannot possibly be grasped and comprehended by us, whereas it is clear to the eyes of everyone else. (W2, 217–18)

Anybody wishing to describe the mind as a centre of pure perception and reasoning would have to overcome the considerable evidence Schopenhauer amasses (from anecdote, general observation and introspection) for the contrary view, that our experience is largely governed by what fits our own aims, instincts, and emotional needs.

Where Schopenhauer shows uncommon insight is in his theory of the unconscious, one of the more important and influential aspects of his theory of the will. Since the will is something that operates independently of our conscious representation of reality, it can be credited with desires, aims, and feelings which are not consciously entertained by the thinking subject, but which nevertheless control his or her behaviour. One example (which he says is 'trifling and ridiculous', but nevertheless 'striking') is that when adding up our finances 'we make mistakes more frequently to our advantage than to our disadvantage, and this indeed without the least intention of dishonesty, but merely through the unconscious tendency to diminish our *debit* and increase our *credit*' (W2, 218). But this is merely a small instance of a wide-spread principle. Schopenhauer says that the intellect is often excluded from 'secret decisions of its own will'. I do not consciously decide what I wish to happen in a particular situation, but at a certain outcome I feel 'a jubilant, irresistible gladness, diffused over my whole being ... to my own astonishment ... (O)nly now does my intellect learn how firmly my will had already laid hold of the plan' (W2, 209).

The will is here a part of the individual's mind which adopts attitudes and guides overt behaviour despite remaining out of sight of the conscious intellect. Schopenhauer even recognizes a process similar to Freud's much later idea of repression:

this will . . . makes its supremacy felt in the last resort. This it does by prohibiting the intellect from having certain representations, by absolutely preventing certain trains of thought from arising, because it knows, or in other words experiences from the self-same intellect, that they would arouse in it any one of the emotions previously described. It then curbs and restrains the intellect, and forces it to turn to other things . . . We often do not know what we desire or fear. For years we can have a desire without admitting it to ourselves or even letting it come to clear consciousness, because the intellect is not to know anything about it, since the good opinion we have of ourselves would inevitably suffer thereby. But if the wish is fulfilled, we get to know from our joy, not without a feeling of shame, that this is what we desired. (W2, 208–10)

In another interesting passage, Schopenhauer sees this mechanism as responsible for some forms of madness:

Every new adverse event must be assimilated by the intellect . . . but this operation itself is often very painful, and in most cases takes place only slowly and with reluctance. But soundness of mind can continue only in so far as this operation has been correctly carried out each time. On the other hand, if, in a particular case, the resistance and opposition of the will to the assimilation of some knowledge reaches such a degree that . . . certain events or circumstances are wholly suppressed for the intellect, because the will cannot bear the sight of them; and then, if the resultant gaps are arbitrarily filled up for the sake of the necessary connection; we then have madness. (W2, 400)

Sexuality and gender

Schopenhauer exaggerates in saying that all previous philosophers have 'ignored' sexual love ('I have no predecessors'

(*W2*, 533)), and his dismissal of Plato's contribution in particular is unwarranted (*W2*, 532). Nevertheless, in talking so bluntly about sexuality, and in making it such a cornerstone of his philosophy, he is again unusually forward-looking for his day. Sex is ever-present in our minds, according to Schopenhauer, 'the public secret which must never be distinctly mentioned anywhere, but is always and everywhere understood to be the main thing' (*W2*, 571). 'It is the ultimate goal of almost all human effort; it has an unfavourable influence on the most important affairs, interrupts every hour the most serious occupations' (*W2*, 533). None of this is surprising on Schopenhauer's theory. The impulse to sexual intercourse is at the very core of our being, as an instinct which is the most direct and powerful manifestation of will to life in our bodies: 'the genitals', he is fond of telling us, 'are the focus of the will'.

Schopenhauer explains instinct as 'an action as if in accordance with the conception of an end or purpose, and yet entirely without such a conception' (*W2*, 540). Sexual behaviour and anatomy are directed at reproduction in a purpose-like manner. Reproduction may at times also be a conscious purpose, of course, but to the extent that his or her behaviour manifests instinct, the individual's conscious purposes are irrelevant. According to Schopenhauer, the procreative 'purpose' which sexual activity and its elaborate, all-pervading surroundings are directed towards, is actually a 'purpose' of the human species, a built-in drive to generate itself over again, for which the individual acts as a mere vehicle. The seriousness with which individuals pursue sexual goals reflects the magnitude of this underlying species-purpose.

Thus Schopenhauer sees the individual's sexual behaviour as at the beck and call of an impersonal force. His most striking way of putting this is to say that it is the will to life of the as yet unconceived offspring which draws a male and female partner together. Their view that they are acting wholly in their own interests out of individual desires towards another individual is a 'delusion' (*W2*, 538), and this delusion itself is a means by which 'nature can attain her end'. The 'longing of love' celebrated in poetry of all ages is on this account truly something external to the lover, and hence so powerful that the individual can scarcely contain it:

this longing that closely associates the notion of an endless bliss with the possession of a definite woman, and an unutterable pain with the thought that this possession is not attainable; this longing and this pain of love cannot draw their material from the needs of an ephemeral individual. On the contrary, they are the sighs of the spirit of the species . . . The species alone has infinite life, and is therefore capable of infinite desire, infinite satisfaction, and infinite sufferings. But these are here imprisoned in the narrow breast of a mortal; no wonder, therefore, when such a breast seems ready to burst, and can find no expression for the infinite rapture or infinite pain with which it is filled. (W2, 551)

Schopenhauer also believes that once the ends of the species are fulfilled between lovers, their rapture and their delusion must eventually ebb away:

Forsaken by [the spirit of the species], the individual falls back into his original narrowness and neediness, and sees with surprise that, after so high, heroic, and infinite an effort, nothing has resulted for his pleasure but what is afforded by any sexual satisfaction. Contrary to expectation, he finds himself no happier than before; he notices that he has been the dupe of the will of the species. (W2, 557)

Of course, individuals will continue to feel sexual desire as a desire of their own directed towards a particular person, and will be conscious of the person's physical and mental attributes. Schopenhauer gives us a detailed list of the qualities that men supposedly look for in women (right age, health, proportion of skeleton, fullness of flesh, beauty of the face—in that order) and that women supposedly look for in men (right age, strength, courage). Looking away from such details, however, all the features of attraction are to be explained in the same way: they result from unconscious principles of selection through which the will of the species works to ensure the character of its next generation. Where the intention of intercourse is expressly not to generate offspring, Schopenhauer is nevertheless determined to explain subjective attraction in terms of life-generating instincts. Even the case of homosexuality does not deter him: such a widespread practice must 'arise in some way from human nature itself', he thinks, though his explanation for it is somewhat desperate. Very young and very old males, he supposes, have deficient semen, and are following an instinct to discharge it in non-procreative fashion, thus still subserving the 'will of the species' for the best possible offspring.

Some may find surprising another of Schopenhauer's convictions: that it is the intellect which we inherit from our mothers, and the will from our fathers. Not many philosophers have thought of the intellect as a female characteristic, and the capacity for emotions as male. Schopenhauer is convinced that there is empirical evidence for his claim, but he also gives another argument in which he shows his true colours. The will is 'the true inner being, the kernel, the radical element', while the intellect is 'the secondary, the adventitious, the accident of that substance' (*W2*, 517). So, the argument continues, we should expect the more powerful, procreative sex to impart the will to its offspring, while the mother, the 'merely conceiving principle', is responsible for the merely secondary intellect. The agenda here is to make sure that the female comes out as superficial and secondary, the male as substantial, radical, and primary. What is inherited from the father is the 'moral nature', the 'character', the 'heart'. The view that the intellect is female in origin thus results from a cross-fertilization between Schopenhauer's doctrine of the metaphysical primacy of the will and his fairly conventional prejudice that the female must be secondary to the male.

Schopenhauer's disparaging view of women, concentrated to most corrosive effect in the short essay 'On Women' (*P2*, 614–26), has earned him some notoriety. To what extent it should single him out from any of his contemporaries and predecessors is debatable. On the one hand, he is perhaps especially worthy of note because of his attempt to imbue gender differences with such metaphysical significance, and because he gives such prominence to sexuality in human life. On the other hand, it may be thought that his actual views are fairly commonplace for his time. What is not in question is the vehemence of his rhetoric on the topic:

Only the male intellect, clouded by the sexual impulse, could call the undersized, narrow-shouldered, broad-hipped, and short-legged sex the fair sex; for in this impulse is to be found its whole beauty. (*P2*, 619)

Throughout their lives women remain children, always see only what is nearest to them, cling to the present, take the appearance of things for reality, and prefer trivialities to the most important affairs. Thus it is the faculty of reason by virtue whereof man does not, like the animals, live merely in the present . . . In consequence of her weaker faculty of reason, woman shares less in the advantages and disadvantages that this entails. (*P2*, 615–16)

There are a few compensating virtues. Schopenhauer allots to women the greater share of humane loving-kindness, which for him is of supreme moral worth; he also thinks they are more down-to-earth and practical than men (the intellect at work again); but he is convinced that they cannot reason very well, and have shallow characters. Their interests are 'love, conquests, . . . dress, cosmetics, dancing'; they regard everything as a means to winning a man; dissimulation is inborn to them 'just as nature has armed the lion with claws and teeth, the elephant and boar with tusks, the bull with horns, and the cuttle-fish with ink that blackens water' (*P2*, 617). Women may be talented, but artistic geniuses can, apparently, only be male: 'generally speaking, women are and remain the most downright and incurable Philistines' (*P2*, 620–1). Occasionally, one glimpses a portrait of the novelist, socialite, and mother, Johanna Schopenhauer:

the original maternal love is purely *instinctive* and therefore ceases with the physical helplessness of the children. In its place, there should then appear one based on habit and reasoning; but often it fails to appear, especially when the mother has not loved the father. . . . Property acquired by the long and constant hard work of men subsequently passes into the hands of women who in their folly get through it or otherwise squander it in a short time. . . . The vanity of women . . . is bad because it is centred entirely on material things . . . and hence society is so very much their element. (*P2*, 625–6)

Conventional male sentiment mixed with personal bitterness—the result is scarcely edifying. But no account of Schopenhauer's philosophy ought to suppress these ideas, which were clearly important to him.

Character

We have seen that in Schopenhauer's view the will is the primary element within us, the intellect only secondary and 'adventitious'. In this, the will often has the role of an impersonal force which is greater than the individual, attaching to the species or to the world as a whole, and expressing itself in each individual equally. However, Schopenhauer also believes that each person has a distinct character. And here too the intellect is secondary. It is not intellectual abilities and traits, or continuity of consciousness, that marks out the true core of one's separate identity as an individual.

The older we become, the more does everything pass us by without leaving a trace. Great age, illness, injury to the brain, madness, can deprive a man entirely of memory, but the identity of his person has not in this way been lost. That rests on the identical *will* and on its unalterable character; it is also just this that makes the expression of the glance unalterable. . . . Our true self . . . really knows nothing but willing and not-willing, being contented and not contented, with all the modifications of the thing called feelings, emotions, and passions. (*W2*, 239)

Each human being's character is unique for Schopenhauer, though since we all belong to the same species, the differences may sometimes be very slight. Individual character comes into its own in explaining and predicting actions. An action follows on from motives, but only in combination with the character of the agent. The same set of objective circumstances, perceived and comprehended in the same way by different people, may lead them to act in quite different ways. Offer a large bribe and some will take it, some will politely decline, and others will turn you over to the authorities. The motive, in Schopenhauer's sense (that is, the external state of affairs as apprehended by the intellect) can be the same in all three cases, and the intellect itself can, if you like, be working in exactly the same way. But the character is what differs. If we knew each persons's character thoroughly, and all the motives they were exposed to, we could predict all their actions without any reminder. In another of Schopenhauer's beloved Latin tags, *operari sequitur esse*, 'acting follows from being': what we *are* partly determines how we act. The principle is no different from that by which we predict the varied behaviour of different natural substances under the same influence: 'the effect of the same motive on different people is quite different; as the sunlight gives to wax white colour and to chloric silver black, so the heat makes wax soft, but clay hard' (*F*, 50). This doctrine of character has consequences for freedom, responsibility, and morality, as we shall discover later.

Schopenhauer sees the character as a person's 'being', something distinct from the collection of all the person's actions put together. The actions follow from the being, each of them bearing the stamp of the person to whom they belong. This may make the character sound mysterious, but Schopenhauer assures us that we only ever learn about it, in other people or even in ourselves, from its empirical manifestations—just the way we learn about the character of wax or chloric silver, in fact. We observe many actions, and come to know someone's degree of honesty, courage, or compassion over the course of time. Similarly with ourselves: until we see how we fare in action, we may be quite wrong about the qualities of character which we possess. So Schopenhauer says that character is *empirical*. It is not identical with the series of actions I carry out, yet is discovered only from observation of those actions.

Schopenhauer maintains that each person's character is both

constant and inborn. We can neither choose nor change what we are. We can be educated to understand the world and ourselves better, giving us better, more refined motives on which to act, but the self that these motives prompt into action really has not altered: 'Under the changeable shell of his years, his relationships, and even his store of knowledge and opinions, there hides, like a crab under its shell, the identical and real man, quite unchangeable and always the same' (F, 51). Schopenhauer thinks that many of our ordinary attitudes bear out this claim: we assume not just identity of the person, but constancy in the moral character as well. When we have gone on trusting someone to behave in a certain way, and have eventually been disappointed, 'we never say: "His character has changed," but "I was mistaken about him"' (F, 52). For example, we say, on this view, not that someone used to be honest and courageous, but is now deceitful and cowardly; rather that the extent of their deceitfulness and cowardice was not fully apparent until now. As further evidence for constancy of character Schopenhauer cites the fact that we recognize others as the same after many years from the manner in which they act, and that we feel responsibility and shame for things we ourselves did forty years before.

With the claim that character is inborn we again find that human beings are to be treated very much on a par with other parts of nature. You would not try to produce apricots from an oak tree, says Schopenhauer. Human beings clearly have inborn species-characteristics. Why are people so loathe to accept that there is inborn courage, honesty, or wickedness at the level of the individual? Schopenhauer's evidence, such as it is, leads him to think that the human individual at birth cannot be a mere blank slate which awaits experience before it forms any character at all. Before we can have knowledge or perceive the world very well, we are creatures of will, reacting with positive or negative feelings to what impinges on us. Even at this stage, there is a basic core to the person which is not moulded by what he or she has intellectually apprehended of the world.

Schopenhauer also has the notion of *acquired character*.

Especially when we are young, we may not correctly understand what our character is. We do not know what we really
like, or want, or can succeed at. Acquired character is a better
self-understanding, which one comes to have by gaining an
insight into one's true constant character—an idea in some
ways reminiscent of Nietzsche's later notion of 'becoming who
you are'. This enlightened idea is, however, at odds with the
rest of Schopenhauer's account. For it seems that before I have
attained the acquired character, I may embark on ventures that
go against my real nature—which ought to be impossible if my
inborn, unchanging character determines all my actions.

Sometimes, however, Schopenhauer says things about the
character which are even more puzzling.

> however old we become, we yet feel within ourselves that we are
> absolutely the same as we were when we were young . . . This
> thing which is unaltered and always remains absolutely the same,
> which does not grow old with us, is just the kernel of our inner
> nature, and that does not lie in time. . . . (W)e are accustomed to
> regard the subject of knowing, the knowing I, as our real self
> . . . This, however, is the mere function of the brain, and is not our
> real self. Our true self . . . it is which produces that other thing,
> which does not sleep with it when it sleeps, which also remains
> unimpaired when that other thing becomes extinct in death. . . .
> The *character itself* . . . is still exactly the same now as then. The
> will itself, alone and by itself, endures; for it alone is unchangeable,
> indestructible, does not grow old, is not physical but metaphysical,
> does not belong to the phenomenal appearance, but to the thing in
> itself that appears. (W2, 238–9)

Here it is unclear what kind of thing the character is. On the
one hand it is unique and attaches to oneself as an individual.
On the other hand it is 'not in time', it is 'not physical but
metaphysical', and even 'remains unimpaired' when the individual dies and his or her subjective consciousness disappears.
The problem, bluntly, is this: is my 'real self', or 'the kernel of
my inner nature', something that attaches to the finite individual that I am, or is it the thing in itself, beyond space, time,
and individuation altogether? If the former, it is neither outside

of time nor unaffected by my own death. If the latter, it does not serve to explain my personal identity at all. Schopenhauer seems to stumble into a quite elementary difficulty. But in a way his confusion has a more profound point behind it. For he wants to claim in the end that our individuality, seemingly so fundamental to us, is not only a source of torment, but some kind of illusion: 'at bottom every individuality is really only a special error, a false step, something that it would be better should not be' (W2, 491–2). The Third and Fourth Books of *The World as Will and Representaion*—its great second half to which we now turn—explore the possibilities of escaping from individuality, and from the will which lies at our core.

6 *Art and Ideas*

Aesthetic experience

Aesthetic experience deliberately reverses the trend of Schopenhauer's book, for in it the will of the subject is suspended. As long as we exercise the will, or are governed by it, we shall be forced to consider a thing in a great mesh of relations to other things and to ourselves: Do we want it? Can we use it? Is it better than something else? What made it the way it is? What will it make happen? Just as our intellects are organs developed to subserve the will, so all the usual connections which we employ in order to understand objects are will-governed: we perceive in order to manipulate, in order to live. Only if we cease to will at all can the object stand out in our consciousness stripped of the relations of time, place, cause, and effect.

Schopenhauer belongs to a tradition which equates aesthetic experience with a 'disinterested' attitude towards its object, and is often cited as one of the chief proponents of such a view. The idea is that to experience something anesthetically, one must suspend or disengage all one's desires towards it, attending not to any consideration of what ends, needs, or interests it may fulfil, but only to the way it presents itself in perception. In Schopenhauer's case, aesthetic experience must always be an extraordinary episode in any human being's life, since he has argued that the will is our essence, and that our 'ordinary way of considering things' is permeated by will:

so long as our consciousness is filled by our will, so long as we are given up to the throng of desires with its constant hopes and fears, so long as we are the subject of willing, we never attain lasting happiness or peace. . . . Thus the subject of willing is constantly lying on the revolving wheel of Ixion, is always drawing water in the sieve of the Danaids, and is the eternally thirsting Tantalus.

When, however, an external cause or inward disposition suddenly raises us out of the endless stream of willing, and snatches knowledge from the thraldom of the will, the attention is now no longer directed to the motives of willing, but comprehends things free from their relation to the will. Thus it considers things without interest, without subjectivity, purely objectively . . . Then all at once the peace, always sought but always escaping us on that first path of willing, comes to us of its own accord, and all is well with us . . . (F)or that moment we are delivered from the miserable pressure of the will. We celebrate the Sabbath of the penal servitude of willing; the wheel of Ixion stands still. (*W1*, 196)

After the brisk formality of the opening book on the world as representation, and the incipient gloom as we descend into the world as will, the Third Book of *The World as Will and Representation* has a character of brightness and joy which testifies to the importance of the aesthetic for its author.

Schopenhauer states the central problem of aesthetics in an acute way—it is: 'how satisfaction with and pleasure in an object are possible without any reference thereof to our willing' (*P2*, 415). (His view of aesthetic enjoyment is similar in some respects to that put forward by Kant in his *Critique of Judgement*, though Schopenhauer makes little of this connection, and does not rate Kant's work on aesthetics as among his best.) In the usual run of events, pleasure or satisfaction arises from the fulfilment of some desire or end. What we call happiness is usually felt on attaining one of our ends, or it may be the temporary absence of anything further to strive for. But these kinds of pleasure and happiness, since they depend on willing, also carry with them the permanent possibility of suffering. In the first place, all willing 'springs from lack, from deficiency, and thus from suffering' (*W1*, 196). Secondly, when any particular desire is stilled, the subject of willing soon experiences another deficiency. Thus to be driven by the will is to oscillate between suffering and satisfaction, and Schopenhauer is convinced that the suffering lasts longer, the satisfaction being only a temporary return to neutral before another lack is felt.

The problem for aesthetics is how there can be any kind of pleasure other than that which is contained in this oscillation. If pleasure is defined as the fulfilment of a lack or the satisfaction of a desire, then a totally will-less state of contemplation ought to be one in which one cannot experience pleasure at all. Clearly, the positive gain of being in such a state would be the loss of the possibility of suffering, and Schopenhauer makes a great deal of this point. But how could a will-less state leave room for real pleasure? Sometimes Schopenhauer writes as if it could not, as if aesthetic contemplation were a state purely of knowledge, a dispassionate registering of objective reality—'we have stepped into another world, so to speak, where everything that moves our will, and thus violently agitates us, no longer exists.... Happiness and unhappiness have vanished' (*W1*, 197). Yet he is also prepared to describe aesthetic experience in terms such as 'peace' and 'blessedness', and as a special kind of pleasure or enjoyment. He even states that when 'all possibility of suffering is abolished . . . the state of pure objectivity of perception becomes one that makes us feel positively happy' (*W2*, 368). These different claims can be reconciled by saying that the usual kind of happiness (and unhappiness) depends on willing, while the aesthetic kind depends on the cessation of willing.

This might be thought sufficient to give aesthetic experience the value which Schopenhauer wishes to assign it. However, his version of the 'aesthetic attitude' theory is unusual in linking the state of will-less contemplation with the achievement of the most objective kind of knowledge. For him, an experience undergone in the absence of subjective desires and aims will be one which distorts the world as little as possible, so he can maintain that aesthetic experience is valuable not only for the calming effect of escaping from one's own will, but because it uniquely displays things as they eternally are. Aesthetic experience, in other words, has high cognitive value, not merely the enriching or therapeutic value of entering into a certain psychological state.

Objectivity and genius

The subject ordinarily experiences material objects that occupy space and time, their causal connections to one another, and bodily acts of will following upon motives. But Schopenhauer believes that we can in exceptional moments gain access to a timeless reality that is not carved up into individuals. Beyond the realm of individual things and events lies the Idea, to which 'neither plurality nor change' belongs: 'While the individuals in which it expresses itself are innumerable and are incessantly coming into existence and passing away, it remains unchanged as one and the same, and the principle of sufficient reason has no meaning for it' (*W1*, 169).

Schopenhauer begins his Third Book with a disquisition on Platonic Ideas and their relation to the thing in itself. His claim will be that artists, and all engaged in aesthetic experience, discern, however fleetingly, the timeless reality of Ideas. Hence he owes us an attempt to set the metaphysical record straight first: what are these Ideas? He calls them 'the most adequate objectivity' of the thing in itself. This sounds obscure but is in fact quite a simple notion. The thing in itself cannot be known; but a knowable object which presented reality to the subject with the least possible degree of subjective distortion would be the 'adequate objectivity' of the thing in itself. Thus Schopenhauer explains:

the Platonic Idea is necessarily object, something known, a representation, and precisely, but only, in this respect is it different from the thing in itself. It has laid aside merely the subordinate forms of the phenomenon, all of which we include under the principle of sufficient reason; or rather it has not yet entered into them. But it has retained the first and most universal form, namely that of the representation in general, that of being object for a subject. . . . Therefore, it alone is the most *adequate objectivity* possible of the will or of the thing in itself; indeed it is even the whole thing in itself, only under the form of the representation. Here lies the ground of the great agreement between Plato and Kant, although in strict accuracy that of which they both speak is not the same. (*W1*, 175)

Some strain is evident in the way that the Idea seems forced to serve as both thing in itself and representation, when these two categories were supposedly mutually exclusive at the outset. Also, although he recognizes that the equation of Kant and Plato would be wrong 'in strict accuracy', he is still prepared to make the extremely dubious statement that 'the inner meaning of both doctrines is wholly the same' (*W1*, 172). Some commentators have regarded the Ideas as an awkward, hasty afterthought. This is not wholly a fair assessment, however, as the Ideas were one of the earliest parts of the system to fall into place, and figured in the account of the will's objectification in nature in the Second Book. What we should hold on to is the notion that nature contains not only a multiplicity of individual things and events, but unchanging single kinds to which they belong. There are not only horses, but the species *horse*, not only pools and fountains but the repeatable molecular structure H_2O, not only many bodies falling to the ground at different times and places, but a ubiquitous gravitational force. Schopenhauer thinks of such kinds as timeless Ideas, and our apprehension of them as the most objective knowledge of the world we can ever attain. Schopenhauer follows Plato in claiming that Ideas exist in reality, independently of the subject. They are not concepts. Concepts are the mental constructs we make in order to grasp reality in general terms; but Ideas are parts of nature awaiting discovery. For Schopenhauer, they are not even discovered by conceptual thinking, but by perception and imagination.

What would consciousness of Ideas themselves be like? Schopenhauer has a dramatic answer. Once we abandon the guidance of the principle of sufficient reason,

we no longer consider the where, the when, the why, and the whither of things, but simply and solely the *what*. . . . [We] let our

whole consciousness be filled by the calm contemplation of the
natural object actually present, whether it be a landscape, a tree, a
rock, a crag, a building, or anything else . . . and continue to exist
only as pure subject, as clear mirror of the object, so that it is as
though the object alone existed without anyone to perceive it, and
thus we are no longer able to separate the perceiver from the
perception. . . . What is thus known is no longer the individual
thing as such, but the *Idea* . . . at the same time, the person who is
involved in this perception is no longer an individual, for in such
perception the individual has lost himself; he is *pure* will-less,
painless, timeless *subject of knowledge* (*W1*, 178–9).

'At one stroke', Schopenhauer continues, the particular thing
'becomes the Idea of its species', and the perceiving individual
'becomes the *pure subject of knowing*' (*W1*, 179). What
Schopenhauer must mean is that I see the particular as embody-
ing a universal Idea, and momentarily lose consciousness of
myself as an individual. His claim is that one cannot know
Ideas if one retains an awareness of oneself as an individual
separate from the object contemplated ('we apprehend the
world purely objectively, only when we no longer know that we
belong to it' (*W2*, 368))—and conversely that one cannot fail to
be knowing an Idea, once one's contemplation turns one into
this 'pure mirror' of reality.

Although Schopenhauer clearly thinks that natural beauty
often gives rise to aesthetic experience (witness the examples of
tree, rock, and crag), it is to art that he gives most attention. He
is fairly orthodox for his day in believing that the production of
art requires something called genius, which must be distinguished from mere talent. But he does give his own account of
what genius is. It consists, he writes, 'in the knowing faculty
having received a considerably more powerful development
than is required by the *service of the will*' (*W2*, 377). The person
of genius has two-thirds intellect and one-third will, the 'normal person' is the other way round. It is not that the genius is
lacking in will—such people usually have strong emotions, for
example—but rather that their intellect is capable of detaching

itself from the will to a much greater extent, and has the power to function autonomously:

the *gift of genius* is nothing but the most complete *objectivity* ... the capacity to remain in a state of pure perception, to lose oneself in perception, to remove from the service of the will the knowledge which originally existed only for this service. In other words, genius is the ability to leave entirely out of sight our own interest, our willing, and our aims, and consequently to discard entirely our own personality for a time, in order to remain *pure knowing subject*, the clear eye of the world; and this not merely for moments, but with the necessary continuity and conscious thought to enable us to repeat by deliberate art what has been apprehended. (*W1*, 185–6)

The genius stands for something impersonal, which Schopenhauer hints at with the metaphor of 'the clear eye of the world'. The genius is not only an individual, but 'at the same time a pure intellect that as such belongs to the whole of mankind' (*W2*, 390). Abandoning the will that manifests itself in this particular individual, and letting the intellect soar free of it, the genius has an uncommon ability 'to see the universal in the particular' (*W2*, 379). It is important that this is a capacity for heightened *perception*. A great painter or sculptor *sees* with more intensity and more detail, and has greater ability to retain and reproduce what is seen. But perceiving merely what is present to hand is not enough: '*imagination* is needed, in order to complete, arrange, amplify, fix, retain, and repeat at pleasure all the significant pictures of life' (*W2*, 379). Thus genius, in whichever art form, may go one better than actual experience: a great work of art may reflect reality all the better when the picture it conveys is a heightened one, having more clarity and definition than is ever contained in ordinary experience itself.

The true province of genius is imaginative perception, and not conceptual thinking. Art which is structured around some proposition, or worked out on a wholly rational plan, is dead and uninteresting by comparison. One example is where pictorial art turns to a symbolic form of allegory, and can be grasped only by deciphering images according to a code, something alien to art as such, in Schopenhauer's view (*W1*, 239). Another is when 'imitators' or 'mannerists' set themselves to produce according to a formula which they note to have been successful in some other work. The result is offensive: prior deliberation can always be discerned, and the constituent elements they have minced together can always be 'picked out and separated from the mixture'. The concept, 'useful as it is in life, serviceable, necessary, and productive as it is in science, is eternally barren and unproductive in art' (*W1*, 235).

Geniuses are rare because they are in a sense unnatural. In the great majority of people, the workings of the intellect are subordinate to the attainment of individual ends, as Schopenhauer's theory would predict. The intellect is an instrument of the will, and is not 'designed' for purposeless imaginative work which grasps and relays eternal Ideas. By the same token, people possessed of genius are commonly viewed as oddities. With its heightened imagination and tendency to distract from the immediate connections of things, genius has some resemblance to madness. Geniuses do not accommodate to the expectations of their own time and place, unlike people of mere talent, who are admired for the ability to produce what is wanted when it is wanted (*W2*, 390). The genius is also prone to impracticality, because of the degree to which his intellect works independently of the end-seeking will. (I say 'his', because Schopenhauer does not recognize female genius, even though the intellect is supposedly a female inheritance. The difference is presumably supposed to be that women's perception always remains superficial and never rises to 'the universal'.)

The arts and their value

Schopenhauer commands respect among historians of aesthetics for his deep and varied knowledge of the arts. While he has a single theory of aesthetic appreciation as the will-less contemplation of Ideas, he appreciates many different art forms, from architecture through painting of different genres, to poetry and drama, and eventually to music, which he sets apart from the rest. His aesthetics is not an inflexible metaphysical monolith: its core is fleshed out with elegance and sensitivity.

Before discussing the various arts, Schopenhauer makes a substantial qualification to his theory. He has claimed that whenever we have an aesthetic experience there occurs both a subjective cessation of willing and an objective insight into the realm of Ideas. However, he now admits that the value of a particular object of aesthetic experience can reside in one or other of these factors almost to the exclusion of the other:

with aesthetic contemplation (in real life or through the medium of art) of natural beauty in the inorganic and vegetable kingdoms and of the works of architecture, the enjoyment of pure, will-less knowing will predominate, because the Ideas here apprehended are only low grades of the will's objectivity, and therefore are not phenomena of deep significance and suggestive content. On the other hand, if animals and human beings are the object of aesthetic contemplation or presentation, the enjoyment will consist rather in the objective apprehension of these Ideas. (*W1*, 212)

In other words, the cognitive import of aesthetic experience may often be quite low. This may invite the thought that the single unifying element in his aesthetics is really the notion of pleasurable will-free contemplation, or even that his aesthetics is not unified. However, he deserves credit for realizing that the arts are regarded both as a release from the pressures of living, and as an intense form of knowledge.

The Ideas form a hierarchy of higher and lower grades of the will's objectification. The lowest are the all-pervading natural forces, the highest the Idea of humanity. Architecture is the art form that deals with the lowest Ideas concerning the behaviour of solid matter: gravity, cohesion, rigidity, and hardness (*W1*, 214). Buildings must also be of practical use, so that their potential to be pure art is, or should be, restricted. But the real core of architecture as an art is the conflict between gravity and rigidity. All the parts of a fine building should be relevant to making this conflict manifest to the observer, and should appear necessary rather than arbitrary: merely decorative elements belong to sculpture, and not to architecture as such. Also, it matters what materials a building is made from. An edifice which turned out to be of wood or pumice-stone would be a kind of sham, because materials less substantial than stone are not suited to bring out the Ideas of gravity and rigidity. We must be able to grasp in our perception the striving of the blocks towards the earth, and the counter-striving of the rigid elements which prevent them from falling. All else is irrelevant—mere beauty of shape is not a peculiarly architectural feature. The only other aspect to architecture that Schopenhauer acknowledges is light. The illumination of a building serves to reveal its fundamental structure more clearly, while that structure, by intercepting and reflecting light, 'unfolds [light's] nature and qualities in the purest and clearest way, to the great delight of the beholder' (*W1*, 216). Similar to architecture is 'the artistic arrangement of water' (*W1*, 217), which is less developed as an art simply because it is less useful than the making of buildings. The construction of fountains, waterfalls, and lakes does for the Ideas of fluidity, mobility, and transparency what architecture does for those of rigidity and cohesion.

Horticulture and landscaping provide a parallel in the realm of plants, although here Schopenhauer reckons that it is predominantly nature rather than art that does the work. Only in depictions of vegetation in painting does art come into its own. Our aesthetic enjoyment of a landscape painting whose subject is entirely vegetative or inanimate is one where 'the subjective side of aesthetic pleasure is predominant', residing in pure, will-less knowing, rather than in apprehending Ideas (*W1*, 218). But painting and sculpture become more concerned with the objective depiction of Ideas when they take animals and finally human beings as their subjects. Schopenhauer sees no important difference between confronting a person or animal face to face, and looking at an artistic representation—except that the abilities of a genius allow art to provide us with exemplars of greater beauty than nature actually provides: the genius 'impresses on the hard marble the beauty of form which nature failed to achieve in a thousand attempts, and he places it before her, exclaiming as it were, "This is what you desired to say!"' (*W1*, 222).

With depicted animals, as with animals themselves, the most beautiful individual is the one most characteristic of the species (*W1*, 220)—the lion, for example, in which we are best able to see the universal Idea of *the lion* embodied. Here, what we enjoy is less the calm of will-less contemplation, more our getting to know the animal which we see in the painting or sculpture: 'we are occupied with the restlessness and impetuosity of the depicted will' (*W1*, 219). With human beings, it is also true that the beautiful individual is the one most characteristic of the species. But there are also considerations of individual character and expression: a portrait ought to bring out the universal Idea of humanity, but of course must render the particular character of the sitter. Is this not an objection to Schopenhauer's theory that the point of art is always to express Ideas? May the strength of a work of art not lie in its conveying something particular and even arbitrary? Schopenhauer attempts to preserve the unity of his theory by maintaining that 'each person exhibits to a certain extent an Idea that is wholly characteristic of him' (*W1*, 224). But if apprehending an Idea is not always apprehending something timeless, universal, and potentially common to many individuals, it surely becomes less clear what sense we may attach to the notion.

Many paintings depict scenes from history, or from some particular legend or biblical story. But again, Schopenhauer urges that what makes them artistically significant is the extent to which they express something universal about mankind. Particular historical circumstances are irrelevant: 'it is all the same as regards inward significance whether ministers dispute about countries and nations over a map, or boors in a beerhouse choose to wrangle over cards and dice' (*W1*, 231). Schopenhauer is fond of contrasting the arts with history. He takes a high-handed line, and often uses the opportunity to disagree with the Hegelian conception of history. In his view, the essential kernel of human beings is always the same, not liable to local variation or change over time. Thus he makes the startling pronouncement that 'The chapters of the history of nations are at bottom different only through the names and dates; the really essential content is everywhere the same' (*W2*, 442). History, he maintains, co-ordinates merely facts about the changing surface of humanity, and can never get beyond this. The contrasting form of discourse is poetry: 'paradoxical as it may sound, far more real, genuine, inner truth is to be attributed to poetry than to history' (*W1*, 245). 'Genuine, inner truth' is supposedly truth about what does not change, that is, the Idea of humanity.

Poetry emerges as the art form which is able to express the Idea of absolutely anything in the world, but which reigns supreme in portraying the diverse characters and actions of mankind. Again Schopenhauer distinguishes carefully between concepts, which are abstract representations formed by the subject, and Ideas, which can be accessed in direct experience and are part of the fabric of nature itself. The task for the poet is to use the conceptual means which poetry has in common with other linguistic practices, towards the distinctive end of revealing an Idea to the mind of the reader. It is this that marks poetry out as an artistic use of language, and as the province of genius—for the writer cannot make an Idea perspicuous to the reader unless he or she first has sufficient objectivity to perceive it. Poetry can be called 'the art of bringing into play the power of imagination through words' (*W2*, 424). It differs from the visual arts not only in using language, but in the degree of work that must be done by the imagination of the recipient. Schopenhauer says much that is of interest about the different genres and styles of poetry: lyric, epic, and tragic, romantic and classical (which he prefers). Sometimes the poet finds the material, the Idea of humanity, in him- or herself, the result of which is lyric poetry. At the other end of the spectrum lies drama, in which the writer depicts humanity from an objective point of view.

Schopenhauer gives particular attention to tragedy, as the 'summit of poetic art' (*W1*, 252). While he is not alone in considering tragedy a supreme art form, it has especial importance for him because it is uniquely able to portray human life in what he regards as its true colours, containing the right degree of unfulfilled desire, conflict, and unmitigated suffering: 'It is the antagonism of the will with itself which is here most completely unfolded at the highest grade of its objectivity' (*W1*, 253). But seeing the Idea of humanity revealed in all its terrible truth is not the end of the matter. Schopenhauer requires that we understand also the ultimate human achievement (as he will later argue it to be) of resigning oneself, and turning against the will to life: 'we see in tragedy the noblest men, after a long conflict and suffering, finally renounce for ever all the pleasures of life and the aims till then pursued so keenly, or cheerfully and willingly give up life itself' (*W1*, 253).

Witnessing the depiction of suffering and resignation in tragedy, we learn by suffering in some measure ourselves. The best kind of tragedy, in Schopenhauer's view (which admittedly leaves out many famous instances of the genre) is where a catastrophe occurs in the course of a more or less ordinary life through no particularly grave fault of the protagonist. This kind of tragedy 'shows us those powers that destroy happiness and life, and in such a way that the path to them is at any moment open even to us. . . . Then, shuddering, we feel ourselves already in the midst of hell' (*W1*, 255). Is there room for pure aesthetic pleasure amid such terror—amid such perturbations of the will? Schopenhauer's answer invokes the Kantian conception of the sublime, in which the contemplation of something potentially destructive, viewed from the vantage point of present safety, brings a pleasurable sense of elevation. Schopenhauer gives this his own twist, however. What we rise to, above our shudderings at the depicted pain and misery of the tragedy, is, he claims, a sense of the serene abandonment of all willing which beckons from the very highest plateau that human life can reach. 'What gives to everything tragic . . . the characteristic tendency to the sublime, is the dawning of the knowledge that the world and life can afford us no true satisfaction, and are therefore not worth our attachment to them' (*W2*, 433–4).

Music

Schopenhauer's philosophical theory of music is set apart from his account of the other arts, and has enjoyed something of a life of its own in musical circles and in aesthetics. It remains one of the most striking theories of the power of music to express emotion, even if, like other attempts to explain this phenomenon, it is not ultimately convincing. Schopenhauer's view is that music is a 'copy of the will itself' (*W1*, 257). Whereas all the other art forms present us with Ideas which are the experienceable manifestation of the will, music bypasses these Ideas, and is 'as *immediate* an objectification and copy of the whole *will* as the world itself is'. The will expresses itself once as the whole world of particular phenomena and universal kinds into which they fall; it expresses itself over again as music. There are two parts to Schopenhauer's view. One attempts to explain the significance of music in terms of states of feeling and striving that we are familiar with in ourselves. The other draws a large-scale analogy between the range of phenomena in nature and the different elements of which music consists.

Here is Schopenhauer's idea about music and conscious strivings:

The nature of man consists in the fact that his will strives, is satisfied, strives anew, and so on and on; in fact his happiness and well-being consist only in the transition from desire to satisfaction, and from this to a fresh desire ... Thus, corresponding to this, the nature of melody is a constant digression and deviation from the keynote in a thousand ways ... (M)elody expresses the many different forms of the will's efforts, but also its satisfaction by ultimately finding again a harmonious interval, and still more the keynote. (*W1*, 260)

Schopenhauer contends that the progression of musical notes through time is immediately understood by the human mind as an analogy of the progress of our own inner strivings. Here are some of the many examples he gives:

as rapid transition from wish to satisfaction and from this to a new wish are happiness and well-being, so rapid melodies without great deviations are cheerful. Slow melodies that strike painful discords and wind back to the keynote only through many bars, are sad, on the analogy of delayed and hard-won satisfaction. . . . The *adagio* speaks of the suffering of a great and noble endeavour that disdains all trifling happiness. (*W1*, 260–1)

The effect of the *suspension* also deserves to be considered here. It is a dissonance delaying the final consonance that is with certainty awaited; in this way the longing for it is strengthened, and its appearance affords the greater satisfaction. This is clearly an analogue of the satisfaction of the will which is enhanced through delay. (*W2*, 455–6)

Many have found these ideas reflected especially in the composition of Wagner's *Tristan and Isolde*.

A popular prejudice is that music expresses the emotion of the composer or performer. But this is decidedly not Schopenhauer's view. Music, for him, has the peculiarity of expressing what might be called impersonal emotions:

music does not express this or that particular and definite pleasure, this or that affliction, pain, sorrow, horror, gaiety, merriment, or peace of mind, but joy, pain, sorrow, horror, gaiety, merriment, peace of mind *themselves*, to a certain extent in the abstract, their essential nature, without any accessories, and so also without the motives for them. (*W1*, 261)

If a person experiences some particular joy or sorrow in life, usually some 'motive' or representation of the way things are gives rise to the emotion. Emotions tend to be about something. But Schopenhauer is proposing that in music we grasp directly and non-conceptually the essential shape, as it were, of feeling joy or sorrow, without any content—without any representation of what the emotion is about. Listeners thus recognize the pure ebb and flow of the will, of striving and satisfaction, in which their own life consists, but without their own desires being engaged, without feeling emotions themselves, and so without any risk of pain. The account remains intriguing, though we may question whether it really captures the essential nature of the emotions, or explains just how the listener is supposed to apprehend them.

Schopenhauer's other central thought about music is that it parallels the world in the range of expressions of will which it achieves. The bass is like the lowest grade of the will's objectification, 'inorganic nature, the mass of the planet' (*W1*, 258). The melody on top is analogous to 'the highest grade of the will's objectification, the intellectual life and endeavour of man' (*W1*, 259). All the parts in between, with their intervals from one another, are the various manifestations of will throughout the inorganic world and the plant and animal kingdoms. Hence, music is not merely an expression of conscious human strivings, but a copy of the will in its great diversity, and hence a re-run of the whole phenomenal world. This idea, though fanciful, is a rather fine one. Whether or not Schopenhauer's views about music can be subscribed to literally, one can understand why musicians have often been drawn to him. No other philosopher has given music such a weighty role, and few have come nearer to the impossible achievement of evoking its pleasures in a purely verbal medium.

7 *Ethics: seeing the world aright*

Against Kant's ethics

In Schopenhauer's view, the ethical sphere parallels the aesthetic in that prescriptive rules, and conceptual thought in general, are not the essential thing:

> Virtue is as little taught as is genius; indeed, the concept is just as unfruitful for it as it is for art, and in the case of both can be used only as an instrument. We should therefore be just as foolish to expect that our moral systems and ethics would create virtuous, noble, and holy men, as that our aesthetics would produce poets, painters, and musicians. (*W1*, 271)

This suggests that people will either have intuitive ethical insight or they will not; and we know that Schopenhauer thinks an individual's basic character cannot be altered. Moral rules, in that case, are useful only in channelling and curbing people's behaviour: you can train an egoistic person so that his or her behaviour has less disastrous consequences, but not make him or her into a good person. Since he takes this view, Schopenhauer's philosophical ethics will not itself be prescriptive. Nor will it attempt to debate whether moral laws are universally binding, or consider what reason one has to obey them, or indeed give any theory of 'moral law' at all.

Schopenhauer's ethical theory does not stand entirely under Kant's shadow, any more than his theory of knowledge or his aesthetics—yet the shadow is always present. Kant's ethics is an ethics of duty, and tries to formulate an imperative to which the actions of the ideally rational being must conform. Schopenhauer's, by contrast, is an ethics of compassion. It tries to explain the difference between good and bad in terms of a divergence of attitudes which individuals may take towards one another, and towards the world as a whole. Morality for Schopenhauer is not a matter of duty or of 'ought'; nor can it be founded in rationality. It is a matter of 'seeing the world aright', to use Wittgenstein's later phrase. But to reach his position Schopenhauer first has to argue with Kant in some detail.

The essay *On the Basis of Morality* contains a succinct and powerful discussion of Kantian ethics, in which Schopenhauer brings forward many objections, chief among them the objection that Kant's idea of an imperative, 'You ought', is a theological notion in disguise. The language in which Kant speaks here has biblical overtones, and, to the atheist Schopenhauer, the very idea of an absolute command either trades surreptitiously on the assumption of an absolute being who may issue it, or it is unfounded. When Kant later tries to show how ethics requires an idea of God, Schopenhauer is reminded of a conjuror who, to our great surprise, pulls out of the hat something which he had planted there all along (*B*, 57). On the other hand, if there is no God, we should not simply swallow the idea of an absolute, universal imperative in the first place.

To whom, in any case, would the Kantian imperative be addressed? Not to human beings as such, but to 'all rational beings'. Schopenhauer is again scathing:

we know *reason* as the exclusive attribute of the human race, and are by no means entitled to think of it as existing outside that race, and to set up a *genus* called 'rational beings' differing from its sole species, 'man'. Still less are we justified in laying down laws for such imaginary *rational beings in the abstract* . . . We cannot help suspecting that Kant here gave a thought to the dear little angels, or at any rate counted on their presence in the conviction of the reader. (*B*, 63–4)

Kant's moral imperative has to be issued to rational beings in the abstract, because his ethics sets out to be non-empirical, and to rest wholly on principles knowable a priori—that is to say, knowable in advance of experience. But this itself is something that should be queried, according to Schopenhauer. Practical morality—decision-making and judgement—is concerned with the actual conduct of individual human beings who occupy the empirical realm. This should also be the focus of the theoretical discussion which Schopenhauer calls 'morals'. He charges that Kant's moral imperative is by contrast purely formal, and so without any 'real substance' (B, 76).

What about the Kantian appeal to rationality? Schopenhauer points out that rational behaviour is not always morally good behaviour: 'Reasonable and vicious are quite consistent with each other, in fact, only through their union are great and far-reaching crimes possible' (B, 83). In other words, if one is evil, rationality will not make one any *less* evil; it may simply make one a more efficient and deadly exponent than an evil person who cannot think straight. Reason is instrumental, concerning the means towards some end which one has. An imperative will therefore motivate a rational being to action, only if he or she has an interest or end already in view. Since *human* beings are material, striving individuals who manifest the will to life, their ends tend to be egoistic. Egoism is the 'paymaster' required to cash out any formal imperative (B, 89): what will rationally motivate me to act in any particular case will be considerations about whether I can achieve *my* own ends.

One final criticism is perhaps worthy of mention. Schopenhauer is affronted by Kant's idea of the 'dignity of man'—our supposed 'unconditioned incomparable value'—and by the idea that human beings must be treated as 'ends in themselves'. One ground for his criticism is that something can be a 'value' or 'end' only if it is the fulfilment of something specific that is willed. 'Unconditioned value' and 'end in itself' would in that case be disguised contradictions. More significantly, Schopenhauer finds this elevation of the human species at the expense of other animals 'revolting and abominable'. Other species are supposed to lack such dignity, and not to be ends in themselves, solely through lacking reason; but the consequence is that, in philosophical morals, animals

are mere 'things', mere *means* to any ends whatsoever. They can therefore be used for vivisection, hunting, coursing, bullfights, and horse racing, and can be whipped to death as they struggle along with heavy carts of stone. Shame on such a morality . . . that fails to recognize the eternal essence that exists in every living thing, and shines forth with inscrutable significance from all eyes that see the sun! (*B*, 96)

Schopenhauer sounds almost our contemporary here. At the same time, his lack of confidence in any special value attaching to humanity or to rationality is an important element in his pessimism. As we shall see, being an individual of the human species is neither a dignified nor a good thing as such.

Freedom and determinism

Schopenhauer believes that actions are caused by a combination of one's unchanging character and a motive occurring in one's consciousness. This is the basis of his claim that all actions are determined, and that, in one important sense, there is no freedom of the will. But his discussion of the issue, especially in its concentrated form in *On the Freedom of the Will*, is of considerable subtlety. As well as arguing for determinism, he makes an important distinction between different senses of 'freedom', and finishes with the reflection that the truth of determinism does not make us any less inclined to feel responsible for our actions—a fact which he rightly says still requires an explanation.

Schopenhauer brings to light a distinction, which is often overlooked, between freedom to will and freedom to act. Freedom to act is the ability to do something, if one wills to do it. This freedom can be removed by external obstacles to action, by constraining motives, laws or threats of various consequences if one acts, or by impairment of the subject's cognitive faculties. Being in prison, being at gunpoint, or having sustained brain-damage are, for example, all ways in which there can be some obstacle to one's doing what one wills. Schopenhauer accordingly lists physical freedom, moral freedom, and intellectual freedom as the three species of freedom to act. The deeper question, however, is whether I have any freedom to *will* this or that course of action. Schopenhauer arrives at his admirably straight answer to this question by examining the only two available sources of evidence: consciousness of ourselves and consciousness of things other than ourselves.

Consciousness of ourselves is powerless to tell us whether we could ever have willed otherwise than we did. In self-consciousness we are aware of doing what we want to do, by being aware of our action itself and of the motives that bring it about. But once I have chosen one course of action, say, going to Frankfurt, can I tell whether I *could* equally have chosen to go to Mannheim? The problem is this:

Everyone's self-consciousness asserts very clearly that he can do what he wills. But since we can conceive of him as willing quite opposite actions, it follows that if he so wills he can also *do* the opposite. Now the untutored understanding confuses this with the proposition that he, in a given case, can also *will* the opposite, and calls this the freedom of the will. . . . But whether in a given case he can *will* the one as well as the other . . . calls for a deeper investigation than the one which mere self-consciousness could decide (*F*, 23).

The question is not whether one can want or wish to do each of two opposite actions, but whether one could will them—remembering that (barring obstacles) willing is acting, for Schopenhauer. I went to Frankfurt, and I am aware that if it had been my will to go to Mannheim, I could have done that. The question is: could that have been my will? Schopenhauer's sensible answer is that, from examining my own knowledge of my actions and motives, I cannot decide this question.

On the other hand, if one looks at the causal relation between the external world and the subject who wills, one is bound to treat the case as one treats any other cause–effect relationship. I cannot regard myself alone as the one part of the world that is exempt from the principle of sufficient reason; so, if the state of affairs which caused me to go to Frankfurt were exactly repeated, it could only cause me to go to Frankfurt. It makes no difference that part of the cause is a process of

rational deliberation. Schopenhauer contends that if my character, and the motive—my representation of reality—were to
remain the same, then I could not have willed otherwise. In this
sense, there is no free will. We think we have it, but all that we
have is the freedom to do what we will, with which it is so
easily confused.

The argument is already cogent, but the way in which
Schopenhauer caps it shows his peculiar skill as a philosophical
writer. Imagine a man standing on the street at six o'clock in
the evening, he says, musing on the following thoughts: 'the
working day is over. Now I can go for a walk, or I can go to the
club; I can also climb up the tower to see the sun set'—and so
on—'I also can run out of the gate, into the wide world, and
never return. All of this is strictly up to me, in this I have
complete freedom. But still I shall do none of these things now,
but with just as free a will I shall go home to my wife.'
Schopenhauer's comment?

This is exactly as if water spoke to itself: 'I can make waves (yes!
in the sea during a storm), I can rush down hill (yes! in the river
bed), I can plunge down foaming and gushing (yes! in the waterfall),
I can rise freely as a stream of water into the air (yes! in the
fountain), I can, finally, boil away and disappear (yes! at a certain
temperature); but I am doing none of these things now, and am
voluntarily remaining quiet and clear water in the reflecting pond.
(*F*, 43)

After stating his case for determinism, however,
Schopenhauer reserves the right to a 'higher view'. 'For there is
another fact of consciousness which until now I have left completely aside', he says: 'This is the wholly clear and certain
feeling of the *responsibility* for what we do, of the accountabil-
ity for our actions, which rests on the unshakable certainty that
we ourselves are the doers of our deeds' (*F*, 93–4). As some
philosophers have said recently, the truth of determinism does
not take away this 'certain feeling' that we are accountable for
our actions, that they are in some sense 'up to us'.

Schopenhauer now turns to a distinction in Kant's ethics,
namely that between a person's empirical character and their

intelligible character, 'one of the most beautiful and profound ideas brought forth by that great mind, or indeed by men at any time' (*F*, 96). This is another aspect of the backbone distinction between appearance and thing in itself with which we have dealt all along:

the empirical character, like the whole man, is a mere appearance as an object of experience, and hence bound to the forms of all appearance—time, space, and causality—and subject to their laws. On the other hand, the condition and the basis of this whole appearance . . . is his intelligible character, i.e. his will as thing in itself. It is to the will in this capacity that freedom, and to be sure even absolute freedom, that is, independence of the law of causality (as a mere form of appearances), properly belongs. (*F*, 97)

The basic idea is quite simple: if I cannot escape from causal necessity as part of empirical reality, then an aspect of me that is beyond empirical reality may do so. Schopenhauer points out that when we hold someone accountable we blame the person for his or her character, or for what he or she *is*, using actions merely as evidence for this. He suggests that I must be responsible for what I am—my intelligible character behind appearances, from which issue all my actions. Freedom is not eliminated, but moved out of the empirical realm.

Here Schopenhauer faces some serious problems. One is that, on his own view, my character is inborn and unchanging. In what sense can I then be responsible for being what I am? Another problem is that *I* seem to disappear from the world in itself. The thing in itself is not split up into individuals—a crucial claim throughout Schopenhauer's philosophy. '*My* will as thing in itself', my intelligible character, ought not to be separate from the world as whole; and so it is hard to see how I could be held responsible for 'what I am in myself'. Schopenhauer is right in saying that we do regard a person as responsible for actions, thinking of the person as their true source, regardless of their place in a causal chain of events. But, although his may be an acute diagnosis of the problem of free will, Schopenhauer's solution is not really credible.

Egoism and compassion

What then is the true basis of morals, according to Schopenhauer? The answer may be given in three stages. One concerns the single principle which, he claims, all moral actions conform to, namely: 'Injure no one; on the contrary, help everyone as much as you can' (which he gives in Latin: *Neminem laede, imo omnes quantum potes, juva*). The second stage of the answer is an attempt to explain the basic psychological attitude which alone can spur people on to moral actions, namely compassion or sympathy. Ultimately, however, the basis of morals is not reached until the third stage, in which we are given a metaphysical account of how the compassionate attitude is both possible and justified.

The *'Neminem laede'* principle can be broken into two parts: 'Injure no one' and 'Help everyone as much as you can'. Actions which conform to the first part Schopenhauer calls instances of voluntary justice, while those which conform to the second are instances of disinterested philanthropy, or 'loving-kindness' towards other human beings (and presumably towards animals too: in line with his earlier censure of Kant, Schopenhauer adduces the fact that we *do* feel compassion towards animals (*B*, 175–8)). No action except those of pure justice or philanthropy can count as having true moral worth (*B*, 138–9). Schopenhauer takes it as a premiss that such acts, however rare and surprising, are acknowledged to occur, and are universally regarded as being good. Examples range from self-sacrifice in battle to someone's returning a lost object which they could have kept without any consequences, or giving alms to a beggar when they stand to gain nothing from doing so. Justice and philanthropy both stem from compassion, which manifests itself either as pure concern to promote the well-being of another, or as pure distress at the suffering of another.

Every human being, according to Schopenhauer, has some element of compassion in their character (*B*, 192). But there are vast differences in the proportion of compassion with which we are endowed. Some are overflowing with it, some have virtually none in them. Schopenhauer thinks that only actions from compassion have moral worth, and that we judge primarily what a person *is*, using their actions merely as evidence. If we follow him in all this, we shall have to admit that some human beings are greatly more good than others, and that some, though they might occasionally act from compassion, are not good. Whether or not that is a problem, it pales into insignificance compared with the difficulty of explaining how, on his view, compassion is possible at all, and how it can be an incentive to action.

If some part of everyone's make-up is compassion, what is the rest? Schopenhauer's claim in full is this:

Man's three fundamental ethical incentives, egoism, malice, and compassion, are present in everyone in different and incredibly unequal proportions. In accordance with them, motives will operate on man and actions will ensue. (*B*, 192)

Schopenhauer helps us with a succinct explanation of the three incentives. Compassion is the incentive to seek the well-being of another (or to alleviate their woe). Malice is the incentive to seek the woe of another; egoism that to seek one's own well-being. We may wonder whether the logic of this triad is quite right: is not malice really a kind of self-seeking, a kind of egoism? In Schopenhauer's defence, the reply must be that some malice at least is not egoistic. Much that we can set down as cruelty is done at the behest of one's own gain in some form or other: it is then a means to an egoistic end. But what Schopenhauer means by pure malice is something as exceptional as pure philanthropy: the kind of depraved or 'devilish' action where the agent sets aside his or her own well-being as an aim, simply in order to harm someone else (*B*, 136)—what one might call disinterested malice. The triad of egoism, malice, and compassion, is thus a genuine threesome, although many cruel and wicked actions do not arise from malice proper.

Nevertheless it is the egoistic incentive that compassion most has to contend with, because it is egoism that makes up the bulk of each individual: 'The chief and fundamental incentive in man as in the animal is *egoism*, that is, the craving for existence and well-being' (*B*, 131). Each individual is a material organism in which will to life expresses itself: hence striving for one's own ends is fundamental to each individual. Indeed, so fundamental is it on Schopenhauer's theory that one must wonder how compassionate action is possible at all. If action is always a bodily striving of the individual towards some end of its own, compassion, which is supposedly the only genuine moral incentive, ought never to move any individual to action. Egoism is 'colossal' and 'natural':

every individual, completely vanishing and reduced to nothing in a boundless world, nevertheless makes himself the centre of the world, and considers his own existence and well-being before everything else. In fact, from the natural standpoint, he is ready for this to sacrifice everything else; he is ready to annihilate the world, in order to maintain his own self, that drop in the ocean, a little longer. This disposition is *egoism*, which is essential to everything in nature. (*W1*, 332)

Egoism 'towers over the world' (*B*, 132) to such an extent that, without the constraint of laws embodied in the State, individuals would be engaged in *bellum omnium contra omnes*, a war of all against all (*B*, 133). All this suggests that action motivated by pure concern for the well-being of others should be not only rare, but so contrary to our nature as to be impossible. Schopenhauer has to admit that compassion is one of the mysteries of ethics. His only choice is to say that compassion is a primitive anti-egoistic trait which, as a matter of sheer fact, is present in us. But how compassion can 'reside in human nature' (*B*, 149) is deeply mysterious given that the human being is a naturally egoistic expression of will to life.

The metaphysics of morals

The final stage of Schopenhauer's ethics, however, seeks to rest the compassionate attitude on a metaphysical foundation. Compassion turns out to reflect a view of oneself and the nature of reality which differs from that implicit in egoism, and is superior to it. Schopenhauer can thus say that compassion is a good thing not only because it tends to decrease the sum of suffering in the world, but because it embodies a truer metaphysical picture.

The initial thought is that it is possible for me to feel compassion only if 'to a certain extent I have identified myself with the other person, and in consequence the barrier between the I and the non-I is for the moment abolished' (*B*, 166). Schopenhauer takes rather literally the idea contained in 'compassion' or 'sympathy' (German *Mitleid*) that one person 'suffers with' another. Thought for my well-being has to yield its place in my motivation to thought for another's well being; and it would be inexplicable how that could happen unless I could make the other's suffering and well-being intimately my own concern. Only if I share your suffering, in some sense feeling it as my own, can your well-being, or the alleviation of your woe, come to motivate me. To be compassionate, someone must, says Schopenhauer, 'make less of a distinction than do the rest between himself and others' (*B*, 204).

But now he can argue that the compassionate person is committed to a different metaphysical view:

The *bad* man everywhere feels a thick partition between himself and everything outside him. The world to him is an *absolute non-I* and his relation to it is primarily hostile. . . . The good character, on the other hand, lives in an external world that is homogeneous with his own true being. The others are not non-I for him, but an 'I once more'. His fundamental relation to everyone is, therefore, friendly; he feels himself intimately akin to all beings, takes an immediate interest in their weal and woe, and confidently assumes the same sympathy in them. (*B*, 211)

Which is the correct view of the world? The appearance/thing in itself dichotomy will tell us. From the point of view of the world of representation, governed by space and time which are the principle of individuation, reality consists of separate individuals, of which any moral agent is one. So the person who thinks 'Each individual is a being radically different from all others . . . everything else is non-I and foreign to me' (*B*, 210), is right about the world of appearance. But beneath this lies the world as thing in itself, which is not split up into individuals, but just is *the world*—whatever there ultimately is. So the supposedly more profound view is the one which considers individuation to be 'mere phenomenon' rather than ultimately part of reality. From this point of view, no one is distinct from anything else in the world, and so can recognize 'in *another* his own self, his own true inner nature' (*B*, 209). Schopenhauer's Indian thoughts come to the fore suddenly: the conception of the world as composed of separate individuals is *Mâyâ*—'i.e. illusion, deception, phantasm, mirage' (*B*, 209), while knowledge of the deeper, more correct, non-individuating view, is expressed in the Sanskrit *tat tvam asi*: this art thou (*B*, 210).

At first sight this idea seems so extreme as to expunge the possibility of compassion altogether. If I really believed that you were not distinct from me, the attitude with which I regarded you could only be a strange kind of egoism. Genuine compassion, on the other hand, surely presupposes belief in distinctness as a minimum condition. An even more graphic objection is that, if the world in itself is without individuation, it does not even contain *me*: it certainly does not contain me as this bodily, willing human being, nor does it contain the thinking 'I' that I regard myself as being from a subjective point of view. It is hard to see how the belief in the illusoriness of all individuals, including the individual which I am, could support a compassionate attitude between the individual that I am and the individual beggar to whom I give money.

But perhaps this is too simplistic a response. What Schopenhauer has recognized is the possibility of an attitude to the world which does not take one's existence as a particular individual to be of paramount significance: a 'universal standpoint' as opposed to a particular one (*W2*, 599–600). In order to adopt this standpoint, one need not abandon the belief in separate individuals altogether. Compassion is supposed to motivate actions which one must carry out as an individual, towards other individuals. What might ground such actions is the idea that, though individuals are separate, there is nothing of any fundamental importance about the individual which I am. If the beggar and I are both equal portions of the same underlying reality, equal manifestations of the same will to life, then from the point of view of the world as a whole, it is a matter of indifference whether my ends are promoted and the beggar's thwarted, or vice versa. This thought seems genuinely capable of grounding a compassionate outlook. The belief that I simply am not an individual separate from the rest of reality is not what does the work here; rather it is that, though being an individual (and naturally egoistic) thing in the world, my perspective does not always have to be one of identification with the individual that I am. As in Schopenhauer's account of aesthetic experience, I need not accept the natural standpoint of individuality as the one from which I must always regard things. In the next chapter we shall see that the individual's renunciation of his or her individuality not only makes aesthetic value and moral worth possible for Schopenhauer, but is the only attitude which can compensate for his or her existing at all.

8 Existence and pessimism

Ineliminable suffering

Awakened to life out of the night of unconsciousness, the will finds itself as an individual in an endless and boundless world, among innumerable individuals, all striving, suffering, and erring; and, as if through a troubled dream, it hurries back to the old unconsciousness. Yet till then its desires are unlimited, its claims inexhaustible, and every satisfied desire gives birth to a new one. No possible satisfaction in the world could suffice to still its craving, set a final goal to its demands, and fill the bottomless pit of its heart. In this connexion, let us now consider what as a rule comes to man in satisfactions of any kind; it is often nothing more than the bare maintenance of this very existence, extorted daily with unremitting effort and constant care in conflict with misery and want, and with death in prospect. Everything in life proclaims that earthly happiness is destined to be frustrated, or recognized as an illusion. The grounds for this lie deep in the very nature of things. (W2, 573)

The Fourth Book of the *World as Will and Representation* is its austere final movement. Schopenhauer's style matches the greater seriousness of the discussion (*W1*, 271), which, together with the topics in ethics we have already looked at, addresses— to use a hackneyed phrase—the human condition itself. Few writers have the insight and eloquence to make a philosophically interesting contribution in this area, but Schopenhauer is undoubtedly one of them.

Schopenhauer looks around the world and finds it full of suffering—frustration, tedium, pain, and misery. It might be thought that this is just a matter of personal propensity. Someone else might point out the occurrence of good fortune, innocent joy, contentment, and reward for honest toil—so is not Schopenhauer merely carrying out a highly selective inventory? If so, his pessimism would be superficial and gratuitous. But this is not the case. Whether we agree with him or not, he has arguments for far-reaching conclusions about the value that can attach to human existence. It must contain suffering, and cannot be preferable to non-existence. It would even have been better for reality not to have existed. These claims make Schopenhauer a pessimist in a philosophically interesting sense.

The first point is that suffering is ineliminably present in the existence of any human individual. As material, living creatures, our ordinary existence is such that we must strive towards ends. But, Schopenhauer argues, a being who strives, and who is conscious of his or her ends and of whether they are fulfilled, is a being who suffers. Part of this can be understood in terms of egoism. Among a multitude of individuals, each of whom must strive in order to exist, conflicts of ends will occur, and, barring the mysterious intervention of compassion, suffering will result. Since compassion is not ubiquitous, nor even widespread, one's life as a human individual among others will be very likely to contain episodes in which one suffers, and episodes in which one brings about suffering.

However, willing itself is closely intertwined with suffering in another way. First, willing could not spring from a state of total sufficiency and contentment. A being strives only if it experiences a lack or deficiency, and experiencing a lack is already a form of suffering. Secondly, in the course of events one does not attain some of the ends for which one strives. If one does not achieve an end, one's original lack is prolonged, which, together with the consciousness of not achieving one's end, is further suffering. Perhaps we can imagine a being that was always successful in its strivings—but that is of little help to Schopenhauer. For what happens when we achieve an end towards which our striving has been directed? The resulting state is called satisfaction or happiness; but, he claims, this state is of value only relative to the deficiency which it removes. Satisfaction can occur only in a being that has suffered, and it has any value only relative to some particular episode of suffering. Schopenhauer puts the point by saying that satisfaction is negative, and pain positive. Pain is something which we feel, but satisfaction is an absence; to be satisfied is simply to return to neutral by wiping out a felt deficiency. And the mere state of feeling no deficiencies, and so having nothing to strive for, has no positive value in its own terms. If it continues for any length of time it is simply boredom, which Schopenhauer often mentions as one of the pervasive features of life. Finally, the attainment of ends never makes striving cease altogether. 'Every satisfied desire gives birth to a new one': whatever striving of ours is successful, we shall soon continue to strive for further ends, and hence to suffer further. Therefore, striving cannot eliminate suffering as such. While we exist, nothing we can undertake to *do* will stop us from willing, or, therefore, from having to suffer.

It is important for Schopenhauer that life's containing suffering is not redeemed by suffering's having any positive point. Many lives, as a matter of fact, strike a balance between suffering and contentment which suffices to make them bearable:

This is the life of almost all men; they will, they know what they will, and they strive after this with enough success to protect them from despair, and enough failure to preserve them from boredom and its consequences. (*W1*, 327)

But if we consider simply that there is suffering, and ask whether existence containing suffering is something good, we cannot say that suffering is redeemed by some good over and above existence itself. If suffering in general is to be redeemed, it must be by its being simply good to exist as a human individual, come what may. And, as we shall see, that is something which Schopenhauer denies outright. But so far, if we accept Schopenhauer's argument, we can at least conclude that the happiness attainable by any human being must be bound up with suffering. To imagine an existence free of suffering is to imagine an existence that is not that of a human individual.

Death

What attitude should any of us take towards the most obvious fact about our existence: that it will cease? We do tend to fear death, not on any good rational ground, according to Schopenhauer, but because we are manifestations of will to life: a 'boundless attachment to life' is inborn in us as much as it is in all animals (*W2*, 465). We might be right to fear dying, if that process involved pain, but then the object of fear would be pain, rather than being dead. Schopenhauer presents a couple of familiar arguments for the view that fear of being dead is irrational. One is the argument from symmetry: we did not exist for an infinite time before birth, and that is a matter of indifference to us, so we ought to regard similarly our not existing again. The other is Epicurus' argument that precisely *because* it involves our non-existence, death should not be feared: to something that does not exist, it cannot matter that it does not exist.

Schopenhauer does, however, offer a more positive consolation. He accepts that death is the cessation of the individual human being, but maintains that this is not the only way in which it should be regarded. The opinion of many in contemporary Europe vacillates between the view of death as absolute annihilation and the notion of immortality. But both opinions are 'equally false' (*W2*, 464). This becomes apparent from a 'higher standpoint' which once again exploits the distinction between thing in itself and phenomenon. The individual that I am is merely part of the world of phenomena. It occupies certain portions of space for a certain time, after which it ceases to exist. From the point of view of the individual, death is annihilation, and it would be absolute annihilation of me, if this particular phenomenal individual were all that I am. However, if I am also something in myself, outside all time and change, then death cannot be my end:

the greatest equivocation really lies in the word 'I' . . . According as I understand this word, I can say: 'Death is my entire end'; or else: 'This my personal phenomenal appearance is just as infi-

nitely small a part of my true inner nature as I am of the world.'
(*W2*, 491)

'My true inner nature' here must refer to the same thing as
'the world', because reality *in itself* is not subject to any
individuation. The 'higher standpoint' thus yields the thought
that I am the world; and, thinking this, one can take the supposedly consoling view that the ephemeral individual to which 'I'
usually refers is really not worth worrying about.

Once again Schopenhauer is trying to loosen the hold of the
usual identification which we make of ourselves with an individual. The world manifests itself as me here and now, but after
I cease to exist, the same world will manifest itself in the same
way as other individuals of the same species, each of which will
find itself as the subject of consciousness, refer to itself as 'I',
pursue its ends, experience suffering and satisfaction, and cease
to exist in turn. Reality in itself, I am supposed to think, is
indifferent between one such manifestation of will and another.
Nature itself does not grieve over the destruction of any
particular part of itself, and will carry on existing without me.
If I share with all other phenomena the same 'inner nature',
then the very core of what I am carries on, regardless of the
passing of phenomena. Indeed, 'carries on' is a misleading way
to put Schopenhauer's point. Reality in itself is eternal in the
sense of timelessness. I have my 'now', and every other
phenomenon that was or will be has its time, which for it is
equally a 'now'. But from the point of view of reality in itself,
time is an illusion. Hence the phenomenal fact that some
particular thing will not exist later than now is not a fact about
reality in itself.

Two concerns arise here: that this may not be convincing
as an exercise in metaphysics, and that it might fail to be
consoling even if it were thus convincing. The notion that the
thing in itself is undifferentiated and timeless stems from
Schopenhauer's idealist doctrine of space and time, and may
well be questioned if we have doubts about that doctrine.
The really troublesome point, however, is the idea that *I* am

somehow present in the timeless, undifferentiated world. Schopenhauer has previously told us that 'I' refers to the material, striving, human being, and to the pure subject of consciousness which we find ourselves as, and which would not exist were it not for the human being with his or her bodily organs. But how could anything to which 'I' refers remain if the human being ceased to exist, taking with it the subject's consciousness? What we said when discussing the compassionate person's non-egoistic world-view applies again to the higher perspective on death: it is impossible to find *myself* in the picture of ultimate reality that it requires.

The question whether Schopenhauer's higher view of death could be consoling is a difficult one. He tries to inculcate the thought that one's own death has no great significance in the order of things. But if one accepted his reasons for taking this attitude, ought one not to think that one's life has just as little significance? And is that a consoling thought? Schopenhauer appears to think so:

death is the great opportunity no longer to be I . . . Dying is the moment of that liberation from the one-sidedness of an individuality which does not constitute the innermost kernel of our true being, but is rather to be thought of as a kind of aberration thereof. (W2, 507–8)

In fact, Schopenhauer recognizes two distinct outlooks for which his view of death might be a consolation. The first, the *affirmation of the will to life*, is the outlook of someone who would, as it were, stand on the earth with 'firm, strong bones':

A man . . . who found satisfaction in life and took perfect delight in it, who desired, in spite of calm deliberation, that the course of his life as he had hitherto experienced it should be of endless duration or of constant recurrence; and whose courage to face life was so great that, in return for life's pleasures, he would willingly and gladly put up with all the hardships and miseries to which it is subject. (W1, 283–4)

This person could be consoled by Schopenhauer's doctrine of our indestructibility by death: 'Armed with the knowledge we

confer on him, he would look with indifference at death hasten-
ing towards him on the wings of time. He would consider it as
a false illusion' (W1, 284). Such a person would think that living
as an individual is fine, but that the cessation of this life is
powerless to detract from that.

Schopenhauer suggests that suicide stems from this same
attitude of affirmation towards life. The explanation of this
(which seems at first bizarre) is as follows: if I regard the pleasures of life as of positive value, despite its pains, I always run
the risk that life's pains will come to outweigh its pleasures. If
I continue to want life for its potential positive side, but come
to believe that only suffering is available, the solution is to stop
living. However,

> Far from being denial of the will, suicide is a phenomenon of the
> will's strong affirmation. For denial has its essential nature in
> the fact that the pleasures of life, not its sorrows, are shunned. The
> suicide wills life, and is dissatisfied merely with the conditions on
> which it has come to him. Therefore he gives up by no means the
> will to life, but merely life, since he destroys the individual phe-
> nomenon. (W1, 398)

Thus the character who wills the endless recurrence of his or
her life (from whom, again, Nietzsche seems to have learned
something), and the character who ends his or her life when
suffering becomes too great, really take one and the same
stance of affirmation. Both, though, would be missing something else: they would not have come to know the truth as
Schopenhauer sees it, that 'constant suffering is essential to all
life' (W1, 283). The alternative outlook, which encompasses
this truth, consists in the *denial of the will to life*. Recognizing
that suffering pervades any existence as an individual manifestation of will to life, and that achieving ends can never be
divorced from suffering, this attitude ceases to look for any
positive value in the life of the individual human being, even
from its passing moments of satisfaction. This provides a
unique attitude to death:

> to die willingly, to die gladly, to die cheerfully, is the prerogative of
> the resigned, of him who gives up and denies the will to life. . . . He

willingly gives up the existence that we know; what comes to him instead of it is in our eyes *nothing*, because our existence in reference to that one is *nothing*. The Buddhist faith calls that existence *Nirvana*, that is to say, extinction. (*W2*, 508)

Denial of the will

The will to life must be denied—'if salvation is to be attained from an existence like ours' (*W1*, 405). Salvation is a religious doctrine, and Schopenhauer is keen to link his philosophical discussion with Christianity, Brahmanism, and Buddhism, claiming that the core of all these religions, leaving aside mythical trappings and recent doctrinal accretions, is really the same. Even God is not to the point: the philosophical import is available to an atheist quite as much as to a theist (*W1*, 385), and is that we must renounce, or say No to, our nature as human beings, if we are to find true value in existing. The real self is the will to life (*W2*, 606), and since this is also what must be denied, salvation lies in self-denial or self-renunciation. 'In fact', he says, 'nothing else can be stated as the aim of our existence except the knowledge that it would be better for us not to exist'. (*W2*, 605)

In 'denial of the will to life', one turns against the particular manifestation of will to life found in oneself, which means turning against the body, and against one's own individuality. Thus one ceases, as much as possible, to strive for one's own egoistic ends, ceases to avoid suffering or to seek pleasure, ceases to desire propagation of the species, or any sexual gratification—in short, one looks down on that willing part of nature which one is, and withdraws from one's identification with it. Such an apparently unpalatable state is made to seem worthy of attainment by Schopenhauer's elevated prose:

we can infer how blessed must be the life of a man whose will is silenced not for a few moments, as in the enjoyment of the beautiful, but for ever, indeed completely extinguished, except for the last glimmering spark that maintains the body and is extinguished with it. Such a man who, after many bitter struggles with his own nature, has at last completely conquered, is then left only as pure knowing being, as the undimmed mirror of the world. Nothing can distress or alarm him any more; nothing can any longer move him; for he has cut all the thousand threads of willing which hold us bound to the world, and which as craving, fear, envy, and anger drag us here and there in constant pain. (*W1*, 390)

Then, instead of the restless pressure and effort; instead of the constant transition from desire to apprehension and from joy to sorrow; instead of the never-satisfied and never-dying hope that constitutes the life-dream of the man who wills, we see that peace that is higher than all reason, that ocean-like calmness of the spirit, that deep tranquillity, that unshakable confidence and serenity, whose mere reflection in the countenance, as depicted by Raphael and Correggio, is a complete and certain gospel. Only knowledge remains; the will has vanished. (*W1*, 411)

Despite its kinship with the tranquil contemplation of the beautiful, the denial of the will is not to be reached by an aesthetic route. It is reached first by a saintly life, one whose justice and philanthropy arise from the insight that egoism, individuation, and the whole phenomenal world are a kind of delusion. The supposed knowledge that all things are identical at the level of the 'in itself' leads to the total surrender of egoism, and to the embracing of all suffering as one's own. This 'knowledge of the whole' then becomes the '*quieter* of all and every willing' (*W1*, 379), and turns the will against its natural state of self-affirmation. Another, secondary route to the same state is through suffering itself. This is more common, according to Schopenhauer, since the saintly life is not only rare, but extremely hard to sustain in the face of the allurements of the will (*W1*, 392). There are those, however, in real life or in tragic art, whose own individual pain is of such duration or intensity that their will to life is broken. Then, as a 'gleam of silver that suddenly appears from the purifying flame of suffering', the state of salvation may arrive in which they renounce all their desires, rise above themselves and above suffering in a state of 'inviolable peace, bliss and sublimity'. (*W1*, 392–3)

Schopenhauer points to numerous practices and experiences which he thinks bear out his descriptions of self-renunciation:

Quietism, i.e. the giving up of all willing, asceticism, i.e. intentional mortification of one's own will, and mysticism, i.e. consciousness of the identity of one's own inner being with that of all things, or with the kernel of the world, stand in the closest connexion, so that whoever professes one of them is gradually led to the acceptance of the others, even against his intention. Nothing can be more surprising than the agreement among the writers who express those teachings, in spite of the greatest difference of their age, country, and religion. (*W2*, 613)

The ascetic, not content with willing the well-being of others, actively seeks to counter the ends of the will as it expresses itself in the body. ('One's own woe' is thus a fourth *incentive* to action, to be set alongside those of egoism, malice, and compassion (*W2*, 607).) Schopenhauer describes the ascetic thus: 'His body, healthy and strong, expresses the sexual impulse through the genitals, but he denies the will, and gives the lie to the body' (*W1*, 380). Voluntary abstention from sexual activity—that most powerful manifestation of will to life—is accompanied by intentional poverty, non-avoidance of injury or ignominy from others, fasting, self-castigation, and self-torture. Since all these occurrences are pursued as deliberate ends, asceticism cannot be identical with total will-lessness. The latter must occur unpredictably as the 'sudden gleam of silver' arising out of suffering; one can deliberately engineer suffering, but true salvation does not come about by intention or design.

Mysticism, meanwhile, is simply 'consciousness of the identity of one's own inner being with that of all things'. Schopenhauer claims to have arrived at a philosophical delineation of the state which mystics achieve in subjective experience. But since this experience cannot be communicated, he arrives at the limits of philosophy:

when my teaching reaches its highest point, it assumes a *negative* character, and so ends with a negation. Thus it can speak here only of what is denied or given up. . . . Now it is precisely here that the mystic proceeds positively, and therefore, from this point, nothing is left but mysticism. (*W2*, 612)

Schopenhauer's book, having begun with the words 'The world . . .', does indeed end with '—Nothing'. The phenomenal world is negated by those whose will has turned against it, and they embrace sheer nothingness in return; but then, from their altered point of view, the whole of this world can be set at nought. Having given up placing any positive value in the human round of happiness and suffering, the will-less subject finds a new value in the very rejection of what has ordinary human value.

However sympathetic or unsympathetic we may be to Schopenhauer's final doctrine, we must surely worry whether it is really coherent at all. We have often enough questioned whether I can think of *myself* as existing in a world deprived of all differentiation between individuals. But, even setting that aside, someone might ask: how can I acquiesce in a tranquil vision of my identity with the kernel of the world, if that kernel is the detested will to life, the very thing which it is so desirable for me to escape? There is, however, a reply to this worry. We must not forget Schopenhauer's distinction between knowing and willing. To *know* the whole world as an all-pervading, purposeless will to life is not the same as colluding with that will as it expresses itself in one's own body—it is not the same as willing on behalf of this particular individual. Salvation is achieved by knowledge for Schopenhauer, but not by knowledge that any good state of affairs obtains. To see the world as a whole from which I am not distinct is of value because it liberates me from the treadmill of striving, happiness, and suffering—but not because I come to understand the world as a good thing. The world is not a good thing, and nor am I, for Schopenhauer. But some value can be salvaged if I stand back and know the terrible place from a universal standpoint, rather than carrying on willing in unquestioning identification with one small part of it.

A final concern about the denial of the will is whether it is always bound to be an act of will. If I have a choice whether to affirm or deny my will to life, then, at some higher level, I must be willing to deny the will. This would not be a contradiction if the 'higher' willing, which discriminates between affirmation and denial, was of a kind not subordinate to the will to life: I could then decide at will to deny my will to life. But if Schopenhauer were to think that all willing is a form of will to life, and that the denial of will to life is something I undertake at will, then his position would be quite incoherent. The best resolution of this problem is to say that denial of the will simply occurs in a subject, and is not a consciously undertaken act. One's natural compassion for every being, or the degree of one's suffering, overcome one's egoism to such an extent that it becomes impossible to strive any longer for the ends that arise out of one's own parochial existence. His other description of this is 'the will to life turning against itself'. At the end of the *World as Will and Representation* he writes not of 'those who have denied the will', but of 'those in whom the will has turned and denied itself' (*W1*, 412). It is important that the agency here is not straightforwardly *mine*. Just as it is not I who originally throw myself into life, so it is not I who turn against the will to life. The 'agent' here is the will to life, which turns against itself. So denial of the will really is *not* an act of will of the person in whom it happens. However, Schopenhauer some-times writes as if it were. Those in whom the will has turned must constantly 'struggle' against affirmation of the will, which is the body's natural state; they must 'strive with all their might to keep to this path by self-imposed renuncia-tions of every kind' (*W1*, 391). The will to life within me is recalcitrant, and reverts to affirming itself, even if it has previ-ously been broken by saintliness or intense suffering, so here is a case where *I* must continue to will its denial after all.

Pessimism

Schopenhauer's philosophical pessimism resides in two con-nected theses: that for each individual it would have been better not to have been born, and that the world as a whole is the worst of all possible worlds. The argument for the first starts from the point that, for the ordinary, striving human being, life must contain suffering, and from the claim that all satisfaction is purely of negative value, being the cessation of suffering. Schopenhauer moves from here to the idea that no satisfaction achievable within human existence can compensate for the suffering that it must also contain. It is as if, in the balance, no satisfaction can weigh anything at all by comparison with any suffering, however small. The mere existence of evil in the world makes it something whose non-existence is preferable to its existence—we should wish, not only not to have come into existence ourselves, but that this world in which we must suffer had not come about (*W2*, 576). All in all, our condition is 'something that it were better should not be' (*W2*, 577).

Now this argument is not one that we have to accept. It is quite plausible that our life has no purpose, that it must contain suffering, and that no satisfactions can ever expunge the evil of any single pain: in this sense the line Schopenhauer quotes from Petrarch, '*mille piacer' non vagliono un tormento*', 'a thousand pleasures do not compensate for one pain' (*W2*, 576), is correct. Also, it may be true that existence is *not guaranteed* to be better than non-existence. And if, as Schopenhauer claims—again with some plausibility—'nine-tenths of mankind live in constant conflict with want, always balancing themselves with difficulty and effort on the brink of destruction' (*W2*, 584), then the total of individual lives that are better than non-existence may be much smaller than we like to think. Still it does not follow that everyone should consider their actual existence worse than non-existence. The crucial premiss needed for this is that *any* suffering contained in a life makes non-existence preferable to it. But this step commits us to thinking that seventy years of contentment are rendered worthless by a single episode of pain—and that is surely incredible. We should question more strenuously the idea that all satisfaction is negative—the idea that while pain is *felt*, satisfaction is a mere restitution of neutrality. It is true that however many parts of one's life are happy, they do not take away the pain of the parts in which one suffers. But it should be equally true that the mere fact of suffering does not take away the value of the parts in which one does not suffer, which may happen to be quite numerous.

Schopenhauer is scathing about optimism, the view that this is the best of all possible worlds—'The absurdity is glaring!' he says (W2, 581). His strongest attack is the argument that this is rather the worst of all possible worlds, which goes as follows: 'Take "possible" to mean "what can actually exist and last". Then, since "this world is arranged as it had to be if it were to be capable of continuing with great difficulty to exist" (W2, 583), we can see that a worse world than this could not continue to exist. Therefore, this is the worst world that is possible'. This is a curious argument. Schopenhauer cites a number of pieces of evidence for the claim that the world is continuing to exist only with great difficulty. Nine-tenths of the human race live on the margins of extinction, many species have entirely disappeared, a very small change in temperature or the composition of the atmosphere would extinguish life altogether, the planet could easily be destroyed by collisions within the solar system, or by the forces beneath its own crust. So perhaps there are many possible worlds that are more remote from catastrophe than the present one—and if so, it may be salutary to be informed of that. But we can clearly imagine many changes distinctly for the worse in this world which would fall short of destroying it or its inhabitants. Many people nowadays believe the environment is becoming gradually less and less favourable for life. But if Schopenhauer were right, this view would be untenable: the end of the world would have to be as nigh now as it ever could be—and there appears no reason to accept this extreme view.

Schopenhauer's arguments for these extreme pessimist doctrines therefore fail to convince. However, his pessimism succeeds in advancing something less extreme and wholly believable, which is this: to think that we are *meant* not to suffer, that we somehow deserve happiness, or that the world owes us the fulfilment of our purposes, is a mistake—as is also the belief that being alive is simply a good a thing, whatever it brings. His protracted, moving discussions of the vanity or worthlessness (*Nichtigkeit*) of life enable us to escape from these optimistic delusions into a view which is harder, but arguably more humane: that life itself has no purpose, that suffering is always part of it, and that its end may sometimes be welcomed.

Despite this, it is sometimes suggested that Schopenhauer is not in the end a genuine pessimist at all. For it is not as if he really thinks that no value is ever attainable in life. Aesthetic contemplation, artistic genius, a life of philanthropy and justice, asceticism, and renunciation of the will, all are supreme values awaiting some human individuals, at least. The individual who escapes from the will achieves nothing less than 'salvation', which seems to be a state whose value is unassailable. All of this is true; but it conflicts with 'pessimism' only if you think pessimism is the view that nothing is of any value at all. It does not conflict with Schopenhauer's views that non-existence would have been preferable and that the world is the worst possible world. The values of will-lessness are genuine, but only by being, according to Schopenhauer, some amelioration of the worst situation possible. Someone might object that a worse world still would be one in which even the salvation of will-less resignation was not open to us. But Schopenhauer's reply would be that in that case existence would be so intolerable that no one who really understood its nature would be able to endure it. It would, in that sense, not be a possible existence.

Finally, even Schopenhauer's notion of salvation must itself be called pessimistic in a definite sense, if we consider that the only value worthy of the name in his scheme of things depends upon self-renunciation. Resignation and aesthetic tranquillity are achieved by an attitude of detachment from the human individual that strives for life, and from the whole tapestry of ends that are woven into life. If this living individual remains *what I am* in the world of representation, and will to life *what I am* in myself—no immaterial soul, no rational essence, no part of any divine plan—then *what I am* is not only worthless, but is the very obstacle that must be broken down before true value is glimpsed. To feel the full weight of Schopenhauer's *solution* to the problem of existence is thus to encounter a kind of self-loathing in which dwells the deepest pessimism of all.

9 *Schopenhauer's influence*

Schopenhauer regarded himself as building a philosophical system which unfolded a 'single thought' (*W1*, xii). But the system, which is vulnerable to many criticisms, has not usually been the basis of his appeal. His lasting importance as a philosopher rests more on his manner of unfettered probing and blunt questioning, on his demolition of traditional certainties and on the new insecurities he confronts. The old ideas of the immortal soul, the divine purpose, and the dignity of man have died, for Schopenhauer, and should not be revived. The human species is a part of nature, and rationality gives it no especially elevated status. The human individual is embodied and restlessly active, an animal who strives and suffers, whose core is sexuality and egoism. The identity of the individual becomes problematic through and through. Our mind is that of an organism adapted to the ends of living, and is split between the conscious, knowing, and seemingly unworldly self with which we try to identify, and the unconscious, natural will which seems alien but is truly what drives us on. Life has no purpose. Being ourselves is not something which has any positive value. Schopenhauer argues himself into a predicament in which existence itself is a problem, and then presents the exceptions of genius and saintliness, aesthetic experience and the submergence of individuality, as the only ways of salvaging value. Such uncomfortable, challenging thoughts represent his distinctive contribution to modern culture.

Although there has never really been a Schopenhauerian school of philosophy, his influence on the history of thought has been both great and varied. In the late nineteenth and early twentieth centuries he was at the forefront of European culture:

his books were widely read, provided the material for many academic dissertations and published treatises, and were seized upon with enthusiasm by intellectuals and artists. He had some philosophical followers, but was perhaps more notable for attracting people who fell in love with his writing, turned over or wrestled with his thoughts, and then put them to their own creative use. In the 1850s Wagner fell under the Schopenhauerian spell, which became a major stimulant in the writing of *Tristan and Isolde* in particular. In the 1860s something similar happened to Nietzsche, and to Tolstoy; in the 1880s and 1890s he was read by Thomas Hardy, Thomas Mann, and Marcel Proust, and in the 1900s by the young Wittgenstein. We find characters in *Buddenbrooks* and *À la Recherche du temps perdu* who read Schopenhauer, or discuss reading him; and he is mentioned in *Tess of the d'Urbervilles*. In all, there are many more notable artworks than can be catalogued here which bear the stamp of Schopenhauer's thinking, some directly, some more obliquely. The list of artists who became involved with his philosophy could continue for example, with Mahler, Richard Strauss, Turgenev, Lawrence, Beckett, and Borges.

Schopenhauer's appeal cannot be divorced from his own stature as a literary writer. His beautiful prose and his grasp of structure and drama—every step in the narrative marked by a powerful image and timed for maximum effect—make the transition from philosophical system to novel or opera stage almost as smooth as it could be. No single doctrine occupied all these writers and musicians equally, but the strongest impressions were undoubtedly made by his aesthetic theory, his philosophy of music, his recognition of the unconscious, his treatment of the overpowering sexual drive, his pessimism, and his questioning of the value of human existence. In some ways, it is strange that the period of Schopenhauer's most intense influence does not stretch much beyond the 1920s, into the decades when many of those we have mentioned had themselves become well-established cultural figures. This time of frustrated strivings in the economic sphere, when the futility of the First

World War was compounded by yet more agonies, and widespread interest in psycho-analysis was changing people's views about the human personality—was this not Schopenhauer's true era? Yet by the middle of this century he was not such a well-known writer, one main reason being that none of the main streams of contemporary philosophy paid him any real attention.

Of those who succumbed to Schopenhauer, the earliest, Wagner and Nietzsche, seem to have been the most deeply affected, and it is in the understanding of these two that an exploration of the link with Schopenhauer is of most help. Wagner was no philosopher, and he sometimes confessed that, despite his constant re-readings, he was struggling to make out what was going on in Schopenhauer's work. Clearly the idea of music as the direct expression of the strivings of the will was one that spoke to him, but so did the idea of the denial of the will. He wrote in a letter to Liszt 'I have . . . found a sedative which has finally helped me to sleep at night; it is the sincere and heartfelt yearning for death: total unconsciousness, complete annihilation, the end of all dreams—the only ultimate redemption.' Wagner clearly felt that Schopenhauer's doctrine crystallized some of his own insights, and gave him a fresh outlook on his own existing work: 'Now at last I could understand my *Wotan*.' He comes closest to Schopenhauer's actual philosophy in his operas when the characters Tristan and Isolde express their deep longing to cease existing as individuals. The capacity of erotic love to overpower the individual is also one of Schopenhauer's themes, of course. Wagner, however, contrives to make the longing for nonexistence turn into the climax of erotic love, instead of the complete negation of it which Schopenhauer calls for—in other words, even at his moment of supreme debt to the philosopher, he does not exactly follow him.

One of the things that brought Wagner together with the young Nietzsche was their devotion to Schopenhauer, whom they had discovered independently. Even though Nietzsche had also experienced a kind of emotional 'conversion' to

Schopenhauer's philosophy, his relationship with it was to be quite different. In his first publication, *The Birth of Tragedy*, Nietzsche uses the pair of symbolic deities, Apollo and Dionysus, to account for the awesome artistic achievement of Greek tragedy. Apollo stands for the beautiful dream-like image of the individual hero, Dionysus for the terrifying but intoxicating glimpse into the cruel world underlying individuation, which will destroy the hero. In attempting to explain this pair of symbols, he calls on Schopenhauer's distinction between representation and will. Although the book is a unique outpouring, much of which has little directly to do with Schopenhauer (as Nietzsche himself later commented), his reading of Schopenhauer was decisive in providing the shape and the impulse of it.

However, it is what happened later that gives Schopenhauer a greater significance for Nietzsche. He turned away from his former 'master', to the extent of saying that he 'went wrong everywhere'. As Nietzsche's own philosophy developed, Schopenhauer continued to be a guiding star of a special kind—the one to steer away from. In the *Genealogy of Morals* he diagnoses Schopenhauer's doctrines as outlets for his own personality, saying in particular that the elevation of aesthetic tranquillity shows Schopenhauer's relief at escaping from his own abhorred sexual impulses; moreover 'he would have become ill, become a *pessimist* (for he was not one, however much he desired it), if deprived of his enemies, of Hegel, of woman, of sensuality and the whole will to existence, to persistence.' Perhaps—but what would Nietzsche have become without his Schopenhauer, his convenient summation of errors? He has already told us in the Preface: 'What was at stake was the *value* of morality—and over this I had to come to terms almost exclusively with my great teacher Schopenhauer.'

Nietzsche is very much concerned with the loss of value. He agrees with Schopenhauer that existence must contain suffering, and is basically without a point. But he revolts against the idea of renunciation and asceticism as a way to salvation. Plumbing the depths of the Schopenhauerian vision is a necessary step, but there must be an alternative to the 'life-denying' attitude of seeking to escape from the will and despising the individual material being that one is. Nietzsche's proposed solution is that of a creative self-affirmation ('Become who you are!), embracing one's pain and even one's cruelty as true parts of oneself. His notion of the will to power, based more than verbally on Schopenhauer's 'will to life', attempts to supplant the latter as a description of the fundamental drive that organizes human behaviour, and, in some way, the whole universe. Will to power is not primarily a political doctrine, but an attempt to find an explanation of human behaviour, cognition, and cultural beliefs by positing an underlying tendency towards increase and mastery, both over the world and over oneself. Though he repudiates Schopenhauer's metaphysical doctrine of the thing in itself, and seeks to discredit philosophical metaphysics altogether, Nietzsche's notion of will to power shows striking parallels with Schopenhauer's conception of the will. In particular, the idea that will to power can be both conscious and unconscious, that it has an organic basis in the individual, and that it is omnipresent, make it appropriate to call it a successor to Schopenhauer's doctrine.

While Schopenhauer is in the forefront of Nietzsche's critique of philosophers, many of the methods for that critique have also been suggested by Schopenhauer. For example, Nietzsche's view that metaphysical doctrines and beliefs about ethical values do not derive from 'pure' reasoning, but are always informed, covertly, by the need to come to terms with suffering and the will to master oneself or one's surroundings, clearly has its origins in Schopenhauer's doctrine that the will shapes our intellectual processes. Schopenhauer's idea that the world is structured by the mind of a particular species of living organism is reflected in Nietzsche's conviction that there are no absolute truths or values, only perspectives and fabrications that help us to cope with life. Schopenhauer also, of course, provides the most naked instance of the ascetic ideal which Nietzsche sees as underlying so much of Western culture—'Man would rather will *nothingness* than *not* will.'

Aside from such doctrinal influences, Nietzsche's writing displays its involvement with Schopenhauer often in fine-grained detail. He will appropriate Schopenhauer's nuances of voice and terminology even at the moment of greatest divergence from his doctrines. To read Nietzsche without a knowledge of Schopenhauer is to lose a recurring sub-text, and one of the key points of orientation in his often bewildering progress.

Among Nietzsche's contemporaries, philosophical interest in Schopenhauer was widespread. He was commonly studied as an important successor to Kant, and philosophers who were significant in their day, such as Hans Vaihinger, and Nietzsche's friend, the orientalist and metaphysician, Paul Deussen, produced new systems which took off from Schopenhauer's. In the twentieth century he was highly thought of by members of the Frankfurt School who were dissatisfied with the optimism of orthodox Marxism, in particular Max Horkheimer. However, it is fair to say that to date the only major philosopher apart from Nietzsche to be influenced by Schopenhauer has been Wittgenstein. Wittgenstein, like Nietzsche, did not come across Schopenhauer's works in an academic setting. He read them as part of the stock of ideas with which Viennese high society was furnished (an illustrative little detail is that Gustav Mahler, another 'disciple', while staying at the Wittgenstein family house a few years earlier, had given Bruno Walter Schopenhauer's complete works as a present). In fact, not to have read Schopenhauer would have been the odd thing for a young person from a cultured family such as Wittgenstein's.

Wittgenstein's earliest philosophical work, leading up to the *Tractatus*, seems at first sight to have little in common with Schopenhauer. He had worked with Frege and Russell in the new methods of formal logic, which became the basis of a movement that attempted to repudiate idealism and the supposed excesses of German metaphysics. It used to be common to apologize for Wittgenstein's interest in Schopenhauer as a youthful aberration. But it was certainly more than that. In the

Tractatus Wittgenstein uses Schopenhauer's images when talking about the 'I': it is an extensionless point, like an eye that
cannot see itself, a limit—not a part—of the world. The 'I' is not
among the facts that make up the world. Nor is there any value
in the world. Value, whether ethical or aesthetic, seems to
come from an attitude to the world as whole, not to any particular facts within it. 'To view the world sub specie aeterni
(under the aspect of eternity)'—another of Schopenhauer's
ideas—'is to view it as a whole', and this is a mystical feeling,
says Wittgenstein. The well-known image of philosophy as the
ladder which one discards after climbing it is also reminiscent
of Schopenhauer's view of the relationship between philosophy
and mysticism.

There hangs over the *Tractatus* the sense that it is about
something that appears only obliquely in the text. Its author
said that the meaning of the book was an 'ethical' one, and in
the book it transpires that ethics cannot be put into propositions, but must show itself. Wittgenstein was clearly troubled
by the thought that once the world had been described in
language, the really big questions, such as what the 'I' was, how
it related to the world, what the point of the world was, and
where good and evil came from, were left entirely untouched.
As he struggled with these issues, the map on which he attempted to plot them was provided to a large extent by
Schopenhauer's philosophy. This is particularly clear from his
early notebooks, where the repeated vocabulary of 'subject' and
'object', 'will' and 'representation', 'world' and 'I' acquires any
semblance of intelligibility only when viewed as an attempt to
think things through with Schopenhauer's help.

Another area where Wittgenstein was clearly influenced by
Schopenhauer is the theory of action. From his earliest writings
through to his mature works, Wittgenstein worried about
whether there is a mental act of will that is separate from
bodily movement. The problem became central to his examination of whether the mental was in any sense 'hidden', and had
a big influence on action-theory in analytical philosophy. The

basic idea that Wittgenstein often seems drawn to is that willing is identical with acting, rather than being some purely
'inner' mental process. It is easy to see that this idea is essentially Schopenhauer's, and, although he does not mention his
predecessor's name very often in this connection, the terms in
which he discusses it reflect its ancestry.

Apart from the arts and philosophy, Schopenhauer's influence also extends into psychology, through his conception of
the unconscious and his idea that sexuality is at the basis of
personality. A very popular work in its day, now more or less
forgotten, was Eduard von Hartmann's *Philosophy of the Unconscious* of 1869. This was a strange hybrid in which the
author tried to combine some of Schopenhauer's ideas with
some of Hegel's, and attempted a kind of *rapprochement* between optimism and pessimism. His chief modification of
Schopenhauer's notion of the unconscious was to suggest that
it must comprise not only will but also Idea, and somehow be
in pursuit of rational ends. This work made the unconscious a
theme for widespread study in the latter art of the nineteenth
century, and served at the same time as a kind of channel for
interest in Schopenhauer. Although Schopenhauer was not the
first or only philosopher to discuss the unconscious, he probably made the greatest contribution before Freud.

Freud himself certainly consulted Hartmann's work, and
does make reference to it. It has often been pointed out, too,
that he must have been familiar with Schopenhauer's ideas
from the academic environment in which he moved. Nevertheless, Freud tried to distance himself from Schopenhauer, saying,
in a well-known passage,

I have carefully avoided any contact with philosophy proper. . . .
The large extent to which psycho-analysis coincides with the
philosophy of Schopenhauer—not only did he assert the dominance
of the emotions and the supreme importance of sexuality but he
was even aware of the mechanism of repression—is not to be traced
to my acquaintance with his teaching. I read Schopenhauer very
late in my life.

One almost hesitates to point out that Freud must have known at some level what to avoid reading, in order to preserve this title to originality. In any case, it is pretty certain that the great attention paid to Schopenhauer in academic and cultural life during this period was an important factor in making Freud's work possible, whether he was aware of it or not.

C. G. Jung is another influential psychologist who was impressed by Schopenhauer. He reports that he read Schopenhauer from his seventeenth year on (putting us, again, in the 1890s), and agreed with his picture of the world as full of confusion, passion, and evil: 'Here at last was someone who had courage for the insight that somehow the foundation of the world was not in the best of ways.' Should we in the 1990s pass a different judgement? Though Schopenhauer's metaphysics is not credible as a system, his doctrines concerning subjectivity, action, striving, suffering, individuality, renunciation, and aesthetic elevation—the troubling or consoling thoughts that have excited so many influential thinkers—are surely still as alive and challenging as ever.

Further reading

A recent full biography of Schopenhauer is:

SAFRANSKI, RÜDIGER, *Schopenhauer and the Wild Years of Philosophy* (London, 1989).

The following are treatments of Schopenhauer's work as a whole from a philosophical point of view:

GARDINER, PATRICK, *Schopenhauer* (Harmondsworth, 1967).
HAMLYN, D. W., *Schopenhauer* (London, 1980).
YOUNG, JULIAN, *Willing and Unwilling: A Study in the Philosophy of Arthur Schopenhauer* (Dordrecht, 1987).

Recent books which focus on certain philosophical themes more than others:

ATWELL, JOHN E., *Schopenhauer: The Human Character* (Philadelphia, 1990).
—— *Schopenhauer on the Character of the World: The Metaphysics of Will* (Berkeley and Los Angeles, 1995).
JACQUETTE, DALE (ed.), *Schopenhauer, Philosophy and the Arts* (Cambridge, 1996).
JANAWAY, CHRISTOPHER, *Self and World in Schopenhauer's Philosophy* (Oxford, 1989).
WHITE, F. C., *On Schopenhauer's Fourfold Root of the Principle of Sufficient Reason* (Leiden, 1992).

For a lively and sometimes idiosyncratic account of the place of Schopenhauer's philosophy in the history of ideas, see:

MAGEE, BRYAN, *The Philosophy of Schopenhauer* (Oxford, 1983).

Two collections of articles reflect a variety of perspectives on Schopenhauer:

FOX, MICHAEL (ed.), *Schopenhauer: His Philosophical Achievement* (Brighton, 1980).
VON DER LUFT, ERIC (ed.), *Schopenhauer: New Essays in Honor of his 200th Birthday* (Lewiston, NY, 1988).

The latter volume contains an extensive bibliography.

Nietzsche

Michael Tanner

Contents

To my father and
in memory of my mother

Abbreviations

After the first mention or so of a particular book of Nietzsche's, I have referred to it by initials, as listed below. All quotations are followed by the initial for the book they come from, and then section or chapter numbers. This can be rather inconvenient in the case of books with lengthy sections, but it is meant to enable readers to consult whichever edition they have to hand.

A	*The Antichrist*
BGE	*Beyond Good and Evil*
BT	*The Birth of Tragedy*
CW	*The Case of Wagner*
D	*Daybreak*
EH	*Ecce Homo*
GM	*The Genealogy of Morals*
GS	*The Gay Science*
HAH	*Human, All Too Human*
NCW	*Nietzsche Contra Wagner*
TI	*Twilight of the Idols*
TSZ	*Thus Spoke Zarathustra*
UM	*Untimely Meditations*
WP	*The Will to Power*

1 *The image of Nietzsche*

Friedrich Nietzsche (1844–1900) was a German philosopher, almost wholly neglected during his sane life, which came to an abrupt end early in 1889. 'Nietzsche' is the figure in whose name people of the most astonishingly discrepant and various views have sought to find justification for them. An excellent recent study (Aschheim 1992) devoted to his impact within Germany between 1890 and 1990 lists, among those who have found inspiration in his work, 'anarchists, feminists, Nazis, religious cultists, Socialists, Marxists, vegetarians, avant-garde artists, devotees of physical culture, and archconservatives,' and it certainly does not need to stop there. The front cover sports a bookplate from 1900 of Nietzsche wearing a crown of thorns, the back cover one of him naked, with remarkable musculature, posing on an Alp. Almost no German cultural or artistic figure of the last ninety years has not acknowledged his influence, from Thomas Mann to Jung to Heidegger.

The story in 'Anglosaxony', to use the term in the title of one book about him which traces his influence in the Western English speaking world (Bridgwater 1972), is similar. Wave after wave of Nietzscheanism has broken over it, though there have been periods when he was in abeyance, being seen as the inspirer of German militarism, and so to be vilified by the Allies. He was extensively, and most inaccurately, translated into English, or a language strangely connected with it, in the early years of the century. For all its archaizing grotesqueness, or partly because of that, it was the only translation of many of Nietzsche's works for almost fifty years.

Then, when his reputation was at its lowest in England and the United States, Walter Kaufmann, an emigré professor of philosophy at Princeton, began retranslating many of the key works, and launched the enterprise with a book that had, for many years after its first appearance in 1950, a determining influence on the way Nietzsche was viewed (Kaufmann 1974). Kaufmann presented a philosopher who was a much more traditional thinker than the one who had inspired anarchists, vegetarians, etc. To widespread surprise, and only slightly less widespread agreement, Nietzsche turned out to be a reasonable man, even a rationalist. Kaufmann sought to establish comprehensively his remoteness from the Nazis, from all irrationalist movements that had claimed him as their forebear, and from Romanticism in the arts. It became difficult, on this version, to see what all the fuss had been about. Thus began the academicization of Nietzsche, one philosopher among others, to be compared and contrasted with Spinoza, Kant, Hegel, and other leading names in the Western philosophical tradition. Reassured by the breadth of Kaufmann's learning, American philosophers, and then increasingly English ones, took him as a starting-point for their studies of Nietzsche on objectivity, the nature of truth, his relationship to Greek thought, the nature of the self, and other harmless topics, at any rate as treated in their books and articles.

Meanwhile in Europe Nietzsche, who had never been in disgrace there, became after World War II a continued object of study and appropriation for existentialists, phenomenologists, and then increasingly, during the 1960s and 1970s, a cynosure for critical theorists, post-structuralists, and deconstructionists. When the latter two movements first gained a foothold in the United States, then took the country over, it was Nietzsche who once more was acknowledged as the major source of their inspiration. Some analytical philosophers, too, found that he was not so remote from their interests as they had assumed, and, in that reciprocal motion that is so characteristic of academic life, congratulated him on having had, in embryonic fashion, some of their insights, while at the same time reassuring themselves about those insights by invoking his authority. There is now a flourishing Nietzsche industry, and almost certainly more books appear on him each year than on any other thinker, thanks to the appeal he has for so many disparate schools of thought and anti-thought.

It is idle to pretend that he would have been entirely displeased by this phenomenon. During his lifetime (and unless I specify otherwise, I shall always mean by that the one that finished when he went mad in 1889, eleven years before his death) he was almost completely neglected, and though that did not make him bitter, as hardly anything did, it caused him distress because he believed that he had vital truths to impart to his contemporaries which they were ignoring at a terrible cost—one of his most accurate prophecies. But he would have looked with scorn on almost everything that has been written or done under his aegis, and the successful take-over by the academic world, though it cannot compare in horror with some of the other appropriations he has suffered, would have seemed to him most like a final defeat, because he wanted at all costs not to be assimilated to the world of learning, where everything becomes a matter for discussion and nothing for action.

Before we move into an account of his views, it is worth stopping briefly and pondering what it might be about his work which has proved so attractive to such diverse movements and schools of thought. Only later will a clearer answer emerge. But it seems, as a preliminary explanation, that it is precisely the idiosyncrasies of his manner that are first found refreshing. His books, after the early *The Birth of Tragedy* (1872) and the *Untimely Meditations* (1873–6), are usually composed of short essays, often less than a page long, and verging on the aphoristic, though, as we shall see, crucially different from aphorisms as normally composed and appreciated: that is, one- or two-line encapsulations of the nature of human experience, demanding acceptance through their lapidary certainty. The number of subjects discussed is vast, including many that it is surprising to find mentioned by a philosopher—such matters as climate, diet, exercise, and Venice. And often his reflections are in no particular order. That means that he is much easier than most philosophers to dip into, and his frequently expressed loathing of systems means that one can do that with a good conscience. Many of his quasi-aphorisms are radical in content, and though one may gain only a vague impression of what he favours, one will certainly find out a great deal about his dislikes, most often expressed in terms that are both witty and extreme. What he seems to dislike is every aspect of contemporary civilization, most particularly that of the Germans, and for the reader that is bracing. His underlying view that if we don's make a drastically new start we are doomed, since we are living in the wreckage of two thousand and more years of fundamentally mistaken ideas about almost everything that matters—in, as it were, the decadence of what was anyway deadly—offers *carte blanche* to people who fancy the idea of a clean break with their whole cultural inheritance. Nietzsche was under no illusions about the impossibility of such a schism.

Even so, the variety of interpretations of his work, which far from diminishing as the decades pass, seems to be multiplying, though in less apocalyptic forms than previously, needs more explanation. It suggests to the outsider that he must have been exceptionally vague, and probably contradictory. There is something in both those charges. But they seem more impressive and damning than they are if one does not realize and continually keep in mind that, in the sixteen years during which he wrote his mature works, from *BT* onwards, he was developing his views at a rate that has no parallel, and that he rarely went to the bother of signposting his changes of mind.

What he more often did was to try to see his earlier works in a new light, surveying his career in a way that suggests he thought one could not understand his later writings without a knowledge of his previous ones, to see how he had advanced; and thus taking himself to be exemplary of how modern man, immured in the decaying culture of the nineteenth century, might move from acquiescence in it to rebellion and suggestions for radical transformation. In 1886 in particular, when he was on the verge, though he could not have known it, of his last creative phase, he spent a great deal of energy on his previous books, providing new, sometimes harshly critical, introduc-

tions to them, and in the case of *The Gay Science* writing a long
new final Book. No doubt this was part of his programme for
showing that nothing in one's past should be regretted, that
there need be no waste. But many commentators have been led
astray by assuming that it gave them licence to treat all his
writings as though they had been produced simultaneously.

Another factor that has made for misreadings and shocking
distortions is a consequence of the fact that, from 1872 at least
but probably before that, Nietzsche must have spent most of
his time writing. The tally of published books is impressive
enough. But he noted down at least as much as he organized
into books, and unfortunately much of this unpublished writing (the *Nachlass*) has survived. It would not be unfortunate if
there were a universally accepted methodological principle that
what he did not publish should under all circumstances be
clearly demarcated from what he did, but almost no one observes that elementary rule. Even those who claim that they
will do this usually slip into unattributed quoting from the
immense *Nachlass* when it confirms the line that they are
taking on him. What makes this a particularly dangerous way
of proceeding is that on some central concepts, among which
the Will to Power and the Eternal Recurrence are perhaps the
most important, his thought remained so undeveloped.
Nietzsche was often so sure he had struck philosophical gold
that he jotted down very many thoughts, but left them
unworked out. This provides a commentator with the possibility of pursuing trains of thought that he is attributing to
Nietzsche, unimpeded by definite statements. Some have even
taken the view that the 'real' Nietzsche is to be found in the
notebooks, the published work being a kind of elaborate—very
elaborate—set of concealments. That absurd attitude is taken
by Heidegger, who is thus enabled to peddle his own philosophy
as deriving from and also critical of Nietzsche.

Like all his other commentators, I shall occasionally quote
from the *Nachlass*, but I shall indicate when I am doing that.
Nietzsche took great pains over the finished form of what he
published, and he was the last person to think that style was an

optional extra. Since he was a natural stylist, his jottings make more elegant reading than most philosophers' finished products. But when one compares his published thoughts with his draft versions of them, the difference is striking enough to make anyone cautious of taking them as being on a par, one would have thought. I emphasize this point because, as we shall see, the manipulation of what Nietzsche wrote has been a major factor in myth-making about him.

None of this explains adequately how Nietzsche could come to be portrayed as the Man of Sorrows, or indeed in many other guises. For all his ambiguities and his careful lack of definition of an ideal, one would have thought there were limits to the extent of possible misrepresentations. All I can lamely say here is that evidently there appear to be no limits. If someone develops a reputation as vast as his rapidly became, once he was no longer in a position to do anything about it, it seems that he will be unscrupulously used to give credentials to any movement that needs an icon. Here, as in some other respects, he does with awful irony come to resemble his antipode, the 'Crucified One'. Almost the last words he wrote were, 'I have a duty against which my habits, even more the pride of my instincts, revolt at bottom: *Listen to me! For I am thus and thus. Do not, above all, confound me with what I am not!*' (*EH*, preface, 1). In the century since he wrote that, few of his readers, fewer still of those who have heard about him, have done anything else.

2 Tragedy
birth, death, rebirth

Nietzsche was a precocious student, but though he wrote copiously from an early age, his first book, *The Birth of Tragedy*, or to give the first edition its full title, *The Birth of Tragedy from the Spirit of Music*, only appeared when he was 27. Its hostile reception in the academic world, where he had received such early advancement as to be appointed Professor of Classical Philology at Basle at the age of 24, should not have surprised him; but apparently it did. It meets no conceivable standards of rigour, let alone those that obtained in the study of the ancient Greeks. A broadside soon appeared over the name of an old enemy from his schooldays, Ulrich von Wilamowitz-Moellendorf, who charged him with ignorance, distortion of the facts, and grotesque parallels between Greek culture and the modern world. Erwin Rohde, a staunch friend, replied in terms at least as pugnacious, and the kind of battle familiar in academic circles directed to those who offend against their canons ensued. Nietzsche had gained notoriety, but it was brief, and was the only kind of fame with which he was ever to be acquainted.

Readers ever since have been divided into those who find its rhapsodic style, and the content which necessitates it, intoxicating, and those who respond with bored contempt. Both are readily understandable. It is a whirlwind of a book, swept along by the intensity of its strange set of enthusiasms and its desire to cope with as many topics as possible in a short space, but masquerading as a historical account of why Greek tragedy lasted for so short a time, and arguing that it had recently been reborn in the mature works of Richard Wagner. Nietzsche had been a fanatical admirer of some of Wagner's dramas since he encountered the score of *Tristan und Isolde*, which he and some friends had played on the piano and quasi-sung when he was 16 (*EH* ii. 6; but see also Love 1963). And he had met the composer and his then mistress Cosima, daughter of Liszt, in 1868, becoming their close friend in 1869, and visiting them often during the years that they lived in Tribschen on Lake Lucerne. There is no doubt that the whole subject-matter of *BT* had been discussed frequently during those visits, and that Wagner contributed substantially to the development of some of its central theses (Silk and Stern 1981: ch. 3). But when he and Cosima received their copy of the book they were nevertheless bowled over by it. However much influence Wagner, who adored pseudo-historical speculation, may have had, there was enough that was new to him in the book for him to find it a revelation.

Generally sympathetic readers of the book have often regretted that its last ten sections are largely devoted to a consideration of Wagner's art as the rebirth of Greek tragedy. Not only does the claim seem to them in itself absurd, but they feel it detracts and distracts from the unity, such as it is, of the first two-thirds of *BT*. That is almost wholly to miss the point of the book's endeavour, and of what Nietzsche spent his life trying to do. For what makes *BT* the indispensable start to Nietzsche's writing career, for those who want to understand the underlying unity of his concerns, is the manner in which he begins with a set of issues which seem to be remote from the present time, but gradually reveals that his underling concern is with culture, its perennial conditions, and the enemies of their fulfilment.

BT begins at a spanking pace, and the momentum never lets up. It is a good idea to read it for the first time as fast as one can, ignoring obscurities and apparent diversions from the central argument (that term being used in a generously broad sense). Such an initial reading certainly involves taking a lot on trust, but to subject it to critical scrutiny the first time through is a recipe for irritation and ennui. It is important to get the sense of flux which the book possesses and which is to some extent also its subject-matter. After the 'Preface to Richard Wagner' which mentions both 'the serious German problem we are dealing with' and the conviction that 'art is the supreme task and the truly metaphysical activity of this life,' Nietzsche begins the book proper with the claim 'We shall have gained much for the science of aesthetics when we have succeeded in perceiving directly, and not only through logical reasoning, that art derives its continuous development from the duality of the *Apolline and Dionysiac.*' So within the space of a very few lines Nietzsche has shown that he is going to be advancing on three fronts. The first mentioned is that of the contemporary crisis in German culture, the second an audacious claim about the nature of metaphysics, and the third a concern with 'the science of aethetics'. (For 'science' Nietzsche uses the word 'Wissenschaft', which covers any systematic investigation, and not what is meant by 'science' in English—this should be remembered throughout his work, or indeed any discussion in German.)

He rapidly moves on to dealing with the 'opposition' between the Apolline and the Dionysiac, but that should not be taken to mean that they are enemies. As his exposition unfolds, it immediately becomes clear that 'These two very different tendencies walk side by side, usually in violent opposition to one another, inciting one another to ever more powerful births,' until they seem 'at last to beget the work of art that is as Dionysiac as it is Apolline—Attic tragedy.' This kind of opposition which yet contrives to be immensely more fruitful than anything that could be produced by either of the opponents going it alone is characteristic of nineteenth-century German philosophy, its leading exponent being Hegel, a philosopher to whom Nietzsche was in general strongly antagonistic throughout his life, no doubt in part because of his attachment to Schopenhauer, whose loathing of Hegel was notorious. But in the elaboration of the opposition and its overcoming Nietzsche does not need any of the dialectical apparatus that Hegel encumbers himself with. For he can work out his scheme by means of images and examples, and that is what he does, though the examples are often used tendentiously.

The idea is that the Apolline is the art of appearance, indeed *is* appearance. Nietzsche invokes dreams to make his point, that at its most representative Apolline art has extraordinary clarity, giving hard edges to what it depicts, exemplifying the *principium individuationis* (the principle of individuation) which Schopenhauer had located as the major error that we suffer from epistemologically—we perceive and conceive of the world in terms of separate objects, including separate persons. As beings with sense organs and conceptual apparatus, we cannot avoid this fundamentally erroneous way of viewing the world; and for Schopenhauer it is responsible for many of our most painful illusions and experiences, though it is unclear that overcoming it should lead to our lives being any less frightful.

Nietzsche traded, in *BT*, on the confusions in Schopenhauer's thought—it is nowhere evident that he was any more aware of them than Schopenhauer himself—to produce his own, somewhat independent, 'artists' metaphysics', as he contemptuously refers to his procedure in the 'Attempt at a Self-Criticism', the magnificent introduction that he wrote to the third edition of the book in 1886, the year of self-reckoning. By that phrase 'artists' metaphysics' he meant partly a metaphysics tailor-made to give art an importance that he later came to regard as preposterous; and partly the use of artistic or pseudo-artistic methods to produce metaphysical views, testing them by their beauty rather than for their truth. One way of looking at *BT* is as a transcendental argument, in Kant's sense. What that comes to in general is the following pattern: *x* is the case—the datum. What else must be the case in order for that (*x*) to be possible? Nietzsche's datum is very unlike that found in any other philosopher, since it gives primacy to our aesthetic experience, normally low on the list of philosophical priorities, when it figures at all. He takes the experiences we have of Apolline art (sculpture, painting, above all the epic) and Dionysiac art (music, tragedy) as his data, and asks how the world must be in order for these experiences to be vouchsafed us. We have seen that he compares Apolline art to dreams; Dionysiac art is aligned rather, as a first indication of its nature, with intoxication, the low way in which the principle of individuation is felt to be overcome, the loss of clarity, and the merging of individualities.

Why do we need them both, once we have grasped that one is the representation of beautiful appearance, while the other enables us to experience reality so far as we can without being destroyed by it? Because we are so constructed that doses of reality must be reserved for special occasions, as the Greeks realized: for festivals (the first Bayreuth Festival was being planned while Nietzsche wrote, though it would not material- ize until 1876). But there is more to it than that. There is nothing wrong with appearances, so long as we realize that that is what they are (this will always be a leading motif in Nietzsche's work). As we saw, the Greek epic is an Apolline art form, and its proudest manifestation is of course the *Iliad*, a work that delights us with its lucidity and its hard edges. The Greeks who lived it were happy to make for themselves fictions of a realm of gods enjoying themselves at their expense—'the only satisfactory form of theodicy,' Nietzsche remarks memo- rably (*BT*, 3). And at this level the formula which occurs twice in the first edition, and is repeated approvingly in the 'Attempt at a Self-Criticism', operates: 'Only as an aesthetic phenom- enon is the world justified' (the formulations vary slightly). Since for the Greeks of the Homeric age existence on its barest terms would have been intolerable, they showed a heroic artis- tic instinct in turning their battle-bound lives into a spectacle. That is why they needed gods; not to console themselves with the thought of a better life hereafter, which has been the usual motivation for postulating another world, but to mark the distinction between any life they could lead and the immortal lives of the gods, which just because they were immortal could be as reckless and irresponsible as Homer shockingly, to us, shows them being. 'Anyone who approaches these Olympians with a different religion in his heart, seeking elevated morals, even sanctity, ethereal spirituality, charity and mercy, will quickly be forced to turn his back on them, discouraged and disappointed' (*BT*, 3).

If we can give a sense, any longer, to the concept of the heroic—something about which Nietzsche had lifelong doubts—it is surely in getting an imaginative grasp on such a vision. This is Nietzsche's first attempt to give force to a phrase that he became addicted to in his later work, 'a pessimism of strength'. He was never callow enough to be an optimist, to think that life would ever become, in a way that a non-hero could appreciate it, wonderful. We, as non-heroes, can only concern ourselves with improving 'the quality of life' (one wishes Nietzsche were around to give what would be the only adequate comment on that appalling phrase). If we feel that it cannot be improved, we become pessimists, but sentimental, or as Nietzsche came to call it 'Romantic' ones, lamenting the miseries of life, and perhaps putting our laments into suitably emollient poetic form.

Nietzsche's celebration of Homer and the heroes to whom he gave his version of immortality by writing the *Iliad* is enough to show that there is nothing intrinsically wrong with Apolline art. But it connives in an illusion, and so is inherently unstable, liable to lapse into something less worthy. As the Greeks became more aware of their relationship to the gods, the age of the epic, which refuses to probe where trouble is likely to be the outcome, gave rise to the age of the tragic. There are many ways in which Nietzsche expresses this momentous transition, most of them influenced by his passionate but short-lived discipleship of Schopenhauer. At the end of section 1 of *BT* he writes: 'Man is no longer an artist [as he had been in creating the gods], he has become a work of art: the artistic power of the whole of nature reveals itself to the supreme gratification of the primal Oneness amidst the paroxysms of intoxication.' At this still early point in *BT* we have the feeling, thrilled or exasperated according to our temperament, that Nietzsche is making it all up as he goes along. He has had a large number of profound and moving artistic experiences, not very many of other kinds, and he is trying to make sense of them in the only way a great critic, at least since the collapse of the Classical tradition in criticism, can do: by composing a work which seems, in its essential movement, to duplicate the strength and richness of those experiences.

In such a mode of procedure, words and phrases come first, then you think what you mean by them. It is a procedure which Nietzsche would use all his writing life, but would soon realize was not fitted to the mode of expression typical of a monograph with the appurtenances of an academic treatise. The passage that I quoted immediately above is a good example of that. Having characterized the Homeric Greeks as artists, thanks to their creative capacities with respect to inventing capricious deities (capacities that they had to have to endure life) he moves on to the idea that they became works of art themselves, but the movement is in the first place on the level of playing with words for a serious purpose. Then he has to justify it, having first explained what it means. The Schopenhauerian notion (which provided the framework in which his thinking could be done) that underlying all individual appearances is a single, fundamentally unchanging Oneness comes to his rescue, and he celebrates the tragedy-producing Greeks for making men into works of art, or in his alternative formulation, 'artists of life'. They realize that to confront reality instead of loving beautiful appearances they must cope with the fact that life is *au fond* eternally destructive of the individual, and allow themselves to abandon their separateness, delighting in the Dionysiac art which was their stronghold against the Dionysiac festivals of the barbarians, at the center of which 'was an extravagant want of sexual discipline, whose waves engulfed all the venerable rules of family life. The most savage beasts of nature were here unleashed, even that repellent mixture of love and cruelty that I have always held to be a "witches' brew"' (*BT*, 2).

Art, that is, always, even at its most Dionysiac, possesses form, and thus up to a point falsifies its subject-matter, which is a formless swirl of pain-cum-pleasure, with pain predominating. But it needs to perform this falsification, for otherwise we would find it unendurable. Thus much later in the book when he is discussing Wagner's *Tristan und Isolde*, Nietzsche claims that it has to be a drama, because in dramas there are characters, i.e. individuals, which means that Apollo is playing his part. In Act III of the drama, Tristan the character interposes between us and Wagner's music; Tristan mediates the experience which causes him to die, and we survive, having come as close as possible to direct contact with the primal reality. So tragic heroes are sacrificial victims, and we achieve 'redemption', a favourite term of Wagner's as well as of Christians, which Nietzsche was shortly to regret having used, though in other contexts it went on serving his purpose.

I have vaulted over the intervening chapters of *BT* in order to show how Nietzsche tries to establish a continuity between Greek tragedy and Wagnerian music drama. The latter is bound, he thinks, to mean more to us than the former can because the music to which the Greek tragedies were performed has been lost, so we can only infer their effects from accounts of how their audiences responded to them: they were put into a state of *Rausch* (intoxication) which is only now once more available to us. This state is impossible except to a community of spectators, whose sense of loss of identity is an upmarket version of that felt by a contemporary football crowd. But we have to concentrate on the way that *Rausch* is produced, otherwise there will be no qualitative distinction between a football crowd and the audience at a tragedy. Before long Nietzsche came to feel, for complex reason, that there was no significant distinction between an audience of Wagnerians and his equivalent of a band of lager louts. But that thought lay in the painful future. For the present he was intent on the regeneration of the spirit of community thanks to its members being united in a common ecstasy. That is 'the seriously German problem that we are dealing with,' Nietzsche at this stage taking it that the Germans were the possessors of a sensitivity to ultimate truths and values which other nations are denied, thanks in large part to the richness of the Germans' musical inheritance.

In between his opening statements about the duality of
Apollo and Dionysus and the extraordinarily involved dialectic
in which they fertilize one another in the closing sections of
the book we get Nietzsche's highly, not to say grotesquely,
schematized version of the peaks (Aeschylus and Sophocles)
and decline (Euripides) of Greek tragedy. His central thesis is
that in the peaks the chorus predominates, so that the audience
sees on stage its own reflection, raised to overpowering heights
of suffering and transfiguration. But when Euripides, whose
plays unfortunately survive in far greater numbers than those of
his superior predecessors, arrives on the scene he manifests an
interest in individuals, in psychology, and worst of all in the
beneficial effects of rationality, or as Nietzsche tends to call it,
'dialectic'. Nietzsche has no doubts that the corrupting influence on him was Socrates, fully deserving his hemlock not for
his power over the youth of Athens, but over what might have
been its continuing tragic greatness. 'Euripides became the poet
of aesthetic Socratism' (*BT*, 12).

The characteristic that makes Socrates so radically anti-
tragic a figure is his belief in the omnipotence of reason—
though one might point out that in the dialogues of Plato which
scholars regard as most likely to be accounts of Socrates' own
views, not much progress is made, except of a negative kind.
But Nietzsche's portrayal of him survives this point:

In this quite abnormal character, instinctive wisdom appears only
to *hinder* conscious knowledge at certain points. While in all
productive people instinct is the power of creativity and affirmation, and consciousness assumes a critical and dissuasive role, in
Socrates instinct becomes the critic, consciousness the creator—a
monstrosity *per defectum*! (*BT*, 13)

The image of Socrates was never to let Nietzsche free; as with
all the leading characters in his pantheon and anti-pantheon,
his relationship with him remains one of tortured ambivalence.
For Nietzsche did not think that the relationship between instinct and consciousness was as simple as he here pretends to.
What he was sure of was

the optimistic element in dialectic, which rejoices at each conclusion and can breathe only in cool clarity and consciousness: that
optimistic element which, once it had invaded tragedy, gradually
overgrew its Dionysiac regions and forced itself into self-
destruction—its death-leap into bourgeois theater. We need only
consider the Socratic maxims: 'Virtue is knowledge, all sins arise
from ignorance, the virtuous man is the happy man.' In these three
basic optimistic formulae lies the death of tragedy. (*BT*, 14)

It is a brilliant indictment, even if it has very little to do
with Euripides. For it can be no accident that the great tradition
of rationalism in Western philosophy has gone with an amazing uniformity of optimism, nor that we have to wait until
Schopenhauer to encounter a philosopher who is a pessimist,
and going with that an anti-rationalist, believing in the primacy
of an irrational Will. The Western tradition has been inimical
to tragedy, thanks to the co-operation of Platonism and Christianity, and its great tragedies, above all those of Shakespeare
and Racine, are either removed from a theological context or in
uneasy relationship to it. Not that Nietzsche is able to countenance Shakespeare as a fully-fledged tragedian, because of the
absence of music. This puts him in an awkward position, which
he deals with by almost total evasion. The one briefly sustained
passage on Shakespeare in *BT* is brilliantly perceptive on Ham-
let, as being a man who, having looked into the Dionysiac
abyss, realizes the futility of all action—he is not a delayer but
a despairer (*BT*, 7). But how that can have the full tragic effect,
if it does, is not something that he explores.

More damagingly still, Nietzsche does nothing to explain
why there are so few musical tragedies; he seems to take it for
granted that Wagner wrote them, though it seems clear to me
that he did not. Indeed, one composer after another has used the
sovereign powers of music to show that, however bad things
may be on stage, they can be saved. What really impressed
Nietzsche was the degree of ecstasy which music, unlike any
other art, can induce. And since he accorded a traditionally high
status to tragedy, as the art form which shows how we can

survive even the apparently unendurable, he effected an amalgam of the two.

It is here that his allegiance to Schopenhauer is most damaging. For Schopenhauer too believed that music gives us direct access to the movements of the Will, since it is unmediated by concepts. But on his general account of the nature of the Will, eternally striving and necessarily never achieving, it is hard to see how or why we should take any pleasure in an art which puts us in immediate contact with it. One would have thought that the greater distance there is between us and reality, the less tormented we would be.

Nietzsche modifies Schopenhauer somewhat by claiming that the Primal One is a mixture of pain and pleasure, but as stated above, pain predominates. What Nietzsche is doing is attempting to answer the traditional question: Why do we enjoy tragedy? He rightly dissociates himself from the traditional answers, viewing them as shallow and complacent. But in his effort to erect tragedy into an agent which transfigures the seemingly untransfigurable, he overshoots the mark, appearing himself to fall into the trap of equating the true and the beautiful, something which he later excoriated in satisfyingly vigorous terms. We want to ask him the question at this point that he was not to ask until more than a decade later: Why truth rather than untruth: What is it in us that urges us always to seek the truth?

It is not as if he has no answers to these questions in *BT*, but they remain obscure. And we shall not find him getting fully to the bottom of these issues until his last phase. What is noteworthy, though, is that he is already embarking on the central quest of his life: How can existence be made bearable, once we grasp what it is really like? The way he approaches it here is by quoting early on a story about Silenus, friend of Dionysus, who said 'Miserable, ephemeral race, children of hazard and hardship, why do you force me to say what it would be much more fruitful for you not to hear? The best of all things is something entirely outside your grasp: not to be born, not to be, to be *nothing*. But the second-best for you—is to die soon' (*BT*, 3). But though Silenus is 'wise', ultimately tragic wisdom (Nietzsche is constantly opposing *Wissenschaft* (knowledge, science) and *Weisheit* (wisdom)), manages to trump even him. It does so, according to some pretty esoteric manœuvres executed late in the book, by an elaborate interplay between the Apolline and the Dionysiac. Then comes his most suggestive remark: 'The pleasure produced by the tragic myth has the same origin as the pleasurable perception of dissonance in music. The Dionysiac, with its primal pleasure experienced even in pain, is the common womb of music and the tragic myth' (*BT*, 24).

One might feel that this is what Schoenberg later called 'the emancipation of the dissonance' with a vengeance. For though we find music without dissonances to be resolved insipid, the world seems to present us rather with incessant dissonance, with odd moments of respite. But it is no good pressing the point at this stage. Nietzsche is indeed providing us with an artist's metaphysic, in which the recalcitrance of the material to be organized is a stimulus to ever-greater feats of creation—but a creation that is also an imitation, so that we can say both that we are presented with reality, but that through being given form it is transformed.

At the beginning of the *Duino Elegies*, Rilke writes: 'For Beauty is nothing | but the beginning of terror, which we are still just able to endure, | and we are so awed by it because it serenely disdains to annihilate us' (trans. by Stephen Mitchell, slightly modified). That, one could fairly say, is the basic thought of *BT*. It is at the least disturbing, and may even be felt to be disgusting (Young 1992: 54–5). It decisively obliterates the long-held distinction between the Sublime and the Beautiful, making the former into an all-important element in the latter. But that may be the least striking of its innovations. More significantly, it announces the determination which Nietzsche maintained throughout his career, and manifested heroically in his life, not to give pain an automatically negative role in life, something which he perhaps felt more oppressed by in the contemporary scene than anything else. At the same time, he was possessed by a vision of the world as a place of such horror that any attempt to give meaning to it in moral terms is simply impossible. That is why in the 'Attempt at a Self-Criticism', having criticized the book more harshly than anyone else had done, saying that he found it 'impossible', he still finds that 'it already betrays a spirit which will defy all risks to oppose the *moral* interpretation and significance of existence' (*BT*, 'Attempt at a Self-Criticism', 5). And a few lines further on he specifies 'Christianity as the most extravagant elaboration of the moral theme that humanity has ever heard.' Though there is hindsight operating here, it is true that he was always sensitive enough to suffering (other people's—he was an incredible stoic about his own) to find an 'explanation' of it in terms of the good it does us, its being a retribution for our wrongdoings, and the rest of the clap-trap that rings down through the millennia intolerable.

BT may well be most of the awful things Nietzsche and others have accused it of, but it has proved a fecund source of inspiration for Classical scholars and anthropologists. It is also, thanks to its highlighting of the Apolline–Dionysiac duality, a book that has had a powerful influence on the vulgar imagination. It gains, too, from rereading; once one has the general movement clear, there are many particular insights that are not to be found elsewhere in Nietzsche. But it will never repay a certain kind of close reading, that which is in vogue today and looks for aporias, fissure, self-subversions, and the rest of the deconstructionist's tool-kit. Only books which apparently achieve a consistency of thought which *BT* undeniably lacks will do that. Its consistency is to be found only in the enthusiasm with which Nietzsche is determined to weld together in a process of feeling his most cherished concerns, and his idols as manifesting them. It is, in other words, a young man's book, less candid than his later ones about its closeness to its author. And, perhaps most strikingly, it is the most optimistic expression of a pessimistic world-view that has ever been penned.

3 Disillusionment and withdrawal

The years which culminated in the writing of *BT* were the happiest in Nietzsche's life, indeed the last that were not dogged by ill health, loneliness, and rejection. When the Wagners left Tribschen and moved to Bayreuth in 1872 Nietzsche's most consistently warm and fruitful relationship(s) were at an end. Without Wagner's presence, Nietzsche began to have doubts about the quality and purpose of his music dramas, on which he meditated to the end of his life. But he was still officially a Wagnerian, recruited to produce more propaganda for a cause that badly needed it. Anxious about the state of German culture, which he soon began to feel he had vastly overrated in *BT*, he embarked on a series of tracts for the times, therefore called *Untimely Meditations*. Thirteen were projected, but only four were written. Probably that is two too many. Upwards of fifty pages in length, as long essays, they show Nietzsche failing to discover a form that is suited to his gifts. Trying to expound and develop an argument in a manner less ecstatic than *BT*, he resorts for the only time in his life to diffuseness and padding.

But there is a more basic problem with *UM* than those. While he directs himself to assessing the health of contemporary culture, with an attack on the aged David Strauss, author of *The Life of Jesus*, but more perniciously for Nietzsche, of *The Old Faith and the New*; to the practice of historiography; and then to celebrations of the genius of Schopenhauer and Wagner, he had not, with the signal exception of the Second Meditation, 'On the uses and disadvantages of history for life', found subjects which coincided sufficiently closely with his concerns. The book by Strauss that he selects for critique in the First

Meditation is so undemanding a pewside read, so unresisting an object for intelligent scorn, that one wonders why Nietzsche is bothering, and evidently so does he. Even so, it is worth reading through; it deals with very much the same topics as Matthew Arnold's *Culture and Anarchy*, and the most profitable way of reading it is side by side with that shallow and influential pamphlet, whose terminology it shares to a surprising degree. And it does contain one of Nietzsche's most inspired coinages, 'philistine of culture', the man who knows about what he should, and makes sure that it has no effect on him.

The Second Meditation is a great work, a real meditation on the extent to which we can cope with the burden of knowledge, specifically historical knowledge, and still manage to be our own men. And it ends with a rousing appeal to us to embrace the Greek concept of culture as opposed to the Roman, the former being that 'of culture as new and improved Nature [*physis*], without inner and outer, without dissimulation and convention, culture as a unanimity of life, thought, appearance and will' (*UM* 2. 10). Excellent, but there is a speech-day quality about these sentiments that nothing in the body of the essay does much to fill out.

The Third Meditation, 'Schopenhauer as Educator', is bewildering mainly because it is so little concerned with Schopenhauer. Nietzsche's discipleship of the compromised pessimist was waning, and what he chiefly has to praise about him is his scorn of university philosophers, but Schopenhauer had done it far better himself in Parerga and Paralipomena. The last Meditation, 'Richard Wagner in Bayreuth', makes painful reading. Even if we had no idea that Nietzsche was, while he wrote it, simultaneously entering in his notebooks grave questions about Wagner, we would feel something was wrong. It is the only occasion on which Nietzsche sounds insincere, trying to recapture a state of mind which had been wonderful while it lasted, but was moving with alarming speed into the past. The only explanation for Wagner's enthusiasm for it—'Friend, how did you get to know me so well?'—is that he was too busy to read it. It makes, in its way, a fitting prelude to the next crucial event (one of the few) in Nietzsche's life: his attendance at the first Bayreuth Festival in 1876, and the break with Wagner.

Most of Nietzsche's commentators greet with relief his becoming an anti-Wagnerian, possibly because they think it exempts them from knowing anything much about Wagner. Of course it does nothing of the kind, since Wagner is the person who continues to feature more often in Nietzsche's writings than anyone else, including Socrates, Christ, or Goethe. But at a serious level they may feel that Nietzsche was not being true to himself when he was a Wagnerian, and became true to himself by causing the extremely painful rift, of which Wagner was not even aware for a long time. To decide what were, in order of importance, the factors which led to it is impossible. No doubt Nietzsche's naïve expectations of what the Bayreuth Festival would be like were shatteringly disappointed; so were Wagner's, but he knew what the practicalities of the situation were. The books had to be balanced, though they disastrously were not; but the attempt meant that the wellheeled had to be wooed, that what was intended to be a festival in which the community celebrated their shared values at minimal cost turned into something in which the fashionable world of philistines of culture was most in evidence, along with crowned heads and other irrelevances.

Nietzsche, horrified by the company, fled into the nearby countryside to recover from his eclipsing headaches. There, and later, he took stock of his relationship with Wagner the man and the artist. He was certainly now in a mood where he did not want to be anyone's disciple, and that must have been a key factor. He may have been in love with Cosima; the evidence is inconclusive but makes the idea reasonable. The least convincing explanation is the one on which Nietzsche put most public weight—that Wagner had become a Christian. Receiving the poem of *Parsifal* was allegedly the last straw. But he had been present in 1869 when Wagner read out the prose sketch, and had heard Wagner talking about the subject, so it cannot have been the bombshell that he claimed it was. Not to be discounted are Nietzsche's own ambitions as a composer, the most embarrassing of his failures. A man who could play his own amateur piano pieces to Wagner, and who could continue to write, until much later, choral pieces that sound like Congregational Church hymns with a few wrong notes but are called 'Hymn to Life' or 'Hymn to Friendship' was evidently not able to judge his own gifts in this respect.

And it is not only as a composer that Nietzsche was frustrated. He was, in a comprehensive way, a creative artist *manqué*. That accounts in large measure for the cavalier way in which he treats the great artists, even the ones he most admires, throughout his work. He is the most distinguished member of that class of writers, who at their best are incomparably insightful, at their worst arrogant and merely distorting; who, unable to produce art themselves, ransack other people's in order to purvey their own vision. Perhaps all the great critics (a very small class in any case) are like that. One certainly does not go to them for accurate accounts of the works with which they deal—that can be left to merely very good critics. But seeing the great artists, whose images in any case tend to become marmoreal as they are routinely categorized as 'classics', in the light of a fervent imagination providing a strange and highly 'interested' slant on them, is exhilarating. It probably accounts better than anything else for the continuing impact of such works as *BT*.

Perhaps the most helpful way to look at the break is that in Wagner Nietzsche had, for the only time in his life, met one of his symbols in the flesh. It is clear from *BT* onwards that almost all proper names in his texts stand not for individuals, but for movements, tendencies, ways of living. This characteristic of Nietzsche's is frequently inspired, occasionally perverse and misleading. The confusion in Wagner's case is that for him Wagner did, in the first place, mean a person with whom he had a 'star friendship' (*GS*), and he was not able to separate, in his writings, what Wagner was from what he came to stand for , so that the degree of ambivalence he shows towards him exceeds that of his other hero-villains. If he had never met Wagner he would still almost inevitably have given him an important role in his works, because Wagner does sum up for him, in the most convenient way, traits in late nineteenth-century culture to which he was mostly bitterly opposed, though not as single-mindedly as he would have liked to be. But the loss of Wagner as friend and mentor, though it was necessary, cost Nietzsche more than he was ever able to come to terms with.

Nietzsche dealt with his problems in the only way that was ever available to him: he wrote prodigiously, producing a new book that in nearly all respects shows his fast-growing powers, and in the mode that from now on most of what he composed would be in. *Human, All Too Human*, subtitled 'A book for free spirits,' is in nine books, with very general titles, and 638 numbered sections, many with their own titles (he was later to publish two very substantial sequels, so that the whole volume is by far the largest of his books). As with all books written in this mode, it makes exhausting reading. Even though the sections are grouped together according to subject-matter, Nietzsche allows himself plenty of latitude, so one is bombarded with particular points which are displaced by others at such a rate that the result is, to one's dismay, unmemorable. The only way is to mark the sections that make a special impact, and return to them later. It is a crucial element in Nietzsche's strategy of writing, though a risky one. Its deployment so lavishly and so suddenly in his writing is the expression of his revulsion from the pseudo-narrtive of *BT*, a book easy to remember despite its turgidity, simply because it does have a connecting thread.

But for all its perennial freshness, there is something about *HAH* which leads one to feel that Nietzsche is not working at the level which is naturally his. The dedication to Voltaire is a warning. For although Voltaire's breezy superficiality was what Nietzsche may have felt he wanted after the sustained effort to plumb the depths of Romantic pessimism, it is hard to think of two temperaments more essentially opposed. *Candide*, Voltaire's critique of optimism, is itself an ineliminably upbeat book. What appealed to Nietzsche in him, as in the French aphorists of the seventeenth century, was the hardness of their style, an Apolline quality which suggests that experience can be tied up in neat, eye-catching little parcels. All good aphoristic writing is tiring to read, because one has to do so much of the writer's work for him. He supplies a sentence, the reader turns it into a paragraph. Nietzsche wrote that he wanted to say in a page what anyone else would take a book to express—and what they even then would not have succeeded in expressing. But the kind of aphorisms and quasi-aphorisms that he aspired to write were ones that would have the effect of transforming the reader's consciousness: in other words, they would have the opposite effect from those of, say, La Rochefoucauld. Nietzsche, at his most characteristic and best, is always producing the reverse of an encapsulation of experience: his subversions, teasings and insults are directed towards making us feel ashamed not only of how we are, but of our complacency in thinking that we possess the best set of categories for the realization of what we might be. They are not weary, nor do they induce weariness, because they lead us to an enhanced sense of the possibilities of escape from the routine of being ourselves. It has been characteristic of the French tradition of moralists that they are observers, reporting elegantly on the perennial human condition. They provide *frissons* of shame in the reader, but no expectation that he might ever be different.

So Nietzsche's lengthy flirtation with them was more a matter of how they said things than of what they said. But that suggests something odd: for he is stickler for the indissolubility of form and content, from the beginning to the end. How else could he have placed such a weight on genre in *BT*, where the fact that a work is a drama rather than an epic poem makes the whole difference to its impact? It can only be explained by his extreme turning-away from Romanticism: everything now had to be seen in the clear light of day, at the same time that it should be infinitely suggestive. In *HAH* he is more preoccupied with the former than the latter, and the result is that one feels, certainly in the light of his later work, that he is constraining himself, surveying the scene—human nature in its manifestations as social life, passion, the psychology of artists, solitude—without the will to transform which is his defining characteristic. So, to take at random one of his *aperçus*:

Thirst for profound pain.—When it has passed, passion leaves behind an obscure longing for itself and even in departing casts a seductive glance. To be scourged by it must have afforded us a kind of joy. The milder sensations, on the other hand, appear insipid; it seems we always prefer the more vehement displeasure to a feeble pleasure. (*HAH*, I. 606)

That is quite deep, and produces a sense, rather than a shock, of recognition. Elsewhere the accuracy can be painful: '*Compelling oneself to pay attention.*—As soon as we notice that anyone has to *compel* himself to pay attention when associating and talking with us, we have a valid proof that he does not love us or loves us no longer' (*HAH*, II. 247).

Writing *HAH*, a book which Wagner said, on receiving his signed copy of it, Nietzsche would one day thank him for not reading, revealed to Nietzsche some aspects of himself he must have been pleased to discover. First, that he belonged to that rare breed on whom nothing is wasted. His range of experience was, in many respects, extraordinarily narrow, but it was adequate for him to view his culture and his acquaintances and produce unnervingly comprehensive accounts of them. In *Ecce Homo*, his bizarre autobiography in which the mood alternates vertiginously between the apocalyptic and the parodistic, he congratulates himself on the possession of a remarkably fine nose, an organ that philosophers have tended to give short shrift to. The first devastating manifestation of its acuteness is in *HAH*. Secondly, it showed him that even under conditions as miserable and deprived as he was in he could work at a level of brilliance which was self-generating. As in *BT*, one feels that it is the momentum of the writing that generates much of what is most impressive in it. Thirdly, and most significant, he was able to dwell on subjects which had occasioned fearful pain and not exhibit the least degree of rancour; *HAH* is a work in which he demonstrates, what he had not yet advocated, that it is possible to turn the most harrowing things that happen to good purposes, and exhibit high spirits without advertising to us that that is what he is doing, a trying tendency in some of his later works.

His next book, *Daybreak*, subtitled 'Thoughts on the Prejudices of Morality', continues the mode of *HAH*, but marks a crucial departure in content, and is much more of a piece with his later works. In beween 1878, when *HAH* was published, to universal indifference, and 1880, when he wrote *D*, his pattern of life changed drastically, and the way in which he was to live for the next decade began. Most of his friends were bewildered by his change of direction, and he was alienated from all but the most loyal. In 1879, several years too late, he resigned his Professorship at Basle, students having lost all interest in his teaching. In that year, too, he had 118 days of severe migraine, rendering him incapable of work. His health had been undermined by the combined attacks of dysentery and diphtheria which he had sustained in 1870, when serving as a medical orderly in the Franco-Prussian War; and it seems most likely that he contracted syphilis from a prostitute sometime in the late 1870s when he was in Italy, which led to his eventual insanity and paralysis. From then on he led a nomadic existence, looking for places which would alleviate his sickness, and permit him the maximum amount of solitude for writing. His preferred places were the towns of northern Italy in the winter, and the Swiss Alps in the summer, though it was not until 1882 that that became his annual routine.

Nietzsche proffers some advice on how to read *D*, though it comes late in the book; 'A book such as this is not for reading straight through or reading aloud but for dipping into, especially when out walking or on a journey; you must be able to stick your head into it and out of it again and again and discover nothing familiar around you' (*D* 454). Which is all very well, but if taken seriously might result in one's never reading it all through. So once more it is a good idea to canter through it, and then to take Nietzsche's advice, if at all. But it is not really good advice, and is probably even meant sarcastically. For this, one of Nietzsche's least studied books, is where he gets back on to the high road of his life's endeavour. It might even seem that it is where he properly begins it, but that is to overlook the extent to which *BT* set the agenda.

4   *Morality and its discontents*

Nietzsche's fundamental concern throughout his life was to plot the relationship between suffering and culture, or cultures. He categorizes and grades cultures by the way in which they have coped with the omnipresence of suffering, and assesses moralities by the same criterion. That is why he was interested in tragedy, but lost interest when he came to feel that it was not a contemporary possibility. It is why he was always passionately preoccupied with the heroic, in life rather than art, and needing eventually to be rebaptized as the *Übermensch* (I shall leave this word untranslated, since I find 'superman' absurd, and 'overman' unnatural). It is the basis of his attack on transcendent metaphysics, and on all religions that postulate an afterlife. And of course it was of primary 'existential' concern to him, because his life was suffering.

Correlative with this preoccupation with how one regards suffering is Nietzsche's interest in greatness rather than goodness. For there is no greatness without a readiness and capacity to withstand, absorb, and use to best purpose an immense quantity of pain. Greatness, one might say to anticipate, involves putting pain to work; goodness involves attempting to eliminate it. All Nietzsche's later works will be devoted to exploring this profound difference. In *D* he presents his first, by no means tentative, analyses of the mechanisms of morality, and of the kind of authority it invokes.

To avoid misunderstanding, it will be useful to quote at length a passage from *D*, which undercuts many of the criticisms that are often made of Nietzsche:

There are two kinds of deniers of morality.—'To deny morality'— this can mean, *first*: to deny that the moral motives which men claim have inspired their actions really have done so—it is thus the assertion that morality consists of words and is among the coarser or more subtle deceptions (especially self-deceptions) which men practise, and is perhaps so especially in precisely the case of those most famed for virtue. *Then* it can mean: to deny that moral judgments are based on truths. Here it is admitted that they really are motives of action, but that in this way it is *errors* which, as the basis of all moral judgment, impel men to their moral actions. This is *my* point of view: though I should be the last to deny that *in very many cases* there is some ground for suspicion that the other point of view—that is to say, the point of view of La Rochefoucauld and others who think like him—may also be justified and in any event of great general application.—Thus I deny morality as I deny alchemy, that is, I deny their premises: but I do not deny that there have been alchemists who believed in these premises and acted in accordance with them.—I also deny immorality: *not* that countless people *feel* themselves to be immoral, but that there is any *true* reason so to feel. It goes without saying that I do not deny—unless I am a fool—that many actions called immoral ought to be avoided and resisted, or that many called moral ought to be done and encouraged—but I think that the one should be encouraged and the other avoided *for other reasons than hitherto*. We have to *learn to think differently*—in order at last, perhaps very late on, to attain even more: *to feel differently*. (D 103)

It is a pity that what Nietzsche tells us 'goes without saying' is something that he thereby rarely bothered to reiterate. For it is a vulgarly and widely held view that he did deny that 'many actions called immoral ought to be avoided and resisted,' etc. Note, though, that in this very careful piece of writing—it is typical of *D*, and makes it all the more surprising that it is so rarely referred to—he does say 'many' actions, but fails to specify which. That is partly, I think, because his views were undergoing radical development at this time, and he may not have wished to commit himself in certain cases. But he is, at this stage, unsure too about how far withdrawing the 'premisses' of morality was going to alter the conclusions. Among the premisses that he immediately goes on to attack are those which define the goal of morality in terms of 'the preservation and advancement of mankind,' about which he asks

Can one deduce from it with certainty whether what is to be kept in view is the longest possible existence of mankind? Or the greatest possible deanimalisation of mankind? How different the means, that is to say the practical morality, would have to be in the two cases! ... Or suppose one conceived the attainment of mankind's 'highest happiness' as being the *to what* and *of what* of morality: would one mean the highest degree of happiness that individual men could possibly attain to? Or a—necessarily incalculable—average happiness which could finally be attained by all? And why should the way to that have to be morality? (*D* 106)

He keeps going at this furious pace, leaving the hapless commentator wondering whether to expound in detail, a valuable enterprise which would result in a very large book, but no larger than the ones awarded many times over to such worthless works as Kant's *Critique of Practical Reason*, surely the most shattering disappointment in the history of philosophy, coming after the *Critique of Pure Reason*, one of its greatest glories. Anyway, that is impossible here. The main thrust of *D*, which also has, as always, reflections on a vast range of subjects, among which contemporary music looms large, is to demonstrate the mess that morality is in. As he puts it succinctly: '"*Utilitarian*".—Moral sensibilities are nowadays at such cross-purposes that to one man a morality is proved by its utility, while to another its utility refutes it' (*D* 230).

What is notable about *D* is the restraint and the modesty of its claims. There is no hint that Zarathustra will soon come down from his mountain, smashing all our moral tablets. Most of the points that it makes seem to me ungainsayable, but clearly that is not how they strike everyone. Thus we still find plenty of people, philosophers among them, who claim, for instance, that morality is a self-supporting system, resting on nothing outside itself; that morality is founded in reason, and that the basis of morality is demonstrable; that, as Nietzsche says, a morality is proved by its utility, or that it is refuted by it. To argue at length about these issues is important, but would be beside the point in considering Nietzsche's development. For all the debates that are current, at least in the anglophone world, about morality assume a great deal that Nietzsche denies. None of them, so far as I am aware, is prepared to see how the various somewhat differing codes of morality that we encounter arise from conflicting views about the nature of the world. It is astonishing, for example, to hear philosophers talking about their 'intuitions' as something to be trusted and left unscrutinized, unless they come into conflict with one another. 'My intuitions are that . . .' is a common way to begin a philosophical discussion, as if one represented the eternal voice of mankind.

It is on this basis, too, if not of one's own intuitions, then of those that 'we' share, that many of Nietzsche's moral positions are routinely dismissed, as being 'élitist', 'anti-democratic', and so forth. This is such a vital issue, and one which must be coped with by any Nietzschean commentator, that I shall quote, also at length, from Henry Staten, who has written what I regard as all told the most illuminating book on Nietzsche:

Our moral beliefs did not fall from heaven and neither are they credentials we can flash like a badge to establish our moral probity. Consider all the rest of human history, including most of the planet at the present moment. What are we to say about this overwhelming spectacle of cruelty, stupidity, and suffering? What stance is there for us to adopt with respect to history, what judgment can we pass on it? Is it all a big mistake? Christianity attempted to recuperate the suffering of history by projecting a divine plan that assigns it a reason in the here and now and a recompense later, but liberalism is too humane to endorse this explanation. There is no explanation, only the brute fact. But the brute fact we are left with is even harder to stomach than the old explanation. So Left liberalism packages it in a new narrative, a moral narrative according to which all those lives ground up in the machinery of history are assigned an intelligible role as victims of oppression and injustice. There is an implicit teleology in this view; modern Left liberalism is the telos that gives form and meaning to rest of history. Only very recently is it possible for someone like Schutte [Ofelia Schutte, who in her book *Beyond*

Nihilism: Nietzsche without Masks castigates Nietzsche for his authoritarianism] to write as she does, with so much confidence that the valuations she assumes will be received as a matter of course by an academic audience, just as much as a Christian homilist writing for an audience of the pious. And only within the protective enclosure of this community of belief can there be any satisfaction in the performance of this speech act, any sense that anything worthwhile has been accomplished by the recitation. When this moral community by means of such recitation reassures itself of its belief, it comes aglow as the repository of the meaning of history, as the locus that one may occupy in order to view history and pass judgment on it without merely despairing or covering one's eyes and ears. There may not be any plan behind history, nor any way of making up their losses to the dead, but we can draw an invisible line of rectitude through history and in this way take power over it. Against the awesome 'Thus it was' of history we set the overawing majesty of 'Thus it *ought* to have been.'

But our liberalism is something that sprang up yesterday and could be gone tomorrow. The day before yesterday the Founding Fathers kept black slaves. What little sliver of light is this we occupy that despite its contingency, the frailty of its existence, enables us to illuminate all the past and perhaps the future as well? For we want to say that even though our community of belief may cease to exist, this would not affect the validity of those beliefs. The line of rectitude would still traverse history. (Staten 1990: 78–9)

Staten is at pains to make clear, after this immensely impressive passage, that he is not criticizing liberalism on a relativistic basis, but only reinforcing Nietzsche's point about the contingency of our historical position, and thus of our values. This must mean that it is not enough to carry out the rituals of horror at his later views, but that they need to be seen as part of an economy of values in terms of which he, in a lonely way, and thus in a frequently and increasingly strident tone, tries to cope with life.

Even though *BT* takes up a spectator's view of tragedy, in part because it is dealing with the dramatic form rather than with human history, it emerges clearly enough that for Nietzsche the dreadfulness of existence is a perpetually present fact. 'Only as an aesthetic phenomenon is life justified'—but we must recall that Nietzsche also says, in the same book, that we ourselves are to become part of the phenomenon. There is not 'life' and then us with ringside seats. If he had thought that in 1871, he would soon be taught his mistake in the most devastating way.

And morality, meaning the variety of attitudes that we find officially espoused in our society? It ministers to our welfare, in its basic form, so that at least we feel safe when our backs are turned on other people. There is no denying that—that is what Nietzsche means by saying he does not deny that many actions called immoral ought to be avoided, etc. But is that not merely a matter of prudence? Of course, Nietzsche says. And the idea that has been touted by many philosophers, beginning with Plato, that on the one (lower) hand there is prudence, and on the other (exalted) hand morality, for which there are sanctions of a transcendental kind, strikes him as high-minded nonsense. So there is the level of morality at which it serves a useful function, and is required by any society that is to survive—though if you are powerful, of course you can get away with a great deal. But that only takes us as far as the continuance of life. What of giving life some point and purpose once we have got that far? The term 'morality' is often used to cover that too, though some people prefer to talk of 'ideals', which they say are essentially individual. Nietzsche does not investigate these matters of nomenclature, but when he is condemning morality or kinds of morality, and when he is calling himself an immoralist, he has the purpose and point of life in mind.

This is where things begin to get complicated. In trying to make them as clear as possible, I shall both depart to some extent from the chronological exposition of Nietzsche, and also rely very heavily on an article by Frithjof Bergmann, on 'Nietzsche's Critique of Morality' (Solomon and Higgins 1988). But it should be reassuring that sometimes commentators agree to the point of holding identical views. In the course of what I have to say, the distinction between morality as convenience and morality as ideal will virtually collapse, along with a good deal else.

The first thing to hold in mind is that Nietzsche does not deny the existence (in some sense) of values. It is a common and amazing mistake to think that he does. But the denial of value is what he primarily means by 'nihilism', the advent of which he dreads above all else. If he sometimes thinks of himself as the prophet of nihilism, it is not in the sense that he is proclaiming its arrival, as something to be celebrated, but in the sense that Jeremiah was the prophet of the destruction of Jerusalem. What he portrays, in book after book, is the gradual but accelerating decline of Western man into a state where no values any longer impress him, or where he mouths them but they mean nothing to him any longer. That is what he sees as imminent. How has this catastrophe, which none of his contemporaries seemed to recognise, come about, and how can it be remedied?

The answer involves looking at two aspects of morality. First, its grounding. Secondly, its content. Morality as it is still practised derives from the Hebraic–Christian tradition, in the largest measure, which means that its origins are to be found in the dictates of the god of a small Middle Eastern tribe, and that its contents remain very much what they were. That immediately transcendentalizes them in two ways. First, their deliverance is a matter of unquestionable commands, for which the punishment for violation was at one time instant divine retribution. Second, since the content was evidently designed for the continuance of the tribe, whose living conditions were vastly different in many ways from ours, it has had to be made more abstract and disconnected from the conditions in which we live. A result has been that morality has in part become unintelligible, and in part has to be coerced into relevance by making us into the kind of beings to whom it would sensibly apply, even though in many respects we know that that is false.

The matter is complicated further by the discrepancies between the Old and New Testaments, and Christ's disingenuousness in claiming that he had come not to destroy the law, but to fulfil it (Matt. 3: 17). Since many of his most impressive precepts are in sharp conflict with the Law, for instance 'Resist not evil', but the Old Testament has remained part of the canon of sacred texts, Christianity has always been in a state of moral identity-crisis. That, though a large factor in the moral bewilderment of the West, is a marginal issue for Nietzsche, whose main interest is in the nature of morality's sanctions in general.

For all sorts of reasons, philosophers of the last three hundred years or so have been concerned to stand by the moral precepts that they have inherited, while attempting to find new foundations for them, including the limiting case of denying that they need foundations. This being so, it is a pity that Nietzsche's Anglophobia led him to attack George Eliot when he was really attacking a tradition in which she plays an insignificant part. The attack comes in *Twilight of the Idols*, one of Nietzsche's last books, but it encapsulates, as so much of that witty and most trenchant of his works does, what he had been saying on the subject for a decade:

They are rid of the Christian God and now believe all the more firmly that they must cling to Christian morality. That is an English consistency; we do not wish to hold it against little moralistic females à la Eliot. In England one must rehabilitate oneself after every little emancipation from theology by showing in a veritably awe-inspiring manner what a moral fanatic one is. That is the penance they pay there.

We others hold otherwise. When one gives up the Christian faith, one pulls the right to Christian morality from under one's feet. This morality is by no means self-evident: this point has to be exhibited again and again, despite the English flatheads. Christianity is a system, a *whole* view of things thought out together. By breaking one main concept out of it, the faith in God, one breaks the whole: nothing necessary remains in one's hands. Christianity presupposes that man does not know, *cannot* know, what is good for him, what evil: he believes in God, who alone knows it. Christianity is a command; its origin is transcendent; it is beyond all criticism, all right to criticism; it has truth only if God is the truth—it stands and falls with faith in God.

When the English actually believe that they know 'intuitively' what is good and evil, when they therefore suppose that they no longer require Christianity as the guarantee of morality, we merely witness the *effects* of the dominion of the Christian value-judgement and an expression of the strength and depth of this dominion: such that the origin of English morality has been forgotten, such that the very conditional character of its right to existence is no longer felt. For the English, morality is not yet a problem. (*TI*, 'Skirmishes of an Untimely Man', 5)

Substitute for 'the English' 'the West' and this whole section seems to me unanswerable. Yet apparently almost the only people to agree with it are Christians, understandably insistent on their faith being seen as a 'system' (in some sense of the word). The most striking endorsement of Nietzsche's argument here, the more impressive for having been written in apparent ignorance of it, is G. E. M. Anscombe's famous (among philosophers) paper 'Modern Moral Philosophy' (Thomson and Dworkin, 1968). Writing as a traditional Roman Catholic, she says

the concepts of obligation, and duty—*moral* obligation and *moral* duty, that is to say—and of what is *morally* right and wrong, and of the *moral* sense of 'ought,' ought to be jettisoned if this is psychologically possible; because they are survivals, or derivatives from survivals, from an earlier conception of ethics which no longer generally survives, and are only harmful without it. (Thomson and Dworkin 1968: 186)

Needless to say, her proposal has not proved to be 'psychologically possible', as she no doubt realized when she wrote those words. And for the same reason that Nietzsche's claims have also been viewed as 'impossible', which is that we have no idea what to replace these terms that 'ought to be jettisoned' with.

As one goes on reading Anscombe's article, one is amazed again and again by the Nietzschean tone of this unwitting disciple. For example:

To have a *law* conception of ethics is to hold that what is needed . . . is required by divine law . . . Naturally it is not possible to have such a conception unless you believe in God as a law-giver; like Jews, Stoics, and Christians . . . It is as if the notion 'criminal' were to remain when criminal law and criminal courts had been abolished and forgotten. (Thomson and Dworkin 1968: 192–3)

Exactly so, and yet that, to Nietzsche's and Anscombe's dismay and contempt, is just how we do contrive to carry on, for the most part untroubled by the conceptual chaos involved, and hardly concealed.

Nietzsche, naturally, has a fundamentally different attitude to what this signifies in the long run, about man throughout history. In *Beyond Good and Evil*, written in 1885, he puts it in the widest context:

The strange narrowness of human evolution, its hesitations, its delays, its frequent retrogressions and rotations, are due to the fact that the herd instinct of obedience has been inherited best and at the expense of the art of commanding. If we think of this instinct taken to its ultimate extravagance there would be no commanders or independent men at all; or, if they existed, they would suffer from a bad conscience and in order to be able to command would have to practise a deceit upon themselves: the deceit, that is, that they too were only obeying. This state of affairs actually exists in Europe today: I call it the moral hypocrisy of the commanders. They know of no way of defending themselves against their bad conscience other than to pose as executors of more ancient or higher commands (commands of ancestors, of the constitution, of justice, of the law or even of God), or even to borrow herd maxims from the herd's way of thinking and appear as 'the first servant of the people' for example, or as 'instruments of the common good'. On the other hand, the herd-man in Europe today makes himself out to be the only permissible kind of man and glorifies the qualities through which he is tame, peaceable and useful to the herd as the real human virtues: namely public spirit, benevolence, consideration, industriousness, moderation, modesty, forbearance, pity. In those cases, however, in which leaders and bell-wethers are thought to be indispensable, there is attempt after attempt to substitute for them an adding-together of clever herd-men: this, for example, is the origin of all parliamentary constitutions. All this notwithstanding, what a blessing, what a release from a burden becoming intolerable, the appearance of an unconditional commander is for this herd-animal European, the effect produced by the appearance of Napoleon is the latest great witness—the history of the effect of Napoleon is almost the history of the higher happiness this entire century has attained in its most valuable men and moments. (*BGE* 199)

This passage of Nietzsche at his most characteristic is likely to evoke mixed reactions. It moves between the highly persuasive, couched in his eloquent rhetorical-argumentative style, and the employment of terms which shock, still, as much as he must have intended that they should, even while they are bound to make most readers recoil from what he is saying. This use of the term 'herd-animal', and its cognates, is upsetting, as is the list of qualities which the 'herd-man' approves, for we approve them too: public-spiritedness, industriousness, modesty, and so on. And we approve them because we are herd-men, and are not at all convinced that we could become anything else, or whether if we could we would want to. And yet we have been made uneasy, since the whole issue of obedience has been raised, and while we are only too pleased to obey what we believe to be right, the question is why we have this belief, when we have abolished the commander—those of us who have. Of course the fact that our moral convictions derive in the first place from the decrees of a god does not mean that, if the god is non-existent, the convictions are wrong. That is 'the fallacy of origins', a well-known and discredited device for discrediting beliefs. But on the other hand it would be foolish not to agree that if we have abandoned the original validating belief, we need something new in its place. For it is all too easy to be like 'the English' and think we know 'intuitively' what is right and wrong—it would be remarkable if we did, since we have no other substantial intuitive knowledge.

At this stage I don't want to look further into Nietzsche's specific views about the content of morality, except in so far as they are inseparable from his claims about the whole institution.

What he begins in *D* he carries on with tremendous panache

in his next book, *The Gay Science*. It is here that he is more obviously preparing the ground for his breakthrough in values, which gets full-dress treatment in *Thus Spoke Zarathustra*. *GS* is his most refreshing book, in that he has the confidence in it to advance beyond the innumerable suggestions of his two previous books, while not yet bearing the prophetic weight that the authorship of *TSZ* put on him. And though the highly effective sniping of his so-called 'positivistic' period continues, one feels a more comprehensive grasp of what he is moving towards. The depth of the plight of post-Christian man is the most conspicuous feature of *GS*, which has, at section 125, the most famous of his announcements, that God is dead.

The section is entitled 'The Madman'. He is considered mad by all those in the market-place who hear him, because they have not the least idea what he is talking about. How could one kill God? It is the expression of Nietzsche's greatest anguish, since he sees as no one else does the consequences of God's death, sees what the long-term effect will be and is appalled at the thought of how people will behave once they have grasped the significance of God's no longer being the linchpin of their world. It does not matter—this is Nietzsche's gist—whether God existed or not. What makes the difference is whether we believe that He does. And over the course of centuries belief in God has eroded without people noticing what was happening. Its deepest consequence will be for values, because, as Nietzsche expresses it in an unpublished note: 'He who does not find greatness in God finds it nowhere. He must either deny it or create it.' And if we have the burden of creating greatness, then most of us, maybe all, will buckle under the weight. And without greatness life has no point, even if the greatness is beyond our reach. We shall explore later the dialectic by which Nietzsche traces God's demise to the inherently contradictory tendencies within Christianity itself. For the moment the important thing is that their result has occurred, that most people don't realize what it means, and that when they do they will no longer find life worth living.

Nietzsche's attitude to Christianity, like his attitude to

most of the things he cared about, was divided at the deepest level. His contempt for the morality it inculcated has been sketched above, and it hardened as the years passed. But though he loathed the smallness of man that is part of Christian doctrine, and the set of virtues which are part of that, he was acutely aware of the achievements that only a Christian culture could have been responsible for. There will never be a Chartres built to celebrate humanist values, nor a Mass in B minor to affirm belief in them. So it looks as if the post-Christian era is most likely to be characterized by men who are smaller than the little Christians they have supplanted. Morality may be terrible, but what is it sensible to imagine replacing it?

5 *The one thing needful*

The first four books of *GS* form a rising trajectory of brilliance and penetration. Book IV begins with a New Year's resolution which went the way that they nearly always do, but still marks the beginning of the surge of affirmation that led Nietzsche to *Thus Spoke Zarathustra*.

I want to learn more and more to see as beautiful what is necessary in things; then I shall be one of those who make things beautiful. *Amor fati* (Love of fate): let that be my love henceforth! I do not want to wage war against what is ugly. I do not want to accuse; I do not want to accuse even those who accuse. *Looking away* shall be my only negation. And all in all and on the whole: some day I wish to be only a Yes-sayer. (*GS* 276)

This passage of intense feeling is carried on in a way that can make one drunk, and it is perhaps unfair to look at it closely. That Nietzsche, our arch-diagnostician, could never look away, and that we would have lost much of his most valuable writing if he had, does something to mitigate the accusation that he never became only a Yes-sayer, and the fact that three of his last five books are attacks, two on Wagner and one on Christ, the only affirmative one being about himself.

For the time being, at least, his mood continues in this exalted way. Then, at section 290, we reach a point where he for the first time makes some clear suggestions as to the kind of people he hopes will replace the small men of late and post-Christianity:

One thing is needful.—To 'give style' to one's character—a great and rare art! It is practised by those who survey all the strengths and weaknesses of their nature and then fit them into an artistic plan until every one of them appears as art and reason and even weaknesses delight the eye. Here a large mass of second nature has been added; there a piece of original nature has been removed—both times through long practice and daily work at it. Here the ugly that could not be removed is concealed; there it has been reinterpreted and made sublime. Much that is vague and resisted shaping has been saved and exploited for distant views; it is meant to beckon towards the far and immeasurable. In the end, when the work is finished, it becomes evident how the constraint of a single taste governed and formed everything large and small. Whether this taste was good or bad is less important than one might suppose, if only it was a single taste! (*GS* 290)

That is not the whole section, but it is enough to be going on with.

The idea that we might become 'artists of life' had been mooted in *BT*, but in a context so different as to make the idea of a continuity specious. What Nietzsche is starting on the road to advocating in *GS* is an extreme individualism, within a framework that does not lead to a scarcely intelligible atomism. But as soon as we are impressed by his vision, we start to wonder too. For the analogy with art, or the art of landscape gardening, which is adumbrated here is clearly one that cannot be worked through straightforwardly. One only lives once (I shall be dealing later with the Eternal Recurrence, which is anyway not going to help here: mistakes made this time round have been, and will be, repeated infinitely). But the artist, with rare exceptions, can tinker with his works indefinitely until he feels that he has got things as right as he ever will. What Nietzsche is proposing is that we carry out a scrupulous survey of our character, assessing it, though we are not told at this stage by what criteria—what are to count as strengths and weaknesses—and give it that unity which is what is called having style. Fitting the elements of our make-up into 'an artistic plan' does rather give the impression that we are less subject to outside contingencies than anyone but a hermit is bound to be.

Despite these preliminary doubts, there is something enticing about Nietzsche's suggestion. It inaugurates his new form of Classicism, where 'it will be the strongest and most domineering natures that enjoy their finest gaiety in such constraint and perfection under a law of their own,' as opposed to 'the weak characters without power over themselves that hate the constraint of style' (i.e. Romantics). And although Nietzsche makes a lot of the idea of individual style, it is evident that he is appealing to a notion of style which exists apart from the individual; if there were not some external criteria then anyone would have style as long as he was distinguishable from other people. The mere use of the concept of style is enough to make us think of given frameworks within which people work, achieving individuality thanks to the support which the framework offers. An obvious case is the Classical Style in music, as manifest from Haydn through Mozart and Beethoven, petering out at some indeterminate point. The constraints of that style were rigorous, but one cannot imagine any one of those three composers thriving without it. They were able to be themselves because so much was already given. It is in the tension between the style which was available to anyone at the time, and which we can see working perfectly satisfactorily without producing works of genius in the hands of, say, Hummel, who owes it entirely to the style available to him that he can be worthwhile at all, and the strongly defined individualities of its great masters that we locate its supreme achievements.

But, the whole drift of Nietzsche's analysis of culture runs, that was then, and now is quite different. There is no longer a common style with which to work in creative tension, so we have to find our own. Clearly in such circumstances the very notion of style is severely strained. The fact that he says that 'Whether this taste was good or bad is less important than one might suppose, if only it was a single taste!' implies that the criteria he is employing here are not only aesthetic but also formal. The nature of the elements takes second place to their configuration. That may make us wonder, again, about whether it matters what the elements are at all, and surely Nietzsche thought that it did. At the end of the section he writes: 'For one thing is needful: that a human being should *attain* satisfaction with himself, whether it be by means of this or that poetry or art; only then is a human being at all tolerable to behold.' But attaining satisfaction with oneself can at best be a necessary condition. There are plenty of people who have attained satisfaction with themselves who are intolerable to behold, and for that very reason.

Such passages as this do raise the question of how far one should press Nietzsche. For all his own tendencies to extremes and exaggerations of expression, he somehow manages to exercise tact, by not pressing in inappropriate places. But the opposite danger is that we call him 'stimulating', which means that we do not take seriously what he says. In this particular case, some tactlessness may be worth risking, because it does contain in embryo thoughts that will be central to his work, but they will be so much more portentous than he is here that it may be better to see him in his human rather than his superhuman dimensions.

So, while leaving open the matter of whether he is giving the man of style *carte blanche* on the issue of the elements of his character, we can agree that one of the things about a person which leads us to say that he has style is his capacity to carry things off, to incorporate disparate and what for most people would be embarrassing or humiliating experiences and make them part of a larger scheme. There is a moving, funny, and memorable moment at the end of Jean Renoir's film *La Règle du jeu* in which, after a shocking shooting incident in which a flying ace is killed during a country-house holiday, the host speaks to the stunned assembled guests with such exquisite taste and carefully chosen words that one of the guests say to another 'He called it an accident. A new definition!' But he receives a rebuke: 'He has style, and that's a rare thing these days.' Quite so. The elegant speech has preserved decorum, kept what is evidently a precarious civilized façade in place, and sent the guests to bed in elegiac rather than recriminatory or inchoate mood. There is strength in such capacity for what may seem like euphemism, the strength to cope with what are,

for any complex person, experiences which could lead to disintegration or at the very least self-loathing.

Nietzsche is candid about what is involved. A few sections
later he asks

How can we make things beautiful, attractive and desirable for us
when they are not? And I rather think that in themselves they
never are ... Moving away from things until there is a good deal
that one no longer sees ... all this we should learn from artists
while being wiser than they are in other matters. For with them
this subtle power usually comes to an end where art ends and life
begins; but we want to be the poets of our life—first of all in the
smallest, most everyday matters. (*GS* 299)

In other, less tactful and tasteful, words: don't be too scrupulous with yourself about getting things right, that is, true. It is
more important that you should make them tolerable at least,
beautiful at best.

I suspect that what Nietzsche has in mind is something
more instinctive than what he gives the impression of recommending—inevitably, since he has to spell out what he would
like us already to know and act on. It is a dilemma he finds
himself in over and over again—should he content himself with
dropping hints, or should he say what he thinks it is necessary
for us to know in skywriting? He wants us to be the kind of
people who only need hints because we are so fine-tuned, but
he knows that we will be deaf to anything less than apocalyptic
thunder—and then accuse him of making too much noise. At
the stage of *GS* he still tries allusive, tantalizing formulas,
leaving us to make the connections between them. The weariness that Zarathustra will often suffer, as he realizes that he is
always going to be misunderstood, has not yet begun to afflict
him. And he is not sure, either, whether one can only educate
people in taste if they are merely ignorant, or if it is possible to
re-educate those whose taste is already formed, and corrupt. *GS*
is, fundamentally, the book of an optimist—the last that
Nietzsche could conscientiously write.

At any rate, this is the relatively relaxed side of Nietzsche, as opposed to what J. P. Stern has justly called 'the moralist of strenuousness'. For if any hint of effort appears in someone's character—if it seems that they are willing their charm, warmth, serenity, at-homeness with themselves—then that is a crucial failure of style. Yet in our hideous freedom from the welcome constraints of tradition, and given the correspondingly large number of ways of living that *seem* to be open to us, far too many of which actually are, we are unlikely to be able to organize 'the chaos within us' without some visible signs of strain. Even Goethe, who comes increasingly to represent Nietzsche's ideal of self-organization, was unable to conceal the effort it cost. He was, of course, a limiting case of unity imposed on diversity, a diversity of interests and impulses that would leave most of us paralysed.

Nietzsche's claim that giving one's character style is 'the one thing needful' (a phrase which is probably intended to parody Wagner, whose chief figures are typically preoccupied with an overriding need) has an unexpected bearing on his critique of pity, one of the most notorious of his insistences, and one of the most consistently maintained. In one of his incredibly brilliant pieces of prose, unfortunately too long to quote in full, he considers 'the will to suffer and those who feel pity'. He asks whether it is good for either the pitier or his object to be in that relationship, and shows in the sensitive discussion that follows that his aversion to pity is nothing to do, at any rate in the way normally taken, with being heartless or ruthless or unfeeling. So far as the pitied person is concerned, he points out that the economy of his soul-states is a delicate affair, that those who notice that he is in distress and therefore hurry to help 'assume the role of fate', and that it never occurs to them that the sufferer may need his anguish, which is intertwined with his joy; 'No, the "religion of pity" (or "the heart") commands them to help, and they believe that they have helped most when they have helped most quickly' (*GS* 338).

It is clear that Nietzsche is not talking about giving a starving person food and drink, or administering anaesthetics to someone about to undergo an operation. His attack is concerned with pity as a full-time occupation of sorting out people's lives, with a noble neglect, as we are taught, of one's own interests. So it is merely vulgar (and very common indeed) to misinterpret him as advocating neglect of others' basic requirements, as his immediately following discussion of the effects of pity on the pitier makes plain. 'I know, there are a hundred decent and praiseworthy ways of losing *my* own way, and they are truly highly "moral"! Indeed, those who now preach the morality of pity even take the view that this and only this is moral—to lose one's own way in order to come to the assistance of a neighbour' (*GS* 338). And he continues eloquently to stress how hard, often how lonely and remote from gratitude and warmth the pursuit of one's own way is. He concludes, tellingly, with 'my morality which says to me: Live in seclusion so that you *can* live for yourself.'

Many people will feel that a morality which insists on their following their own way is one which they simply cannot follow, for the obvious reason that they don't have 'a way'—they have competences, needs, anxieties, and problems, but nothing that for them is an individuating goal. In suggesting that each person becomes the artist of his own life, Nietzsche is probably operating with the rather exigent view we now have, or had until very recently, of what constitutes a work of art, originality ranking high among its desirable, or even its necessary, qualities. And that seems just absurd as a wish about human beings, let alone an injunction; it presupposes that most people have it in them to be unique in a fairly strong sense, an assumption that, if he held it, Nietzsche should certainly have given prominence to.

In fact he is thinking of, at the lowest, those people who can read him with understanding—not that he says that, so far as I am aware; but if one could not do that, the chances of summoning up the kinds of energies required for following 'one's own way' would be nugatory. That already limits the number of people he is talking about to a tiny proportion of the population. What about the rest? How can he condemn herd-men when they have no capacity for being anything else? But he does not condemn them; he is simply not interested in them. That raises the whole issue of his politics, or lack of them, which gives rise to more canting among commentators than any other single feature of his thought. I shall deal with it later. But what about people who can read him with understanding but still feel that there is no special way that is theirs? Is it Nietzsche's view that they are deluding themselves in order to have an easy time of it, or that they may be right? If the first, he seems to be holding a rather surprising, for him, estimate of the possibilities of people. If the second, then what he says about giving one's life style is irrelevant, and one may wonder what they are supposed to do with themselves—those gifted, intelligent, cultivated, sensitive, receptive people who have no inclination to develop a high profile, because despite their gifts they are essentially passive. Or is no one essentially passive? More questions for later in the agenda.

One other outstanding question needs to be looked at before we leave the matter of style, endlessly discussable as it is. One of the finest of Nietzsche's commentators, Alexander Nehamas, has raised it (Nehamas 1985) and failed to come up with a remotely satisfactory answer. It is this: Can someone who has, by standards that one can imagine few rejecting, certainly not Nietzsche, a wholly deplorable character still pass his tests for having style? If Nietzsche's criteria were purely formal, that is, all the bits fit together and it does not matter what they are individually, then the appalling answer would seem to be yes. Nehamas writes 'I think that there is something admirable in the very fact of having character or style' (Nehamas 1985: 192). What about Goering? His style is undeniable and unmistakable, but one hopes he has few admirers. Nehamas:

It is not clear to me whether a consistently and irredeemably vicious person does actually have a character; the sort of agent Aristotle describes as 'bestial' probably does not. In some way there is something inherently praiseworthy in having character or style that prevents extreme cases of vice from being praised even in Nietzsche's formal sense. (Nehamas 1985: 193)

This is embarrassing: the only way Nehamas could push through his claim would be by blatant linguistic stipulation, which is what this passage comes to.

It is not necessary to wriggle like this on Nietzsche's behalf. As I said, what he proposes in *GS* is to be taken as preliminary moves towards a goal of which he was not yet at all confident. He is bracing himself for his *chef d'œuvre*, and the last two sections of Book IV, the end of the first edition of *GS*, are pregnant with the book on which he staked his fame. The penultimate section, 'The greatest weight', introduces the notion of the Eternal Recurrence, as an idea too horrifying for any but the strongest to bear. But those who are the strongest will exult in it. Then the final section, 'Incipit tragoedia', is almost word for word the same as the opening of *Thus Spoke Zarathustra*, a trailer for that work, and unintelligible except in that capacity. It is, one must concede, Nietzsche's least subtle effort to give his life's work a unity.

6 *Prophecy*

For a long time Nietzsche's most famous book was *Thus Spoke Zarathustra*. It is not, I think, any longer, and on the whole that is a development I applaud. Written in short bursts of inspiration, it shows all too clearly the worst signs of that state, though it also contains some of his best writing. What Nietzsche was trying to do in it was to establish himself as a philosopher-poet, and for that purpose he employed a set of idioms that reveal dismayingly what his idea of poetry was. He uses a great deal of imagery and allegory, but he does that elsewhere too, and to much better effect. One's initial impression is of pastiche: most obviously biblical pastiche, ranging from staightforward echoes of the Bible to parody—the range of moods is easily overlooked by the reader somewhat numbed by the reiteration of 'Thus spoke Zarathustra' at the end of each section. There are poems, some of which have became famous, and have been employed by many composers, of whom the most successful have been Mahler and Delius. One can see why the poems should have had the appeal they did for those two composers in particular, men of extraordinarily strong will-power who spent much of their time evoking the earth in its fullness and beauty, enduring, in contrast with the poignant brevity of human life. But their success betrays an element in Nietzsche-Zarathustra which he was at pains to disown: nostalgia.

The most genuine tone of *TSZ*, which surfaces in surprising places, is one of regret. The least convincing tone is of exaltation and affirmation, the qualities that Zarathustra is at such pains to inculcate, since they are necessary to prepare the ground of the arrival of the *Übermensch*, whose prophet

Zarathustra is. But he is a prophet who is intent on not having disciples, a desire which he is keen to stress, since it singles him out from all other prophets. But one might ask whether someone who speaks the truth should not want disciples, as many as possible. The answer would seem to be that Zarathustra is not at all sure of the truth which impels him to leave his mountain and to 'go down' or 'go under'—a carefully calculated ambiguity on Nietzche's part. The magician in Part IV gives voice to the melancholy that is Zarathustra's constant companion, when he sings '*That I be banished from all truth, Only fool! Only poet!*' Again, in the last section of Part I, 'On the gift-giving virtue', Zarathustra speaks to his disciples in words that Nietzsche was so proud of that he quotes them at the end of the Foreword to *Ecce Homo*:

Truly, I counsel you: go away from me and resist Zarathustra! And even better: be ashamed of him! Perhaps he deceived you . . . One repays a teacher badly if one always wants to remain nothing but a pupil. And why do you not want to pluck at my wreath? . . . you say you believe in Zarathustra? But what matters Zarathustra? You are my believers—but what matter all believers? You had not yet sought yourselves: and you found me. Thus do all believers; therefore all faith amounts to little.

It is a powerful passage, but for all its ponderable wisdom it is strange coming from a prophet. For prophets do not argue, they announce. And so by what methods are the disciples to discover what is true and what false in Zarathustra's teaching? The refusal to accept homage that is not justified by independent checks on the truth is admirable, and clearly meant as part of Nietzsche's running battle with Christ. But it leaves us in the dark as to how to cope with Zarathustra's teaching, for decadent as we are, we are not in the best position to criticize.

The trouble with a self-doubting prophet, one who advises caution as to anything he says, is bad enough: we are in the presence of an incarnate oxymoron. But the dangers of being a poet, to which Zarathustra is not the first to alert us, only compound the problem of how to deal with a philosopher-artist, who seems more than incrementally suspect. All we can do, under these inauspicious conditions, is to try and share Zarathustra's visions, and see to what extent they command our imaginations, always remembering that those are corrupt. But then if it turns out that the vision itself is vague and opaque, we shall have to do what in the end I am convinced is the only thing that one really can do with the book, which is to savour it in a picaresque way.

There are enough wonderful things, despite all the caveats I have depressingly entered, to make reading it a memorable experience. It begins impressively, with Zarathustra's descent from his mountain, and what one might call his Sermon off the Mount is written with genuine inspiration. But Zarathustra soon gets on to his central theme: 'Behold, I teach you the *Übermensch*. The *Übermensch* is the meaning of the earth. Let your will say: the *Übermensch* shall be the meaning of the earth! I beseech you, my brothers, *remain faithful to the earth*, and do not believe those who speak to you of otherworldly hopes!' (*TSZ* I, Prologue, 3). That introduces the first of Zarathustra's three major concepts. And his injunction to be faithful to the earth is one of Nietzsche's great recurring themes, and one with which I feel the greatest sympathy. But what we now wait for is some illumination about how the *Übermensch* is the meaning of the earth, what steps might be taken to bring about his arrival, and what he will be like when he appears. Unfortunately we get very little information about any of these matters. There are crude misunderstandings which can be quickly cleared up, such as that the *Übermensch* would be an evolutionary phenomenon. There is no reason to think that he will not be human in form, but that is minimally enlightening. He seems to be defined in large part in terms of the second of Zarathustra's announcements, that of the Eternal Recurrence. The *Übermensch* is the being who can joyfully embrace that doctrine, for doctrine, or dogma, is what it is. And the third of Zarathustra's teachings is the Will to Power, the fundamental reality of existence. Once more, the *Übermensch* manifests it in its purest, most impressive way: as self-over-coming, whatever that comes to.

One of the things it comes to is made clear during the course of Zarathustra's progress. Zarathustra, it may be worth pointing out, is the herald of the *Übermensch* but is not himself one. Yet they share many characteristics, and it seems often that the best handle we can get on the *Übermensch* is that he is a heightened version of Zarathustra.

When, for instance, in Part IV, the soothsayer tells Zarathustra what his final sin is, it turns out to be pity for man. The *Übermensch*, one takes it, would realize without being tempted that this is the ultimate seduction. He would be able to accept that man suffers, but it would not make him suffer—and to what point, if he did? We have been so infused with suffering, and with the view that it is the most ineradicable element in existence, as indeed for us it is, that we take it that in some way it is the deepest state there is. Because joy is always ephemeral, we regard it as superficial too—or that is the temptation. The only joy we have heard about that is eternal is the joy of the next world, which we have no grasp of. For understandable biological reasons, we regard joy, or pleasure, as the terminus of a process and thus as displaced as soon as the next process, or the next stage of the same process, begins. To that extent we are all modified Schopenhauerians, Schopenhauer having taken the more extreme line that pleasure is *nothing* more than the temporary cessation of pain. By this stage in his career, Nietzsche was wholly opposed to Schopenhauer, who is along with his former idol Wagner, one of the gallery of more or less ludicrous figures thinly disguised in *TSZ*. It is Zarathustra's teaching—and does he want his disciples to disagree?—that joy is deeper than suffering, as we learn in the chapter in Part IV called 'The Drunken Song' (that, at any rate, is how it appears in the English translations; the German in the new Critical Edition is 'Das Nachtwandlers-Lied'—'The Sleep-walker's Song'):

The world is deep,
Deeper than day had been aware.
Deep is its woe;
Joy—deeper yet than agony:
Woe implores: Go!
But all joy wills eternity—
Wills deep, wills deep eternity.

It is not, even in German, distinguished poetry. But its basic sentiment is moving, and has, for Zarathustra, the closest connection with the Eternal Recurrence. Earlier in the same section Zarathustra had made that clear:

Have you ever said Yes to a single joy? O my friends, then you said Yes too to *all* woe. All things are entangled, ensnared, enamoured; if ever you wanted one thing twice, if ever you said, 'You please me, happiness! Abide, moment!' then you wanted *all* back. All anew, all eternally, all entangled, ensnared, enamoured—oh, then you *loved* the world. Eternal ones, love it eternally and evermore; and to woe too, you say: go, but return! For *all joy wills eternity*.

This is Nietzsche's lyrical, not to say gushing, version of his elsewhere more austerely expressed view that saying Yes to anything is saying Yes to everything, since the causal network is such that any state depends on the rest of Nature being in the condition it is. That is, at least initially, the view of the Eternal Recurrence that he promulgates. The *Übermensch* is the being who is prepared to say Yes to whatever comes along, because joy and sorrow are, as always for Nietzsche, from the Primal Oneness of *BT* onwards, inseparable. So despite the horror of existence up to now, he is prepared to affirm it all. That, at any rate, is how I understand it, and him.

But that is only the beginning of an account of *Übermenschlichkeit*. For having expressed his unconditional acceptance of existence to the point where he wills that everything should be repeated, exactly as it has been, in eternal cycles, there still remains the question of what the *Übermensch* does with his time. Something, presumably, very different from man, who is defined early on as 'a rope, tied between beast and *Übermensch*—a rope over an abyss' (*TSZ I*, Prologue, 4). He will be as different from us as we are from the beasts. Whatever he does will be done in a mood of affirmation, but what will it be? We know what it won't be—anything small, reactive, resentful. There is a strain of antinomianism in Zarathustra which suggests that if you have the right basic attitude you can do what you like. That comes out clearly in the chapter entitled 'On Chastity', where he says

Do I counsel you to slay your senses? I counsel the innocence of the senses. Do I counsel you to chastity? Chastity is a virtue in some, but almost a vice in many. They abstain, but the bitch sensuality leers enviously out of everything they do. Even to the heights of their virtue and to the cold regions of the spirit this beast follows them with her lack of peace. And how nicely the bitch sensuality knows how to beg for a piece of spirit when denied a piece of meat.

There is a touch of puritanism there, but it is shrewd, especially the last sentence, and in the generally imperative tone of *TSZ* it comes as a relief. But there is a dominant line, apart from tone, which leads in the opposite direction—not one of repressiveness, but a stress on arduousness and hardness, above all with oneself. That is what we would expect, given that Nietzsche's primary concern is with greatness; and comfort, satisfaction, sensual gratification are inimical to greatness. In what way will the *Übermensch* be great? Nietzsche always has at least one eye on artistic achievement, so one might expect stupendous works of art from him, but on that subject *TSZ* is strangely silent. It is, of course, fruitless to meditate on works of art that have not yet been created, as it is not to dwell on scientific achievements still to be realized, since in the latter case we know what it is we want answers to. But in art there are no questions in that sense. Furthermore, the idea of a group of *Übermenschen* all being artists does seem ridiculous. But then what will they be? It is no good speculating further because Nietzsche provides us with no clues on the subject. Indeed, it seems that he was unable to make any progress with it, and although he is as famous for coining the term as for anything else, it does not occur again in his work, except in the self-celebrations of *Ecce Homo*, where he goes on about *TSZ* much longer than about any of his other books, saying 'Here man is overcome at every moment, the concept *Übermensch* here becomes the greatest reality' (*EH*, 'Thus Spoke Zarathustra', 6).

But that is a sad piece of wishful thinking. Nietzsche has succumbed to the besetting temptation of creators of ideals—the ideal is so far removed from the squalidly real that all that can be done is to dwell on the ghastliness of reality and say that the ideal is nothing like that. One is reminded of Swift's portrayal, in *Gulliver's Travels*, of the disgusting Yahoos (us) and the approvable Houyhnhnms, about whom Leavis justly remarked that 'they may have all the reason, but the Yahoos have all the life . . . The clean skin of the Houyhnhnms, in short, is stretched over a void; instincts, emotions and life, which complicate the problem of cleanliness and decency, are left for the Yahoos with the dirt and the indecorum.' There is an uncanny resemblance here to man and *Übermensch*, though perhaps it is not so surprising, given the difficulties that anyone trying to indicate an ideal that transcends and negates humanity is bound to encounter.

Early on in *TSZ* there is an alternative, or maybe it is meant as a complementary account of the progress of what is there called 'the spirit'. It is the first of Zarathustra's Speeches, at which stage he still seems uneasy with figurative language, to judge from the clumsiness of this passage, which induces, as Erich Heller remarks, 'a sense of extreme zoological and spiritual discomfort' (Heller 1988: 71). The spirit here begins as a camel, that is to say modern man, weighed down by the accumulation of the values it has to bear, a whole oppressive tradition of obligations and the guilt attendant on their inevitable violation. Speeding off into the desert, the camel staggers; but finally revolts and metamorphoses into a lion, with the intention of fighting a dragon. The dragon is named 'Thou shalt' and is thus the creator of the camel's intolerable burden. It claims that 'All value has long been created, and I am all created value.' The lion resists, intent on replacing 'Thou shalt' with 'I will'. But though the lion can fight, all he can create is the freedom for new values; he cannot create the values themselves. He says a sacred 'No', and that is the end of him—he has served the only purpose he can. So far so clear. The last transformation is a surprise: for it is a child.

Why must the preying lion still become a child? The child is innocence and forgetting, a new beginning, a game, a self-propelled wheel, a first movement, a sacred 'Yes.' For the game of creation, my brothers, a sacred 'Yes' is needed: the spirit now wills his own will, and he who had been lost to the world now conquers his own world.

This must be, among other things, Nietzsche's version of Christ's 'Except ye become as little children, ye shall not enter into the kingdom of heaven' (Matt. 18: 18). And elsewhere Nietzsche uses the phrase 'the innocence of becoming'. At moments of stress in his writing, he sometimes resorts to formulations which are oxymoronic or in the deepest sense sentimental, because he knows that one element in the combination is too deeply embedded in us to be withdrawn, while the other is what would redeem it, despite its manifest incompatibility. Thus as early as *BT* we hear of 'a Socrates who practises music', whereas it is of the essence of the Socrates that Nietzsche has idiosyncratically portrayed that he is antimusical. And in an unpublished note he writes of 'the Roman Caesar with Christ's soul'.

Are these merely touching attempts to square the circle, or can they be forced to mean something? There are good reasons for saying the former, because Nietzsche was a desperately divided man. He could not help admiring far more about Socrates than he officially should; and as we shall see, *The Antichrist* gets almost out of control as his portrayal of the alleged 'ideal decadent' takes lyrical wings. And, to return to *TSZ*, his general attitude to life is what video libraries call 'highly adult', yet he is entranced by the thought of a child wholly absorbed in play, serious and rapt, innocent but also ignorant. Can he have wanted his *Übermensch* to be like Wagner's Siegfried, brought up with no knowledge of the world—and coming to grief for want of it? It seems unlikely. That phrase 'a new beginning' is dangerous. For it is usually Nietzsche's distinction as a connoisseur of decadence to realize that among our options is not that of wiping the slate clean. We need to have a self to overcome, and that self will be the result of the whole Western tradition, which it will somehow manage to 'aufheben', a word that Nietzche has no fondness for, because of its virtual Hegelian copyright, and which means simultaneously 'to obliterate', 'to preserve' and 'to lift up'. Isn't that just what the *Übermensch* is called upon to do, or if we drop him, what we, advancing from our present state, must do if we are to be 'redeemed'? The ideal of being a child, or as a child, has, apart from its Christian affiliations, Romantic ones which it is strange to see Nietzsche endorsing. The element which he wants to stress, I am sure, is the unselfconsciousness that young children possess. But for us, or an advance on us, to achieve that now is hardly imaginable.

So we are back with the *Übermensch* as embracing the Eternal Recurrence. And that has proved the most riddling of all Nietzsche's views. Is it meant simply in a 'What if . . . ?' spirit, or as a serious hypothesis about the nature of the cosmos? In the penultimate section of Book IV of *GS* it is certainly the former. But in his notebooks, including especially those that were posthumously edited as *The Will to Power*, he tries giving proofs of it as a general theory, based on the fact that if the number of atoms in the universe is finite, they must reach a configuration that they have been in before, and that will inevitable result in the history of the universe repeating itself. This is one of the least rewarding areas of his speculation, and his failure to publish these experimental thoughts is a cause for rejoicing—or would be if scholars were not intent on scanning them for clues to what he really thought. They are encouraged by his own excitement at the idea, which occurred to him in the Swiss Engadine, 'six thousand feet above man and time' and which he regarded, evidently, as one of those intuitions in which one is convinced that there is something deep and true, though one cannot say precisely what it is.

The cosmological view of the doctrine has not in general been regarded favourably. Yet commentators are so impressed by Nietzsche's own enthusiasm for the doctrine, or at any rate its name, that they use their ingenuity to explain what he really meant by it. I can only say here that in trying to render it intelligible and interesting what they produce makes one wonder why Nietzsche should have given it so misleading a nomenclature. Tersely: if by 'Eternal Recurrence' he did not mean Eternal Recurrence, why did he not call it what he did mean?

So we are left with the 'What if . . . ?' approach. My initial reaction was to say that I wouldn't give a damn, thus surprisingly qualifying for *übermenschlich* status, on the verificationist ground that if each cycle is, as it has to be, precisely the same as the previous and successive ones, then we have no knowledge of what happened, and especially not of what we did, last time round, so can neither take steps to avoid the consequences of what was disastrous, nor think with horror or joy of what lies ahead. If the Eternal Recurrence were true, this would be the *n*th time I was writing this book, but that would do nothing to lead me to alter its contents. That would seem to be that. But for many people with whom I have discussed the idea, though they agree that it can make no difference to anything, they are still reluctant to say that it has no effect on how they feel about things. As someone asked me recently: which is worse, a universe in which Auschwitz occurs once, or one in which it occurs infinitely many times? It seems to need, to say the least, an unfeeling person to say that it does not matter. Recurrence, even if it makes, in practical terms, no difference, still invests with a terrible weight what *does* happen.

Kundera, in what has now become a rather famous passage at the beginning of his novel *The Unbearable Lightness of Being*, has this as the core of his brief but pregnant thoughts on the subject:

Let us therefore agree that the idea of eternal return implies a perspective from which things appear other than as we know them: they appear without the mitigating circumstance of their transitory nature. This mitigating circumstance prevents us from coming to a verdict. For how can we condemn something that is ephemeral, in transit? In the sunset of dissolution, everything is illuminated by the aura of nostalgia, even the guillotine. (Kundera 1984: 4)

The key, or give-away clause there, is the first one. The reason why people's imaginations are so gripped by the idea is that they take up a perspective outside any one cycle, so that they can visualize it occurring again and again. It may perhaps even be the shift from seeing oneself as locked in the cycle, and viewing the whole thing from a god's-eye point of view, that generates the thrill, and the sense of intolerable weight, or, if one is an arch-yes-sayer, the rapture of return.

I remain a sceptic; it does nothing for me either way, though I can appreciate the inspiration that it has given great artists, such as Yeats in his 'A Dialogue of Self and Soul':

> I am content to live it all again,
> and yet again . . .
> I am content to follow to its source
> Every event in action or in thought;
> Measure the lot; forgive myself the lot!
> When such as I cast out remorse
> So great a sweetness flows into the breast
> We must laugh and we must sing,
> We are blest by everything,
> Everything we look upon is blest.

Those lines, inconceivable if Yeats had not read and been profoundly impressed by Nietzsche, are also a good example of how he can influence people who have only a vague and inaccurate idea of what he is saying—something one sometimes suspects of Nietzsche himself. And they contain much that Nietzsche is most ardent in his advocacy of, most particularly the idea of casting out remorse. But he arrives at that view in his later writings not via Eternal Recurrence, but through penetrating psychological analyses of the effects of remorse and backwards-looking in general.

There is one further line on the Eternal Recurrence which is worth mentioning briefly, because it renders it something of a joke, though by no stretch of the imagination does it count among Nietzsche's best. That is that it is a parody of all doctrines of another world whose relationship to this one—this 'preposterous, pragmatical pig of a world', to quote Yeats again—is one of ontological and axiological superiority. Instead of heaven and hell, or the world of unchanging Platonic forms, it suggests this world made eternal through meaningless repetition. Whereas otherworldly doctrines allege that this world only gains value through being related to another world, the Eternal Recurrence teasingly suggests that this world is deprived of value by a process analogous to that whereby a sentence is repeated until it becomes nothing more than a series of noises. To return to Kundera: weight is attached to incidents by the thought that they happen more than once, whereas 'Einmal ist keinmal' ('Once is nothing', or better: 'Try anything twice'); but weight is one thing, value another. Kundera, in this respect a faithful disciple of Nietzsche, manages a nimble dialectic between lightness and heaviness, meaning or value and futility. Do we, should we, does it make sense to ask whether we should, value something more on account of its uniqueness or because it is representative, at the limit of an infinite series? The shortest answer is that it depends on what your temperament is. Nietzsche, with his all-too-protean temperament, was inclined to answer 'Both' and also 'Neither'.

The third of Zarathustra's cardinal teachings is that of the Will to Power. It gets its first mention in the chapter in the Part I called 'On the Thousand and One Goals', which recounts how Zarathustra visited many nations, finding that each needed to esteem, but something different from their neighbour. And then:

A tablet of the good hangs over every people. Behold, it is the tablet of their overcomings; behold, it is the voice of their will to power.

Praiseworthy is whatever seems difficult to a people; whatever seems indispensable and difficult is called good; and whatever liberates even out of the deepest need, the rarest, the most difficult—that they call holy.

And later in the same chapter, stressing the connection of power with value: 'To esteem is to create: hear this, you creators! Esteeming itself is of all esteemed things the most estimable treasure. Through esteeming alone is there value: and without esteeming, the nut of existence would be hollow.' But at the end of the chapter he says 'Humanity still has no goal. But tell me, my brothers, if humanity still lacks a goal—is humanity itself not still lacking too?' How the will to power is tied in with valuing is better discussed later. That is still clearer from the other brief mention of the will to power, in the chapter in Part II called 'On Self-Overcoming'. There Zarathustra says 'Indeed, the truth was not hit by him who shot at it with the word of the "will to existence": that will does not exist [a swipe at Schopenhauer] . . . Only where there is life is there also will: not will to life but—thus I teach you—will to power.'

And that is virtually all that Nietzsche says on the subject in *TSZ*. Once more we find, in other words, that Zarathustra is a prophet more of what his author will be writing later than of anything worked out and seriously discussable. His problem is that he is resolutely opposed to systems and system-builders, as many remarks show. But it is not clear how he can avoid a system if he is to promulgate a new table of values. This dilemma leads him to make the worst of both worlds: he drops tantalizing hints, which lay him open to multiple interpretations and misunderstandings. But though the hints imply a huge submerged richness of thought, we are denied that and told that we must disagree, if we can, with thoughts expressed too fragmentarily for us even to know what to disagree with. That is the harshest estimate of *TSZ*. Much less harsh ones are defensible. But I prefer to move on to his post-Zarathustra works, where his powers are at their height, and he does not have to cope with looking dignified in his prophetic mantle.

7 *Occupying the high ground*

Thus Spoke Zarathustra was written in the aftermath of the single most devastating experience of Nietzsche's life: his rejection by Lou Salomé, to whom he proposed marriage through his friend Paul Rée, only to discover that they were closer to one another than they were to him. Lou was an immensely gifted woman, who went on to become Rilke's mistress and later one of Freud's most valued disciples; he pays tribute to her in uncharacteristically generous terms for her discoveries in the area of anal eroticism. Nietzsche briefly envisaged a partnership in which he could carry on his work, understood and aided by a woman whom he could regard as an equal. There is a bizarre photograph, taken at his insistence, in which he and Rée are drawing an ox-cart, while Lou stands in it brandishing a whip over them. It provides an unexpected slant—whether or not the connection ever occurred to Nietzsche is immaterial—on that notorious remark in *TSZ*, when an old woman says to Zarathustra 'Are you going to a woman? Do not forget your whip!'

The rejection humiliated Nietzsche to the point of utter despair. Writing to one of his closest friends, Franz Overbeck on Christmas Day 1882, he says:

This last *morsel of life* was the hardest I have yet had to chew, and it is still possible that I shall *choke* on it. I have suffered from the humiliating and tormenting memories of this summer as from a bout of madness—what I indicated in Basle and in my last letter concealed the most essential thing. It involves a tension between opposing passions which I cannot cope with. That is to say, I am exerting every ounce of my self-mastery; but I have lived in solitude too long and fed too long off my 'own fat,' so that I am now being broken, as no other man could be, on the wheel of my own passions . . . Unless I discover the alchemical trick of turning this—muck into gold, I am lost. Here I have the most beautiful chance to prove that for me 'all experiences are useful, all days holy and all people divine'!!! (Middleton 1969: 198–9; the passage in inverted commas is from the epigraph to the first edition of *GS*, derived from Emerson.)

It was on that basis that he set about writing *TSZ*, and his agonies doubtless contributed to the exalted mode which sometimes makes the book hard to bear. But given his disappointment and his loneliness, the effort to perform the alchemist's trick is impressively successful. His torments are probably responsible, too, for the equivocal tone of much of *TSZ*, which I paid no attention to in my remarks on it. But Zarathustra is prone to depressions, collapses, coma, and paralysing self-doubt, all of which make identification of him with his author irresistible.

Nietzsche's characterizations of *TSZ* as by far the most important book that mankind has been given so far, etc., indicate that however critically he advised his disciples to take it, self-critique was not in his line, at least then. All the more upsetting that the publication of the first three parts was a non-event in the cultural life of Europe, and that Part IV was brought out privately at Nietzsche's own expense in 1885. It shows how far removed he was from a close understanding of the state of his contemporaries that he should have been in the least surprised. If his previous books had fallen like stones, what could be made of a work which was more innovative in one way, more archaic in another, than anything produced by a 'philosopher' since Plotinus?

What must seem astonishing is that Nietzsche's writing went on unabated, but mostly in the mode established by the books that had preceded *TSZ*. He insisted that everything he wrote after *TSZ* was a commentary on it, but that seems to have been more in the nature of an attempt at self-reassurance than a genuine assessment of their nature or quality. For one thing, the *Übermensch* is never heard of again; the Eternal

Recurrence rarely recurs; and the Will to Power simmers away alternately on and under the surface. For another, the progress through the first post-Zarathustra book, *Beyond Good and Evil*, through his masterpiece *The Genealogy of Morals*, to the torrential pamphlets of the last year, has little to do with anything stated or adumbrated in *TSZ*.

It strikes me rather that with the writing of *TSZ* Nietzsche got a great deal out of his system in one go—and fortunately so. However indefensible they may have been, the grotesque and earnest parodies of Nietzsche which constituted the cults I referred to in Chapter 1 all took their inspiration from that book—they could not have taken it from any of the others, where the tones of mockery and tentativeness, which continue right up to the end, amid stridencies and denunciations, foreclose on the possibility of doctrine. All Nietzsche's books demand close attention, but to profit from *TSZ* one needs to be flexible and vigilant in a way that few readers, confronted with the orotundities of the opening pages, are likely to be. Without his prophet, there would have been no chance of Nietzsche's sister Elisabeth clothing him in a white robe for exhibition to tourists, after he had reached a state of advanced insanity, as himself 'the transfigured prophet'. Nor would his friend Peter Gast have been able to say, as Nietzsche's body was lowered into the ground, 'May your name be holy to all future generations!' when Nietzsche had written in the last Chapter of *Ecce Homo* 'I have a terrible fear that I shall one day be pronounced *holy*: one will indeed guess why I bring out this book *beforehand* . . . I do not want to be a saint, rather even a buffoon' (*EH*, 'Why I am a Destiny', 1).

His first book after *TSZ* is given a deliberately misleading title: *Beyond Good and Evil*, whatever may be said by Nietzsche or his commentators, suggests a transvaluation of *all* values, and not just a man preparing to replace those we have with a new set, however drastic. It is this that provides what excuse there is (none, if one reads carefully) for thinking that Nietzsche was intent on eliminating value from the world. There is no value to be discovered in the world, but it is therefore all the more imperative to endow it with value. But how is that to be done? We have, Nietzsche insists, always done it, but up until now that is not what we thought we were doing. And the movement from imagining that we are finding what in fact we are inventing, to a full realization that that is what we are doing, has to be negotiated with the utmost combined lightfootedness and caution if we are not to fall headlong into the abyss of nihilism.

The initial movements of thought in *BGE* are cunningly designed to create the maximum sense of unease about where we stand with repect to what we take to be our fundamental value: truth. If he can make us share some of his doubts about what our will to truth comes to, we are putty in Nietzsche's hands, because there is nothing more basic to which we can appeal. It is a typical move of his, to proceed from truth to the will to truth, to psychologize our relations with the world. He puts it in riddling form, as he acknowledges by saying that it is hard to know who is Oedipus here and who the Sphinx. 'We asked rather about the *value* of this will. Suppose we want truth: *why not rather* untruth? and uncertainty? even ignorance?'

It is not only millennia of attachment to an ingrained set of values that makes this so odd. For the sheer idea of wanting, that is knowing that one want, untruth, has a zany quality about it. It is perfectly acceptable to say that one wants to remain in ignorance of some matter, or is uninterested in what the truth about it may be. We often do. But to say or claim that one wants the untruth about something smacks of a logical paradox. It is a quite different matter from being inertly complacent about the lack of rigour with which one looks for truth, as almost everyone is on all important issues. And it is also different from wanting to believe what is in fact false, though we do not know that. There is nothing odd in saying 'Many of my beliefs are false,' which any sane person would agree to. But there is terminal oddness in saying 'Many of my beliefs are false, including the following: . . .' and then providing a list. For in saying something is false one is saying that one does not believe it.

I am making a meal of this point because Nietzsche does

seem to suggest that we can investigate the question of why we have a will to truth, i.e. to assenting to propositions the truth of which we have, or think we have, ascertained. If he does mean that, he is confused. Suppose that he is not, what does he mean? He keeps on (a characteristic ploy) changing the subject at such a rate that we lose grip, if we aren't careful, of what he is investigating. So in section 2 he moves on to a wide range of issues, the most searching of which is the metaphysician's 'faith in opposite values'. He shrewdly points out that metaphysicians, whom he has been attacking since he stopped being one himself in *BT*, though they tend to claim that they doubt everything possible, do not call in question the possibility of deriving something from its opposite. Since, for example, they deny that selflessness could emerge from selfishness, purity of heart from lust, truth from error, they posit 'the lap of Being, the intransitory, the hidden god, the "thing-in-itself",' since nothing less imposing will do for the source of our values. In other words, ones which Nietzsche does not use here, but often elsewhere, Plato has called the tune. There is falsity, ugliness and wickedness ('appetite') in the mundane; so their opposites must originate in the supra-mundane.

By contrast, Nietzsche doubts:

whether there are any opposites at all, and secondly, whether these popular valuations and opposite values on which the metaphysicians put their seal, are not perhaps merely foreground estimates, only provisional perspectives . . . frog perspectives, as it were, to borrow an expression painters use. For all the value that the true, the truthful, the selfless may deserve, it would still be possible that a higher and more fundamental value for life might have to be ascribed to deception, selfishness and lust. It might even be possible that what constitutes the value of these good and revered things is precisely that they are insidiously related, tied to, and involved with the wicked, seemingly opposite things—maybe even one with them in essence. Maybe! (*BGE* i. 2)

Speculating at this rate is dangerous, and Nietzsche does not let up. Plodding behind, let us notice to what extent he has already changed his focus from the opening section. For now he is scrutinizing not our will to truth, but our will to think that certain kinds of statement are true, those that contrast things we hold in low esteem with things that we value. What he is doing is giving examples, which he hopes we will find unwelcome but will not be able to counter, of how what we take to be the basic value of truth is in fact derivative from other, more instinctive, values. Truth, we take it, certainly if we are philosophers, is a matter for conscious reflection. But, vaulting on to his next point, Nietzsche puts the greater part of the philosopher's activity on the instinctive level, and claims that the conscious thoughts of philosophers are dictated by their inclinations, 'valuations, or more clearly physiological demands for the preservation of a certain kind of life' (*BGE* i. 3). This sounds like bad news; but in yet another piece of intellectual demoralization, Nietzsche goes on

The falseness of a judgment is not for us necessarily an objection to a judgment; in this respect our new language may sound strangest. The question is to what extent it is life-promoting, life-preserving, species-preserving, perhaps even species-cultivating . . . To recognise untruth as a condition of life—that certainly means resisting accustomed value feelings in a dangerous way; and a philosophy that risks this would by that token alone place itself beyond good and evil. (*BGE* i. 4)

Such a philosophy would place itself beyond good and evil by dint of its denial of the grounds that we give for our value-judgements. It would also, I think it is part of Nietzsche's intention to intimate, make us into anthropologists of the whole human scene, so that we would be beyond good and evil in the same way that anthropologists of primitive tribes are 'beyond' the concepts of the tribes they study. But this is to place us very high indeed—us new philosophers: *BGE* is subtitled 'Prelude to a Philosophy of the Future'. Anyone who is concerned with so far-reaching an enterprise as Nietzsche since he embarked on his 'Thoughts on the prejudices of morality' in *D* is bound to feel himself taking up a loftier and loftier position as he realizes that everything about morality is prejudice, but that does produce acute problems as to how he is to achieve and then maintain so exalted a perspective. He is in a way in the reverse position from what is known as 'the anthropologist's dilemma'. That is of how to understand a tribe whose concepts one does not share—for understanding is in part a preparedness to apply the same concepts to the same situations; and if one's disagreements are as comprehensive as ours with a tribe that practises witchcraft, based on a set of views about the causal relationship between formulas and rituals performed by some members of the tribe, and the resultant state of some other members, then it looks as if in some way we cannot grasp what is going on—or at least that has been thought by some anthropologists and theorists of the subject.

But Nietzsche, in trying to take up an anthropological stance to his own society, and the central traditions of Western culture, is in a different but perhaps more worrying plight. For he is the first person to insist that there is no such thing as a substantial self, which can view the world with dispassion, uncontaminated by its environment. We are, he is ever more anxious to point out, nothing over and above our drives, our memories, and the other states and dispositions which grammar (and deriving from grammar, philosophy and theology) leads us to attribute to a subject, which turns out to be mythical. And these mental states are determined by the society in which we grow up, to a point where we are unable to stand apart from ourselves and take a look at what we would be like if we had independence from what constitutes us. So what enables him to achieve a god's-eye view of the human condition, from which he can make judgements beyond good and evil?

He never answers this question directly, though he is certainly aware of it. His solution, in so far as it is meant to be that, lies in what has become in recent years one of his most celebrated views, thanks to its being so congenial to deconstructionists. He does not believe that there are such things as facts without interpretations, though his strongest claim on that score is to be found in his notebooks (printed as section 481 of *WP*). In his published work, his most explicit statement is 'There is *only* a perspective seeing, only a perspective "knowing"; and the *more* affects we allow to speak about one thing, the more complete will our "concept" of this thing, our "objectivity" be' (*GM* III. 12). So what interprets and what is interpreted are both in a different position from that which a naïve epistemology would attribute to them. We are bound to see things from our point of view, so it is a good idea to take up as many points of view as possible. We shall never get to 'the things themselves', because of us and also because we have no reason to think that, in the sense that traditionally has been given to that phrase, there are such things.

Nietzsche never worked out his own epistemology in detail, nor is there any reason to think that he would have particularly wanted to. As always, his overriding concern is with culture, and he says what he does about perspectives—not nearly enough to make possible an uncontroversial account of his view—in order to stress that our beliefs, specifically about value, are never free from the place we occupy in the world. If one tried to press his perspectivism harder than that, it would seem very dubious. That is no doubt the reason for the plethora of inverted commas sprouting round tricky works in the quotation above from *GM*. But so far as values are concerned, he demonstrates in his own practice how one can take up various attitudes to a particular problem, never arriving at the truth concerning it, because that would be to suppose that in the world of values there are truths—and thus, also, to give that privileged place to truth that he is keen to dispute.

But there does seem to be one criterion, which makes its début in his first book, and continues to the end of his work, by which all else is finally judged. That is: life. We have seen him saying in *BGE* that the falseness of a judgement is not necessarily an objection to it, the question being to what extent it is life-promoting, life-preserving. And in the same year as he wrote *BGE* he produced many versions of prefaces to some of his previous books, *BT* included, in which again 'life' is taken to be the measure of all things: 'to look at science in the perspective of the artist, but at art in that of life' is what, in 'An Attempt at Self-Criticism' he says was 'the task this audacious book dared to tackle for the first time.' Life as opposed to what? That is not something that Nietzsche ever gives a clear answer to, any more than other distinguished artists and philosophers have. He is certainly not concerned with the *quantity* of life around— if anything, he would prefer there to be much less, and of a superior order. But what is a superior order of life? Well, the *Übermensch*, one imagines. But we have seen that one has to imagine all too much about the *Übermensch*, that blank cheque which Zarathustra issues without any directions about cashing it, for him to be helpful. Power? Certainly that is heavily involved, since life is Will to Power; but not all power is approved by Nietzsche; it could not be, or he would approve of everything. And power and life are, in his philosophy, two terms that inhabit so much the same conceptual region that rather than one illuminating the other, they both seem to stand in need of some independent light.

All the great advocates of life as an ultimate criterion— Christ, Blake, Nietzsche, Schweitzer, D. H. Lawrence, for a few—have been vigorous in their condemnation of an enormous amount of it, on behalf of other, more precious forms or varieties. And in a way one sees what they all mean, though if bacteria could speak they would no doubt have claimed every bit as much right to live as the larger organisms in whose favour Schweitzer was eliminating them. And what the five people I mentioned counted as being 'on the side of life' or 'life-denying' varies in many respects sharply. Yet they do not seem to be saying *nothing* when they speak on behalf of life, vague and often unhelpful for making decisions as they are. Often what Nietzsche means is something close to vitality or even liveliness. That becomes increasingly clear in his judgments on art, where the test is, in the later and last writings, whether it manifests an overabundance on the part of its creator, or whether it is the product of need and deprivation. It is for being an exemplar of the latter that Wagner is condemned, to take the ubiquitous case.

It is at least clear that vitality is a necessary, if not a suffi-cient, condition for Nietzsche's approving of anything in his later work. A figure such as Goethe (subject to some mytholo-gization by Nietzsche, naturally) is venerated because of the number of diverse impulses he was able to organize and mobi-lize, in the course of a life of almost unexampled productivity in a wide variety of fields. And yet (to go back for a moment to style) everything he did bears his stamp. But there is, lurking just under the surface of Nietzsche's criterion, a strong and disturbing tension. Henry Staten, whose superb book, already quoted from at length, is organized round this tension, puts a crucial part of it tersely:

On the one hand, there is an overall economy that includes both health and decay; on the other hand, Nietzsche cannot deny him-self the satisfaction of sounding the note of strong ascendancy over the forces of decay. And the question of the relation between these forces is also the question of Nietzsche's identity. (Staten 1990: 30)

Which is to say that Nietzsche is drawn to overall affirmation, as the Eternal Recurrence shows, if it shows anything. But the movement of affirmation is powerfully countered by a fastidi-ous revulsion from almost everything he encounters, certainly among his contemporaries. This tension is fairly closely paral-lel to the one regarding life: all of life, or only the noblest, best, strongest kind?

It is amazing that, so far as I can discover, Nietzsche never noticed this rending cleavage in his work, all the more so in that it must reflect crises that he experienced in trying to cope with his horribly painful life. And it can be seen, too, as an extrapolation from Apollo and Dionysus in *BT*. For Apollo presents life in a way that is tolerable, through exclusion of the chthonic depths; while Dionysus ignores nothing, forcing us to face the fundamental terrors of existence. If Nietzsche had not found himself, for many reasons, having to abandon the artist's metaphysics of *BT*, he would have had set up for himself a system which did justice to the conflicting impulses in his make-up, and an account of why he had them.

But it was not long before 'the terrible,' that which we are hardly able to bear, came to have a quite different significance for Nietzsche from that portended in *BT*. In that book it is spectacular, a matter usually of suffering, sometimes of joy, on a primal scale. To affirm it is glamorous as well as almost impossible, except to the greatest tragedians. This is where Nietzsche shows most blatantly his immaturity and lack of experience. But when experiences came along, all too many too soon, it turned out that though some of them were appalling in a way that could, with not too much inflation, be seen under the aegis of Dionysus, the vast majority were of a kind for which no allowance had been made in *BT*, and which left Nietzsche at a loss: they were trivial, small, no more glamorous than suffering from a large number of insect bites. It turned out that what is hardest to face, at least if you are Nietzsche, is the quotidian, that which it would be an insult to the artistic gods to ascribe to either of them, Hence he is unable to fit the nineteenth-century art form *par excellence*, the realistic novel, into any artistic category. There is of course also the novel's antipode, instrumental music, flourishing in a way and on a scale unprecedented in Western culture. But music fulfilled its truest role when it was part of tragedy. Now we have a ghastly split between the mundane, apparently unsusceptible to any form of artistic transfiguration, and 'pure' music whose splendour and misery are that it is uncontaminated by 'reality'. The attempt to bring them together has resulted in the charlatanry of Wagner, the most painful, because most deceptive, of contemporary phenomena. No one else even appears on the horizon to unite what should never have been separated. (Nietzsche's last-minute proclamation of the genius of Bizet in *Carmen* is, given the gravity of the situation, bathetic. Nietzsche needed a work in which significance was pervasive, whereas, as Adorno has argued, *Carmen* uncompromisingly refuses meaning to any event.)

Zarathustra says at one point in Part III, when he temporarily returns to his mountain home for refreshment:

Down there all speech is vain. There, forgetting and passing by are the best wisdom: *that* I have learned now. He who would grasp everything human would have to grapple with everything. But for that my hands are too clean. I do not even want to inhale their breath; alas, that I lived so long among their noises and vile breath! (*TSZ* III, 'The Return Home')

And he continues with a horrified account of the empty unavoidable chatter he encountered at ground level. That was, I'm sure, Nietzsche's usual reaction to his urban surroundings. But to exclude almost the whole of human life was an odd move for the unqualified affirmer. He tries to duck what he glimpsed, it seems, as an inconsistency in his outlook by talking of 'forgetting and looking away', just as at the opening of Book IV of *GS* he had said '*Looking away* shall be my only negation.' But what if what you have to look away from is so ubiquitous that you either have to live in a cell or leave the world behind and ascend to your mountain cave? That shows a despair more crushing than mixing with banality and denouncing it. And when Nietzsche has that thought, or something like it, he resolves instead that one way or another he will affirm everything. There is, after all, something less than impressive in a philosophy of unlimited yes-saying which begins by ruling most things out of bounds. That is recognised by Zarathustra when he says that the biggest objection to the Eternal Recurrence is the thought that the small man will recur. Nietzsche puts it with his own brand of desperate humour in *EH*, where he writes 'I confess that the deepest objection to the Eternal Recurrence, my real idea from the abyss, is always my mother and my sister' (*EH*, 'Why I am so wise', 3; this passage was suppressed by Elisabeth and only published in the 1960s).

There is, too, a further worry about affirming everything. Although Nietzsche was attracted by formulas such as *amor fati* he was also aware of the nearly inevitable tepidity of them. For there is not an easily specifiable difference between affirmation and resignation—or rather, one can say that their modality differs but it is hard to know in practice what that comes to. Is it a matter of beaming versus shrugging? And is that enough? To affirm life in all its richness, which includes on the comprehensive reading in all its poverty, does not, I take it, involve actually doing any particular things; at most it involves taking up an attitude which welcomes whatever it finds. But if what it overwhelmingly finds is smallness, spiritual squalor, it would seem to be required of the affirmer to intervene and raise the tone of the world. That is the gravamen of Adorno's succinctly expressed objection to Nietzsche (Adorno 1974: 97–8). It is also what is working away beneath the surface of a great deal of Nietzsche himself, nowhere more acutely than in *BGE*. It means that he has to move on once more, propelled by the aporia presented in one book to resolve it in the next—the characteristic movement that drives him from work to work (see Peter Heller 1966). But though his next book is his most magnificent, it fails, thanks to Nietzsche's intransigent honesty, to lessen the tension, indeed it screws it up even further, leaving the books of the last year, 1888, to oscillate between unexampled anathemas and furious exaltation.

8 Masters and slaves

Nietzsche subtitled *The Genealogy of Morals* 'A polemic', and the next page announces that it is 'A sequel to my last book, *Beyond Good and Evil*, which it is meant to supplement and clarify.' It is in a different form, at least superficially, from his other works, in that it consists of three titled essays, divided into sometimes quite lengthy sections. It has some of the appurtenances of an academic essay, but that is Nietzsche teasing. It is much better regarded as a send-up of academic procedures, though it is, in its content, a work of extreme seriousness. It is easily Nietzsche's most complex text, at least for the first two essays, performing dialectical reversals at a rate that only just prevents the virtuosic from sliding into the chaotic.

It is worth noting that it was after he heard Eduard Hitschmann read excerpts from *GM* in 1908 that Freud said Nietzsche 'had a more penetrating knowledge of himself than any other man who ever lived or was likely to live' (Jones 1955: ii. 385). Since *GM* is Nietzsche's most sustained and profound attempt to make sense of suffering, and of how other people have tried to make sense of it, it may not be surprising that Freud, who devoted his life in a radically different way to the same enterprise, should have been stirred to this remarkable compliment. The astounding twists and turns of *GM*, occasionally issuing in downright contradiction, are the result of Nietzsche's constant brooding on the variety of methods which people have developed for coping with it. So (to anticipate one of his lines of thought) the ascetic imposes one kind of suffering on himself in order to escape from many other kinds. By itself that is not to be judged. But when, in the Third Essay, 'What is the Meaning of Ascetic Ideals?', he begins to examine the varieties of asceticism practised by artists, philosophers, priests and their flocks, evaluations proliferate and enter into relationships with one another whose complexity suggests that Nietzsche has reached a point of subtlety, often disguised by the crude vigour of its expression, which admits that the phenomena are no longer susceptible of intelligible ordering.

The movement of the book as a whole is from a simplicity of contrasts which, both in its form and content, induces incredulity, to a collapse of categories which hovers around incomprehensibility. The initial postulate of the First Essay, 'Good and Evil', 'Good and Bad', is of 'the noble', those who are entitled to be legislators of value because of their position, 'who felt and established their actions as good, that is, of the first rank, in contradistinction to all the low, low-minded, common and plebeian. It was out of this *feeling of distance* that they first seized the right to create values and to coin names for values: what had they to do with utility!' (*GM* I. 2). It is here that Nietzsche makes fully explicit another force of the phrase 'beyond good and evil'. For they are now said to be the categories of the slaves, who regard their masters as evil, and define 'good' by what is unlike them. By contrast, the original nobles first define themselves, and then call 'bad' whatever lacks their qualities. Clearly Nietzsche thinks that the latter procedure is superior to the former, which is inherently reactive, a product of negation. The trouble with these proto-nobles is that in the simplicity of their approach to life they are boring. Incorrigibly healthy, indifferent to suffering, uninterested in condemnation of those unlike themselves, they are the creators of value without having any of the materials to work on which make evaluations pointful.

In *BGE* Nietzsche had repeatedly stressed the necessity of vigilant evaluation—life depends on it. But how is it to operate simultaneously with the unrestricted affirmation which sometimes seems to be the only positive value, and which the noble once came closest to? This takes us back, as it should, to the aporia of *BGE*. To live without regrets or nostalgia, for instance, sounds in a way wonderful. And yet how can one not regret wasted time, missed opportunites, failure, as well as happiness of a kind that one can never know again? And how can one avoid, in these regrets, going in for a lot of comparison and contrast, the bases of evaluation? In general, some of Zarathustra's most pregnant words seem to settle the matter:

And you tell me, my friends, that there is no disputing of taste and tasting? But all of life is a dispute over taste and tasting. Taste— that is at the same time weight and scales and weigher; and woe unto all the living that would live without disputes over weight and scales and weighers! (*TSZ*, ii, 'On Those Who Are Sublime')

So it is clear that the noble, the original 'masters', are not for Nietzsche an unequivocal subject of praise. Equally, the 'slaves', those who resent the masters, are more likely, in their industrious enquiries into the sources of their misery, to emerge with interesting answers. But the answers become too interesting, and any possibility of heroic simplicity is lost. Since there is no question but that it has been lost, irrecoverably, we late men, decadents, must have the courage of our lateness and pursue the argument wherever it leads. To abbreviate Nietzsche's most searching points in a brutal way (it is hopeless to try to summarize *GM*): the slaves found that by being subtler than their masters (no difficult feat) they could exercise their Will to Power in ways that, though despicable from the noble perspective, were effective; even, finally, to the extent of converting the masters to their own values. That was the inevitable progression from the Jews in captivity to Christianity, the greatest moral coup ever perpetrated. Among many other things, that is what is traced in the Second Essay, '"Guilt", "Bad Conscience", and the Like'. By condemning worldly values such as pride, prosperity, satisfaction with oneself, and replacing them by modesty, humility, and the rest, Christians succeeded in making their rulers as small as they were. But to do that they cultivated values which contained the seeds of Christianity's own destruction. Nietzsche quotes one of the most persuasive passages in Book V of *GS* near the end of *GM*:

Christian morality itself, the concept of truthfulness taken more and more strictly, the confessional subtlety of the Christian conscience translated and sublimated into the scientific conscience, into intellectual cleanliness at any price. To view nature as if it were a proof of the goodness and providence of a God; to interpret history to the glory of a divine reason, as the perpetual witness to a moral world order and moral intentions . . .—that now seems to belong to the *past*, that has the conscience *against* it . . . (*GS* 357)

And he continues *GM* with one of his most stupendous passages:

All great things bring about their own destruction through an act of self-overcoming: thus the law of life will have it, the law of the necessity of 'self-overcoming' in the nature of life—the lawgiver himself eventually receives the call: Submit to the law you yourself proposed. In this way Christianity as a *dogma* was destroyed by its own morality; in the same way Christianity as a *morality* must now perish too; we stand on the threshold of this event. (*GM* III. 27)

And his very last remarks in this book are about the collapse of morality, hijacked by Christianity, as the will to truth gains self-consciousness.

Note: 'all great things' and then an account of Christianity's self-destruction. *GM* is Nietzsche's most balanced book not by virtue of the sobriety of its style—Nietzsche is no longer interested in that—but by its taking contraries to extremes and giving them all their due; so that he presides over a battle, or rather several, in which he delights in arming both sides as powerfully as possible and lending all the assistance he can to getting them to fight it out. That enables him to indulge in the studied unfairmindedness of his last books. *GM* is both a creative retrospective and a point of departure for his next phase, which was to be abruptly cut off.

This retrospective dimension of the book is what gives the Third Essay, 'What Is the Meaning of Ascetic Ideals?', its strange structure, seemingly wandering far from the points he has been making earlier. For in it he conducts a survey of what ascetic ideals mean to various groups of people who have always been important to him, in the light of their self-inflicted sufferings. Life is dreadful anyway; so why make it worse by practising asceticism, the voluntary increase in what one would expect people to avoid? Suffering that is merely contingent, visited on us without explanation, is unendurable. But if we inflict it on ourselves we can understand it, and extend our understanding to the whole of life.

Artists are the first to be scrutinized; but that soon comes down to a consideration (not one of Nietzsche's big surprises) of Wagner, and of what Nietzsche took to be his embracing of chastity in his old age. In the course of it Nietzsche says 'one does best to separate an artist from his work, not taking him as seriously as his work ... The fact is that *if* he were it, he would not represent, conceive, and express it: a Homer would not have created an Achilles nor a Goethe a Faust if Homer had been an Achilles or Goethe a Faust' (*GM* III. 4). The conclusion is that the artist is conscienceless, adopting any pose that will further his work. He uses experience for the purpose of creation, which may have little to do with 'the truth'. 'What, then, is the meaning of ascetic ideals? In the case of an artist, as we see, nothing whatever!'(*GM* III. 5). Having at the outset of his career said that 'art is the true metaphysical activity of this life' and then abandoned metaphysics, Nietzsche is by now not disposed to think that there are any intimate relations between art and reality. In a late note he writes: 'For a philosopher to say "the good and the beautiful are one" is infamy; if he goes on to add "also the truth", one ought to thrash him. Truth is ugly. We have art lest we *perish of the truth*' (*WP* 822). And yet he always takes art as the paradigm of human activity. So it seems—a further aporia, not addressed—that artists are inherently suspicious characters, while art is a life-preserving evasion of the truth, often presented—certainly by Wagner—as the truth. Any artist who merely tries to produce a report on reality is roundly condemned. Apart from them, the rest 'have at all times been valets of some morality, philosophy or religion' (*GM* III. 5). So as far as understanding ascetic ideals goes, 'let us eliminate the artists' (ibid.).

Nietzsche next turns to philosophers. To be a philosopher is to practise asceticism for one's own benefit. But here asceticism comes to no more than, in the first place, being single-minded and denying oneself various pleasures for the sake of a single-mindedly pursued goal. Whereas the *compulsion* to asceticism is the result of horror at the possibility of enjoyment of life, because one does not deserve it. There is asceticism chosen and asceticism imposed, and they are utterly separate phenomena. Those who practise it at the behest of priests do not do it to achieve any good for which it is a prerequisite, but because the guilt the priests have made them feel drives them to an increase of suffering which they deserve: the hideous cruelty of explaining to them why life is painful by inflicting more pain on them: they are responsible for their own suffering.

Such a bizarre phenomenon clearly both fascinates and appals Nietzsche, just as he is amazed at people's capacity for turning their backs on the whole thing and dwelling in a state of frivolous misery. 'Man is the sick animal,' but it seems that all available remedies have been tried and found wanting. Hence Nietzsche's growing impatience, expressed in the telegraphic prose of his last year, and his longing for total revolution. As his own sufferings became more acute, which they did at an alarming rate during 1887 and 1888, he got less tolerant of any view of things that tried in any way to claim a meaning for them; and that is how he conceives morality during this period, as no more than a collection of frequently terrifyingly adroit moves to persuade people that behaving well and prospering are connected. At the close of *GM* he allows himself the hope that 'there can be no doubt that morality will gradually perish.' But he cannot have believed that. For so much of *GM* has been devoted to showing the infinitely resourceful ways in which the priestly, who need not, of course, be actually in the service of the Church, contrive to keep morality going. And as we become smaller—without Christianity there is the possibility of becoming bigger, but the overwhelming probability that we shall cling to our Christian-based morality, claiming that it only needs a few adjustments to bring the heaven on earth of utilitarianism—we will lose even the capacity to recognize greatness, supposing it were any longer possible. Slave-morality has triumphed. We are content to be slaves even when there are no masters. The brilliant last section of *GM* sums it all up without simplifying or making crude:

Man, the bravest of animals and the one most accustomed to suffering, does *not* repudiate suffering as such; he *desires* it, he even seeks it out, provided he is shown a *meaning* for it, a *purpose* of suffering. The meaninglessness of suffering, *not* suffering itself, was the curse that lay over mankind so far—*and the ascetic ideal offered man meaning!*. It was the only meaning offered so far; any meaning is better than none at all . . .—man was *saved* thereby, he possessed a meaning, he was no longer like a leaf in the wind . . . he could now *will* something; no matter at first to what end, why, with what he willed: *the will itself was saved.*

We can no longer conceal from ourselves *what* is expressed by all that willing which has taken its direction from the ascetic ideal: this hatred of the human, and even more of the animal, and more still of the material, this horror of the senses, of reason itself, this fear of happiness and beauty, this longing to get away from all appearance, change, becoming, death, wishing, from longing itself —all this means—let us dare to grasp it—*a will to nothingness*, an aversion to life, a rebellion against the most fundamental presuppositions of life; but it is and remains a *will!* . . . And, to repeat in conclusion what I said at the beginning: man would rather will *nothingness* than *not* will.—(*GM* III. 28)

With those words Nietzsche ends the last truly original book he was to write. It is extraordinary how exhilarating it is, since it contains almost no messages of hope. But diagnosis carried out at this level strikes one—however illusorily—as being half-way to cure.

1888, the last year of Nietzsche's sane life, was very productive, but in an increasingly odd way. What was to have been the most important of his books, *The Transvaluation of All Values*, was begun and abandoned, not, one may suspect, for lack of stamina, but because in the end Nietzsche found himself at a loss. The often-used phrases about the return of innocence, the birth of a new consciousness, and so on, must have seemed to him ever more hollow, if he could not incarnate them in artistic form. So he devoted himself to further polemics, written in a style of hard clarity which even he had never attained before. It is quite wrong to claim, as some commentators have, that he cheapened what he had been saying by reducing it to slogans.

These polemics, though, take on again and again an elegiac ring, as he settles accounts with the great figures who had preoccupied him throughout his life. There are two pamphlets on Wagner, the impact of whom, personal as well as artistic, he had never managed to shake off. The first of them, *The Case of Wagner*, is shrewd and hilarious, and its total effect, as its most intelligent commentators, such as Thomas Mann, have pointed out, is of curiously inverted eulogy. Quite a lot of the eulogy is not even inverted. It seems that at the end, when he surveyed his whole range of artistic experience, the work that meant most to him was, as it had been in *BT*, *Tristan und Isolde*. Certainly he never managed anything more eloquent than his account of its effects on him—still. The attack on Wagner as a decadent, portraying in mythic dimensions characters who belong in Flaubert, can all too easily be used for a *tu quoque*: 'Transposed into hugeness, Wagner does not seem to have been interested in any problems except those which now preoccupy the little decadents of Paris. Always five steps from the hospital. All of them entirely modern, entirely *metropolitan* problems. Don't doubt it' (*CW* 9). And Nietzsche? He is surely presiding over proceedings inside the hospital.

The second anti-Wagner polemic, *Nietzsche Contra Wagner*, is a collection of sections from his earlier books, from *HAH to BGE*, slightly modified. It is strangely called by Walter Kaufmann 'perhaps Nietzsche's most beautiful book', which is not to say it does not contain beautiful passages, but it is an album rather than an organized work and is anyway only twenty pages long. As much as anything else, it is part of Nietzsche's self-mythologization, in which he represents himself as 'being condemned to Germans', with Wagner providing an apparent contrast with the rest of them, until he too 'suddenly sank down, helpless and broken, before the Christian cross' (*NCW*, 'How I broke away from Wagner', 1). He portrays Wagner as the great antipode to himself, what he might have become if he had not had the strength to realize what dangers were involved in being a fully-fledged Romantic. The density of insight into music, Wagnerian music-drama, the nature of Wagner's genius, is flabbergasting, and the gathering together of these passages adds to their impact. But more than anything it is testimony to the abiding love of Nietzsche for forbidden things.

That could be claimed as even more true of *The Antichrist*, which, in the centre of its strident but effective polemics gives a portrayal of Christ as the 'great symbolist, [in that] he accepted only *inner* realities as realities, as "truths"—that he understood the rest, everything natural, temporal, spatial, historical, only as signs, as occasions for parables' (*A* 34). This passage, as it continues, reaches heights of ecstatic lyricism which make one wonder how Nietzsche is going to be able to beat a retreat. He contrives it via an attack on Christendom of which Kierkegaard might have been proud, and another on St Paul from which he would have vehemently dissented. But Nietzsche's outrage at what the priests have made of Christ's teachings is glorious in its passion, its expression of his nausea at corruption. And he revealingly says: 'only Christian *practice*, a life such as he *lived* who died on the cross, is Christian. Such a life is still possible today, for certain people even necessary: genuine, original Christianity will be possible at all times' (*A* 39). But not for strong spirits, because it depends on faith. 'Faith makes blessed: consequently it lies' (*A* 50). This is from the inveterately puritan Nietzsche, the man who thinks that 'the greatest suspicion of a "truth" should arise when feelings of pleasure enter the discussion of the question "What is true?"' (*A* 50). One might agree, though Nietzsche seems to be putting into abeyance his questioning of the will to truth. And earlier in the same book, in the middle of a devastating attack on Kant's ethics, he writes 'An action demanded by the instinct of life is proved to be *right* by the pleasure that accompanies it; yet this nihilist [Kant] with his Christian dogmatic entrails considered pleasure an *objection*. What could destroy us more quickly than working, thinking, and feeling without any inner necessity, without any deeply personal choice, without *pleasure*—as an automaton of "duty"?' (*A* 11). Though there is not a straightforward contradiction here, there is that characteristic tension between Nietzsche the man who is determined to face everything and not flinch, and Nietzsche the high-flying hedonist.

The most lively, witty, and altogether exhilarating product of 1888 is *Twilight of the Idols*, the title a parody of Wagner's doomladen *Twilight of the Gods*. It manifests the freedom of complete mastery, though it was written on the very verge of collapse. And it contains Nietzsche's longest, most ardent paeon to Goethe, who had more and more, as Nietzsche gave up on the *Übermensch*, become the prototype of the 'higher man', a concept which gratefully yields examples; while Zarathustra was insistent that 'there has never yet been an *Übermensch*'. But though every specimen of higher manhood has some reservations entered about him, at least we are able to grasp what Nietzsche is celebrating. So what Goethe 'wanted was *totality*; he fought the mutual extraneousness of reason, senses, feeling and will (preached with the most abhorrent scholasticism by

Kant, the antipode of Goethe); he disciplined himself to whole-ness, he *created* himself' (*TI* 'Skirmishes of an Untimely Man', 49). Nietzsche awards him the highest of all his honours: 'Such a spirit who has *become free* stands amidst the cosmos with a joyous and trusting fatalism, in the *faith* that only the particular is loathsome, and that all is redeemed in the whole—*he does not negate any more.* Such a faith, however, is the highest of all possible faiths: I have baptized it with the name of *Dionysus*' (ibid.). There are striking departures here—we have never before heard from Nietzsche that 'only the particular is loath-some', and wonder what to make of it. But we have heard a great deal, though to very different effect, about Dionysus, never wholly absent from Nietzsche's pantheon, but now mak-ing a major come-back in this last year. As always, he is the god of unlimited affirmation. But the context in which he affirms has changed so that the kind of affirmation required is one with little in common with *BT*.

And this is Nietzsche bravely talking about the joys of heaven from a position in hell—for this last year he says No as never before. One might even say that *his* affirmations are only, and this is his tragedy, the negations of negations. His faith—and it is remarkable to find him talking of faith at all in a positive way—is that it is possible to be someone who does not need to negate first. But he could never be that person, and the more dialectical cartwheels he turns, with wonderful and en-trancing dexterity, the further he is removed from that ideal. The only Dionysus we can identify him with is the one torn into innumerable agonized fragments.

References

ADORNO, THEODOR (1974), *Minima Moralia* (NLB, London).

ASCHHEIM, STEVEN E. (1992), *The Nietzsche Legacy in Germany 1890–1990* (University of California Press, Berkeley and Los Angeles).

BRIDGWATER, PATRICK (1972), *Nietzsche in Anglosaxony* (Leicester University Press, Leicester).

HELLER, ERICH (1988), *The Importance of Nietzsche* (University of Chicago Press, Chicago).

HELLER, PETER (1966), *Dialectics and Nihilism* (The University of Massachusetts Press, Amherst, Mass.).

JONES, ERNEST (1955), *Sigmund Freud, Life and Work*, ii (Hogarth Press, London).

KAUFMANN, WALTER (1974), *Nietzsche* (4th edn., Princeton University Press, Princeton, NJ).

KUNDERA, MILAN (1984), *The Unbearable Lightness of Being* (Faber and Faber, London).

LOVE, FREDERICK R. (1963), *Young Nietzsche and the Wagnerian Experience* (University of North Carolina Press, Chapel Hill, NC).

MIDDLETON, CHRISTOPHER (1969) (ed. and trans.), *Selected Letters of Friedrich Nietzsche* (University of Chicago Press, Chicago).

NEHAMAS, ALEXANDER (1985), *Nietzsche: Life as Literature* (Harvard University Press, Cambridge, Mass.).

SCHUTTE, OFELIA (1984), *Beyond Nihilism: Nietzsche without Masks* (University of Chicago Press, Chicago).

SILK, M. S. and STERN, J. P. (1981), *Nietzsche on Tragedy* (Cambridge University Press, Cambridge).

SOLOMON, ROBERT C. and HIGGINS, KATHLEEN M. (1988) (eds.), *Reading Nietzsche* (Oxford University Press, New York).

STATEN, HENRY (1990), *Nietzsche's Voice.* (Cornell University Press, Ithaca, NY).

THOMPSON, JUDITH J. and DWORKIN, GERALD (1968) (eds.), *Ethics* (Harper and Row, Cambridge, Mass.).

YOUNG, JULIAN (1992), *Nietzsche's Philosophy of Art* (Cambridge University Press, Cambridge).

Further reading

The amount of writing on Nietzsche in English alone is now growing at a rate that is both a tribute and a threat. The most magisterial book on him, by someone deeply sympathetic yet firmly critical, is Erich Heller's *The Importance of Nietzsche* (University of Chicago Press, Chicago, 1988). A book somewhat similar in tone, but following patiently through Nietzsche's development, is F. A. Lea's *The Tragic Philosopher* (Athlone Press, London, 1993). Originally published in 1957, it is a trail-blazing work, written, like Heller's and unlike almost everyone else's, with notable grace and a Nietzschean passion. Unfortunately Lea uses old and discredited translations for quotation; and he ends surprisingly by finding that Nietzsche rediscovered the teachings of Christ *and* Paul for our time. Walter Kaufmann's ill-organized transformation of Nietzsche into a liberal humanist has its place in the history of Nietzsche reception (*Nietzsche* 4th edn., Princeton University Press, Princeton, NJ, 1974).

Of more recent works, the most acclaimed, often setting new standards in detailed analytic working-through of Nietzsche's positions, is Alexander Nehamas's *Nietzsche: Life as Literature* (Harvard University Press, Cambridge, Mass., 1985). It is a demanding but rewarding book, but Nehamas relies too heavily on unpublished notebooks of Nietzsche's. More impressive still, as I have indicated in the text, is Henry Staten's *Nietzsche's Voice* (Cornell University Press, Ithaca, NY, 1990), a moving and profound series of meditations on some basic themes in Nietzsche. A less demanding and more critical work on an aspect of Nietzsche which has received little in the way of book-length attention is Julian Young's *Nietzsche's Philosophy of Art* (Cambridge University Press, Cambridge, 1992). Young finds a lot to be indignant about, but his criticisms, in their downrightness, are thought-provoking. A full-length book on *BT* by M. S. Silk and J. P. Stern is *Nietzsche on Tragedy* (Cambridge University Press, Cambridge, 1981), which leaves no stone unturned, so far as the biographical background, the accuracy of Nietzsche's account of Ancient Greece, and so on, are concerned. The essence of the work itself, and the source of its fascination, eludes them, but this is a mine of absorbing information. Nietzsche's politics, or rather his seeming lack of them, are dealt with at length in two overlong but intermittently helpful books, both rather badly written. Tracy Strong's *Friedrich Nietzsche and the Politics of Transfiguration* (expanded edn., University of California Press, Berkeley and Los Angeles, 1988) ranges very widely, and contains a particularly bizarre account of the Eternal Recurrence. Mark Warren's *Nietzsche and Political Thought* (MIT Press, Cambridge, Mass., 1988) distinguishes between what Nietzsche's political views, never presented systematically, were, and what they should have been, from the standpoint of the Frankfurt School of Critical Theory.

There are many collections of essays by various commentators: one that has some excellent contributions to the reading of particular books is *Reading Nietzsche*, edited by Robert C. Solomon and Kathleen M. Higgins (Oxford University Press, 1988). The way that Nietzsche tends to be read in France now is usefully illustrated in a book of translations of Derrida, Klossowski, Deleuze, and so on: *The New Nietzsche*, edited by David B. Allison (Delta, 1977). I find Gilles Deleuze's celebrated *Nietzsche and Philosophy* (trans. Hugh Tomlinson, Athlone Press, London, 1983) quite wild about Nietzsche, but interesting about Deleuze. Many people swear by it. And we are in for an invasion of works from France, where Nietzsche has been idiosyncratically cultivated since World War II.

A note on translations

All decent translations of Nietzsche into English or American date from after 1945. Walter Kaufmann was the pioneer of excellence, and his translations of *BT* and everything from *GS* onwards are classics, though his commentaries are obtrusive, self-referential, and lacking insight. R. J. Hollingdale has translated for Penguin and Cambridge University Press the books that Kaufmann did not, and several that he did. They are also serviceable. Introductions to the Penguin series are by me. Kaufmann and Hollingdale joined forces to translate *WP*, which anyone interested in Nietzsche will want to read, and find out for themselves what Nietzsche did not publish, but might or might not have.

Index

Expand your collection of
VERY SHORT INTRODUCTIONS

Available now

Available soon

Visit the
VERY SHORT
INTRODUCTIONS
Web site

www.oup.co.uk/vsi

➤ **Information** about all published titles

➤ News of **forthcoming books**

➤ **Extracts** from the books, including titles
not yet published

➤ **Reviews** and views

➤ **Links** to other **web sites** and main
OUP web page

➤ Information about **VSIs in translation**

➤ **Contact** the editors

➤ **Order** other **VSIs** on-line

ARISTOTLE
A Very Short Introduction
Jonathan Barnes

The influence of Aristotle, the prince of philosophers, on the intellectual history of the West is second to none. In this book Jonathan Barnes examines Aristotle's scientific researches, his discoveries in logic and his metaphysical theories, his work in psychology and in ethics and politics, and his ideas about art and poetry, placing his teachings in their historical context.

'With compressed verve, Jonathan Barnes displays the extraordinary versatility of Aristotle, the great systematising empiricist.'

Sunday Times

www.oup.co.uk/vsi/aristotle

ANCIENT PHILOSOPHY

A Very Short Introduction

Julia Annas

The tradition of ancient philosophy is a long, rich and varied one, in which a constant note is that of discussion and argument. This book aims to introduce readers to some ancient debates and to get them to engage with the ancient developments of philosophical themes. Getting away from the presentation of ancient philosophy as a succession of Great Thinkers, the book aims to give readers a sense of the freshness and liveliness of ancient philosophy, and of its wide variety of themes and styles.

> 'Incisive, elegant, and full of the excitement of doing philosophy, Julia Annas's Short Introduction boldly steps outside of conventional chronological ways of organizing material about the Greeks and Romans to get right to the heart of the human problems that exercised them, problems ranging from the relation between reason and emotion to the objectivity of truth. I can't think of a better way to begin.'
>
> **Martha Nussbaum, University of Chicago**

www.oup.co.uk/vsi/ancientphilosophy

LOGIC
A Very Short Introduction
Graham Priest

Logic is often perceived as an esoteric subject, having
little to do with the rest of philosophy, and even less to do
with real life. In this lively and accessible introduction,
Graham Priest shows how wrong this conception is. He
explores the philosophical roots of the subject, explaining
how modern formal logic deals with issues ranging from
the existence of God and the reality of time to paradoxes
of self-reference, change and probability. Along the way,
the book explains the basic ideas of formal logic in simple,
non-technical, terms, as well as the philosophical
pressures to which these have responded. This is a book
for anyone who has ever been puzzled by a piece of
reasoning.

'This book is terrific. ... It covers a lot of ground, but in
a wonderfully relaxed and interesting way.'

Simon Blackburn, University of North Carolina

'This is a delightful and engaging introduction to the basic
concepts of logic. Whilst not shirking the problems, Priest
always manages to keep his discussion accessible and
instructive.'

Adrian Moore, St Hugh's College, Oxford

www.oup.co.uk/vsi/logic

LITERARY THEORY
A Very Short Introduction
Jonathan Culler

Literary Theory is a controversial subject. Said to have transformed the study of culture and society in the past two decades, it is accused of undermining respect for tradition and truth, encouraging suspicion about the political and psychological implications of cultural products instead of admiration for great literature. In this Very Short Introduction, Jonathan Culler explains 'theory', not by describing warring 'schools' but by sketching key 'moves' that theory has encouraged and speaking directly about the implications of cultural theory for thinking about literature, about the power of language, and about human identity. This lucid introduction will be useful for anyone who has wondered what all the fuss is about or who wants to think about literature today.

> 'It is impossible to imagine a clearer treatment of the subject, or one that is, within the given limits of length, more comprehensive. Culler has always been remarkable for his expository skills, and here he has found exactly the right method and tone for his purposes.'
>
> **Frank Kermode**

www.oup.co.uk/vsi/literarytheory

PSYCHOLOGY
A Very Short Introduction
Gillian Butler and Freda McManus

Psychology: A Very Short Introduction provides an up-to-date overview of the main areas of psychology, translating complex psychological matters, such as perception, into readable topics so as to make psychology accessible for newcomers to the subject. The authors use everyday examples as well as research findings to foster curiosity about how and why the mind works in the way it does, and why we behave in the ways we do. This book explains why knowing about psychology is important and relevant to the modern world.

'a very readable, stimulating, and well-written introduction to psychology which combines factual information with a welcome honesty about the current limits of knowledge. It brings alive the fascination and appeal of psychology, its significance and implications, and its inherent challenges.'

Anthony Clare

'This excellent text provides a succinct account of how modern psychologists approach the study of the mind and human behaviour. ... the best available introduction to the subject.'

Anthony Storr

www.oup.co.uk/vsi/psychology

THEOLOGY
A Very Short Introduction
David F. Ford

This Very Short Introduction provides both believers and non-believers with a balanced survey of the central questions of contemporary theology. David Ford's interrogative approach draws the reader into considering the principles underlying religious belief, including the centrality of salvation to most major religions, the concept of God in ancient, modern, and post-modern contexts, the challenge posed to theology by prayer and worship, and the issue of sin and evil. He also probes the nature of experience, knowledge, and wisdom in theology, and discusses what is involved in interpreting theological texts today.

www.oup.co.uk/vsi/theology

CPSIA information can be obtained at www.ICGtesting.com
Printed in the USA
BVOW030153101211

277960BV00004B/5/P